SAN FRANCISCO
The Story of a City

PLAN
OF PORT
St FRANCISCO,
IN CALIFORNIA
Point de Reyes in 37°58′ of Latitude North & 124°54′.
Longitude — West.
The soundings are expressed in Spanish fathoms, of two vares or six Castilian feet.

A. Punta des Almexas.
B. Laguna de la Merced.
C. Laguna del Presidio.
D. Pta del Cantil Blanco.
E. Presidio de San Francisco.
F. Pequena Laguna.
G. Mission de San Francisco.
H. Laguna de los Dolores.
I. Isla de Alcatrazes.
J. Isla de Ierba buena.

K. Isla de los Angeles.
L. Pta de San Antonio.
M. Isla del Carmel.
N. Ensda des Carmelites.
O. Ensda de Consolacion.
P. Pta de S. Carlos.
Q. Pta de S. Iaco.
R. Pta de Reyes.
S. Islets.
T. Sand Island.
V. Sand Ie look'n aground.

SAN FRANCISCO
The Story of a City

John Bernard McGloin, S.J.

PRESIDIO PRESS
San Rafael, California & London, England

Copyright © 1978 by Presidio Press

Published by Presidio Press of San Rafael, California,
and London, England, with editorial offices at
1114 Irwin Street, San Rafael, California 94901

Library of Congress Cataloging in Publication Data

McGloin, John Bernard.
  San Francisco, the story of a city.

  Bibliography: p.
  Includes index.
  1. San Francisco—History.   I. Title.
F869.S357M32 1978   979.4'61   78–9968
ISBN 0–89141–045–7

Book design by Hal Lockwood

Cover design by Mark Jacobsen

Printed in the United States of America

Contents

Preface   vii

PART 1
BEGINNINGS THROUGH THE NINETEENTH CENTURY

1   Geography: Lay of the Land   3
2   Origins: Presidio, Mission and Pueblo   11
3   From Yerba Buena to San Francisco: 1835–1847   23
4   Days of "Old, of Gold, of '49"   31
5   Religious Beginnings   37
6   Education and Culture: 1847–1862   45
7   The Vigilance Movements: 1849, 1851, 1856   53
8   Six Fires of the Fifties   67
9   The Terry-Broderick Duel   77
10 The Bonanza Age: 1860–1900   83
11 William Chapman Ralston: Builder of a City   95

PART 2
SAN FRANCISCO LANDMARKS

12 Golden Gate: The People's Park of San Francisco   107
13 The Story of the Cable Cars   117
14 1906: Earthquake and Fire   131
15 Relief and Reconstruction   143
16 The Panama-Pacific International Exposition, 1915   155
17 The Civic Center   163
18 Under the Hills of Home: Five Tunnels   173
19 The Age of the Ferry Building   183
20 The Port of San Francisco   189
21 Symphonies in Steel: Bay Bridge and the Golden Gate   195
22 The "Muni" Railway to BART   207
23 Water: From Lobos Creek to Hetch Hetchy   217
24 The San Francisco Airport: 1919 to Now   223

PART 3
PEOPLE, LABOR AND POLITICS

25 Adolph Sutro and the San Francisco Story   235
26 Denis Kearney, Agitator Extraordinary   243
27 The Teamsters' Strike of 1901   253
28 San Francisco's "Consecrated Thunderbolt": Father Peter
   C. Yorke   261
29 Corruption: Abe Ruef and Eugene Schmitz   267
30 The Streetcar Strike of 1907: Labor's Defeat   279
31 Contrasting Administrations: Edward R. Taylor and P. H.
   McCarthy, 1908–1912   287
32 Perennial Mayor: "Sunny Jim" Rolph   295
33 The Mooney-Billings Case   303
34 Maritime and General Strike of 1934   309
35 San Francisco's City Charters and More Mayors   321

PART 4
MORE MODERN TIMES

36 Host to the World: San Francisco and the Birth of the
   United Nations Organization, 1945   345
37 Social Changes in the City: Beatniks, Hippies and the
   Haight-Ashbury   351
38 Changing Skyline   359
39 Reflections on the Contemporary Scene   369
40 A Survey of San Franciscana   381
   Bibliography   395
   Sources and Notes   399
   Index   435

Preface

A FEW WORDS about the building of this book. It comes, essentially, out of long experience in teaching local history at the University of San Francisco. In 1950 I started a course which I have now given twenty times to over fourteen hundred students. The resulting lectures, discussions, and research papers have prompted me to record some of the findings in this more permanent form. I have long held the conviction that San Francisco is sufficiently different from other cities, and is so full of flavor and color that it deserves a special, topically-oriented historical treatment, presented, I hope, in simple, readable language. That is what I have tried to do here.

For twenty-five years now, the University of San Francisco catalog has listed a course in the history of San Francisco as follows: "A study of the factors which have contributed to the rise of San Francisco from Spanish settlement to modern metropolis." In presenting such a sweeping panorama (which makes no pretense to being a complete or definitive historical treatment), it is necessary to keep both perspective and focus in mind; to neglect this would be to expose the result to the understandable charge of excessive parochialism. San Francisco does not need such treatment, for it can well stand on its own merits and storied past. That those who live in San Francisco are "citizens of no mean city" is a truism that is shared by many nonresidents who also love the city.

The time is overdue to shed some of the legends and indefensible assertions about San Francisco which are still spawned and, by some, even cherished, as I have found out on more than one occasion. Too long now have the legend merchants passed along downright untrue or unproven assertions about San Francisco's past. What I have in mind here will be evident to those who read these pages: I will make an honest attempt to correct the record where this can and should be done.

I once heard my former teacher, the distinguished Professor Herbert Eugene Bolton, remark in one of his Berkeley seminar sessions that "some of my students have written my best books." He went on to explain that a number of his better students had provided him with key ideas as a result of their detailed research and thus inspired him to delve more deeply and, eventually, to come up with a book of his own. For more than twenty-five years now, I have had a similarly delightful experience, as a number of splendid students have provided me with seminal ideas and much primary information about matters San Franciscan; I have used the fruits of their research here while trying to join them with my own ferrettings in this field. To all the unsung and unnamed, my sincere gratitude. Finally, I think I may say that, with imperfections freely acknowledged, these pages have been (in an old expression which still has meaning) a labor of love. My hope is that they will add to the legions of those who truly love the City of the Golden Gate.

John Bernard McGloin, S.J.
Professor of History
University of San Francisco, 1978

PART 1

BEGINNINGS THROUGH THE NINETEENTH CENTURY

CHAPTER 1

GEOGRAPHY:
The Lay of the Land

M ANY WHO WRITE about San Francisco make at least passing reference to the geographical features of the city. Frequently, though, such mention consists mostly of praise of the "imperial city" because of its distinctive geographical features. However, I have yet to see anywhere a detailed breakdown, given with as much scientific accuracy as possible, of these same geographical features; I propose to furnish just such a listing here. It is logical that, before Portola, Anza, and others are brought into sight, some attention be paid to setting the scene and indicating the stage upon which the drama of San Francisco has been acted.

First of all, we must remember that San Francisco is situated upon a peninsula and, looking at the Latin derivation of this word, *paene insula,* "almost an island," we reflect that perhaps one reason why it takes a lot of water to impress a San Franciscan is because he lives almost entirely surrounded by it. Ascending Twin Peaks, on a day of good visibility, he can gaze upon the beauty of the bay, or, if he prefers, can see the Pacific Ocean to the west. So it is correct to say that such a person is never really far from the watery aspects of the area of land that he calls home.[1] Which brings us immediately to another point: what, actually and accurately, is the area that we call San Francisco? Almost legendary is the facile and frequently given information (but inaccurate, nevertheless) that "San Francisco is about 42 square miles." However, according to official figures furnished by the city engineer's office, the city and county of San Francisco, which have been coterminous since the Consolidation Act of 1856 (i.e. that which is the "city" is also the "county" and vice versa), has as its exact limits 129 square miles, of which the land mass comprises 46.38 square miles and the watery area, 82.38 square miles.[2]

At the top of Mount Davidson, highest elevation in San Francisco. Brother A. A. Grosskopf, S.J.

For ordinary purposes, therefore, it seems sufficiently accurate to refer to the *land* area as comprising about 47 square miles and the water area, about 83 square miles.

Mount Davidson (formerly called Blue Mountain) remains the highest point of land within the city and county of San

Francisco; its elevation is 927 feet. The lowest point in the city, as reported by the engineer's office, is the southwest corner of Fifth and Berry streets which has a minus (i.e., below sea level) figure of 5.71 feet.

Two locations should be mentioned when identifying the geographical center of San Francisco: that of the *mainland* of the city, at the southeasterly line of Grandview Avenue between Alvarado and 23rd streets (the city engineer reports the location as Latitude N. 37° 45'10"—Longitude W. 122° 26'27"); and that of the geographical center of the *entire* city and county, at the southwest corner of Fulton and Baker streets (Latitude N. 37° 46'33"—Longitude W. 122° 26'24").

Three natural lakes fed by springs and augmented by rainwater are situated within San Francisco. First and foremost is Lake Merced which was named by Franciscan Padre Palou when the Heceta expedition of which he was chaplain arrived on its shores on or about September 24, 1775, the Feast of Our Lady of Mercy. Two things seem certain about the lake itself which has long been divided into two sections by a manmade causeway that forms part of the access to an adjacent golf course. First, Lake Merced is a natural lake; second, early maps indicate that at one time it emptied into the Pacific Ocean; it seems that some natural cause, perhaps a mild earthquake, closed this entrance. Second of the lakes within city limits is Mountain or Presidio Lake *(La Laguna de la Presidio de San Francisco)* which is in a considerably abbreviated form now because of fill placed on its shores during the construction of Park Presidio Boulevard as a main access road to the Golden Gate Bridge. A third lake, adjacent to Sloat Boulevard, is still marked on city maps as *Laguna Puerca,* the "Pig Lake," so called by the first Spanish explorers; it also answers to the later names of "Pine Lake" and "Crest Lake." (*Laguna Honda,* once a natural lake, has long been concrete-lined and serves the purposes of a reservoir—the name means "Deep Lake.")

Historically there have been other lakes and some vagrant lagoons as well, such as *Laguna Seca,* "Dry Lake," which is marked on an 1867 map of the city and which seems to have been in the general direction of Twin Peaks. Lake Geneva was once located where Geneva Avenue now runs between San Jose Avenue and Alemany Boulevard. Although indicated on a 1913 map of the city, it has since vanished from the scene. (It is not difficult for a building operation to dispose of a relatively shallow lake by simply covering it with dirt fill.) Other vagrant lagoons have included Washerwoman's Lagoon in the North Beach region, so called because it was used for laundry purposes in Gold Rush days, and the *Laguna de los Dolores* which was a shallow lake located at Mission Dolores; it once extended to the bay but it has long since disappeared.

We now approach the interesting question of the number of the "Hills of Home" in San Francisco.[3] On September 27, 1967, the city engineer, Clifford J. Geertz, wrote to the author:

> This question we can answer in any way you might like. It depends on what may be deemed to constitute a hill. "Fourteen," said one of my predecessors, "Forty-two" says the book entitled *The Hills of San Francisco!* "Thirty-two," said Robert O'Brien in an article written for the *San Francisco Chronicle* in the early '50's; "Twenty-four, give or take a few" say I after counting what I arbitrarily termed "major crests" on a relief map hanging on the east wall of my office.

The (unlisted) authors of *The Hills of San Francisco* are closest to accuracy with their count of forty-two hills in San Francisco. Certainly this is more correct than the inexact data of the incurable romanticists who write: "Just as Rome rose upon its seven hills (which, incidentally, are hard to find in modern Rome) so, too, does the City by the Golden Gate rise upon seven hills!" It might help here, before proceeding, to define a "hill" for the special reason that, even though the term "mountain" is used to describe certain elevations in San Francisco, there is no height that attains even to 1,000 feet. Our elevations had better be considered, then, as "hills" with this term being defined as a "conspicuous natural elevation" which is to be distinguished from a mountain, defined as a "lofty elevation of rock, or earth and rock, usually having a small summit area, standing either singly or forming part of a series." It will help here to list with their heights in feet ten of the forty-two "Hills of Home," which may be called "major crests" of special importance.

Mount Davidson (927); Twin Peaks South (910.5); Twin Peaks North (903.8); Golden Gate Heights (758); Buena Vista Park (569); Mount Olympus (561.22); Lone Mountain (392); Nob Hill (338); Russian Hill (294); Telegraph Hill (273).

Nineteenth century Portsmouth Square

Inquiries are sometimes made concerning a number of assorted points connected with the man-made topography of San Francisco. Here are some items that may prove of interest in this regard: in 1975, the tallest building in San Francisco was the Transamerica Pyramid (853 feet) which exceeds the Bank of America World Headquarters by 53 feet. The tallest structure (as distinguished from building) is the Mt. Sutro Tower (981 feet). This rises from Sutro Crest (909 feet) to make the total elevation from sea level 1,890 feet. (The two towers of the Golden Gate Bridge rise to a height of 746 feet.)

The most winding thoroughfare in the city, which is frequently called the "crookedest street in the world," is Lombard Street between Hyde and Leavenworth, with its nearest rival being Vermont at 20th Street in the Potrero Hill district. The steepest street open to traffic was along First Avenue, between Irving and Parnassus Avenue, but this has now disappeared and a building of the University of California Medical Complex is in its place; now there appear to be two rivals for the above-mentioned distinction: Filbert Street between Leavenworth and Hyde streets and 22nd Street between Church and Vicksburg. The oldest street in the city is Grant Avenue between Clay and Washington streets which was originally laid out in 1835 as the *Calle de Fundacion* and formed the western boundary of the old Plaza now generally referred to as Portsmouth Square. When the calle was first designated, the newly created *Pueblo de Yerba Buena* had fewer than fifty inhabitants.

The chief geographical features described in this chapter will serve to set the stage for the human occupants who came to explore and settle on that part of the peninsula now called San Francisco.

CHAPTER 2

ORIGINS:
Presidio, Mission, and
Pueblo

M OST CITIES SETTLE for one date of origin. How-
ever, San Francisco, distinctive even in its beginnings, can hardly
settle for less than three. The historical record makes it abundantly clear that it was founded in three separate stages: first as
a presidio, soon after as a Franciscan mission, and, finally as a
pueblo, *Yerba Buena,* from which, certainly, most of the modern
city by the Golden Gate has developed.

Each year, on June 29, San Franciscans, in impressive numbers,
gather at Mission Dolores for an anniversary Mass commemorating the "birthday" of their city; they next go to the Officers' Club
at the Presidio for a luncheon and nostalgically impressive program which includes a birthday toast to the city. However, the
record is clear that this date, June 29, is not the *real* birthday of
San Francisco. What happened on June 29, 1776, was the celebration of Mass by Father Palou on the feast of Saints Peter and Paul
on the shores of what had been named *La Laguna de Nuestra Senora
de Los Dolores;* Palou and others had encamped there two days
previously to await, in the sheltered area protected from fog by
the Twin Peaks, the arrival of supplies that were to be used in
establishing the Presidio.

It is of utmost importance that the intentions of the founding
authority be examined when we have conflicting dates given in
a matter such as the establishment of San Francisco; the record
is clear that Juan Bautista de Anza had been sent to our peninsula
to establish what Professor Herbert E. Bolton aptly described as
an "Outpost of Empire"—i.e., a presidio or military post—for
many pressing reasons not unknown to students of California's
past. Hence the date of September 17, 1776, has priority here, for
on that date the Presidio, a primitive but real structure (and
surrounding area) was dedicated with the celebration of Mass

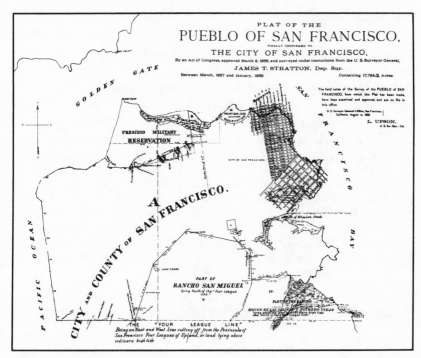

Pueblo of San Francisco

accompanied by the usual ceremonies employed by Spain on such formal occasions. The convincing words of Maynard Geiger, O.F.M. are quoted here to settle the matter:

> Since the present city of San Francisco grew out of the development of the mission, the presidio and the later Yerba Buena, all three of which grew into one, the date of the beginning of that community stems from the day of the first definitely established place within it. That place was the presidio, formally established on September 17, 1776.[1]

On March 29, 1776, Captain Juan Bautista de Anza had designated a site for the future Presidio of San Francisco. Standing somewhere in the vicinity of what came to be called the *Cantil Blanco,* the "White Cliff" (which was to disappear when Fort Point was built between 1853 and 1861 and the cliff considerably cut back) Anza designated an area of about 3,000 varas (a vara is roughly equivalent to a yard); it is, perhaps, a legitimate use of historical imagination to envision this sturdy soldier using his Spanish sword as the instrument of such designation.[2] Thus began the significant story of a military outpost of empire which has had, among other distinctions, that of never having fired a shot in hostility—this certainly must please the peaceful St. Francis. Pedro Font, O.F.M., who is called by Bolton the "Prince of Diarists," for his precise account of his visit in 1776 to the *Cantil Blanco,* wrote these quotable lines concerning what he saw from the top of that same *Cantil Blanco:*

> The Port of San Francisco is a marvel of nature and may well be called the harbor of harbors and I think that if it could be well settled like Europe, there would not be anything more beautiful in all the world—for it has the best advantages for founding in it a most beautiful city with all the conveniences desired by land as well as by sea—with that harbor so remarkable and so spacious in which may be established shipyards, docks and anything that may be wished.[3]

Bolton comments eloquently on Font's prophetic words:

> Font's dream has come true. San Francisco has grown to be more, perhaps, and doubtless something different from anything that Font could have imagined. But, from then to now, it has been true to its original character as an Outpost of Empire.[4]

Designation of a presidio site was not enough to bring it into being; this was helped along by the arrival through the Golden Gate, on July 25, 1776, of that same San Carlos which had first made it into the bay on August 5 in the previous year. Aboard were the necessary tools and supplies that had been sent for the construction of the Presidio; soon an enclosure that formed a 275-foot square with walls of redwood palisades was hammered together. (In two years, this temporary structure was replaced by an adobe building with walls of solid dimensions.) One cannon, courtesy of the *San Carlos,* slung over its side and delivered to the *Cantil Blanco,* was mounted to command the strait, and the future city had its presidio and its fortress. Later, probably about 1791, the headquarters of the comandante was erected within the palisade; today what is left of it (very little indeed and certainly not enough to be called a "building") has been long claimed (see

The Presidio of San Francisco in 1856. Southern Pacific

Some of the original bricks; inside Officers' Club.

the sign outside the modern Officers' Club) to be the "oldest building in San Francisco," which it assuredly is not.[5]

Several fortresses succeeded each other on *Cantil Blanco,* one in 1792 and a more substantial one in 1794 which was called the *Castillo de San Joaquin.* The first garrison consisted of a corporal in command of six men, and the armament was eight twelve-pounders that had been cast in Peru. It appears that neither the foundation out on the cliff nor its firepower commanded the respect of foreign visitors; indeed, Otto von Kotzebue, visiting the area in 1824 as commander of the Russian man-of-war, *Rurik,* reported that a few well-directed shots from his vessel would have reduced the castillo on the *Cantil Blanco* to ruin and rubbish. The fortress was constantly in need of repairs and its exposure to the fogs that mark the area made it extremely unpopular duty with the Spanish, and later Mexican, soldiers assigned to it. In 1813, an earthquake severely damaged it; there followed a re-building in 1817, this time partly in brick and stone, and, by 1820, a certain respectability came when twenty guns were mounted, among them three twenty-four pounders. Change came in 1822 when Spain's flag yielded to that of the newly independent Mex-ico. Apparently the Mexican government came to regard the San Francisco Presidio as a sort of minor penal colony for recalcitrant soldiers; while the officers were of a more trustworthy sort, some of the ordinary soldiers were, at times, serving out periods of punishment which came from infractions of military discipline. It can easily be imagined that Mexican soldiers, used to a warm climate, had a special dislike for their stay on a cliff frequently swept by dense fogs.

On February 2, 1848, the treaty of Guadalupe Hidalgo saw the Presidio, with all the rest of California, becoming American. (Ac-tually the flying of the American flag at the Presidio was not the first such on the peninsula for, on July 9, 1846, Captain John B. Montgomery, commanding the U.S.S. *Portsmouth,* had caused the flag to be raised in the public square at *Yerba Buena* during the progress of the conquest of California, as a part of the Mexican War.) The enterprising Americans decided that the quaint fanci-ful Spanish-Mexican days of the old fort had gone and they soon planned new fortifications. *Cantil Blanco* was cut back to increase the area designated for an American fort of different dimensions. The present Fort Point, whose official name, since 1882, is Fort Winfield Scott, was occupied, though not yet entirely completed, as early as 1857 and it is regarded as an imitation, in great part, of the famous Fort Sumter in Charlestown, South Carolina. It was considered an outstanding example of engineering skill when finished in 1861. After much neglect for many years, the old fort

Artist's drawing of Presidio, 1816.

came at last into its proper place in our civic story with its designation, on April 14, 1971, as a National Historical Site.

The second of the three-pronged origins of San Francisco is the Franciscan mission known as "Mission Dolores" although its official name has always been *San Francisco de Asis*. A plaque on the wall of the entrance to the mission unfortunately does not satisfy those interested in accuracy in historical matters. Its inscription reads as follows:

Mission Dolores
Founded June 29, 1776
by Rev. Francisco Palou, O.F.M.
Cradle of San Francisco

Even though, as mentioned, the title "Mission Dolores" is commonly used and is quite acceptable, it is not the correct name of the Mission, which was dedicated to St. Francis of Assisi, founder of the Franciscan Order. Secondly, it was not founded by virtue of the Mass offered by Padre Palou on the shores of the lagoon on June 29, 1776: as will be indicated, the correct foundation date is October 9, 1776. Finally, it is wrong to call Mission Dolores the "cradle of San Francisco"—it is so only in the religious sense and must share honors with the earlier presidio and later pueblo. Until recently there was nowhere an indication that the building which the visitor enters after viewing the plaque is not the original built in 1776—yet not only is it a completely new structure but it is located several city blocks from the original mission.[6]

On March 12, 1975, through the efforts of the California State Society, Daughters of the American Revolution, a new and accurate plaque was placed on the outside wall of Mission Dolores—on the side facing the cemetery. Here is the inscription:

> Mission San Francisco de Asis (Mission Dolores). This edifice, the construction of which was started in 1788, was dedicated August 2, 1791. An adobe structure in use since that time, it is the oldest building in San Francisco. Original adobe brick walls and roof tiles are still in place.

> (It was the author's privilege to bless this plaque on the occasion mentioned above; now, at last, there is an accurate inscription concerning this most important building.)

The record indicates that Father Palou had actually blessed a small wooden church on October 3, 1776, and offered Mass within its walls on the next day, the Feast of St. Francis, while he awaited the return of Lieutenant Jose Joaquin Moraga who was exploring some of the East Bay area, before the official dedication and opening of the mission, which took place on October 9. Of great importance is the fact that the building in question was located, not at the present site at 16th and Dolores streets but at what is now the corner of the block-long street appropriately called "Camp Street"—since it was, indeed, the camp site for the few soldiers there. The small church served until 1783 when another was built on the present site, more remote from the waters of the laguna;[7] this would also allow the former site to be used for agricultural purposes. However, before this transfer, Palou erected another small wooden church. The story grows a bit more complicated with the mention in official reports located in Mexico City's National Archives that Palou built yet another temporary chapel at the present site while laying the foundations there of what was to be

the present and permanent church. By the end of 1783, therefore, three small churches had been built before the present
mission came into being. In 1785, Father Palou returned to
Mexico while Pedro Cambon, his Franciscan successor, began
work on the present church, in the construction of which over
25,000 adobe bricks were used. Finally on August 2, 1791, the
present and still serving Mission Dolores was dedicated.

For the first few months, no converts were made at this latest
of the California spiritual outposts of empire; indeed, the priests
met hostility from the Indians for whose benefit Dolores had
been established. Only on June 24, 1777, is there recorded the
baptism of three Indian neophytes; however, the subsequent
total is sufficiently impressive as, from 1777 to 1833, when the
mission came to a practical end because of secularization, 6,536
baptisms were recorded on mission registers.

When one comes to the vital part played by Captain William
A. Richardson (1795–1856) in the founding of that pueblo of
Yerba Buena which was to contribute considerably more to the
growth of the modern city than either the presidio or the mission,
one is perplexed at the relatively small amount of information
printed about him. Bolton has properly memorialized the part of
Anza and Moraga in the military phase of the foundation of the
city, while the Franciscans Engelhardt and Geiger have done well
concerning Serra and the entire Franciscan story in California.
But no such complete treatment has yet been accorded to Captain
Richardson.[8] Here I hope to provide some details that will set the
record straight in his regard.

However, the Pioneer of the Pueblo has not been entirely neglected, as an unobtrusive tablet mounted on a wall outside 827
Grant Avenue near Clay Street testifies:

The Birthplace of a Great City
Here, June 25, 1835, William Richardson, founder of Yerba Buena
(later San Francisco) erected its first habitation, a tent dwelling,
replacing it in lumber, 1835, by the first wooden house and, on
this ground, he erected the large adobe building known as Casa
Grande.

Richardson was born in London on August 27, 1795. After some
years spent at sea, he entered the Golden Gate as first mate of the

English whaler *L'Orient* on August 2, 1822. He decided to remain and married Maria Antonio Martinez, the daughter of the comandante of the Presidio. He quickly became a prominent personage because of various skills and received permission from the Mexican governor to establish a dwelling on the shore of the cove of *Yerba Buena;* this he did on June 25, 1835. He later moved to Sausalito where he died on April 20, 1856.

Earlier, Father Geiger was quoted in proof of the fact that the foundation date of the Presidio—September 17, 1776—is the best date to be used as the proper birthday of San Francisco; it should also be observed that modern San Francisco owes more to its civil or pueblo phase than to either its military or religious origins. From this it follows that the day on which Captain Richardson pitched his tent in the area known as *Yerba Buena*—June 25, 1835 —seems to have special importance in this discussion of origins. There is a sense, then, in which this latter date may well be considered the foundation date of modern San Francisco.

Now that the three-pronged origins of San Francisco have been established, we shall go on to the consideration of the beginnings of civil government in the city. This will be the story of its transition from the *Pueblo de Yerba Buena* (June 25, 1835) to its change of name to San Francisco on January 30, 1847.

SOME EARLY DATES IN THE SAN FRANCISCO STORY

September 28, 1542—Juan Rodriguez Cabrillo entered what is now San Diego Bay; he is known as the "discoverer of Alta California." (On November 16, 1542, Cabrillo sighted the Farallon Islands which, since 1872, have been part of the city and county of San Francisco.)

November 6, 1595—Sebastian Rodriguez Cermenho entered a bay on the Marin Coast which he named *La Bahia de San Francisco,* the present Drake's Bay. This is the first recorded use of the name that was later to be applied to San Francisco itself.

October 31 to November 4, 1769—Discovery of the present San Francisco Bay by Gaspar de Portolá with the help of Sergeant Jose Ortega and companions.

August 5, 1775—Captain Juan Manuel Ayala, commanding the *San Carlos,* sailed through the Golden Gate, anchoring off what is now called Angel Island.

March 29, 1776—Juan Bautista Anza, having previously scouted the peninsula of San Francisco, designated the site of a presidio of that name.

June 29, 1776—Franciscan Padre Francisco Palou offered Mass at the site of what was to become the Mission of San Francisco de Asis.

September 17, 1776—Padre Palou offered Mass at the formal dedication of the newly constructed Presidio of San Francisco.

October 9, 1776—The dedication of the first "Mission Dolores." (The present structure, dedicated on August 2, 1791, is the oldest building in San Francisco.)

June 25, 1835—William Anthony Richardson, establishing residence in the cove of Yerba Buena, effectively established what was to be called the *Pueblo of Yerba Buena;* the name was changed to San Francisco on January 30, 1847.

CHAPTER 3

FROM YERBA BUENA TO SAN FRANCISCO: 1835–1847

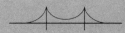

I N LESS THAN fifteen years, Captain Richardson's settlement on the shores of the cove of *Yerba Buena*[1] was destined to be catapulted into worldwide greatness by the discovery of gold by James W. Marshall at Sutter's Mill situated at Coloma about 140 miles northeast of San Francisco. Before gazing out the Gate in those stirring "days of old, of gold, of '49" to welcome the ships who made it white with approaching sails, let us briefly recreate what transpired in the relatively quiet days of a sleepy pueblo.

Although Spanish policy had always been wary of allowing foreign visitors to its ports in New Spain or elsewhere, this same policy was sometimes honored more in the breach than in the observance. For example, from 1776 to 1848, a number of interesting and observant foreign visitors entered the Golden Gate: on November 14, 1792, Captain George Vancouver arrived from England in H.M.S. *Discovery* in the first recorded visit of a foreign vessel to San Francisco Bay. About a decade later, on August 12, 1803, the first American vessel, the *Eliza,* commanded by Captain James Rowan, entered the harbor. On April 8, 1806, Count Nikolai Petrovitch Rezanov arrived in the Russian vessel *Juno.*[2] The Russians returned on October 2, 1816, when Otto von Kotzebue, commanding the *Rurik,* entered the bay. Later accounts by him indicate that he had a haughty contempt for the Spanish he saw on this visit to the future San Francisco. Between this Russian visit and the next, California became a province of Mexico (April 11, 1822); this expected event caused the oath of allegiance to Mexico to be administered at the Presidio only two days later. On November 6, 1826, the English Captain, Frederick William Beechey, commanding the H.M.S. *Blossom,* entered the harbor and successfully sought permission to make a survey of what he saw.

He drew a map which is still of interest, exchanged courtesy visits, and sailed after a seven-week stay during which he visited most of the bay region. His ungenerous conclusion was that the sleepy little settlement was both "tedious and insipid." However, Beechey wrote in colorful detail about mission life as he saw it, noting that the Presidio garrison was composed "of a ragged lot." The next year, 1827, France entered into the picture with the arrival of a trading ship, *Le Héros,* commanded by Captain Auguste Huhaut-Cilly. So, it will be seen that the sleepy pueblo was not entirely unknown during its quiet years. What a change was soon to come.

With regard to the beginnings of civil government in the future San Francisco, it should be mentioned that, on December 7, 1824, the first *ayuntamiento,* or town council, was organized, with Francisco de Haro declared the first *Alcalde* after a not very large electorate had so indicated. Although the civil pueblo, according to normal Spanish procedures adopted by the Mexican authorities, would have emerged from the "Presidial Pueblo of San Francisco," this did not occur because of the deterioration of that same presidio which made it incapable of giving birth to anything— much less to a civil pueblo. Also, Captain Richardson had obtained leave from Mexican officialdom to start his own quasi-pueblo on the shores of the cove, as already described in Chapter 2.[3] It so happened that Alcalde de Haro lived in the vicinity of Mission Dolores, but the "pueblo" of which he was given nominal charge (a charge confirmed by Governor Figueroa) does not loom as large in our civic past as does that of Captain Richardson.[4] A brief summary of the civil government picture of the time puts it as follows:

> Between 1834–8, efforts were made to adopt a form of local government consisting of an Ayuntamiento (a 6 man council) and an Alcalde (a combination of mayor and chief justice). The effort was short-lived, however, since the village lacked the 4,000 residents required by the Mexican government to be a self-governing seaport. Thereafter alcaldes were apparently the Mexican military authorities in Monterey.[5]

If indeed, then, it was the intention of the Spanish governors of California to have San Francisco emerge from the so-called "presidial Pueblo," it seems that this intention, still-born because of circumstances, was destined never to be fulfilled.

The circumstances that resulted in a renaming of *Yerba Buena* came from the important event of July 9, 1846, when Captain John B. Montgomery caused the American flag to be raised in the Yerba Buena Plaza. The ready cheers with which the local citizenry greeted this event told of their desire to live under that flag; a twenty-one gun salute followed from the *Portsmouth* out in the bay and the old Plaza was renamed Portsmouth Plaza, as seemed most appropriate. On January 9, 1847, Yerba Buena's first newspaper, the *Star,* appeared and, on January 29, an Ordinance of Naval Lieutenant Washington A. Bartlett (who had been appointed by Montgomery as the first American *Alcalde*) was printed in the *Star;* its importance merits full quotation here. *The Annals of San Francisco* thus records the change of name:

> . . . A highly important announcement, which pleased all but the inhabitants of the place, appeared in the *Star* of January 30, 1847:
>
> An Ordinance
> Whereas the local name of Yerba Buena, as applied to the settlement or town of San Francisco, is unknown beyond the district and has been applied from the local name of the cove on which the town is built; THEREFORE, to prevent confusion and mistakes in public documents and that the town may have the advantage of a name given on the public map—IT IS HEREBY ORDAINED that the name of SAN FRANCISCO shall hereafter be used in all official communications and public documents or records appurtaining to the town.
>
> Published by order:
Washington A. Bartlett,
Chief Magistrate.[6]

The events connected with the establishment of civil government in the Spanish-Mexican *Yerba Buena*–San Francisco, are best summed up in three separate periods. The first was the period of Spanish settlement and Mexican rule extending from September 17, 1776 (founding of the Presidio), to the raising of the American flag on July 9, 1846. A second transition period followed, from the American conquest of California, ratified by the Treaty of Guadalupe Hidalgo on February 2, 1848, to the adoption of the first city charter for San Francisco on April 15, 1850, which action

Bosqui print: View of San Francisco in 1846–7. California Historical Society

was ratified by the State Legislature on the following May 1. The third period ended exactly one year later with the adoption, on April 15, 1851, of a revised second city charter. Because of the interesting circumstances that, in 1856, made the city and county of San Francisco coterminous, it should be noted here that it became a county (one of the original 27 in California which now has 58 counties) on February 18, 1850; it was officially made a city on April 15, 1850; finally the consolidation act passed by the State Legislature declared the city and county of San Francisco coterminous as of April 19, 1856.

When, on February 22, 1847, Alcalde Bartlett was allowed to resign his office and return to his naval duties, General Stephen W. Kearny, American military governor in Monterey, appointed Edwin Bryant as his successor. After four months he was replaced by George Hyde, also a Kearny appointee. At this time the *Star* printed the following figures as to those resident in the area: "Total = 459 of whom 228 have been born in the United States while 182 are under forty years of age." There seem to have been "politics as usual" from the earliest days in San Francisco and these intrigues centered, in part, around the person of John White Geary (1819–1873) who bears the distinction of having served as the last American *alcalde* and the first American mayor of San Francisco. Born in Pennsylvania, Geary was appointed postmaster of San Francisco, a political plum given to him because of services rendered in the army during the Mexican War. He arrived in the city on April 1, 1849, but did not have much opportunity to care for the mail, for soon the presidential elections resulted in the Democrat Polk being succeeded by a Whig President, Zachary Taylor. This meant Geary's replacement, so he resigned to stand successfully for the now elective post of *alcalde*. Since he was also appointed "Judge of First Instance" for San Francisco by military governor Bennett Riley, Geary had the distinction of being, for a while, the only local law administrator in the city. On May 1, 1850, following the ratification of the city's first civil charter, Geary was elected first mayor of San Francisco. Serving for one turbulent year, and plagued by a lack of funds with which to administer civic affairs, in 1851 he refused to run again. His other more compelling reason was that he hoped to become senator from California with the idea of occupying the seat left vacant by John Charles Fremont. Geary did not succeed here, and returned to Pennsylvania in February 1852. Later, in 1873, after serving as a major general in the Civil War, Geary became governor of his native state where he died several weeks after finishing his term. He had been quite interested in the early charters of San Francisco and his service in the city, while short, was significant. One of the major thoroughfares of the city bears his name.

Between 1835 and 1847 the future city of San Francisco began to take shape. The beginning of the pueblo of *Yerba Buena* and the first private land grant occurred in the same year, 1835. The next decade witnessed further distribution of land and settlement outside *Yerba Buena* itself. The ranchos were controlled by native Californians who wished to combine a place of residence with large ranches. Between 1835 and 1847 there were about twenty individual grants within the boundaries of San Francisco; while most were minor in area and of small fame, others were of paramount importance. The first private grant was the *Rancho la Laguna*

John W. Geary. San Francisco Archives, Public Library

de la Merced which was granted, on September 23, 1835, to Jose Antonio Galindo. (He was an ex-soldier and the grandson of one of Anza's original expedition, Nicolas Galindo.) The second major grant was made to another descendant of Anza's expedition, Jose Cornelio Bernal. In 1839 to 1840, he was granted the *Rancho Rincon de las Salinas y Potrero Viejo.* Quite extensive, this grant covered much of southeastern San Francisco, and within its boundaries were included the future Bernal Heights and Hunters Point.

In 1841, the first major grant was given to an American. Governor Juan Alvarado granted Jacob B. Leese the *Rancho Canada de Guadalupe Rodeo Viejo y Visitacion* in the area of mid-southern San Francisco. This large grant comprised some 8,880 acres in San Francisco and, later, in San Mateo County as well. In 1844, *Rancho Potrero de San Francisco* was granted to Francisco and Ramon de Haro. This became known as *Potrero Nuevo.* The *Rancho San Miguel* was perhaps the wealthiest within the future city. Granted in December, 1845, by Governor Pio Pico to Jose de Jesus Noe, it was located in what later came to be regarded as the geographical center of San Francisco. On this rancho, Noe kept 2,000 cattle and 200 horses. On March 30, 1857, the Land Board confirmed 4,443 acres to Noe. Although other smaller grants were made, those mentioned here comprised the major ranchos of the future city and county of San Francisco. By the time of American occupation in July 1846, virtually all the available land had been assigned both within the pueblo of *Yerba Buena* and throughout the outlying districts.

CHAPTER 4

DAYS OF "OLD, OF GOLD, OF '49"

T

HERE IS CERTAINLY no lack of literature about the discovery of gold in California in 1848. This epochal and classical discovery (there had been other "preclassical," i.e. not so well-known finds of the precious metal before that of James Wilson Marshall on January 24, 1848) was destined to change San Francisco from relative obscurity to a bustling metropolis of the Gold Rush. It is but a truism to state that our modern city developed most of all from this onrush of gold-seekers. Indeed, a number of things distinctively San Franciscan claim their origin from these same years.

Before the Marshall discovery at Sutter's Mill at Coloma on the American River, California could muster only 15,000 persons in the entire territory: in 1857, this figure had yielded to 500,000 with many more yet to come. In the still newly named San Francisco, as nearly as one can come on substantially accurate figures, the population, in early 1848, was about 1,000; by the summer of 1848, several months after Marshall's discovery, the peninsula was practically deserted, at least as far as able-bodied males were concerned. A local Gold Rush had set in that was to have its effects on San Francisco long before the more celebrated international rush. Many of those who went to the gold country were back in the city by the fall of '48, some with rheumatism and other ills contracted from the working conditions; soon San Francisco would have to brace itself for the anticipated increase as more and yet more gold-seekers came by sea (around the Horn and across the isthmus of Panama) from all parts of the world and over the plains and mountains from the eastern and middle-western parts of the country. By February 1849, the population of San Francisco was about 2,000 but, by July, this had risen to 5,000 while the end of the year saw it grow to about 20,000.

(Here, indeed, was the city's first population explosion.) While absolute accuracy in this matter has long been conceded as impossible, some knowledgeable things have been written on the subject; among the best is George Groh's interesting analysis from which the following quote is taken:

> Various trail counts and harbor master reports provide a basis for reasonable guess. Conservative figures place the 1849 movement at between 30,000–35,000 who arrived in California by land while approximately 20,000–25,000 came in through the Golden Gate. For the entire Gold Rush years, generally considered to be from 1848–1852, California's population went from 15,000 to 250,000.[1]

The figures concerning the number of those who came by sea enjoy greater accuracy than those for the arrivals by land, for harbor master reports were detailed and based upon the shipping lists of passengers aboard, whereas no such check was kept on land arrivals. For example, from the middle of April 1849, to the end of January 1850, 805 vessels entered the Golden Gate; of these, 487 were American and 318 were of foreign registry. On board were almost 30,000 American males and 919 females; foreigners numbered about 8,600 males and 502 females.[2] (These interesting statistics say a number of things to those who enjoy examining their implications; for example, the preponderance of males "on their own" with regard to providing meals and the like, undoubtedly contributed much to the quick growth of the number of eating places in San Francisco—and this is one of the reasons why the city has always had a reputation in this regard. Even today, one may dine in "almost any language and at almost any price" in the epicurean City by the Golden Gate.)

It would be nice to think that all the arrivals were impressed with what they saw but the record is clear that in a number of cases the opposite was true; for example, a passenger on the S.S. *Lenore* wrote home: "Just arrived—San Francisco be damned!" Still others were more optimistic, such as the bard who sang:

> I soon shall be in San Francisco
> And then I'll look around,
> And when I see the gold lumps there,
> I'll pick them off the ground.

Verandah Saloon, Washington & Kearny streets, 1856.

Others took a more realistic approach. Thus Theodore T. Johnson's appraisal of what he saw appeared in his volume published in New York in 1851:

Rising abruptly from the water, an amphitheatre of three or four ugly, round-topped, barren hills form the site of the notorious town of San Francisco. These hills serve a twofold purpose: the miserable, sandy clay soil produces a weed which a starving jackass will scorn and a fine dust for the eyes which no eyelid is proof against—while ravines and ridges afford full sweep to the perpetual gales from ocean and bay in the summer and a place for rivulets and ponds in the winter.[3]

Yet another revealing picture of San Francisco as it appeared to one observer in August 1849, is to be found in these lines:

San Francisco, formerly Yerba Buena, is a queer place. It contains at this time (diary entry for early August, 1849) a dozen adobe structures and perhaps two hundred roughly constructed frame buildings, mostly shipped around Cape Horn. The beach, for a space of two miles, is covered with canvas and rubber tents and the adjacent sand hills are dotted to their summits with these frail but convenient tenements of the prospective miners. The population, numbering

Wallowing in the mud on Montgomery Street, 1849. Southern Pacific

perhaps 5,000, is as heterogenous as their habitations. Such a meeting of languages and jargons and of tongues the world has seldom seen. It is a modern Babel.[4]

For practically all those who came by land or by sea, San Francisco was the mecca of their dreams; their arrival quickly made of the seaport town a veritable emporium of the Gold Rush; all kinds came, the good, the bad, and the in-between; all were, if briefly, funnelled into the city before being spewed forth to the gold country. And San Francisco has never been quite the same since.

CHAPTER 5

RELIGIOUS BEGINNINGS

NOW THAT WE have indicated the beginnings of civil government in the San Francisco that was so radically changed by the Gold Rush, we shall turn to the matter of religion as a phenomenon of the emerging frontier. It is necessary to do this since it is sometimes assumed, with unwarranted oversimplification, that California in general and San Francisco in particular were in earlier days (from the religious and moral standpoints) really jungles, where those who considered themselves somewhat west of the commandments of God and of man busied themselves with little else than getting rich in a hurry. Closer investigation will reveal the shallowness of this view; while making full allowances for the freedom (and even license) attached to frontier societies, there were in San Francisco, and this most certainly, devoted men of the laity as well as clergymen of many faiths who gave the lie to any such "jungle thesis." The *Daily Alta California* thus expressed scorn for those who distorted the truth:

> One who has "seen the elephant" writes home to the New York *Tribune:* "San Francisco is a God forsaken place, nearly given over to gamblers, professional idlers and tipplers. They seem a band of outcasts met in a brotherhood of woe. Daily arrivals of fancy sporting men, pugilists and genteel loafers and abandoned women from the states are rapidly swelling their ranks."
> This is another of those absurd statements culled from California Correspondence which we are repeatedly called on to contradict and which cannot even aspire to the propriety of a sober, one-sided view of the subject which it professes to elucidate. For such wanton perversions, their authors deserve to be held up to ridicule, pointed at by the finger of incredulity and kicked out of their positions as writers for the press by the insinuating toe of ineffable contempt.[1]

So at least, according to the eloquent editor, it seems untrue that all the Argonauts parked their morals on the east side of the Sierra or threw their equivalents into the Golden Gate as they approached the promised land by sea. No less an authority than the distinguished Harvard philosopher Josiah Royce (born in Grass Valley, California) declared that, on the whole, the California clergy of the time were "remarkably faithful, intelligent, laborious and devout." Finally, the contemporary testimony of the authors of the *Annals of San Francisco* may be mentioned here: "We have said enough, we hope, to prove that not all, or nigh all, the citizens of San Francisco are lost to everything but reckless dissipation. No city of equal size—and few of ten times its age—can present such a list of men and institutions who have accomplished such real good with so little of cant or hypocrisy."[2] So it appears, therefore, that religious and other cultural values were in evidence during the period of which we now treat; indeed, any attempt (and there have been such, of course) to exclude such values from a telling of the past of San Francisco becomes immediately suspect.

The Franciscan phase of religious activities, as evidenced in the Mission Dolores story, has already been indicated; here it is proposed to confine the discussion to the first years of what may be called the American period of San Francisco's past. That period as applied to California started effectively with the discovery of gold. The American period of Roman Catholicism in California may be dated from December 6, 1850, when the American vessel *Columbus* entered the bay bearing a new bishop appointed to California, Joseph Sadoc Alemany, O.P. He bore the title of Bishop of Monterey (his jurisdiction included all of California, though) from 1850 to 1853 and was named first archbishop of San Francisco in the latter year, serving in that important capacity until 1884. One who examines the Alemany years is quickly forced to the pleasant conclusion that the earlier Franciscans such as Serra, Palou, Lasuen, and others, had a worthy successor in the humble Dominican friar who ruled the Catholic church in San Francisco for thirty-four years.[3]

Three pioneer Catholic parishes were established in Gold Rush San Francisco. The first is the patronal parish of the city, that of St. Francis of Assisi, founded in 1849. Even before the stirring days of "old, of gold," Mission Dolores had slept in the sun of its decayed grandeur, its heart eaten out by the worm of secularization. Catholics arriving in San Francisco in 1848 and seeking spiritual succor found that Padre Prudencio Santillan, a Mexican Indian priest in charge of the mission, neither knew any English nor wanted to communicate with those whom he looked upon after the Mexican War as hardly his friends. It remained for two secular priests, both French Canadians, to come from the Oregon country to improve the condition of Catholicism in the city. They were John B. Brouillet (1813–1884) and Anthony Langlois (1812–1892) and the result of their joint apostolic endeavors was the dedication of a small frame church on Vallejo Street where the first Mass was offered on Sunday, June 17, 1849. Soon sermons were being given in several languages, with the small building frequently crowded to capacity. Eventually, in 1860, a permanent church was built and, in essence and despite a gutting of the interior which was its lot in 1906, this is the same St. Francis Church of today which has appropriately been called the "Queen of the [Columbus] Avenue." It holds a unique place in the story of San Francisco's Catholic past.[4]

The second Gold Rush parish was that dedicated to St. Patrick which was established by the Reverend John Maginnis (1797–1864) in 1851. Admittedly this was founded as an Irish parish and the beautiful St. Patrick's Church on the Mission Street of today (between Third and Fourth streets, dedicated in 1872, is a lineal descendant of the first one which stood on the present site of the Palace Hotel. St. Patrick's was the first parish established by Bishop Alemany, who found St. Francis Church already established on his arrival in late 1850. On September 7, 1851, the young prelate blessed a small frame building on Market Street in the area known as Happy Valley. In 1854, a more commodious structure was built and this same building has the unique distinction of having "travelled west" several times until finally, in 1891 it came to rest in its present location on Eddy Street between Scott and Divisadero; it served as Holy Cross Church there for some years and now is preserved alongside a more modern church; it is the oldest frame church edifice in all San Francisco.[5]

The third pioneer Catholic church in San Francisco has the distinction of having been the first cathedral here. Known now as "Old St. Mary's" and located on California Street at Grant

Avenue, it was dedicated by Archbishop Alemany at Christmas
Mass in 1854. There was some difficulty in obtaining building
materials as much of the stone was quarried and cut in China and
shipped to San Francisco to be assembled for the foundation
according to prefabrication plans. The brick for the walls was
brought from New England around the Horn in sailing ships.
Many were the difficulties that were met and surmounted in its
construction and it was a legitimately proud Archbishop
Alemany who, as celebrant of a pontifical Mass at midnight,
made the Christmas of 1854 memorable in local Catholic annals.
Small wonder that the delighted Alemany thus wrote to his
mother in Vich, Spain:

> The Cathedral is large, not so large as that of Vich, and all were
> surprised to find it as full as an egg. One hour before the ceremony,
> the people were hurrying to the bell tower and to the galleries. I do
> not remember having seen a church more crowded.[6]

Although not yet complete, the structure reverberated that
night in frontier San Francisco to the sound of music as majestic
as could be heard in the cathedrals of Europe. Suffice it to remark
that within its sacred walls have been written some of the more
substantial pages of the Catholic history of San Francisco. St.
Mary's served as the cathedral church until 1891 when a second
St. Mary's Cathedral was dedicated on Van Ness Avenue at
O'Farrell Street; the first cathedral became known as Old St.
Mary's Church. At the present time, under the devoted care of
the Paulist Fathers, it remains a major factor in the continuing
work of Catholicism in the city.

When one turns to early Protestant activities in San Francisco,
he finds that various denominations hold honored places in its
religious past. Sam Brannan, an elder in the Mormon church,
preached a sermon in San Francisco, possibly in the open air, on
Sunday, August 2, 1846. Less than a year later, on April 25, 1847,
the Reverend James H. Wilbur held a service aboard the bark
Whiton in "Yerba Buena Harbor." He was a presiding elder in the
Methodist Church. In September 1848, the Reverend Elihu Anthony, a Methodist minister, preached in a schoolhouse in Portsmouth Square. The event was thus noted by an attendant, E.C.
Wetmore, a local jeweler:

I arrived in San Francisco via Honolulu in August, 1848 and, on the first Sunday after my arrival, which was September third, I attended religious services in Portsmouth Square conducted by Mr. Anthony, an exhorter, who is a blacksmith by trade. Episcopal services were also held at the schoolhouse several times later, Captain Stout, in charge of the Pacific Steamship Company's work in San Francisco and Captain Thomas, an English Episcopalian, officiating.[7]

On November 2, 1848, undenominational Protestant religious services in San Francisco in charge of a locally paid, full-time pastor began. Reverend T. Dwight Hunt, a Congregational missionary in the Sandwich Islands, finding himself with little to do, because most of his people had deserted for the gold fields of California, obtained a few months' leave of absence from the Islands to see what could be done in a religious way in California. His advent is thus recorded by the Protestant historian, W. W. Ferrier:

> His arrival was opportune. The need was great. People rallied about him in welcome at once and on the second of November 1848, engaged him at a salary of $2500 a year to conduct, for one year, undenominational services in the Public Institute building on Portsmouth Square. His official title was "City Chaplain." Dr. Hunt's duties were those of a regular pastor of a church with preaching services and Sunday school on Sundays, prayer meeting on Wednesday evenings and the full round of church activities during the week.[8]

The Baptist church was early represented in San Francisco with the arrival, on February 28, 1849, of the Reverend O.C. Wheeler. He began preaching in a private home which was quickly filled with those who wished to hear his message. He was followed by the Reverend Albert Williams, a Presbyterian minister, who arrived in early April, 1849. On Sunday, April 8, accepting an invitation extended to him by the Reverend Hunt, he preached in the Public Institute building on Portsmouth Square. It was the Reverend Williams who, after successful preliminary endeavors, founded the first Presbyterian church in San Francisco. On May 20, 1849, six charter members had affixed their names to church rolls and, on Saturday, August 18, they pitched a large tent on the west side of Dupont Street which was "neatly furnished with pulpit, chandeliers and seats to accommodate 200 persons." The

Reverend Williams thus recorded details of the first service in the tent:

> When, on that bright Sunday morning of the nineteenth of August, the crowded congregation for the first time worshipped in the Church Tent, no lofty cathedral with nave, aisles, arches and ornaments could have yielded more real delight.[9]

Both Trinity Episcopal Church and the First Baptist Church date from July 1849; on July 8, the Reverend Flavel S. Mines conducted the first Protestant Episcopal services in San Francisco in the dining room of the American House on Stockton Street. A small church was erected on the southwest corner of Powell and Jackson streets and the first service was held there on October 28, 1849. The Reverend J.L. VerMehr, who had been sent to California by the Episcopal church in the East, arrived in San Francisco a few weeks after the arrival of Mr. Mines. Although he found the field already occupied, he decided that there would be ample need for two Episcopal churches in the area and he proceeded to organize the Grace Episcopal Church. A change came in late July, 1849, when Dr. Hunt was persuaded to change his status from a nondenominational preacher to founder of the first Congregational group in San Francisco. Accordingly, the First Congregational Church was officially organized on July 29, 1849, with the Reverend Hunt as first pastor. Only a week later, on August 5, the Baptists dedicated a church edifice on Washington Street, between Dupont and Stockton streets, furnishing yet another bit of evidence of Protestant religious activity.

These activities seem to have had a highly significant bearing on the trend of life in San Francisco when set against the overall background of social conditions. If there were little good and even outright evil in Gold Rush San Francisco, there is also solid evidence of constructive efforts by dedicated laity and clergymen of both the Catholic and Protestant faiths. Owen C. Coy in *Gold Days,* remarks:

> At the time of the discovery of gold there was little active interest in religious matters. At that time there were in California about a dozen clergymen of the Roman Catholic faith, besides a few lay preachers of the Protestant faith. It is wonderful, therefore, to think that these few Christian leaders were able to turn the quiet village of Yerba

Buena into San Francisco and to establish in the midst of the seething stream of recklessness a highway for the worship of God.[10]

Jewish congregations also date from these pioneer times of San Francisco. Between 1840 and 1850, a number of Jews came to the Pacific coast. (The San Francisco City Directory for 1850 contains a good number of Jewish names.) Likewise, Jewish benevolent societies and small congregations were known in some of the mining towns of the Mother Lode. When the first Pacific Mail steamer arrived in San Francisco, on February 29, 1848, several Jews were listed among the passengers. The first religious services of the newly arrived Jewish people were held in the autumn of 1849, with the total number of worshippers probably not exceeding one hundred. Indeed, there seem to have been two separate services, one held in the second story room of a Montgomery Street building and the other taking place in a tent room occupied by Mr. Louis Franklin on Jackson Street near Kearny. About forty or fifty were at the first-mentioned service while only ten were at the latter. Almost immediately the two groups thought of uniting to form the first synagogue in the city. This took the form of Congregation Sherith Israel, ground for which was purchased in 1852 on Stockton Street between Broadway and Vallejo Street. The dedication of San Francisco's first synagogue took place on September 8, 1854. The building had been erected at a cost of a little more than $10,000. The congregation was composed largely of Polish, English, and German Jews. Temple Emanu-El was the second congregation to be formed in the city, with most of its adherents of German extraction. Meeting temporarily in a building on Bush Street, the group finally saw its synagogue rise on Broadway between Powell and Mason streets. Although its congregation had first met in 1850, the date of dedication was September 14, 1854.

CHAPTER 6

EDUCATION AND CULTURE:
1847–1862

IN A CLASSICAL essay entitled "The Mission as a Frontier Institution in the Spanish American Colonies," Herbert E. Bolton made the point that, in addition to being places of worship, the Franciscan Missions were the first schools in California.[1] They were trade schools, with manual training of various kinds taught to the neophytes, and they were, in a very true sense, the earliest schools in California. Obviously, Mission Dolores was no exception. While one who visits it now may think of it only as a church with adjacent cemetery, this was far from the complete picture when San Francisco's patronal mission was in the full vigor of planned activity. To place the beginning of educational efforts in San Francisco at a different place or later date is an error. With this point made concerning the oldest "school" in the city, we may now turn to a consideration of other schools that were born in San Francisco in the 1840s and 1850s.

The chartered ship *Brooklyn* put into Yerba Buena Cove on July 31, 1846; aboard were 238 exiled Mormon home-seekers under the direction of the redoubtable Sam Brannan. One hundred of these "Pacific Pilgrims" as they were called, were Yankee children from either New England or Atlantic seaboard states who were accustomed to attending school. These new arrivals more than doubled the population of the little hamlet on the cove that welcomed them. However, they created an acute housing shortage, which is why several of the larger families quickly made their way to the secularized Mission Dolores, four-and-a-half miles southwest of the cove. In a dilapidated outbuilding of this mission, school bells soon began to ring. Miss Angelina Lovett, a twenty-one-year-old spinster, was employed as the first teacher. (Several months later, in an outbuilding at Mission Santa Clara nearly fifty miles to the south, a certain Mrs. Isobel taught the children of military families stationed there; she also accepted some Indian children.) These were the first schools in California where English was taught; however, the Lovett enterprise was opened prior to that of the one to the south. It would appear to add up to a real "first" in the history of education in northern California.

In a matter of only a few months, Sam Brannan had a large house built adjoining Portsmouth Plaza; he gave the rear of his home lot for the site of the first formal schoolhouse. Classes opened there early in 1848 and it was duly licensed by the Town Council, or *ayuntamiento,* which agreed to pay $400 a year toward its maintenance, with particular interest shown in indigent children who needed financial help. Six pupils comprised the first class which was taught by Thomas Douglass, a graduate of Yale. In 1848, the discovery of gold broke up this school soon after it was opened when schoolmaster Douglass answered the call to the gold country. However, now that the educational ground had been broken, it was only a matter of time before both public and private schools were founded in Gold Rush San Francisco. Such, for example, was a private institution opened in the fall of 1854 under the supervision of the Reverend C.B. Wyatt, who was the rector of Trinity Episcopal Church. He put in charge a twenty-three-year-old Englishman, A.S. Lowndes, who had just returned from the gold country. Taking a room on Dupont Street (now Grant Avenue) between Pine and California, Lowndes soon had a class of about twenty boys. Soon he was joined by another Englishman, Cambridge educated, who had already had some teaching experience; together, they opened the Trinity Grammar School "in a building in the 300 block of Post Street near the present Union Square—which then was but a sandy hillock."

> Recalling those days more than three decades later for a writer on the Overland Monthly magazine, Lowndes mentioned that Geary Street was cut through only to Powell with the latter street consisting of a deep ravine which had a considerable stream coursing down it. Lowndes' house was near the corner of Geary and Powell.[2]

Like other such schools, Trinity Grammar continued in existence for only a year, 1854 to 1855. Then the building was sold and moved to Stockton and Pacific Avenue where it was converted into a butcher shop. However, answering the requests of some interested parents, the two men later opened a boarding school (Trinity had been only for day scholars) on Bush Street between Mason and Taylor. With the addition of some small structures alongside, they named their school "San Francisco College." It was not surprising, though, that the shifting nature of the population saw some of the students remaining only a few months. However, in the City Directory for 1863, San Francisco College could boast of a "faculty of six and a student body of one hundred and thirty." In the same directory, four other schools were mentioned—St. Mary's College, then newly founded and located in San Francisco; Santa Clara College dating from 1851; Union College, at Second and Bryant streets, which called attention to the "commodious buildings and well-ventilated dormitories"; while the California Collegiate Institute for Young Ladies stressed that its students were "instructed in needlework." So it seems that an educational frontier was already established in the San Francisco of post–Gold Rush days.[3]

The modern University of San Francisco, which has borne the name since 1930, is the direct descendant of the Saint Ignatius College that opened its doors on the site of the present Emporium on Market Street on October 15, 1855. Since, until recent years, it was the only university in the city, we shall here furnish details of its origins and early development.

On December 8, 1849, two Italian Jesuits, Michael Accolti and the future founder of Santa Clara College, John Nobili, entered the Golden Gate five days out of the Oregon country, bent on lending spiritual aid to the many who had crowded San Francisco in search of gold. Their stay in the city was rather brief, though, for Bishop Alemany assigned Father Nobili to the parish church in San Jose while Accolti was recalled to the Oregon Jesuit mission to be Superior there. So it was that the Jesuit Apostolate of Education in San Francisco did not begin until November 1, 1854, when Father Anthony Maraschi, accompanied by two other Jesuits with teaching experience, came through the Golden Gate in answer to a request from Archbishop Alemany to found a school of the Order in San Francisco. First came a little parish church, dedicated to St. Ignatius Loyola and opened on July 15, 1855, at the Market Street site already mentioned.

The Third Street Ignatius Church and College, 1880–1906.

Next came "St. Ignatius Academy," (1855–1859) a one-room wooden structure immediately adjacent to the equally small church; a third structure served as a residence for the several Jesuit fathers. Like most pioneer foundations, although the seeds of future progress were sown that day, they took some time to increase and multiply. "Master Richard McCabe" and two others were the first to answer the call to Jesuit education on that Monday morning, October 15, 1855. After the usual pioneer vicissitudes, which are almost routine in such ventures, the infant school had sufficiently progressed to merit chartering by the state of California as "Saint Ignatius College" under the date of April 30, 1859; it was a source of pleasure for Father Maraschi to read these encouraging lines in a local newspaper for August 1, 1859:

> The Reverend Anthony Maraschi, President of St. Ignatius College, is eminently qualified for the position, being a finished scholar and a man of high moral character. He has labored incessantly to advance the interests of those placed under his charge and the examination of the several classes exhibited the complete success which has attended his efforts.[4]

St. Ignatius Church today.

By 1862, it was possible to erect an imposing brick building adjacent to the original wooden church; the auditorium served as the second St. Ignatius Church with the rest of the structure devoted to the work of the still young college. This second college was to serve for almost twenty years until the Golden Age of Saint Ignatius College began when a magnificent new church and college were dedicated at Hayes Street and Van Ness Avenue. The story so far will suffice to indicate why the Jesuit Fathers of the University of San Francisco with their present campus on Ignatian Heights near Golden Gate Park feel that their predecessors have written an integral and pioneer page in the history of education in San Francisco.[5]

When we come now to a brief history of early cultural efforts in pioneer San Francisco, it is interesting to note that the authors of the *Annals of San Francisco* seem to blow hot and cold on the subject. Already quoted is their opinion that "not all or nigh all the citizens are lost to everything but reckless dissipation." Yet the same authors, describing the city as they saw it in 1851, called it "a community lawless and reckless, passion actuated and fancy governed, wild, desperate and daring—pregnant with vices and barren of virtue."[6] Evidently, Reverend William Taylor, pioneer Methodist minister, thought even this too mild for his liking; in a stern denunciation, he cried: "The city of San Francisco may, with propriety, be regarded as the very citadel of his Satanic Majesty." As usual it seems that the truth lay somewhere in between. As will be indicated, almost from the beginning of, at least, the American period of its history, San Francisco never lacked a cultural dimension.

The historical record is sufficiently clear to assert that, by the end of 1849, San Francisco, though still a frontier town, was on its way to becoming a cosmopolitan and somewhat sophisticated city. Earlier we asserted that it would be unrealistic to think that truly religious persons would completely abandon their beliefs and practices by virtue of their arrival in Gold Rush San Francisco; the story of the almost dozen pioneer religious congregations established during the decade of the 1850s seems to make this abundantly clear. Equally unrealistic would be the assertion that those Argonauts who were educated in traditions of culture before their arrival (and there were many such) would not soon want to bring about the establishment of theatrical productions and other evidences of culture.

On June 22, 1849, in an abandoned schoolhouse that had already been used as a hall, an actor, Stephen C. Massett, gave the first theatrical performance ever to be given in English in San Francisco, thus inaugurating what has come to be regarded as a distinguished cultural and theatrical tradition in the city. An account notes that the audience seemed to have a good time, and the enterprising Massett netted $500. Perhaps this was what inspired Joseph A. Rowe to open a circus on Kearny Street above Clay, with the first performance staged on October 29, 1849. Despite the undoubtedly large number of persons who wanted more earthy forms of entertainment, Shakespeare first came to San Francisco with the staging, on February 4, 1850, of *Othello*. Competition to such presentations was liberally afforded by the goings-on in such saloons as the Bella Union which was both famous and notorious, depending on one's point of view. On July 4, 1850, Dr. D.F. "Yankee" Robinson, opened "Robinson's and Evrards Museum"; his first show, done with amateurs, was called "Seeing the Elephant." Since this was a melange of the experiences of those who had come to California in quest of gold, it proved to be of considerable interest to its auditors. The next impresario was an illiterate cab driver named Tom Maguire; it was he who, despite discouraging disappointments when several earlier ventures were destroyed by fire, opened his Jenny Lind Theatre III on October 4, 1851, in the vicinity of Portsmouth Plaza. A contemporary newspaper described this event:

> The Jenny Lind Theatre, a new and really magnificent establishment, was opened on Saturday night to a densely crowded house. An opening address was spoken with admirable taste and correctness by Mrs. D. Woodward:
>
>> Beneath this lofty dome . . . we greet tonight,
>> The witching form and grace of beauty bright;
>> Ye patrons of the drama, one and all . . . we'll
>> Strive to win your praise. . . .
>
> The address was greeted with great applause after which the curtain rose for the business of the evening: "Faint Heart never won Fair Lady" and "All That Glitters is not Gold."[7]

The success of the Jenny Lind caused Dr. Robinson to open his American Theatre some weeks later; the Jenny Lind was still out in front, though, when the celebrated tragedian, Junius Brutus Booth, played there for two weeks. When the Jenny Lind was sold for service as a city hall, Tom Maguire opened a fine new theatre, which came to be called Maguire's Opera House and which contributed much to the growing cultural tradition. By the early 1850s, then, San Francisco could already boast of rivalry with some of the great theatrical centers of the East. More complete accounts of the ever-growing cultural tradition of stage and theatre indicate that the momentum gained by Robinson and Maguire and others never slowed down entirely, and history here amply testifies that culture was not unknown to the San Francisco of Gold Rush days—and after.

CHAPTER 7

THE VIGILANCE MOVEMENTS: 1849, 1851, 1856

IT HAS ALREADY been indicated that no support will be found here for any of the exaggerated facets of what has been called the "jungle thesis" with regard to San Francisco's past. At the same time, proper perspective and historical balance require the frank admission that among the multitudes arriving in the city in Gold Rush years were many who were already proficient in crime including some, notably but not entirely, from the penal colony of Australia who had served jail sentences. Some were quite willing and even prepared to resume their criminal careers amid the, to them, favorable circumstances that marked a frontier civilization swollen and disorderly because of the continuing search for the riches of El Dorado. From these off-scourings of society were to be expected the perpetration of crimes and it was not long before the gold country of California, and San Francisco in particular, became acquainted with these persons and their deeds. Many writers still maintain that the Vigilance Movements and/or the two Committees in San Francisco that resulted from this tense state of affairs were completely justified and that they represent frontier justice at its very best; before entering into this controversial area, it may help to indicate briefly some of the background of our story.

In California history, San Francisco does not have the unenviable distinction of having first hanged criminals, for the record reveals that such hangings were not unknown in the Mother Lode and other rural areas of California. Still told, for example, is the dramatic story of how one Juanita, a Mexican national, was hanged in 1851 in Downieville, while modern Placerville, once called "Hangtown," was so named because of some similar incidents. However, the main movements connected with vigilance centered in San Francisco in the three years 1849 to 1851, and, more notably, 1856, when the so-called "Great Committee" was formed there.

When the "Sydney Ducks," many of them ex-convicts, arrived in the city from Australia in 1849 and 1850, they could hardly have been impressed by any legal compulsions stemming from the treaty of Guadalupe Hidalgo (February 2, 1848) between the United States and Mexico which had brought the Mexican War to an end: in awarding California to the victorious United States, the treaty had stipulated that Mexican law usages should be honored until such time as they would be replaced by American law. The very presence of any convicted criminals in California flaunted a Mexican law that explicitly prohibited just such entries into her territories. In place of concern for the fulfilling of such a law, some of the newly arrived decided to take the authority unto themselves and to "go respectable" at least in external appearances. From this determination came a unique organization, which these same assorted undesirables called the "Society of Regulators" (quickly dubbed the "Hounds") who, although professing a desire to see law and order prevail, were called by an early appraiser of their assorted activities, "the veriest rogues and ruffians that ever haunted a community, a band of self-licensed robbers." The special object of their antipathy seems to have been the "Chilenos," a group of Spanish-speaking natives of Chile who, even as the Regulators, had come in search of gold and who, like their future tormentors, lived at the base of Telegraph Hill in a kind of tent village.

Racism seems to have had a long history in San Francisco for, certainly, this was the underlying cause of the Regulators' contempt, hatred and, eventually, murderous attacks on the inoffensive foreigners. Assorted frictions led to the bloody events of Sunday, July 15, 1849, when the Chilenos were assaulted by a group of the Regulators, the brawl centering around what is now Post Street between Grant Avenue and Kearny Street. Some of the Regulators murdered a protesting Chileno mother and criminally assaulted her daughter. A group of irate citizens demanded summary action from Alcalde Leavenworth and Sheriff Ellis; their demands resulted from a speech given by Sam Brannan the next morning when he addressed an indignant crowd from the roof of the Alcalde's office on the Plaza. A counterorganization was formed, to be known as the "Law and Order" group; quickly, Sheriff Ellis swore in one hundred and fifty citizens as his deputies, and nineteen of the Regulators were arrested and incarcerated in the hull of the U.S.S. *Warren* in the harbor. A tribunal was constituted and found eight of the nineteen guilty of disturbing the peace and other more reprehensible activities. While there were no hangings, sentence of banishment was passed on the convicted; in effect, this germ of the first official Vigilance Committee, which was to be formed in two years, served notice in 1849 (a full year before the admission of California into the Union) that criminality would not be condoned in San Francisco. On the key historical issue as to whether the convictions and sentences were justified as dealt out by the group, it should be observed that the local system of courts had either not been set up or had already proven ineffective so that the irate citizens simply responded in what they considered, with abundant reason, to be a crisis in civic history.

If the relieved citizens of San Francisco thought that prompt action against the Regulators would bring lasting peace to their city, they were due to be quickly disillusioned. It was not long before more criminality broke out—and the city was to continue to suffer from such things in 1850 as well as today. Thieves, murderers, and other undesirables went unpunished, with local government showing little or no effective desire to bring an end to such intolerable conditions. It would take a particularly objectionable crime to organize, once more, the forces of decency. This came on February 19, 1851, when a prominent merchant, C.J. Jansen, was beaten in his store while his safe was burglarized. This plus other signs of increasing unrest, including pillaging after another large fire in the city, brought into being the first official Vigilance Committee in San Francisco's short history—that of 1851.

As a prelude, well-intentioned but ineffectual to this committee, a group of genuinely public-spirited and concerned citizens, many of them merchants, had organized a night patrol. Under the captaincy of F.W. Macondray and operating in shifts, they patrolled various parts of the menaced city, especially the business district between Portsmouth Plaza and the waterfront; however,

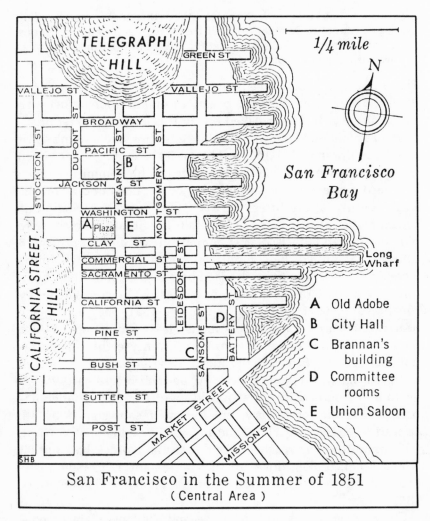

San Francisco in the Summer of 1851
(Central Area)

San Francisco in the Summer of 1851.

despite such valiant efforts, crime continued to increase; on May 4, 1851, the sixth fire to afflict the wooden city brought in its wake the usual pillaging and other terrifying effects. On June 8, 1851, an anonymous but effective letter appeared in the *Daily Alta California* calling for immediate action and a "war of extermination" against all miscreants. Urging the formation of a Committee of Public Safety, the letter said:

Let us set about this work at once. Without this or some similar plan, the evil cannot be remedied and, if there is not spirit enough among us to do it, then, in God's name, let the city be burned and our streets flow with the blood of murdered men.

That same afternoon, three men met in a house on the corner of Bush and Sansome streets and began the organization of just such a committee as had been called for by this letter. The first president was Selim E. Woodworth, while a leading and moving spirit was Sam Brannan. At the height of its activities, over seven hundred men were enrolled on the roster of this committee which had headquarters on the second floor of a frame building on the west side of Battery Street between Clay and Pine. Some unsolved crimes plus the case of a certain Jim Stuart, who chose to hide out in San Francisco after committing a murder in the gold country, catapulted the committee into action. Although courts were operative at the time, the members of the committee chose, for the most part, to take the law into their own hands; when they concluded their activities in September 1851, they had made nearly ninety arrests and were responsible for four hangings. Also they had whipped one man, sentenced twenty-eight to deportation, handed over fifteen to the authorities for trial, and dismissed charges against forty-one others. While their record hardly adds up to an irresponsibility that would merit complete condemnation, the verdict of history, not by any means shared by all, appears to be that, with local courts operative and not all corrupt, the committee overreached itself. Law and order had not, it would seem, broken down to such an extent as to have justified the activities of this well-meaning Vigilance Committee of 1851.[1]

Only five years passed before a second Vigilance Committee—usually called the "Great Committee"—was formed in San Francisco. The half-decade had not seen the presence of sufficient law and order in what was still a frontier city; there had been about a thousand unpunished homicides in the city between 1849 and 1856. The same years saw many corrupt civic officials firmly entrenched in their positions of influence and peddling their favors to those prepared to pay for them. Out of these conditions, coupled with other unfavorable circumstances, came the second official call to vigilance in the city. It will ever be associated with

Montgomery Street in 1856.

the names of its two most famous victims, Charles Cora and James Casey. Those who died on the receiving end of the Cora-Casey bullets were, respectively, United States Marshal William H. Richardson (not to be confused with that William A. Richardson already mentioned as the pioneer of the pueblo of *Yerba Buena*) and the celebrated journalist, James King of William. Richardson received mortal wounds from the gun of Charles Cora, a local gambler; the former had uttered some sneering remarks at a theatre performance when he saw that Cora was accompanied there by his mistress Belle. Cora vowed vengeance and, on Saturday, November 17, 1855, he claimed it on Clay Street near Montgomery with a well-directed shot. The trial that resulted finished with a hung jury because many of the jurors thought that Cora had received sufficient provocation from the public insult given to him and his companion. Cora might well have gone free had it not been for the events of Wednesday, May 14, 1856.

James King of William (1822–1856), so called to indicate that he was the son of William King, had come to San Francisco from his native Washington, D.C., in 1847, and at the end of several years, had become a successful banker. However, reverses came

Market Street in 1865.

in the hard times that hit the city in the early fifties and King next turned to journalism. Helped by a few friends, he became the founding editor of the *San Francisco Bulletin* and determined to make his mark in an overcrowded field by resorting to sensational and muckraking editorials and news articles with a view to increasing circulation and as a guarantee against another failure, which he could not afford since he had a wife and six children to support. Fair (or unfair) game for his pointed and even poisonous pen was furnished by various persons whom he decided to attack and whom he did attack viciously and, at times, without proof of their being guilty of what he accused them. It quickly became apparent that King was at his best when heaping personal abuse on those persons or conditions or institutions that he disliked. Included were priests and nuns, for he entertained a special malevolence toward the Catholic Church; the deservedly respected Archbishop Alemany was the occasional object of his remarks, as was Father Hugh Gallagher, a prominent priest of the city; King sneered at the purported chastity of the esteemed Sisters of Mercy who staffed Saint Mary's Hospital, and thus made himself thoroughly obnoxious to many of the solid citizenry who, with reason, suspected that King was a self-appointed demagogue who could be counted on to offend many persons. (This should all be remembered when one reads the accepted and yet generally uncorrected accounts that call King "San Francisco's martyr of the freedom of the press," words of high praise for one who was, at least at times, hardly more than a journalistic mountebank who frequently asked for hot lead in his vitals and who, eventually, got just that as a result of what might best be called a frontier feud.)

One of the prime targets of King's abuse was James Casey (1829–1856) editor of a smaller paper, the *San Francisco Sunday Times*. Casey had come west from New York City after serving some time in Sing Sing prison and, latterly, he had engaged in some adroit ballot box stuffing, which had resulted in his election to the Board of Supervisors. This last detail justified some of editor King's comments in his paper; however, when he dug too much, in Casey's estimation, into the latter's past (which Casey thought had been amply atoned for by a completed jail sentence) he told King to cease and desist or face the consequences. This caused King to take the highest of ground and to proclaim that he would continue to harass Casey until he had been banished from the local scene. This brings us to that Wednesday May 14, 1856, a date already mentioned. Casey had visited King in the latter's editorial office and, reiterating his demand that he be spared further journalistic attacks, he had been met by the firm rejoinder that his adversary would continue to "do his duty" as a public-spirited editor. (King mentioned in an editorial in the *Bulletin* that he went armed and was prepared to defend himself against all enemies, including rival editors.)

The not unexpected confrontation came in the late afternoon when King was crossing Montgomery Street after leaving the *Bulletin* office. Customary and oft-repeated accounts of what transpired speak of the "assassination" of King by a skulking James Casey who acted more as a sniper than otherwise: however, one

St. Mary's Hospital on Bryant Street, at South Beach, 1866. Southern Pacific

who subjects to examination the party line accounts that abound in this area of written San Franciscana may be permitted to have his doubts. First of all, witnesses testified that Casey, in full sight of King, said, in the almost classical words of a challenge: "James King of William, are you armed?" When King reached under his half cloak to pull out his derringer in answer to his adversary's question, Casey fired first and King sank to the ground groaning "Oh my God, I have been shot!" Casey then ran up to Portsmouth Plaza and later sought sanctuary in a police station.

King was carried into the lobby of the nearby Montgomery Block (now the site of the Transamerica Pyramid) and, it should be noted, it was commonly agreed upon that Casey's bullet had lodged in a fleshy and nonvital area of King's body. Actually, he did not die (in Room 207 of the Montgomery Block) until six days had passed and it appears evident that he died, at least in part, of "consultation," for a bevy of about a dozen doctors attended him in the lobby of the Montgomery Block Building where, at first, he was placed upon a pillow and blankets. Each seems to have had his own opinion as to the specifics to be prescribed. Later, Dr. Beverly Cole incurred the wrath of his medical peers with the written assertion that, when he was called to attend Mr. King when he was first shot, he diagnosed the wound as merely a fleshy one that was not at all dangerous adding that, with ordinary care, there "would not have been the slightest danger to the life of the wounded man." It would seem that the legitimate anxiety of King's friends was such that they quickly called other physicians which made Cole withdraw from the case almost immediately. He stated, though, that he knew for a fact that a sponge was left in the wound for at least five days and it was his professional opinion that this had been a major cause of King's death. So it would seem from this testimony that it was not Casey's bullet alone that caused the death of the "martyred editor" who had "been cruelly assassinated because of his defense of liberty of the press." (As a matter of record, either Casey's aim at a short distance was quite poor or his intention, as happened more than once in the code of duelling, was merely to wound his opponent, thus "teaching him a well-needed lesson.") Certainly, it seems that the wound was not an overly severe or mortal one. This is not to justify entirely what seems to have been, in effect, more of a duel than a covert assassination; the moral, if such there be, seems to be that a crusading editor with a designedly reckless pen should, under the frontier conditions prevailing in the San Francisco of the middle 1850s, be prepared to die suddenly. Such a respected author as John S. Hittell in his *History of San Francisco*, remarks of the *Bulletin*'s attacks as penned by King: "Many were not sustained by any proof or even plausible testimony and others were even unjust . . . but good motives were attributed to Mr. King."[2]

Whatever verdict may be most correct about what has been told here, the fact remains that the Casey-King affray sparked a somewhat dormant Vigilance Committee to renewed life. William T. Coleman, later immortalized in literary form as the "Lion of the Vigilantes" and already a veteran of the 1851 committee, served as president of the second committee. At the height of its acknowledged power, this committee had several thousand citizens on its roster. Organized along military lines in companies of one hundred, the members were convened by the tolling of a bell on the top of their headquarters, called "Fort Gunnybags" which was located on Sacramento Street between Davis and Front.

On Sunday, May 18, 1856, with King yet hovering between life and death, a large group of the second Committee of Vigilance marched silently to the county jail on Broadway where they demanded the persons of Casey and Cora. The men were delivered into their hands and were conveyed, with equal solemnity and as an indication that this was not a mob but a responsible group of concerned citizens, to Fort Gunnybags. When James King died on Tuesday, May 20, the fates of both Casey and Cora were sealed and it was evident that they would both be condemned to hang. On the afternoon of King's funeral, Thursday, May 22, which took place from the Unitarian Church on Stockton Street followed by the longest funeral procession in the city's history, with the burial at Lone Mountain Cemetery, a decision was made at Vigilante headquarters to advance the date of the two executions which had been set for Friday, May 23rd. A contemporary newspaper account related that more than twenty thousand persons hastily gathered in the vicinity of Fort Gunnybags when they heard the tolling of the death knoll for Cora and Casey. At about 1 P.M. workmen hastily erected gallows outside the building at the second story level; inside, a sort of a trial had previously been held with the foregone conclusion that death would be the prescribed penalty. (Critics of the process have indicated that an undeniable bias was shown when Archbishop Alemany's first request to provide spiritual ministration for both men, who were Catholics, was denied; finally, and with reluctance, he was allowed to visit them several days before their death.) On the day of the execution itself, Father Anthony Maraschi, already mentioned as the founder, in the previous year, of St. Ignatius Academy on Market Street, attended Casey, while his Jesuit confrere, Father Michael Accolti, attended Cora. (An interesting detail is to be found in an unpublished manuscript in the Bancroft Library in Berkeley that was written By William T. Coleman: "Father Accolti who was in constant attendance upon Cora, as Father Maraschi was upon Casey, refused to give absolution unless Cora gave evidence of repentance by marrying Belle, his mistress with whom he had been living at the time of his arrest." The marriage, accordingly, was performed a short time before Cora's execution.) On the scaffold Cora appears to have remained much the more composed of the two, uttering not a word. When Casey launched into an impassioned speech, Cora stood behind him seemingly unmoved and, even when the rope was placed around his neck, he remained quiet. Casey quickly seized the opportunity offered him to speak about the unfortunate circumstances that had brought him to the scaffold at the early age of twenty-seven; his opening words possessed an eloquence of their own:

> Gentlemen: I hope this will be forever engraved on your minds and on your hearts: I am no murderer. Let no man call me a murderer or an assassin. Let not the community call me a murderer. Let no editor slander my memory by calling me a murderer. My faults are because of my earlier education for, where I belonged, I was taught to fight and to resent wrongs was my province; I have always resented wrong and have done it now. Gentlemen, I pardon you as I hope God will forgive you, as I hope He will forgive me, Amen, Oh God, have mercy upon me and my poor mother.[3]

The remains of both Charles Cora and James Casey are now in the old Mission Dolores Cemetery. On Casey's tombstone, which identifies him as a member of one of the companies of the San Francisco Fire Department, may be read the words: "May God have mercy on my persecutors." Belle Cora joined her husband in death in 1862 and is buried at his side.

This was the peak of the committee's activities; after this it became less and less important, and finally was disbanded.

It appears that, even now, one who is inclined to criticize the Vigilantes of earlier days in San Francisco is sure to be criticized himself for these same views. However, the tide in this regard is slowly, but surely, turning. For example, in 1971, an excellent study was published with the title: *The San Francisco Vigilance Committee of 1856; Three Views: William T. Coleman, William T. Sherman, James O'Meara.* Walton Bean, professor of California History at the University of California at Berkeley, made some quotable comments about this much needed publication:

> To have reprinted these accounts . . . with good editorial notes, would have been useful in itself but Professor Nunis (Doyce B. Nunis, Jr. the editor and himself an authority on California's past) has done much more by adding . . . an historiographical essay that is a model

of thoroughness and fairness. In it he describes the published materials on the San Francisco vigilance committees from the pamphlets of the 1850's all the way up to recent writings. That the views of Richard M. Brown (critical) and Roger Olmstead (favorable) are almost as conflicting as those of most earlier writers suggests that the controversies over the merits of vigilantism will long remain unsolved. As Nunis says, "a judicious history of the Vigilantes has yet to be written." He states his own general view at the end of his introduction: "In a day when law and order is a critical national problem, it would do no harm for all of us to contemplate quietly and rationally the consequence of invoking extralegal means as a tool for social or political redress." . . . Every serious student of California history must form his own judgements about the vigilantes, and every student of the vigilantes will find Nunis's book essential.[4]

It may be that much of the indiscriminate praise heaped upon the San Francisco Vigilance Committee of 1856 is undeserved, with some of it stemming from that pietism which comes largely from genealogical or familial considerations. Crucial to the whole issue is whether or not the ordinary and accepted practices of law and order had so broken down in San Francisco that it was necessary for an aroused citizenry to take matters into their own hands, with the awesome responsibility that comes from sending persons to the gallows without the usual authorized trial processes. If these processes went unobserved when they might have been invoked, and this appears to be so, it is difficult to justify the actions of the "Peoples Court" of that day. However, I would join others in welcoming a detailed and, if possible, an objective study of the phenomenon of Vigilantism; it has certainly not been published as these lines are written.

CHAPTER 8

SIX FIRES OF THE FIFTIES

AS ALL SAN FRANCISCANS know, their city was spectacularly visited by an earthquake followed by many fires beginning on Wednesday, April 18, 1906, and continuing during the two following days. In the glare cast by these grim days of destruction, they may be inclined to pass over some earlier fires in their civic past. However, because of their importance, these earlier occurrences must be mentioned. Here is one, heavy with history, that comes as somewhat of a shocker even now: between December 24, 1849, and June 22, 1851—a period of only eighteen months—San Francisco was burned six times and about 3,000 structures were destroyed at an estimated value of about $30 million which, when updated to present monetary values, would probably come to about $150 million. By mid-1851, the phoenix, that fabled bird of ancient Egypt which was supposed to live for five hundred years and then, after being consumed by fire by an act of self-destruction, to rise again with youthful freshness from its own ashes, had a permanent assignment in frontier San Francisco.

It is not at all surprising that the San Francisco of 1849 was a city of paradoxes. While wealth was not absent, it was hardly a planned city; rather, like Topsy, it "just grew!" The fact that the Boom Town of '49 underwent its sixfold and cruel baptism by fire in a year and a half was responsible for this only in part.

In January 1847, San Francisco consisted, essentially, of twenty-two subnormal and temporary "buildings" (some would dismiss them as "shanties") together with thirty-one frame houses and twenty-six adobes. That same month saw the first recorded fire in the history of the city. The first, however, was a mere brush fire and it was not until Christmas Eve, 1849, that the classical cry of "Fire" aroused the city. Dennison's Exchange, a gaming house on the east side of Kearny between Clay and Washington streets, caught fire, with the painted cotton ceiling and tarred roof providing ample fuel and, soon, the neighboring buildings also caught, including the equally inflammable United States Restaurant. The adjacent Portsmouth Plaza quickly filled with the curious but was depopulated on the double when rumor had it that a nearby hotel, the Parker House, had powder stored in its basement. The authors of the *Annals of San Francisco* inform us that the excited stampede of the people on their way out of the area was a scene almost as terrible as that of the advancing fire.[1] "By noon of that memorable Monday an entire block on Washington to Montgomery had been destroyed; it was there checked by an unfinished brick building. In all, the blaze had burned the entire block bounded by Washington, Clay, Kearny and Montgomery streets with an estimated loss of $1,500,000." Fifty buildings were burned. Yet, within a few days, reconstruction was begun. With regard to this and subsequent fires, it was commonly thought and as frequently asserted, that the criminal elements of San Francisco gleefully and wilfully applied the torch to at least some of these six fires: certainly, they were set to profit by the ensuing disorder.

Several months passed until, on Saturday morning, May 4, 1850, the same dread cry of "fire" rang out once more. Another gambling house and saloon, which had replaced the gutted Dennison's on exactly the same spot, burst into flames. Again, the entire block was destroyed. A certain salvation was brought to the menaced area by an expedient somewhat unique, it would seem, in the annals of fire fighting. Citizens plus fire fighters tore down every house on Dupont Street (now Grant Avenue) between Washington and Jackson streets, a rather small area but pivotal in the defense of the city with regard to this fire. By this action, the uphill progress of the flames was stopped; the estimated loss was about $4 million, with three hundred buildings destroyed and three lives lost. Obviously, the first fire of 1850 was more disastrous than its predecessor; equally obvious was the fact that there was a lack of available water as well as of fire-fighting equipment. Not a structure stood in the gutted block bounded by Dupont, Jackson, Kearny and Washington streets. Soon the city council ordered construction of a 12,000-gallon cistern in Portsmouth Plaza. However, the undermanned and underequipped volunteer fire department of the time consisted of only three engines (with a total complement of ninety men) together with a hook and ladder company manned by forty fire fighters, all of them on a volunteer basis. Surely, San Francisco was not yet prepared to successfully withstand further trials by fire.

The third fire was bigger if not better: it came on Friday, June 14, 1850, with a recorded loss of $5 million coupled with the destruction of yet another three hundred structures. Beginning in the Sacramento Bakery at the rear of the Merchants Hotel at Clay and Kearny streets, the fire destroyed practically everything between Clay, California, and Kearny streets to the water's edge which then curved up from California and Sansome to Clay and Montgomery streets. This, unlike the former fires, included much more of the residential district as then constituted and thousands were for the first (but not the last) time made homeless in San Francisco. This graphically taught a long overdue lesson—that the city could not hope to be spared further holocausts if its buildings were not improved. Brick buildings were encouraged and given official sanction and encouragement while those of immediately combustible materials were completely forbidden. The hills of San Mateo County were stripped for all available redwood, ditches were filled in, and preparations made for a more efficient response to the next visitation by fire. Additionally, Mayor John W. Geary signed an ordinance for the proper organization of a fire department on July 1, 1850, a date that may be considered to be the natal day of such a department in San Francisco. Only a few months passed before yet another fire visited the city.

This fourth fire struck on Tuesday, September 17, 1850, when the block bounded by Montgomery, Washington, Dupont streets, and Pacific Avenue again went with a loss, though the least of any thus far. Total damage and loss came to an estimated $550,000, with one hundred and fifty buildings destroyed. In retrospect, this fire can be seen as a mere prelude of what is generally called the "Great Fire" which occurred on Saturday, May 3, 1851, starting on the south side of Clay Street opposite the Plaza. A westerly wind drove the flames toward the bay, and a resultant sudden change of wind carried them back to the heart of the city. The blaze raged all night and its eerie reflections were visible in the sky of San Francisco and adjacent areas including, some said, the more distant area of Monterey. The morning sun rose on smoking ruins which covered an area three-quarters of a mile in length, and one-quarter of a mile in width. Sixteen entire blocks had gone with parts of seven others; obviously, the heart of the growing metropolis had been ravaged in the fiery holocaust. Property loss amounted to somewhere between $10 and $12 million, with more than one thousand buildings destroyed. Even the newly built Custom House, situated on the northwest corner of Montgomery and California streets, was gutted, to the special grief of those who had so proudly hailed its completion. Also destroyed were some hulks of Gold Rush days which, grounded, had been used as warehouses, among them the well-known *Niantic.* A macabre scene resulted when some unfortunate persons decided to put to a test the newly designed "fire proof" building which had been built of iron on the northwest corner of Sacramento and Montgomery streets; these people elected to stay inside the building where they died of suffocation when heat from the adjacent flames caused the doors to expand so they could not be opened. Eventually even the iron doubled up in an almost grotesque caricature as the building collapsed. Hubert H. Bancroft reports that at this fire's height and greatest heat water from the small hoses of the day (with little pressure behind them) vaporized on contact with the flames and did but little good. This, then, was the Great Fire of 1851—with almost the entire center of the city gone either in whole or in part.

The new San Francisco which was to result from the Great Fire of 1851 was to be more than a little different. Further and successful searches were made for building materials that were as noncombustible as possible. These included granite, some of which came from the quarries of far-off China as well as bricks from the Atlantic states and even from remote Australia; the granite mentioned was supplemented, of course, with some quarried in northern California. Public reaction to the Great Fire took the form of a determined search for arsonists, with Sam Brannan organizing a volunteer police department to aid in such investigations. However, the end was not yet.

On Sunday, June 22, 1851, a house on Pacific Avenue below Powell Street burst into flames. Before this fire was extinguished between four and five hundred houses had been burned at a cost of more than $3 million. This fire consumed some blocks that had been burned before. The City Hall at the northwest corner of Kearny and Pacific Avenue, was gutted, with the Jenny Lind Theatre being right on schedule, for this structure had suffered in each of the preceding fires. Among the buildings destroyed was that which housed the congregation of the First Presbyterian Church on the west side of Stockton below Pacific and Broadway. Additionally, an old adobe near Portsmouth Plaza which had served as the Customs House for both Mexicans and Americans was destroyed. Oddly enough, the main business section of the city, so afflicted seven weeks earlier, was not damaged anew. However, some houses that had escaped the Great Fire were levelled at this time. Seven lives were lost, three by burning, two by police action when looters were discovered at work, while two were beaten to death by an enraged crowd on suspicion of arson. Negative aspects included the fact that some available reservoirs were discovered practically empty, and some citizens failed to cooperate with firemen. For the sixth time San Francisco set about the task of reconstruction. In many places, large houses constructed of brick, considerably more fireproof than their predecessors, sprang up. Their worth was proven on Tuesday, November 9, 1852, when another fire broke out near the Plaza; however, its flames were quickly halted by some heavy brick walls which had been erected on Washington and Montgomery streets, and little damage resulted. (An interesting detail was printed in the columns of the *Alta California* on the next day: under the title of "Destructive Conflagration": "Rev. Bishop Alemany of the Catholic church worked zealously all evening with the Empire Co. n.1 and did good service.")

So ended the most trying eighteen months in the city's history. While preluding the ultimate in destruction, which was to come over a half century later, these conflagrations of the fifties affected the lives and fortunes of the many who had already cast their lots with San Francisco.

Some mention should be made here of the formation of the early volunteer fire departments of San Francisco which were

Fireman's Memorial: Coit Tower. Redwood Empire Association

born of real necessity. In the modern Washington Square facing Columbus Avenue there is an impressive monument commemorating the San Francisco volunteer firemen of an earlier era. It consists of a bronze group of three such volunteers with the accompanying inscription: "Dedicated to Volunteer Firemen, 1849–1866." It was placed in the square in 1933 as a result of a bequest of the famous Lillie Hitchcock Coit who, always in love with fire fighting, had been made an honorary member of her beloved Volunteer Company Number Five. The earliest firemen in the city, while enjoying a certain status such as firemen customarily do, were unpaid volunteers and worked, of course, with very primitive equipment. The first fire engine arrived in San Francisco on December 9, 1849, aboard the S.S. *Magdalen.* Called the "Martin van Buren" since it had been used to water the lawn on the upstate New York estate of the former president, it was quickly employed in fighting the fires of the fifties. The available supply of water was at first limited to a single well located on the western slope of Telegraph Hill. However, by August 1853, after sad experience, thirty-eight cisterns had been built at strategic points in the city. The first fire engines were hand drawn, and

Monumental Engine House on the Plaza, 1856.

answering calls frequently meant dragging equipment several miles; at night, young lads, hired to do such duty, ran before the firemen with illuminated torches. Members of the various volunteer groups were quite proud of the distinctions that were theirs, as increasingly they became identified with the social life of the city; many important and influential men of the city considered it both an honor and a privilege to serve as volunteer firemen. In appreciation of their hard work and devotion, on March 25, 1853, the California State Legislature passed an act exempting the volunteer firemen throughout the state from jury duty and military service. Among the local pioneer groups of volunteers was the "Empire Number One," composed mostly of men from New

York, the Empire State; this group was organized right after the first fire of December 24, 1849. Other companies included "Social Number 3," mostly from Boston; "Knickerbocker Number 5," composed of Unionists and opposed to "Monumental Number 6," whose ranks consisted largely of Southern sympathizers.

The history of these groups, whether engaged in fighting fires or in friendly rivalries, is a colorful page in San Francisco's past. The death knell of the volunteers came, though, with the arrival, in 1862 from New York City, of the first steam fire engine in San Francisco. Earlier, in 1861, the transcontinental telegraph system reached San Francisco; then horses took the place of men to pull the equipment and paid fire departments became more common on the American scene. Some volunteer companies lasted until December 2, 1866, when, by previous arrangement, a bell's tolling noted the official passing of the volunteers from the San Francisco scene. By that date, the "paid" city fire department already numbered several hundred men who, arranged in shifts, manned an engine company, three hook and ladder groups, as well as three hose companies. Despite the proud history of its present fire department which remains outstanding in efficient performance as well as equipment, San Francisco owes a great debt to the volunteer firemen of its past.

CHAPTER 9

THE
TERRY-BRODERICK
DUEL

T

HE END OF the turbulent decade of the 1850s in San Francisco was marked by a celebrated duel—the last of its kind in California—which found a United States senator matched with his political opponent in the California Democratic party who, up until his resignation the day before the duel, had served as Chief Justice of the California Supreme Court. The two principals were David C. Broderick and David S. Terry.

Broderick, destined to die as a result of his duel with Terry, was born in Washington, D.C., of Irish parents on February 4, 1820. On moving to New York City, he lost no time in entering into the activities of the Democratic party. The young Tammany Democrat seems to have become adept in all the tricks of political chicanery and used the approved methods to build a political machine. However, after suffering a defeat in a try for Congress in 1846, he settled for a change of location and although already a successful saloon keeper, followed through on his plan of self and political reform by emptying his casks in the street and vowing that he would never again sell a drink of liquor, smoke a cigar, or play a card. Taking passage for California, young Broderick reached San Francisco in June 1849. It was not long before he was once more immersed in the local political scene. Elected state senator, he served briefly as Lieutenant Governor of California. His overpowering ambition was to return to the nation's capital as United States senator from California and his ambition in this regard was fulfilled by his election to the Senate in 1856. March of the following year saw him seated in the Senate in Washington; he was then only thirty-seven years of age.

Among his California political opponents was another Democratic politician who was a proslavery Southerner, David S. Terry, formerly of Tennessee. There was deep antagonism be-

tween them centering about the control of their party in California. Terry, frequently intemperate in speech, made a point of
stating his low opinion of Broderick. The immediate cause of the
duel that resulted in Broderick's death was an address, made by
Terry (then Chief Justice of the California Supreme Court) before
the Democratic State Convention in Sacramento during which he
called Broderick a traitor and condemned him on several other
counts. When Broderick read the speech in San Francisco, he
announced that he now withdrew some complimentary things
that he had said about Terry, adding these words: "I take back
the remark I once made that he was the only honest judge on the
Supreme Court. Had the Vigilance Committee disposed of him as
they did of others, they would have done a righteous deed!"
Letters were exchanged, and Terry issued a challenge which
Broderick was not exactly anxious to accept (for the duelling skill
of Terry was well known). Finally a meeting on the so-called
"field of honor" was arranged for Monday, September 12, 1859,
near the boundary line of San Francisco and San Mateo counties.
A great deal of publicity followed, as was to be expected, and,
since their encounter was clearly against a state law which prohibited duelling, Police Chief Martin J. Burke of San Francisco
arrested the two men at the site; however, a local police judge
dismissed the men with the comment that no misdemeanor had
been committed. Immediately the word got around that the principals intended to have their encounter the next morning, this
time in San Mateo County so as not to face the opposition of
Chief Burke. Since there was some attempt to conceal the exact
locality (it was right over the line that separated the two counties), the result was that in the early hours of Tuesday morning
a good number of horses and carriages were lost in the general
vicinity of Lake Merced as they endeavored to locate the scene.
However, twenty buggies containing sixty-seven persons (as
counted by reporters) finally arrived at the right spot which was
described the next morning as "a small valley surrounded by low
hummocks or hills. The sun rose clear in a bright blue sky and
illuminated the scene with his cheerful rays as if in mockery of
the bloody work he was to witness. Little birds hopped merrily
about in the stunted herbage and, warmed into life by the beauty
of the morning, chirped blithely and happily their matin songs."[1]

UNITED STATES SENATOR DAVID C. BRODERICK
AND
JUDGE DAVID S. TERRY
FOUGHT A DUEL ON THIS GROUND IN THE EARLY MORNING
OF TUESDAY, SEPTEMBER 13, 1859. SENATOR BRODERICK
RECEIVED A WOUND FROM WHICH HE DIED THREE DAYS LATER
THE AFFAIR MARKED THE END OF DUELING IN CALIFORNIA.

SENATOR BRODERICK, FACING WEST, OCCUPIED THE POSITION
MARKED BY THE SHAFT FARTHEST TO THE SOUTH, WHILE JUDGE
TERRY FACING EAST, STOOD IN THE POSITION DESIGNATED
BY THE SHAFT IN THE FOREGROUND. SPECTATORS OCCUPIED
THIS EMINENCE.

ERECTED BY HISTORIC LANDMARKS COMMITTEE,
NATIVE SONS OF THE GOLDEN WEST
1917.

Site of the Terry-Broderick Duel.

What followed quickly demonstrated that Senator Broderick was hardly a match for his challenger. The duelling pistols were chosen by Terry, examined by the judges, and declared acceptable for use; what seems to have escaped Broderick, however, was that both of the weapons had hair triggers which would discharge the contents of the pistol at the slightest touch. The next morning the *San Francisco Times* reported what happened:

> Both men were perfectly cool and manifested no uneasiness. The bearing of Judge Terry, though he assumed a more practiced and motionless attitude, was not one jot more that of an iron-nerved man than was that of Mr. Broderick. At a quarter before seven o'clock, Mr. Coulton pronounced the words: "Are you ready?" "Ready," responded Judge Terry and "Ready" was uttered by Mr. Broderick immediately after. "Fire! One, Two!" was pronounced in moderately quick time. Mr. Broderick raised his pistol (both weapons were set with hair triggers) and had scarcely brought it to an angle of 45 degrees from its downward position and in a bee line towards his opponent, when, owing to the delicacy of the hair trigger, it was discharged, the ball entering the ground about four paces in front of him. Judge Terry fired a few instants later, taking deliberate aim. There was a perceptible interval in the two reports. At that instant, Mr. Broderick was observed to clap his left hand to the right side of his breast when it was seen that he was wounded. He reeled slowly to the left and fell (not heavily) to the ground still grasping his weapon.[2]

Broderick was taken to a friend's home at Black Point in the Fort Mason area where he expired three days later. His death caused much excitement in San Francisco and his many political partisans called it a cold-blooded murder on Terry's part because of his choice of a hair trigger revolver with which Broderick was not familiar. Since the fallen senator was a Catholic, he called for and received the last rites of his church with both Father Anthony Maraschi, S.J., and Father Hugh Gallagher in attendance upon him. (However, he had lost the privilege of church services and ecclesiastical burial because of deliberately choosing to participate in a duel which was clearly against the regulations of his church.) His remains were visited by thousands as they filed past his bier in the lobby of the Union Hotel directly across from Portsmouth Plaza; since it became evident that it would be impossible to accommodate the crowds within the hotel, the remains were brought across the street to the Plaza where thirty thousand had gathered to hear the funeral oration delivered by Senator Edward D. Baker of Oregon, one of the outstanding orators of the day. He thus concluded a moving address in which, as expected and even demanded by the many present, he awarded civic canonization to the fallen Broderick:

> But the last words must be spoken and the imperious mandate of death must be fulfilled. O Brave Heart, we bear thee to thy rest! Good friend! True heart! hail and farewell!

A slightly different note marked the address that Father Hugh Gallagher delivered about 5 P.M. that same afternoon when the extensive funeral procession arrived at Lone Mountain Cemetery, the Laurel Hill of later days. The priest explained why it was that Broderick had been denied burial in consecrated ground, declaring that he passed no judgment on his ultimate worth as a politician and senator except to say that the record was clear that he had served honestly in both capacities and therefore merited the words of praise which the priest chose to utter. Expressing the hope that the whole regrettable incident might mark the end of such public duelling in California (it seems to have done so), Father Gallagher declared that Broderick had been completely reconciled to his church and had received the final rites. His final words were generous indeed: "Peace to thy ashes, joy to thy spirit, truest and most unselfish of friends, and most moral of public men."

His victorious opponent, Judge Terry, was tried in San Rafael on charges of manslaughter after claiming a change of venue from San Francisco, but the charges were dismissed probably on the grounds that what had transpired could best be called, essentially, but another frontier feud between politicians. In retrospect, neither Terry nor Broderick seems to have been much more than an ordinary ambitious politician; as happens in such events, Broderick was at his best in his going; while writing a colorful page in the history of a colorful city, it would seem excessive to claim that he was a martyr any more than, three years previously, had been James King of William.

CHAPTER 10

THE BONANZA AGE:
1860–1900

BY 1876, SAN FRANCISCO had reached the respectable age of one hundred, since both presidio and mission date from 1776. Now the infant pueblo which had been catapulted into worldwide significance because of the discovery of gold, had arrived securely at a place in the sun of civilization. The four decades between 1860 and 1900 carried on the pace and excitement thus begun. Vibrant personalities and interesting events marked these fascinating decades.

As will be seen, San Francisco had a bit of just about everything during these years, including its share of civic characters. Perhaps one such, Joshua A. Norton (1819–1880) the famous "Emperor Norton I" should find immediate mention. His story will always remain high on the list of San Franciscana. He was an English Jew who, after amassing considerable wealth in rice speculation in San Francisco, lost it all in a sudden financial reverse. This induced a genial form of self-delusion which caused him to proclaim himself as "Norton I, Emperor of North America and Protector of Mexico"; soon, accompanied by his two faithful dogs, Bummer and Lazarus, he walked (perhaps "processed" would be the more accurate term) the streets of San Francisco dressed in a bedraggled uniform complete with epaulets and a cocked hat. Until his sudden death in 1880, the "Emperor" formed a colorful part in the daily life of a city that had never, at least since Gold Rush times, been without color; all these years, Norton was the object of charity for he never paid for his meals or lodging but simply left signed chits to take care of such material considerations. It will probably never be settled whether the "Emperor" was as demented as he seemed: there are some who think that he was pretty much of a shrewd operator who knew a good thing, and city, when he found both combined. Whatever the truth, it

Emperor Norton.

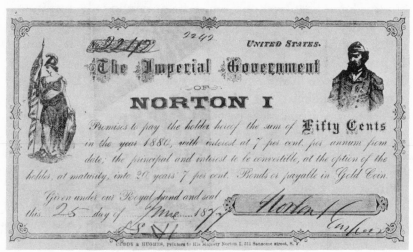

Norton Currency.

Gray & Gifford's Sketch Map of San Francisco in 1868. Southern Pacific

should be remarked that, perhaps, the chief merit in the San Francisco story of Emperor Norton is that he probably could not have lived out such a life anywhere else; he would have been quickly disposed of on vagrancy or other charges. Never did this happen to the "Emperor" in the center of his "kingdom," or elsewhere within its royal confines. (At least two lives of Emperor Norton have been written, while he is continually mentioned even today.)[1]

San Francisco did not sleep through the 1860s. With the discovery of vast silver deposits on what became known as the Comstock Lode in the Virginia City, Nevada, area, the city became the beneficiary of a bonanza. Much of the wealth was absorbed in various ways by San Francisco, so much so, indeed, that it was sometimes referred to as the Silver City during this and the following decades. (An examination of the career of Billy Ralston, which follows in the next chapter, will bring out the connection between the Comstock Lode in Nevada and the San Francisco story.) The decade was almost complete when the city was given a rehearsal of the earthquake that was to come thirty-eight years later, in 1906. On Wednesday, October 21, 1868, a severe earthquake was felt in the city. Three years earlier, in October 1865, there had been such an occurrence but the 1868 quake was much more serious; in fact, it was the most severe yet recorded in the city, and the rather light loss of lives, amounting to only five persons, was attributed to the fact that schools and office buildings were not yet in use since the quake came just before 8 A.M.

Another date of distinction of the sixties was that which marked the completion of the transcontinental railroad, Monday, May 10, 1869. When the Central Pacific and the Union Pacific railroads met at Promontory Point, Utah, 24 miles west of Ogden, California and San Francisco became much more accessible to commerce from the eastern states. However, the results quickly proved that San Francisco was to be more than a little disappointed in the overall effects of its new transcontinental connection; although a good number of passengers arrived "by the cars," more freight than people came, not an unwelcome ecnomic dividend but not exactly what was counted on at the time. However, on September 6, 1869, the first "transcontinental train" arrived on the eastern shores of San Francisco Bay, with a pleasant ferryboat ride ahead to finish the trip.

In San Francisco, the 1870s witnessed the amassing (and, in some cases, the flamboyant) exhibition of wealth by some emerging tycoons. By 1870, the population of San Francisco was about 150,000, and some quite wealthy persons and families were represented in this figure. On August 6, 1871, the *Morning Call* listed 122 men of the city who, collectively, controlled $146 million of local capital. Among those in the top bracket were Leland Stanford (railroad king, $10 million), Ben Holladay (stage coach monarch, $7.5 million), James Phelan, Sr. (real estate and liquor tycoon, $2.5 million), and William C. Ralston (banker, $1.5 million). Their wealth manifested itself in the building of some notable and occasionally even magnificent dwellings on Nob Hill and in the vicinity, especially after it became accessible by cable car in the middle 1870s.

The newly made rich built their palatial dwellings along Stockton, Powell, Mason, Post, Van Ness, Bush, and Pine streets. Among others, Ralston built a city house on Pine Street near Leavenworth at a cost of $140,000; the Flood mansion was built on the site currently occupied by the Pacific Union Club on California Street; the Crocker mansion was on the site now occupied by Grace Cathedral on the same street; the Leland Stanford

Charles Crocker Home on California Street. Now the site of Grace Cathedral. Southern Pacific

mansion was on the southwest corner of California and Powell streets, now the site of the Stanford Court Hotel. Mark Hopkins built a sort of architectural monstrosity on the site of the present Mark Hopkins Hotel. (Gertrude Atherton's remark about this house was as follows: "It looked as if several architects had been employed and fought each other to the finish!")[2]

Despite the opulence just described, which might let one conclude that all was distinguished about San Francisco, the city did have occasional visitors who were critical of what they saw. Thus, in 1872, a twenty-nine-year-old lady en route to the Orient wrote home to her family in Philadelphia after some days in the City by the Golden Gate. Commenting that she found the city built almost entirely of wood and that it even had wooden sidewalks, she added that she thought all this extremely ugly:

> It is on hills, some of them extremely steep, and, for several days, my limbs pained from ascending and descending them. The houses are

built in almost every style of architecture and are generally surrounded by gardens with lovely flowers. The climate is the same all
year—only it rains all winter and blows all summer! The houses look
old, the brick buildings are hideous but, down in the business centers,
things are not so bad.[3]

The same young lady mentioned how cosmopolitan was the
population of what ended up as not her favorite city. "It contains
the most nondescript population. Digger Indians, miners, a whole
city of Chinese, many French, Italians, plenty of Germans—and
each build their houses, keep their stores or do their work at
home. We visited the famous Woodwards Gardens and saw the
sea lions. The flowers were lovely and luxuriant but around were
those desolate gloomy hills making the city like Jerusalem." (At
least her report home can help the aficionado of San Francisco
from over-indulging in that excessive patriotism of which such
are frequently accused!)

By 1880, there was a substantial increase in the population of
San Francisco which the federal census then reported as 233,939;
this figure was up over 75,000 from ten years previously. (This
impressive figure, in fact, represented about one-fourth of the

Hopkins and Stanford Residences.

total population of California and probably helped to give birth to that sobriquet, "The City," which many residents still use to the occasional dismay and/or irritation of those from different parts of the state.) The decade was also marked by the mostly benevolent but always present political rule of Boss Chris Buckley (1845–1922). He was the proprietor of a Bush Street saloon who, although almost blind, controlled the politics of San Francisco with skill for many years. He was a genius in seeing to it that the tax rate remained low, a telling point with the electorate, while not above collecting abundant tribute from the underworld to finance multifarious and far-reaching activities in his shadowy but real control of government in the city. (To his credit it may be said that he was neither violent nor countenanced violence in his followers.)[4]

Mention could well have been made earlier in treating of the 1860s and 1870s that San Francisco in general and the Jesuit Order in particular were then the better for the presence in the city of a very distinguished scientist and scholar. This was Joseph Neri, S.J. (1836–1919) who was responsible for notable contributions in the field of electrical research during most of these years when in the east, Thomas Edison and others were seeking for some means to produce electric light for general use. In 1869, Father Neri, then professor of physics at St. Ignatius College on Market Street, devised an electrical lighting system which was used successfully in the exhibition hall of the college and which attracted much attention. The system made use of carbon electric lights and was in operation fully a decade before Edison invented the incandescent lamp. In 1874, the priest-inventor followed with the installation of a searchlight in the St. Ignatius tower whose rays could be seen for 200 miles under favorable circumstances. In his experiments, Neri first used large batteries, then magnetic machines and, finally, dynamos. His was the distinction of first using the brush machine, the storage battery, and the pioneer magnetic electric machine in California. On July 4, 1876, he commemorated the centennial of the city by treating its inhabitants to the first public exhibiton of electric lights when he strung wires outside the college where the Emporium now stands and illuminated the adjacent areas as well. When, in August, Father Neri exhibited the "Physical Cabinet of St. Ignatius College" at

the Eleventh Industrial Exhibition of the Mechanics Institute at
their Eighth and Mission Pavilion, he merited this inclusion in the
official report of the Exhibition:

> We may congratulate ourselves in possessing in our midst in this city
> and state such facilities for scientific research as St. Ignatius College
> affords. In our rising generation, such a cabinet is second to none in
> the United States.

Mention has been made of the centennial year of 1876; not
surprisingly, it was marked by some impressive celebrations both
on the civic and religious level. Under the date of September 16,
1876, Archbishop Alemany issued an invitation to attend such a
celebration:

> On the eighth of next October will be celebrated the Centenary
> of the Foundation of the Mission and Presidio of San Francisco.
> This hundreth anniversary will be commemorated with due pomp
> at the Mission and at the Mechanics Pavilion of this city. The
> ceremonies will begin with a Pontifical Mass and sermon at the
> Mission at ten in the morning and then the procession will form
> to go to the Pavilion where, at about one o'clock, will take place
> the exercises proper to the civic celebration. You are respectfully
> invited to the said ceremonies.

An impressive commemoration was had, as planned, with Archbishop Alemany and General Mariano G. Vallejo joining oratorical forces in two lengthy addresses at the outdoor Mass in the
garden of Mission Dolores which was offered by Bishop Eugene
O'Connell of the diocese of Grass Valley, with Archbishop
Alemany the presiding prelate. Actually, various aspects of the
celebration continued for three days.[5]

The decade of the 1890s was a crowded one in San Francisco's
civic past. It marked the final phase of a great epoch in the city's
development as well as the accumulation of a half century of
steady and impressive growth which had begun with the abrupt
transition from a frontier town to a sophisticated city. In 1890,
San Francisco had almost 300,000 inhabitants while, by the turn
of the century, this number had grown to 342,782. By 1890, San
Francisco had become the eighth largest city in the United States
as well as by far the largest on the Pacific Coast. Civic spread
found the city expanding in a combination of what could be

called the Westward Movement joined with some growth also in a southern direction. By this time, Portsmouth Plaza had pretty well been relegated to the realm of history since perimeters had spread out from it in various directions. Because of the earlier fires of the fifties, many of the homes were built of brick or stone. However, with the improvement of the water system and a better fire department, inhabitants began to allow themselves more latitude in planning their dwellings with the more imaginative, prevailing use of wood. (Many of the so-called "Victorian dwellings," sometimes referred to as "San Francisco Gothic," date from this period.) The new residential districts such as the Western Addition and Hayes Valley, saw this style prevailing, and there are still some notably impressive examples to be seen which were spared in the holocaust of 1906. The downtown trend during the last quarter century was more toward steel frame construction, such as the Phelan building, the Emporium, the Baldwin Hotel at Powell and Market which, however, despite masonry walls, burned in 1898. In 1890, the first "skyscraper" was built in San Francisco: this was the Chronicle building at the corner of Market and Kearny streets, later known as the de Young building. The year 1897 welcomed the city's first "high rise," Claus Spreckels building on Market Street, a respectable eighteen stories high. (It has since been rebuilt as the Central Tower.) For years, it had the distinction of being the loftiest landmark (man-made) in the whole city.

If San Franciscans have always loved parades, they have also always had a special place in their civic affections for expositions and fairs. Hence, when 1894 saw the opening of the Midwinter Fair in Golden Gate Park, San Franciscans beamed with anticipation and children squirmed at the thought of good things and good days to come. The fair was mounted as a private-enterprise and consisted of over one hundred buildings erected in the park on a 200-acre site between the present 8th and 12th avenues centering around the area now marked by the bandstand and the de Young Museum. The fair went on for six months with a total attendance of 2,225,000. After all the buildings had been demolished except the Egyptian style museum which, now gone, long served as the nucleus for an expanding museum, the fair was declared an unqualified success.[6]

It remains but to chronicle two further events of the 1890s; they were the activity and excitement that marked 1897 when another Gold Rush, this one to the Klondike area of Alaska, took place in San Francisco, which served as a staging area for both transportation and supply. The next year, the city was again to serve as a staging area when, for the first time but not for the last, it was a supply depot for both men and supplies in the Spanish American War. There was a large encampment in the Presidio and in that part of the Richmond district which lies between California Street and Golden Gate Park. Peace came on December 10, 1898, but the intervening months had caused many soldiers to become acquainted with San Francisco and environs, as was to happen again after World War II.

CHAPTER 11

WILLIAM CHAPMAN RALSTON:

Builder of a City

No man possessed to a more eminent degree than he the sincere geniality which endears an individual to his followers. With him has passed something that mere money cannot replace. His was the vast vision of the builders and his like shall never pass this way again.

San Francisco Daily Alta California, August 28, 1875.

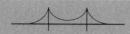

J

UST AS SOME key events are essential in recreating San Francisco's past, so also are certain pivotal personalities. There can be no argument as to whether or not Billy Ralston belongs to the latter category. Since his story is so much a part of San Francisco's past, we shall recall it here, and make an appraisal of his lasting importance in the city.[1]

William Chapman Ralston was a fourth-generation American of Scotch Irish descent. He was born in 1826 on a farm near Plymouth, Ohio; as a young man he was a clerk on a steamboat on both the Mississippi and Ohio rivers where he picked up the rudiments of navigation. He was twenty-two years old when the news of the discovery of gold in California reached him and he quickly decided to join the Argonauts who were en route to El Dorado. His turned out to be a delayed arrival in San Francisco, though, for upon his arrival in Panama City on the west side of the isthmus, he decided to remain there, at least for a while, entering into a partnership in a banking business with two men from Louisiana, Messrs. Fretz and Garrison. Quickly, the firm became engaged in the more profitable enterprise of transporting persons across the isthmus to Panama and thence by steamer to San Francisco. Ralston first arrived in the city on September 20, 1851, but he did not settle permanently there until 1854. In that dramatic manner which was to become part of him, he "skippered" the 1,100-ton steamer *New Orleans* from Panama in through the Golden Gate; evidently his earlier and limited experience of inland waters had endowed him with that massive self-confidence which was also to form a part of his being. The years between 1851 and 1854 were spent in profitable travel between San Francisco, Panama, and New York. In 1852, he fell in love with Louisa Thorne, the nineteen-year-old granddaughter of gruff Commodore Cornelius Vanderbilt, who was not at all favorably impressed by Ralston and let him know so with characteristic vigor. To effectively destroy the budding romance, Vanderbilt dispatched Louisa to Europe for an extended stay apart from her earnest suitor. Returning ill, Louisa died prematurely the next year. Although Ralston later married, he never forgot Louisa (for whom he named his first child, a daughter who died in infancy) or forgave Vanderbilt. Later on, he repeatedly took special delight in opposing the Commodore and his family in business transactions.

On December 1, 1855, a notable change came in the Ralston fortunes when, deciding to remain permanently in San Francisco, he opened an office in the city with the help of three other associates. The name of the firm was the Accessory Transit Company and its stock was largely controlled by Ralston himself. In 1858, he was married to Elizabeth Reed Fry in a ceremony that took place in Calvary Presbyterian Church; his wife, to be known as Lizzie Ralston, presented him with five children, three girls and two boys. She proved herself to be a good and dutiful wife who deliberately sought the shade in any of the Ralston episodes on his "Journey with Banners." While a devoted mother to her family, she did not enjoy living in San Francisco society and there seems to have been some sadness in her life because of this. (A novel note was introduced after the wedding when the entire wedding party of fourteen joined in a honeymoon stay near Bridal Veil Falls in Yosemite Valley.)

In 1861, Ralston, still on the rise, formed part of Donohoe, Kelly, Ralston and Company, established as a banking enterprise in San Francisco. Always what might be called a constructive visionary and practical dreamer, Billy Ralston spent much time and money in planning great things for the city that he loved so much. With continued success, he acquired an extensive estate at Belmont on the peninsula. It was not long before he had added on to the elegance of the main building he had purchased, and this same structure, now called Ralston Hall and long a part of the College of Notre Dame, is still a beautiful building visited by many because of its architectural distinction. In 1864, Ralston was the moving spirit in the opening of the Bank of California in San Francisco which replaced the earlier Donohoe, Kelly, and

Ralston enterprise. Darius Ogden Mills was made president, with Ralston himself serving first as cashier and later assuming the presidency. At the height of its economic power, the Bank of California, which is still an important part of the banking picture in California, was easily the most important financial institution on the Pacific Coast. It came into its own a few years after the 1859 Comstock Lode discoveries of much silver and some gold in Nevada; the financial center of the Comstock was not in Virginia City or Gold Hill in Nevada but rather in the conference rooms of the Bank of California in downtown San Francisco.[2] Again, as had happened in 1849, the city became the center of the necessary financial aids, this time for the mines of the Comstock Lode. Through her harbor once more passed men and equipment as the silver wealth of the Comstock poured back into San Francisco.

The branch of the Bank of California that was established in Virginia City became one of the busiest of its kind in all the west. It was headed by William Sharon, destined to become Ralston's nemesis. He was a shrewd but unscrupulous businessman who, after witnessing and weathering the first economic depression on the Comstock in 1864, determined to enrich the Bank of California by forming a company to buy and operate holdings which had come to the bank by foreclosures. (This would serve to eliminate the necessity of dividing the profits from these holdings with the stockholders of the bank.) Hardly honest either in intent or execution, the Sharon scheme soon resulted in the Union Mill and Mining Company with Mills, Ralston, and Sharon serving as its directors; this was one of the earliest monopolies on the Comstock Lode and it did not exactly endear its progenitors to those living there who felt that they had, in effect, been victimized when they could no longer keep their properties.[3] When Sharon added control of the new Virginia City, Carson City, and Truckee Railway, it appeared that the partners would have long and prosperous years ahead. With these and other financial gains, Ralston became interested in many different real estate transactions and it was because of this part of his colorful career that he has been called, with reason, the "Man Who Built San Francisco." Anything that would bring beauty plus permanence plus personal profit interested him; since San Francisco had already become the city of his heart, he was determined to leave his mark upon it as

Palace Hotel from Mission Street, 1879. Southern Pacific

a result of the transactions that now occupied him. Envisioning a great hotel for a truly great city, his dream was to give San Francisco its famous Palace Hotel which was opened on October 3, 1875, several months after Ralston's death. In keeping with his dream of keeping San Francisco the financial center of the West, Ralston loaned money and encouraged many enterprises which he thought fit for his grandiose schemes. Gladly did he watch the progress of the city under his benevolent protection which was joined with the resources of the mighty Bank of California. Truly these were happy years in the life of Billy Ralston.

While perhaps not as well known as are the names of the "Big Four" Railroad Kings—Stanford, Huntington, Crocker, and Hopkins—the names of the "Big Four" of the mining operations which centered both in Nevada and San Francisco are of prime

Open Court of Palace Hotel in 1875. Southern Pacific

importance. These men, Flood, Fair, O'Brien, and Mackay—commonly called the "Bonanza Kings"—were just as important in their field as were the Big Four of the transcontinental railroad. All of them rose from humble beginnings to financial and national distinction; their rise, however, indirectly hastened Ralston's early and tragic death. Forming a seemingly unbeatable combine to buy some neglected and, it was believed, generally mined out properties on the Comstock, the Bonanza Kings were richly rewarded when, in 1873, what came to be called the "Big Bonanza" was discovered there and extensive silver deposits were found on their properties: soon the halcyon days of '49 and

'59 began to live again. For two years this new wealth of Nevada poured into San Francisco as the mining exchange in the city witnessed an orgy of speculation of truly fantastic proportions. Eventually, though, the inevitable blow fell as rumors were passed (perhaps deliberately) that the Big Bonanza was almost exhausted and that those holding stock in any of its operations or who were in debt because of them would soon be left bereft of their resources. This resulted, as always, in a panic of stock selling as prices dropped alarmingly; it was not long before the discovery that there was no great or ready reserve of cash on hand in, among other banks, the Bank of California, which was the most heavily involved. The resultant run on the resources of the bank which Ralston now headed brought about its failure. The Board of Directors, many of whom had been made prominent by Ralston himself, met on August 27, 1875 (ever after to be known as "Black Friday" in San Francisco's history); their obvious purpose was to check the condition of the bank and then to decide what to do; a quick check of the books revealed that Ralston's unsecured liabilities amounted to nearly $5 million. His resignation was demanded immediately in a dramatic scene in which it became evident that Ralston was to be made the scapegoat in the whole crisis. It was now evident that the directors, and most of all William Sharon, would not only not aid him but would sacrifice him, as they soon did. Ralston presented his resignation as head of the bank; it was accepted within the hour and Ralston walked out through the portals of the bank which he, in large part, had made. Outside, he happened to meet Dr. John Pitman, his personal physician, whom he informed that he was on his way for a swim at his favorite club at North Beach. He reported there, changed, and prepared for a swim in the bay and was seen by a few onlookers to swim some distance offshore when he appeared to go limp in the water and finally to disappear from sight. All accounts of Ralston spend considerable time speculating as to what really happened—was his death a deliberately planned suicide under the pressures of a disastrous situation, or was his death the result of natural causes? With the passage of time, the suicide theory seems to have yielded to the more plausible opinion that he had suffered either a heart attack or some form of apoplexy and that, accordingly, he had died of natural causes. Added proof that Ralston had so died comes from the fact that at the required autopsy his brain was found to be "congested," probably the result of a cerebral hemorrhage or stroke. As a result of these findings, the New York Life Insurance Company paid a policy of $65,000 to his wife.

On the corner of California and Sansome streets, in the heart of the financial district of downtown San Francisco, there has long stood a classically designed structure which is the main office of the Bank of California. Built of California granite in the post-earthquake years after 1906, the building suggests little, if anything indeed, of the dramatic story of its founder, the "Man Who Built San Francisco." Perhaps a better way to recapture his saga is to visit his former estate in Belmont where the spirit of William Chapman Ralston is still in evidence.

PART 2

SAN FRANCISCO LANDMARKS

CHAPTER 12

GOLDEN GATE:
The People's Park of San Francisco

. . . The people of the State of California do enact as follows: The land designated upon a map of the Outside Lands of the City and County of San Francisco, by the word "Park" to wit: Extending from Stanyan Street of the East to the Pacific Ocean, is hereby designated and shall be known as the "Golden Gate Park."

An Act to Provide for the improvement of Public Parks in the City of San Francisco. Order 800, Board of Supervisors.

ALTHOUGH SAN FRANCISCO'S Golden Gate Park now has few critics, this was not so from the beginning; when land was acquired for it, a Santa Rosa newspaper commented:

> Of all the white elephants the city of San Francisco ever owned, they now have the largest in Golden Gate Park, a dreary waste of shifting sandhills where a blade of grass cannot be raised without four posts to keep it from blowing away.[1]

Golden Gate Park, San Francisco's largest municipal recreational area, containing 1,016 acres, is a parallelogram approximately three miles long by one-half mile wide, extending west from Stanyan Street, between Fulton Street on the north and Lincoln Way on the south, to the Great Highway and ocean front; it also includes a parkway annex or corridor one block wide, called the "Panhandle," which extends eastward eight blocks between Oak and Fell streets to Baker Street.[2] The park is an outgrowth of the city's legal battle, begun as early as 1853, to establish its title to the "four square leagues" granted municipalities under Mexican law by a decree dated November 9, 1833, and issued by the departmental legislature in Monterey. The first decision of the courts, granting only 10,000 acres, left the title unsettled as to all land west of Divisadero Street, a district then mainly occupied by squatters. Upon appeal, the city's title to the larger area was confirmed in 1866, and the state legislature authorized the conveyance to squatters and other claimants of "all land not needed for public purposes." As early as 1855, Frank Soule, one of the authors of the *Annals of San Francisco* had commented:

> Over all these square miles of contemplated thoroughfares there seems to be no provision made for a public park—the true "lungs" of a large city. The existing Plaza, or Portsmouth Square, and two or

three other diminutive squares, seem the only breathing holes intended for the future population of hundreds of thousands. This is a strange mistake.

By the middle 1860s, agitation had already begun for a large public park and the city authorities, taking advantage of the proviso just mentioned, made a compromise settlement with the squatters whereby the latter relinquished to the city 10 percent of their holdings in exchange for clear title to the remainder. In this way, the city retrieved lands for Golden Gate and Buena Vista parks, a cemetery, and numerous public squares, totalling 1,347 acres. In 1868, Mayor Frank McCoppin ordered the Board of Supervisors to begin plans for a system of city parks. Envisioned was a large park to encompass a land mass of about a thousand acres. Since some substantial difficulties remained with regard to the squatters, Mayor McCoppin appointed a committee to make an appraisal of the land desired for the park. The group chosen reflected future San Francisco street names: Cole, Stanyan, Ashbury, and Clayton were four citizens so named. The committee appraised the land for a suprisingly high evaluation of $1.3 million. The squatters were offered $810,595 which they accepted, thus making available land that was, ultimately, to become one of the most beautiful parks in the world.

In 1870, Golden Gate Park finally came into being through the creation, by the state legislature, of a five-man Park Commission. (It is interesting to note that, from 1870 to 1900, the Park Commissioners were appointed and their acts controlled by the State of California rather than by the city and county of San Francisco.) Appointed as "Surveyor," or equivalently a Superintendent, was William Hammond Hall (1846–1934) with Patrick Owen as park keeper. Hall has been pretty well eclipsed in the story of the park which he effectively brought into being; most of the fame is now given to John McLaren, an impressive person indeed, but the name of William Hammond Hall deserves more than the relative oblivion that it has received. While McLaren deserves much credit as the long-term and successful landscape gardener, it is Hall who was the planner, the dreamer, and the principal architect of Golden Gate Park.

Hall was born in Maryland on February 12, 1846. In 1853, he

moved to California with his parents and settled in Stockton. His formal education in engineering was received there through a private tutor. On its completion, he was employed by the U.S. Army Engineers during the Civil War, 1861–1865; specifically his task was to map the west coast surrounding San Francisco Bay for possible defensive positions. During his tenure with the Army Engineers, young Hall was engaged in the plans and construction of Fort Point. In his topographical surveys along the coast of San Francisco, he had many opportunities to study the sandy waste-lands, known on early maps as "The Great Sand Bank." In 1870, the twenty-four-year-old engineer received a contract from the Park Board to survey the proposed area; in 1871, he produced detailed maps which he entitled "Proposed Park Improvements for the Eastern Portion of the Park and Avenue": they showed considerable expertise because of his intimate knowledge and study of the terrain. Hall was not a trained gardener; however, his engineering talent was an absolute prerequisite for the topo-graphical maps and the general design and layout of the entire park from Stanyan Street to the Pacific Ocean. His design was only slightly altered as the park completed its march to the Pa-cific. With Hall's knowledge of engineering and Patrick Owen as his chief gardener, Golden Gate Park as we know it today, was designed and brought into being. (After serving as superinten-dent from 1870 to 1876, Hall became an engineer for the Bank of California and the first engineer of the State of California. He died aged 88, on October 16, 1934. He most certainly deserves top billing in the story of the beginnings of Golden Gate Park.)

The primitive and undeveloped area selected for the site of Golden Gate Park was about the most undesirable in San Fran-cisco. It was a section of sand dunes, ice plant, and other succu-lents which could derive but meagre sustenance from the air and sand. The logical place to begin the extended battle to conquer this wasteland was in the panhandle area protected from exces-sive winds by Lone Mountain on the north and covered sparsely by willow and scrub oak. Native plants and sand-hugging grasses were tried there with soil and leaf mold worked into the sand to form a necessary base for the roots of the shrubs and trees then being planted. While this process was being implemented by Patrick Owen, Hall was at work surveying boundaries and roads.

(An interesting sidelight indicating Hall's precise thinking is that all the boulevards running east and west were designed wide enough to allow parking and at the same time were curved suffi- ciently to break the force of the strong winds from the Pacific Ocean.)

When careful planning and experimentation saw the begin- nings of the park successfully taking root in the panhandle, an- other crucial problem had to be faced: this was how to stop the progress of the sand that blew in from the beach. Without a plan, the prevailing westerly winds would soon bury the entire park under tons of sand, as they had for centuries. Hall determined to break the offshore wind by building a wall across the entire westerly or ocean side of the park. Accordingly, he had two fences constructed three feet apart in which rock, leaves, and other compost were deposited. (This first "sea wall" was some- where between six and ten feet in height and was built at almost the identical spot where the concrete wall now stands along the ocean beach.)

A problem of immediate urgency concerned the water supply for the park. For seven years, 1870–1877, the Spring Valley Water Company supplied the park with 100,000 gallons daily. In 1877, the Park Commission proposed drilling exploratory wells and, in 1885, a successful well was drilled near the beach which, by 1910, was supplying 1.5 million gallons a day to a storage reservoir located on Strawberry Hill, 412 feet above sea level. In 1902, construction was completed of the first windmill, called the Dutch windmill, which cost $25,000. In 1905, its mate, called the Murphy windmill after a San Francisco bank president named Samuel G. Murphy, was built. This second windmill had the distinction of being the largest in the world. Both windmills, powered by the ever-present westerly wind, pumped a combined 70,000 gallons of fresh water an hour for use in the park.

Less than a decade after its beginnings, Golden Gate Park had already begun to form that integral part of the city which it has been ever since. In 1878, Langley's City Directory referred to its attractions by pointing out that "seven lakelets, grottos, mounds and rustic benches" awaited the visitor. By that same year, more than two miles of roads and paths had been built and more than 135,000 trees and shrubs had been planted, with 32,000 being

Conservatory in Golden Gate Park in 1887. Southern Pacific

raised in the park's own nursery. All this makes it evident that when John McLaren (1847–1943) took full charge in 1890 the park had already progressed extensively. McLaren had the shrewdness and good sense to follow Hall's basic plan and vision, which was to present the park as a quiet countrylike oasis quite different from the city itself. In general, this atmosphere has been preserved in the present park, although there have been some departures from the idea. Both Hall and McLaren shared the desire that the park be a sylvan retreat where the only intrusion would be the footpaths. Vegetation, lakes, and any available cliffs or hillocks would be planted to represent a setting as true to nature as possible.

In 1887, Hall, who had returned as park superintendent for one year on an unpaid, part-time basis, brought in this promising young Scotchman, John Hays McLaren, to serve and train under him as assistant superintendent of the park. In 1890, McLaren

Midwinter Fair in Golden Gate Park, 1894. Southern Pacific

was appointed superintendent of Golden Gate Park—he was to serve as such until his death in 1943—a period of fifty-three years. (Small wonder that, for many years, McLaren referred to Golden Gate Park as "My Park!") Born in Sterling, Scotland, on December 20, 1846, McLaren was early associated with gardening in his native country. In 1869, he left for the United States, arriving in San Francisco from New York via the Isthmus of Panama. He was to leave a lasting mark on the history of his adopted city. McLaren was first employed in some of the larger estates on the peninsula; by 1887, his skill had attracted the attention of Superintendent Hall who saw to his appointment as his assistant and eventual successor. The many years of service of the man who came to be known as "Uncle John" McLaren found him loved (as well as, at times, feared) by those who came up against his stubborn and imperious ways. On balance, McLaren was a definite asset both to the park and to San Francisco and, although he must share this honor with William H. Hall, in a very real sense the modern Golden Gate Park is McLaren's monument.

At the Corner of 33rd Avenue and Anza, looking Southwest: Richmond District in 1910 (top) and 1969.

An "invasion" of Golden Gate Park which was not favored by Superintendent McLaren came between 1892 and 1894 when a group of San Francisco businessmen organized the California Midwinter Fair. Against the violent reactions of McLaren and others equally opposed, the fair covered a two-hundred-acre site at the eastern end of the park. When it closed in July 1894, most of the buildings and the trees and shrubs that McLaren had been forced to plant were removed. Among the remaining evidences of the successful fair are the Japanese Tea Garden and the music concourse to which was added, in 1900, the "Claus Spreckels Temple of Music."

An unplanned use of park space came in 1906 when much of its area was devoted to the temporary housing of refugees who had been burnt out in the fateful days of April. Statistics reveal that over forty thousand people were given shelter within its confines. Occupancy lasted until early 1907; when some of the slower evacuees attempted to establish "squatter" claims upon the land, McLaren, with a force of park laborers and some court orders, forced them all to leave. John McLaren would have no one trifling with his park.

On January 12, 1943, McLaren died at the age of ninety-six and San Francisco officially mourned his passing; funeral services took place in the rotunda of City Hall. His successor, Julius L. Girod, who had been McLaren's assistant, served with distinction until his own sudden death in 1957; his years of service in the park had numbered forty-three.

Between 1900 and 1950, tremendous urban growth was recorded in the Richmond, Sunset, and Parkside districts. At the turn of the century, San Francisco had a population of about 300,000: by 1950, this figure had increased to an all time high, 776,000; by 1960, withdrawal to suburbs by many as well as other causes brought the figure down to 763,000. As available land within city limits became more scarce, the area closest to Golden Gate Park claimed the highest prices. The unsurpassed recreational facilities of the "People's Park" brought about this appreciation of land values.

In 1970, the centennial of the founding of Golden Gate Park was duly observed. Parades, musical concerts, and other events marked the ten months' long commemoration. All concerned felt legitimate and continuing pride in the park which was so much a part of San Francisco. In 1888, Frederick Law Olmstead, world-famous landscape architect, wrote in a letter to Park Commissioner R.P. Hammond:

Sunset District in 1950.

. . . Let me counsel you to remember that your Park is not for today but for all times: so long as you have a city. Its development is an interesting problem, no longer obscure, to be sure, but to be studied in a careful and sustained manner. You have your present population to satisfy and please . . . but it is expected that future populations will be more intelligent and more appreciative.[3]

While present generations who visit and make maximum use of Golden Gate Park may or may not be "more intelligent," the record is obvious that they much enjoy and claim as their own their "People's Park."

CHAPTER 13

THE STORY OF THE CABLE CARS

I T WOULD BE neither possible nor acceptable to tell the story of San Francisco's past without some account of how her "peculiar institution," as it has been called, came into being over a century ago. Added interest in this phase of the city's history stems from the fact that, if the cable car is to die, (which is not at all evident) it will have to die where it was first born—in the United States—for San Francisco is the only city in the entire world with cable cars, strictly so called. Local residents speak with affection of their "Ride on the Rope" while a few others have, seemingly, developed a sort of love-hate relationship toward the little cars as they loudly proclaim how they will welcome the day when the "little coffin fillers"—as an indignant letter-writer in the *San Francisco Chronicle* called them—will be banned from the hills of home. Several times reports of an imminent demise have been made. As far as cable car fans are concerned, they are in solid agreement with the one who rhetorically asked: "Breathes there a San Franciscan with soul so dead/ Who never to himself has said/ 'Lets take a ride on the Rope!' " On, now, to this distinctive story high on the list of San Franciscana.

It is not surprising that San Francisco's transportation "system," if, indeed, it merited such a name, was not exactly planned. Before 1850, there simply were no public conveyances. Those who did not walk rode horseback or in the few available carriages. The dislocations brought about by the Gold Rush saw the first beginnings of a transportation system in the growing city when a wooden plank toll road was built between Mission Dolores and Portsmouth Plaza. This proved to be an expensive project and tolls, for that day, were high—25¢ to ride from one end of the line to the other in a carriage-wagon behind four horses. The decade of the 1850s necessarily saw increased empha-

South Park Station, 1865.

sis placed upon transportation problems, with the real start of the story coming in 1852 when an "omnibus" (i.e. a vehicle resembling a stage coach) line commenced running from Kearny and Clay streets to the old Mission; a 30-minute headway was maintained as the coaches, which contained room for many passengers, careened along the precarious wooden road with a one-way fare set at 50¢—which fare was doubled on Sundays. This was known as the "Yellow Line Number Two" to Mission Dolores by Folsom and 16th streets (1854), while the next year, still another line started operations between Townsend Street and Meiggs Wharf, which was located at the foot of Mason Street. Soon competition brought about the "Peoples" or "Red" Line which, to the delight of its riders, standardized its fares at 10¢ a ride. Their "omnibus" seated eighteen persons who were hauled by either two- or four-horse teams, whose drivers received $2.50 for a 12-hour day which included the feeding and care of their horses. Next there followed the horse-car period which was at its zenith from 1860 to 1873; the first incorporated line was the San Francisco Market Street Railway, which began operations on July 4, 1860, with its main line going from the waterfront to Market and Valencia streets. By 1863, San Francisco's population had risen to an impressive 94,000 and added transportation facilities

Kearny Street Terminus of Clay Street Cable Car Route, 1873. Southern Pacific

were needed; this came about steadily if gradually with four more horse-car lines in operation by 1870. By 1875, eight railway companies were in competitive operation in the city, including the new-born Clay Street Cable, about which more presently. By that same year, San Francisco could boast of 220 cars running on 80 miles of track which employed 700 men and used the services of 1,700 horses.

The rectangular street pattern which had been devised for the city's downtown streets by Jasper O'Farrell and others had imposed some steep grades which were not easily negotiated by horse cars, although some attempts were made in this direction. Consequently, most of the city's wealthy people chose to live south of Market Street, many in an area known as South Park which came to be the location of some of the earlier mansions of the city. Presumably, some of that generation must have wished to live on the side or crests of one or another of San Francisco's spectacular hills but, for the most part, access to these areas was denied to them because these natural eminences remained inaccessible. Added to this was another difficulty: any horse-car line that dared to ascend these hills, such as that which came to be called "Nob Hill" on California Street, would have had to face the fact that, in inclement weather, the horses would have had unsure traction on wet streets and other difficulties. In this connection it appears that the words of John P. Young are true: "No city in the world has been more affected by an improvement in transportation facilities than San Francisco." As will be seen, it was the coming of the cable car that was to make the difference.[1]

The advent of the cable-car system in San Francisco will always revolve around the name of Andrew Smith Hallidie who contributed significantly to its birth and development, although he should not be regarded as the only one who did so. Born in London of Scotch parentage in 1836, Hallidie was given the name of his father, Andrew Smith, to which he later appended "Hallidie," the surname of his uncle and godfather who at one time was a royal physician. Following in the footsteps of his inventive father, he worked in his brother's machine shop in London, acquiring skills and experience that were to serve him well in far-off California, and especially in San Francisco. He also continued engineering studies at night and, when too much activity and concentration brought about a state of impaired health, following his mother's death, he and his father decided to move to California. Father and son arrived in San Francisco on May 4, 1852, on the S.S. *Brutus* from Panama. During his first five years in California young Hallidie wandered to various mining camps and towns where four times he almost lost his life in various accidents. At the age of nineteen, a change came when he designed and built a 220-foot wire suspension bridge and aqueduct across the middle fork of the American River. His father was one of the inventors of wire rope and, in June 1856, the son drew on his father's expertise to construct a wire rope-making machine, the product of which was used to pull mine cars up a track. This was the first

Andrew Smith Hallidie, 1836–1900.

wire rope made on the Pacific Coast, a significant breakthrough
that would have bearing on San Francisco's future cable cars. The
next year, 1857, Hallidie celebrated his coming of age by moving
to San Francisco where he transported his wire-making plant.
The next decade found him and his business associates busily
designing and constructing wire-rope suspension bridges; among
the profitable inventions that came from a well-trained and inge-
nious mind was that called the "Hallidie Ropeway" which became one of the several types of aerial tramways used by mine

operators in California and throughout the Far West. In 1871, one of his numerous patents concerned what he described as an "endless ropeway" which proved to be an important prelude to his cable-car planning. Later on, he wrote how he was induced to action in this regard by "seeing the difficulty and pain the horses experienced in hauling cars up Jackson Street from Kearny to Stockton; with a view to obviating these difficulties and for the purpose of reducing the expense of street railways, I devoted all my time to a careful consideration of the subject." Much reflection and consultation with such friends as Joseph Britton, Henry L. Davis, and Jackson Moffitt convinced him that his plan to pick California Street between Kearny and Powell as his first experimental cable railway should yield in favor of Clay Street from Jones to Kearny, a distance of 2,800 feet down a grade amounting to 307 feet. This decided, he and the above-mentioned friends became business associates with their formation of the Clay Street Hill Railroad Company which was incorporated on August 15, 1872. David F. Myrick, an acknowledged authority in western transportation history, makes a pivotal point in discussing the matter:

> Contrary to a general impression, it appears that Hallidie did not invent the cable car; instead, the honor belongs to Benjamin H. Brooks. With his associates, Brooks did considerable planning and secured franchises for a "street railroad" (which the *San Francisco Bulletin* referred to in part as "a steep grade endless rope") but they were unable to finance the construction, so they sold the entire project to Hallidie for a nominal sum. The preamble to the incorporation papers of Hallidie's company cites the franchises which the supervisors granted to Brooks et al. in 1870 and 1871. Hallidie faced the same monetary difficulties and it was only because E. Willard Burr, president of the Clay St. Bank, had confidence in the project that the Savings and Loan Society advanced $30,000 on a ten year, 10% interest loan.[2]

Even though it appears that Hallidie must not be regarded as the inventor of the cable car, the evidence is abundantly clear that it was he who devised, constructed, and put into actual operation in San Francisco the first cable street railroad which provided public transportation and overcame the many mechanical problems of operating up and down hill in the public streets without interference with other vehicular traffic; also, his is the distinction of operating the system with a marked financial profit. Hallidie's accomplishments, then (in the face of abundant skepticism) in carrying to completion an undertaking involving mechanical and financial problems of no small moment can leave no doubt as to his mechanical ability, resourcefulness, energy, determination, and courage.

The details that surrounded the first operation of the Clay Street Hill Railroad Company have been told many times; surprisingly, though, except in one or two accounts, the date of this first operation has been incorrectly stated. Practically all printed accounts (as well as the inscription in what appears to be imperishable bronze on the plaque at Kearny and Clay streets) give the date as August 1, 1873. For example, the San Francisco Municipal Railway's official brochure thus pictures the scene:

> The morning of August 1 (1873) was cool and damp. Fog rolled in from the ocean beyond Point Lobos in swirling cloudbanks. The rails were damp and everyone feared for the brakes. Only a handful of people climbed out of their beds to watch a small group of men anxiously tinkering with the brightly painted wooden trolley standing at the top of Clay Street. No crowds cheered or bells rang as the first cable car in history made its maiden run that day.[3]

> Nothing demonstrated the Scotsman's complete confidence in his own design better than the fact that he chose to make the initial trip from the top (of Clay St.) down (to Kearny St.)—a distance of six city blocks. An ordinary man would have started at the bottom of the hill. Then, if things did go wrong, he wouldn't be streaking down six blocks of near precipice to land in a heap of splintered wreckage! Some such thoughts must have passed through the first grip-man's mind as he boarded the little car poised on the crest. According to reports, he took one long look down the steep, fog-shrouded hill, turned pale and disappeared. Hallidie stepped forward, waved a cheery farewell to the small crowd, took hold of the grip wheel himself—the original grip was tightened by a screw—and began to turn it. The car slowly "took the rope" and rolled smoothly over the brink and down the 20% grade at an even nine miles an hour. Thus was set in operation the first cable line in the United States, the Clay Street Hill Railroad.[4]

Most probably, this account is substantially correct; however, an examination of several San Francisco newspapers reporting the

California Street Cable Car, 1879. Southern Pacific

event in their Sunday (August 3, 1873) issues reveals that they are unanimous in stating that the event took place on the previous day, i.e. Saturday, August 2. Actually, Hallidie's franchise demanded that he start operations on or before August 1; it would seem that, because of some unforeseen difficulties, he obtained permission to extend the date by one day and made his successful descent of the Clay Street hill on Saturday, August 2, 1873.[5]

With this significant beginning in San Francisco, the United States entered upon the age of the cable car. As the idea developed, it spread to other cities in California (Oakland, Los Angeles) and, eventually, to the entire country—Kansas City, Chicago, St. Louis, Philadelphia, and New York. Other lines augmented the original operation, and London and Sydney, Australia, joined the list of cities with cable operations.

With regard to the subsequent events connected with the saga of the cable cars in the city, it should be noted that its immediate success caused much activity in San Francisco. Such tycoons as Leland Stanford and Mark Hopkins were led to establish their own cable-car operations after obtaining the necessary franchises from city government. By 1890, the city's population of about 300,000 was served by eight cable car companies which operated six hundred cars over one hundred miles of single cable track and employed 1,500 men. Additionally, there were still some twenty-five miles of horse-car lines as well as two steam lines, on either side of Golden Gate Park, which carried passengers to Ocean Beach. Between 1891 and 1894, the eight lines mentioned above were merged into the Market Street Railway Company; however, several other operations such as the California Street Railroad, the Presidio and Ferries Railroad, Sutter Street Railroad, and the Geary Street, Park, and Ocean Railroad remained independent operations. Obviously, the proliferation of these successful enterprises served, among other things, to change the population trend to the south of Market area, for it was now possible to ascend the heights of Nob and other hills with comfort and safety. The cable car then, may claim credit for the building of many homes in the northeast area of the city as well as in some of the valleys beyond. This was referred to by the then Chief Justice Earl Warren when, on October 1, 1964, he was the principal speaker at a ceremony marking the inclusion of the San Francisco Cable Car System among the national historical landmarks. In this ceremony, which took place at Victorian Plaza, Hyde and Beach streets, the Chief Justice remarked:

> This occasion is of great significance to the citizens of San Francisco but it is also one which will attract the attention of people who hear about it all over the world. There is an affection for San Francisco's cable cars in many lands. They are truly world-renowned.
>
> My appreciation of these cable cars is based upon a host of memories. When I was a freshman student at the University of California,

California Street from Nob Hill, 1890. Southern Pacific

Looking Northeast from Masonic Avenue and Fulton Street, 1895; McAllister Street Car House. Now Petrini Plaza. E. Dressler

I first rode the cable cars on the San Francisco hills. I associate them, as hundreds of people do, with stimulating experiences, superb views of the Bay and the sheer excitement of being in "everyone's favorite city."

Some of the Chief Justice's enthusiasm and affection for cable cars in the city seem to have been captured by an editorial writer for the *San Francisco Chronicle,* who wrote several days after the Victorian Plaza ceremony:

The San Francisco cable car, invented out of necessity arising from the city's steep and frequent hills, has now climbed to the peak of esteem and respectability. The perky, noisy, woefully archaic little contraption is now the revered symbol of a metropolitan city, but has attained national recognition—and protection—as a national monument. This obsolete, creaking, inadequate, slow, expensive to operate, money-losing—and uniquely San Franciscan—piece of last century machinery has risen in the world like a Horatio Alger hero and is now a tourist attraction that brings thousands of visitors and millions of dollars to this community annually.[6]

The firm hold that the cable car system has upon many people had been demonstrated earlier on November 10, 1967, when the "Cable Car Barn" at the corner of Mason and Jackson streets was dedicated. Originally built in 1887, this structure, while gutted in the fire of 1906, had since been sufficiently restored to enable it to be returned to service some years later; however, with the cessation of several cable car operations, the "Barn" gradually became the only source of power for the operation of the remaining three lines. In a wise decision, it was decided to add an attractive Visitors Gallery where the operation of the system could be observed at close range and from where the interested could go on to an inspection of a cable car museum upstairs which includes the areas where the cable cars are stored between use. Annually, thousands visit this working area and see for themselves the actual operation of the entire system.

A final mention must be made here of the well-planned and equally well-executed commemoration, in 1973, of the centennial of San Francisco's cable cars. There were several appropriate events in connection with this centennial which climaxed on the centennial date, August 2, 1973, with a reenactment of the origi-

Cable Car with Alcatraz in the distance. California Mission Trails

nal run of the first cable car a century before. Since Clay Street had long since lost its cable-car line, the run was made down it in a "cable-car cavalcade" which featured several cable cars running on rubber tires and powermotored; at Portsmouth Square, where the first run had terminated, a nostalgic ceremony, presided over by Mayor Joseph Alioto, was held with various addresses featuring the cable car "in history," "in print," in song," "in my day" (speech by a senior gripman), "in my life," and "in San Francisco." Several hundred attended this early morning ceremony which took place at about 6 A.M. All of which caused the *Chronicle* to again editorialize:

> Andrew Hallidie created the cable car system, August 2, 1873, to the great relief and convenience of persons having a need to go up and down Nob Hill but lacking a private equipage in which to negotiate it. From that day to this is a whole century of clang-clang—a period of uninterrupted joy and satisfaction with this mode of transportation. No American city ever found a more delightful way of getting

people up and down a hill or a more appealing trademark recognizable the world over. May the San Francisco cable car ever successfully resist profane hands that would snatch it out of its slot and replace it with "modern, and efficient" (i.e. smoke and noise polluting) buses.[7]

CHAPTER 14

1906:

Earthquake and Fire

. . . Seismologically it was a number nine quake (number ten being complete devastation) but I think that "A 1" would be a better name for it. . . .

George Davidson to
Gertrude Atherton on the
San Francisco earthquake
of April 18, 1906.

H IGH ON THE wall of the rotunda of San Francisco's City Hall are inscribed the words which are among the finest of the literary legacies that Mayor Edward R. Taylor (who served from 1908 to 1910) bequeathed to his city. They read as follows: "San Francisco, Glorious City of our Hearts, which has been tried and not found wanting—go Thou with like Spirit and make the future Thine." The reference is to the four fateful days, April 18–21, 1906, during which the City by the Golden Gate was subjected to its most severe trial and time of testing—a destructive earthquake which was followed by several days of fires.

Before turning attention to this San Francisco 'quake, remember that earthquakes are an integral part of the earlier history of California. These lines are to be found in a book published in San Francisco in 1876:

> So far as is known, California has always been "shaky on her pins." The Spanish records make mention of earthquakes in the latter part of the last (18th) century and an account of a very severe earthquake shock that occurred in 1812 is among the Spanish archives. This shook down the tower of the old Spanish Mission, San Juan Capistrano, burying a number of natives in the ruins. Always, for a few days succeeding any severe shock, there are numerous slight tremblings at intervals of a few hours. . . . The average number of shocks per year in San Francisco is probably fifteen. Some are scarcely perceptible, while others are sufficiently vigorous to remind one of the old Jesuit [!] prophecy that foretold the sinking of the whole peninsula, and engulfing a large city beneath the waves of the ocean. . . .[1]

An earlier mention of this same phenomenon was recorded by the authors of the *Annals of San Francisco,* published in 1855; in the light of subsequent happenings, the lines seem almost prophetic:

It may be mentioned that since the earlier earthquakes of 1812, 1829, 1839, no serious occurrences of this nature have happened at San Francisco. . . . God help the city if any great catastrophe of this nature should take place. Her huge granite and brick palaces, of four, five, and six stories in height, would indeed make a prodigious crash, more ruinous both to life and property, than even the dreadful fires of 1849, 1850, and 1851. This is the greatest, if not the only possible obstacle of consequence to the growing prosperity of the city . . . such a terrible calamity, however, as the one imagined, may never take place. Sufficient for the day is the evil thereof! This maxim satisfies the excitement-craving, money-seeking, luxurious-living, reckless heaven-earth-and hell daring citizens of San Francisco.[2]

While it is evident, then, that earthquakes are not exactly new in California, it must also be observed that there were, and are, "earthquakes—and earthquakes." For example, those which shook San Francisco on Sunday, October 8, 1865, and on Wednesday, October 21, 1868, were two of the greatest seismic disturbances ever recorded in California. *Lights and Shades in San Francisco* furnishes vivid details of both earthquakes; that of 1868 was much the more severe but neither was minor, either in impact or in the fright each inspired in San Franciscans. In B.E. Lloyd's colorful and even florid language:

> The quake (of 1868) continued for forty-two seconds and was even more vigorous than the shock of '65. The excitement was intense. Mothers could be seen in their night garments wringing their hands and weeping, while the little bright-eyed babies at their breasts cooed and clapped their tiny hands in an ecstasy of joy (!) Strong men grew ashy pale and quaked with fear, for there was a power manifesting itself with which it were useless to contend. O that was a sad day for the inhabitants of San Francisco! . . . There was not one, perhaps, in that city of 150,000 souls but felt for the moment that they had finished their work and would now be hurled into Eternity. . . .[3]

Since 1906 was to witness a considerable amount of damage from earthquake and the many fires that broke out immediately afterwards, it should be mentioned here that the earlier "preview" of 1868 resulted in the deaths of five or six killed outright by falling walls or cornices, while the number of injured was recorded at between forty-five and fifty. The estimated damage to property was about $400,000.

After these preliminary words to sketch some of the previous

Before the Earthquake, Market Street east from Sansome to the Ferry, 1905.

history involved, we now turn to what is sometimes thought of as the "villain of the piece" in San Francisco's past—the well-advertised San Andreas Fault. A fault is defined as a fracture in the earth's crust. The one called the "San Andreas" is the "master" fault of an intricate network of such faults that cut through the coastal region of California. This fault is a high fracture about 600 miles long and extending almost vertically into the earth to a depth of at least twenty miles. It forms a continuous break from Northern California southward to Cajon Pass in San Bernardino County. What is of more immediate pertinence is that the San Andreas Fault lies entirely outside the limits of the city and county of San Francisco. Hence it is but legend to say that the city is built above such a fault—it is more correct to say that San Francisco is adjacent to this fault, but, obviously, it is sufficiently close to it to respond dramatically to any of its movements or convolutions.

Seismologists always stress the fact that no one can predict, with absolute accuracy, when earthquakes will occur. Hence there was no special reason to think that the Wednesday in Easter

Telegraph Hill at Green & Taylor streets, April 6, 1906.

Week, April 18, 1906, was going to be a decisive day in the history of San Francisco. Yet this was to be a day of destiny in its history for, on that morning, the seismograph located at the University of California in Berkeley recorded a major seismic disturbance which lasted for forty-eight seconds, from 5:12:06 A.M. to 5:12:54 A.M. The main shock (there were no warnings or previous shocks) was felt in the city at 5:16 A.M. when, among others, the clock of the Ferry Building stopped. The local disturbance was part of a more general one which extended up and down the San Andreas Fault centering around the town of Olema in western Marin County. One hundred-twenty separate shocks were recorded on April 18, through a long and frightening day, with further complications coming from a burning city. However, it should be pointed out immediately, that the earthquake damage amounted, in the end, to only about 20 percent of the total damage to the stricken city and that it is considerably more than merely local patriotism to claim that it was fire that destroyed the vitals of San Francisco rather than earthquake. Loss of life from earthquakes is usually quite high; when Tokyo was so afflicted in 1923, about 100,000 were killed in a frightful holocaust. The most accurate figures concerning the total loss of life in San Francisco (this includes those who died as a result of the fires) estimate that approximately 667 were casualties of either fire and earthquake, with about 352 listed simply as missing.[4] The comparatively light loss of life is partially explained by the fact that, just as in 1868, most of the inhabitants of the city were at home in their wooden frame dwellings (by 1906, about 90 percent of the homes in the city were of wooden construction) and these stood up well, despite creakings and groanings, when the quake came. While bricks and stone facades and the like are liable to shake and fall, frame buildings have the capacity to "ride out" an earthquake without too much damage except to the composure of their inhabitants. It seems that many of the deaths in San Francisco happened in the flimsy waterfront hotels built upon filled ground which collapsed around their unfortunate occupants. Of more importance is the fact that the massive shock which came at approximately 5:15 A.M. triggered a set of events that involved San Francisco in three days and nights of terror and destruction.

The chain reaction went somewhat as follows: the great shake or quake immediately caused a breakage of major water mains, one of 30 and another of 40 inches, both coming from Spring Valley Lakes through Baden, near Holy Cross cemetery, in San Mateo County. With these major breaks, one of the principal sources of water was destroyed. Obviously, this was to be of key importance in the tragic hours that now lay ahead of San Francisco. Before turning to a consideration of these hours, mention should be made of an official report made later on which summed up the damage that came to the city from the earthquake:

> The physical effects of the earthquake in and upon the city of San Francisco were 1. The displacement of the earth's surface in the Region of "filled" or "made" ground over water or former swampy area. 2. The demolition of a few buildings that were already verging on collapse and the injury to other buildings by the fracturing of brick or stone walls and the movement of frame buildings upon their foundations. 3. The rupture of underground pipes in the neighborhood of the earth's displacement. This was the most serious in the case of the water pipes which were used to carry the city's water supply from the reservoir twenty miles away. One of these pipe lines was laid along the "fault line" for a distance of six miles and was practically totally destroyed. Other pipe lines crossed marshy and filled ground and were broken at such points. 4. The causing of numerous fires, due to broken gas connections, crossing of electric wires, the breaking of chimneys, overturning of stoves, the liberation of chemicals (principally in drug stores) and like effects. . . . It is recorded that fifty-two fires occurred, most of which were extinguished while incipient.[5]

It has already been indicated that San Franciscans are sensitive on the point of how most of the damage was done to the city in 1906. However, facts amply support the position that, had it not been for the fires that followed the quaking of the earth, San Francisco would have recovered rather quickly from any and all earthquake damage.

It is also a fact that fire, which consumed so much of the city, gave it the distinction, if such it may be called, of being the scene of the greatest conflagration in the recorded history of cities, even exceeding the famous Chicago fire of 1871. As will be seen, approximately 4.11 square miles, comprising 514 city blocks, were burned in the 1906 conflagration. This furnishes the sober reflection that the heart of the city was burned away in the three days and nights of fire that followed the early morning quake of April 18, 1906.

The first and most massive shock caused some small fires, and this same shock wrecked the electrical system controlling fire alarms because the Central Fire Alarm System, which was located on Brenham Place, directly behind Portsmouth Plaza, was among the first to go out of commission since the dry cell units, which were in jars and which generated the current for the alarms, fell off their shelves and became completely inoperative at this most critical of moments. The result was that not one of the city's fire companies responded to call as a result of the fire alarm system; however, a good number of the commanding officers stationed in the various fire houses rightly ordered their companies to fight the fires as best they could, operating under emergency rules.[6]

Edward Livingston's *Personal History of the San Francisco Earthquake and Fire,* which was published in 1941, is one of many such accounts that confirm the fact that it was the scourge of fire, rather than the force of the earthquake, which brought devastation to San Francisco. His words are:

> The actual earthquake damage, though appalling to those who experienced the shock, was not, as a general rule, so serious as far as appearances went. The damage was mostly to tall chimneys, church towers, plaster and flimsy frame structures. Observation of the unburned Western Addition, and also photographs taken between the earthquake and the fire, make it clear that San Francisco was far from being destroyed by the quake, but that the great damage was done by the numerous fires which broke out as a consequence of the terrific shock. . . .

Fifty-two separate fires were counted on the fateful morning of Wednesday, April 18. Gradually these merged into two main conflagrations, one north of Market Street and the other to the south of that thoroughfare. Each of the two fires moved generally in a western direction; although the wind never, at least according to official records, exceeded a velocity of ten miles per hour, it was enough to fan the flames. Both fires seem to have taken their origins along the Embarcadero, which was then known as East Street; the north fire had, as an added contributory cause, the fallen and live electric wires in what was then called the commission district, the area to which farm produce was brought for distribution to the city's markets. By midday, the flames were eating away at the vitals of this district with firemen finding it impossible to extinguish them because of lack of water. The south fire spread even more rapidly because of the absence of any natural geographical barriers—flat areas and congested housing conditions made it easy for this fire to expand. By Wednesday afternoon, the south fire had reached Eighth and Market streets, while the north fire had progressed to Fourth, Ellis, and Stockton streets. Wednesday evening and night in the city resembled a scene from Dante's *Inferno;* dismayed and terrified citizens huddled together on hilltops to view the city that burned below them; many quickly became prophets of doom and destruction with their predictions that just about the entire city was destined to be consumed in the merciless maw of fire. Their predictions seemed to be on the way to tragic fulfillment as the south fire bore down relentlessly on the Mission district, while its counterpart to the north roared toward the Western Addition; 120-foot-wide Van Ness Avenue was yet to be tested as a firebreak.

Thursday found the city in the throes of absolute crisis; indeed, even more tragedy was to come for, as the north fire reached Leavenworth Street, four blocks east of Van Ness Avenue, it was joined, at about Ellis or Eddy streets, by a third blaze which had originated in the Hayes Valley district on the day before and which was already responsible for the gutting of St. Ignatius College located at Hayes Street and Van Ness Avenue.[7]

The unhappy union of these two fires (north and Hayes Valley) promised even greater destruction to the city. Having joined fiery forces east of Van Ness Avenue, they now, like animated things, moved westward as if determined to hurdle the wide street and thus attack the Western Addition, which consisted almost entirely of wooden buildings. There were feverish attempts to control it around Clay Street and Van Ness Avenue using dynamite set off by soldiers from the Presidio as they endeavored to created a firebreak in the area. However, the first attempts found black powder being employed in this dangerous operation and it quickly developed that this served only to generate more heat and start other fires. Another unlooked-for result came with the burning of several houses as a result of ignited pieces of wood which, like flaming torches, were blown across Van Ness Avenue. Among the buildings attacked were the Crocker mansion as well as the steeple of St. Mary's Cathedral, which, since 1891, had been at the corner of Van Ness Avenue and O'Farrell Street. Although the cathedral was spared (until it was destroyed by fire on September 7, 1962), due to the successful efforts of Father

Charles Ramm and others to extinguish the blaze in the belfry, five square blocks across Van Ness to Franklin, from Clay to Bush streets, were burned.[8]

Other developments on that same Thursday, which was the second day of destruction in San Francisco, witnessed the south fire extending itself as far as Market and Dolores streets with its farthest point of penetration in this direction being reached at about 20th and Dolores streets, on the east side of Dolores only (with the venerable Mission Dolores remaining exempt from any fire damage while the wooden Notre Dame Convent, located directly across the street, was destroyed).[9] By midday of Thursday, the north fire seemed to have subsided; however, it broke out again in the evening when a section around Clay and Van Ness Avenue, not yet entirely burned, started to burn. Further complications came when a wind, blowing eastward from the Golden Gate, backed the fire in the direction of Russian and Telegraph hills, which had previously been spared in the former progress of the north fire.

Friday and Saturday were to bring some overdue respite from the two previous days; after continuing to burn during most of the day, the north fire died on Saturday morning when it simply ran out of combustible materials after being pretty well contained on the east side of Van Ness Avenue. The south fire had come under control on Thursday evening with the use of a tank containing ten thousand gallons of water which was located at 22nd and Church streets. (This tank had been known but it was too far away to be of use until the fire came to its vicinity.) By Saturday, April 22, it was apparent that the worst was over; to some extent, this meant only that so much had been destroyed that the "objectives" of the three main fires might be said to have been attained.

With the eventual publication of official reports concerning the extent of damage that resulted from the fiery holocaust to which San Francisco had been subjected, it developed that, within the over 500 city blocks that had been visited by fire, 28,188 separate buildings, many of them private dwellings, had been burned. The assessed loss was later placed at $52,504,000 but, actually, the loss was much greater than this figure indicates for it covered only buildings as such and not all of these either, since it excluded public buildings such as the City Hall as well as churches and some other buildings not on the tax roll; also, the figure does not include personal property loss which, naturally, was very high in the burned areas. This consisted of 3,400 acres which meant, that, in a city of comparatively small size, 4.11 square miles were destroyed, comprising the very heart of the city. Later, insurance experts estimated that about four-fifths of the property value of San Francisco had gone up in smoke, while they tabulated the total loss suffered by the city and its inhabitants at between $350 million and $400 million. Small wonder, then, that Charles E. Banks and Opie Read in their *History of the San Francisco Disaster* (Chicago, 1906) call the San Francisco disaster the "greatest conflagration in historic times." At least, there appear to be no rivals to San Francisco's claim to this dubious distinction.

Reference will be made later to the efficient service rendered by Mayor Eugene Schmitz during the days of earthquake and fire. More explicit mention should be made now of the fact that, at no time, and this despite many assertions to the contrary, was martial law imposed upon San Francisco: at all times, the military and other federal and state forces were, while efficiently rendering much needed services, under civil jurisdiction. Because some still seem willing to dispute this point, it may help to destroy, once and for all, the legend about San Francisco being subjected to martial law. This type of law is defined as "an arbitrary law proclaimed directly from the military power" and it is easy to establish that this sort of law was never the case in San Francisco at this time. Always and ever, the civil government, headed by Mayor Schmitz and other responsible and capable public officials, was at the helm during the emergency. The mayor quickly formed a Committee of Safety, which, with him, governed the city but, as indicated, it was always a municipal administration and not a military one. A later official report of Major General Adolphus Greely, commanding the U.S. Army's Pacific division, included another report of his subordinate, Brigadier General Frederick Funston, in which the latter made it explicit that, in the earlier absence of his superior officer, General Greely, he had dispatched 500 soldiers from the Presidio to report to the mayor for any necessary and needed services. His statement was that "the troops continued, during the day (April 18) to assist the police and fire department in every possible way." A final quotation from the important Greely report may be mentioned here:

> ... My instructions and directions all tended to complete subordination to the civil power and to urgent public needs, from which policy the slightest deviation was never sanctioned.[10]

We shall next turn to the relief and reconstruction phases that followed the unforgettable days of 1906 in San Francisco.

CHAPTER 15

RELIEF AND RECONSTRUCTION

. . . I am a citizen of No Mean City, although it is in ashes. Almighty God has fixed this as the location of a great city. The past is gone, and there is no use of lamenting or moaning over it. Let us look to the future and, without regard to creed or birth, work together in harmony for the upbuilding of a greater San Francisco.

Address of Archbishop Patrick W. Riordan at meeting of Citizens Committee, Friday, April 27, 1906.[1]

I

T SHOULD BE noted how fortunate San Francisco was in the person of its mayor, Eugene Schmitz, in its days of utmost crisis. As an example of the firm administrative actions that marked his rule of the city at this time, we may mention the incisive proclamation which he issued on the very day of the earthquake:

PROCLAMATION BY THE MAYOR
The Federal Troops, the members of the regular police force and all special police officers have been authorized to *kill* any and all persons found engaged in looting or in the commission of any other crime. I have directed all the gas and electric lighting companies not to turn on gas or electricity until I order them to do so; you may therefore expect the city to remain in darkness for an indefinite time. I request all citizens to remain at home from darkness until daylight of every night until order is restored. I warn all citizens of the danger from fire from damaged or destroyed chimneys, broken or leaking gas pipes or fixtures or any other like cause.

E.E. Schmitz, Mayor[2]

When he found the City Hall uninhabitable because of earthquake damage, Mayor Schmitz set up temporary headquarters in the Hall of Justice by Portsmouth Plaza. This served only a few hours, for it was not long before this structure lay directly in the path of the advancing flames. A quick removal was made to the newly completed Fairmont Hotel, but this building also had to be abandoned as the flames advanced toward it; the hotel was gutted and later had to be extensively restored. Next, Franklin Hall at Fillmore Street near Hayes served as City Hall for several weeks, with yet another removal to the Whitcomb Hotel on Market Street which, until recent years, kept a remembrance of its several years' service as the site of administration in the city with the two words "City Hall" which were inscribed above its front entrance.

Another example of prompt action witnessed the appointment by the mayor of a "Committee of Fifty" to aid him, and it is significant to note that he named former Mayor James D. Phelan, no political friend, to head it as chairman. (This and other like examples attest to the fact that tragedies and disasters have a way of bringing all concerned together; they are simply not times for "politics as usual.")

It was not long before the mayor, with the aid of his committee, formulated some early measures of relief. That commendable provision was quickly made in this direction is testified to by a memorandum that was signed under date of May 18, 1906, exactly a month after the earthquake, by Lieutenant Colonel Evans, commanding the Fifth Infantry. He had been placed in charge of "permanent camps," those destined to be such until later developments would render them unnecessary. Evans reported that during the month twelve permanent camps had come into being which housed 12,660 persons with room for 1,515 more. As might be expected, too, a sympathetic nation sent immediate aid to the stricken city in the form of necessary foodstuffs. Three days after the 'quake, the House of Representatives appropriated another $1 million in addition to the first $1 million already voted almost immediately after word had been received of San Francisco's hour of need. This first sum had been designated for immediate relief to any and all distressed, while the second was programmed for medical supplies and the words of the resolution added that some of it might be used "for steel frames." President Theodore Roosevelt issued a proclamation asking that money be contributed to the American Red Cross for distribution in San Francisco. Secretary of the Treasury Leslie M. Shaw authorized the transfer of $10 million from the New York subtreasury to San Francisco's own subtreasury. Cash was deposited in New York where it was paid out on order of the San Francisco banks that were entitled to it. Cars and ships loaded with aid of all sorts were quickly on their way to the city; an interesting gesture, among many such, was that of five hundred Americans living in London who forwarded $12,500 to San Francisco for purposes of relief.

Two letters of Mayor Schmitz deserve partial quotation here. The first, dated three weeks after the fateful days, was addressed by him to "My unfortunate fellow citizens living in tents" and reminded them, "The United States Army is endeavoring in every possible way to provide proper accommodations for the housing and feeding of those who are destitute." Schmitz called attention to the fact that the decision had been made that it was necessary for people to come together in large camps rather than to continue to live outdoors in small family clusters with the resultant complications of sanitation and so forth. "The large camps," the mayor went on, "such as Golden Gate Park, Presidio Reservation and those at the foot of Van Ness Avenue and at the Potrero, have the best of sanitary conditions and are arranged in such a manner as to give the best possible results. Therefore, those living in tents separated from the large camps are requested and directed to immediately move when ordered to do so and to take up their living quarters in one of those large camps supervised by the proper military authorities." Some stern words followed in which the mayor called attention to some who were hoarding supplies or obtaining more than they needed and "for those committing this dastardly crime" the mayor threatened prompt prosecution upon their apprehension. Some final words of exhortation read as follows:

Again I say to those in need, keep up your spirits and determination to help the authorities in helping you, and let us upon all occasions extend to our brother man the same kind feeling and assistance that we should expect under like conditions extended to us.

E.E. Schmitz, Mayor.[3]

In late May, a second letter went to President Roosevelt in Washington:

My Dear Mr. President:

The people of San Francisco have shown a remarkable courage in the hours of this great calamity, and the determination which each and every one exhibits to build a better and a greater San Francisco speaks well for the true American spirit centered in the breast of every Californian. Our people know not what it is to be discouraged and, with God's help, Mr. President, within the next five years we will return to the nation her greatest seaport on her western shores.

In the name of the brave people whom I am proud to represent, I extend to you my sincere gratitude for the prompt and loyal action that you have taken in endeavoring to help to relieve the suffering of our afflicted people. . . . I cannot speak in too high praise of the magnificent help given the municipal authorities by the U.S. troops

stationed here and, I might say, the devoted assistance of Major
General Greely and General Funston. Mr. President, as an American
citizen, I am proud to be able to certify to their work, and I am proud
that we have men of such calibre in the ranks of the United States
Army.

> Eugene E. Schmitz,
> To the President of the United States,
> Theodore Roosevelt.[4]

As might have been expected, there were several examples of
thieves at work while the city was in its hours of crisis. Indeed,
six such were shot when caught at their nefarious tasks, although
the mayor later reported that rumors about the number of such
executions were considerably exaggerated. Although isolated incidents of drunkenness were reported, there was nothing in the
nature of an orgy in this respect for Schmitz had been prompt in
prescribing the closing of every saloon in the city for a period of
three months, which action, surprisingly enough, seems to have
been generally approved by the saloon-keepers themselves.

The problem of relief in San Francisco was a staggering one,
even judged by modern standards. A city of 350,000 had been
made almost entirely dependent upon outside provisioning. Almost all had to be cared for and sustained and, here again, the
record is clear that, with some few exceptions, the task of immediate and later relief was well taken care of by those concerned
with it. Quickly, the entire city was divided into seven sections
for purposes of "food relief distribution." Within several weeks,
about 70,000 persons were living in tents and temporary dwellings in the Presidio, of which number about 35,000 were in the
general vicinity of the present Presidio Golf Links. Here again the
military proved of the greatest help in issuing rations and blankets to those in need; in all, there were, in the beginning, about
one hundred camps in the city; some were large, as indicated, and
others, at first, were quite small; of these, fifty were under some
form of military supervision (all subject to civil approval,
though); when the military officially withdrew from this work in
favor of the Red Cross and other agencies, Mayor Schmitz was
quick to express his gratitude for "the magnificent work which
has been done in the matter of taking care of our homeless and
destitute."[5]

Since relief measures are meant to be but temporary, the real test of San Francisco was to come with the emergence of the multiplicity of problems that were the city's when reconstruction was discussed. How, in retrospect, did the city pass this test? With the amassing of historical evidence to buttress the assertion, it is felt that San Francisco passed, and with flying colors, the tests that came with the rebuilding of the city from 1906 to 1909. (So much progress had been made in fact, that, in the latter year, the city decided to celebrate its rebirth and proceeded to do so quite successfully.)

It should perhaps be noted that the average San Franciscan never seemed to have entertained serious doubts as to whether his city would rise again. Really, it was not a question of "whether," but rather one of "when." However, there were quite serious and different problems and perplexities to be faced in a city whose heart including, notably, its business section, had been pretty well destroyed by fire. It was evident that some months would have to pass before there could be anything resembling "business as usual." Consequently, temporary steps were quickly taken for the orderly transfer of many business firms from downtown to the Western Addition as well as to the Mission district beyond 20th Street. Both became natural centers, then, of resurgence in the city; both became islands of rebirth as the first months went by after the disaster. Van Ness Avenue quickly changed its character, at least in part, from residential to commercial as some old-time firms moved there on a temporary basis. Such large stores as the White House, the City of Paris, and Shreve moved west to Van Ness; also such well-established firms as W. and J. Sloane, Nathan-Dohrmann, and S. and G. Gump found new locations along Van Ness Avenue.

A quotable example of the spirit that animated Raphael Weill of the White House appeared as follows in the *San Francisco Call* on August 5, 1906:

> The best sermon that a businessman of SF may give to the people of this city at this time must be framed, not in words but in actions. The duty of the hour is not speech but deeds. Let us all in our own field do the best that is in him to rebuild SF, to place her not where she was. . . . We are building a city that must be among the greatest in the U.S. . . . We must profit by one of the costliest lessons ever

given to a modern civilized community, and then we may go forward in confidence to the building of a city that will be splendid in its beauty and prosperity.

Soon some of the better known San Francisco restaurants, such as the Old Poodle Dog and Techau Tavern, moved to new sites. Most of these transfers were made within several months after the great catastrophe. Other firms, like Livingston's, went even farther west—"all the way out" to Fillmore Street; what was formerly a minor shopping district soon had some famous commercial enterprises relocated along its main and subsidiary thoroughfares. Also, many private homes in the unburned areas soon had commercial signs outside as smaller firms sought likewise to open for business. So it was that the prognostications made by occasional pessimists with regard to San Francisco's future were rendered false.

The ruins of San Francisco had hardly cooled before the first phase of reconstruction, necessarily a negative one, began: this consisted in the removal of debris, ruined stone walls, and masses of twisted steel. All this would have to be done before streets could be reopened and communication resumed between various areas. It was not long before temporary railroad tracks were laid on Market Street and other key streets; whereas, earlier, in the 1850s, the "Steam Paddies" had first removed sandhills to establish Market and other streets, now these earlier engines yielded to newer vehicles of reconstruction. Steam shovels and mechanical cranes vied with the steady old horse and wagon, hundreds of each, to collect debris and haul it away as quickly as possible from areas that were to be restored. Estimates have it that about $20 million were spent in this first phase of the reconstruction of San Francisco. (An interesting problem concerned the opening of some safes and bank vaults. Sad experience quickly proved that a considerable period of cooling off was necessary before these safes and vaults could be opened, because the contents would burst into flame on contact with outside oxygen. When necessary precautions were taken, however, it was found that, at least with properly built safes, the contents were in generally satisfactory condition; as expected, however, various degrees of charring of paper records was observed.[6])

It would be expected that Mayor Schmitz would again be heard from in his observations and hopes for the rebuilding of his beloved city. Under the date of June 15, 1906, his office issued a statement; after reminding his fellow citizens that they had been party to one of the greatest scenes of destruction in history, Schmitz invoked the "never-give-up" determination of the pioneers who had founded San Francisco while expressing his complete confidence that a newer and better city would rise from its ashes. Referring to the proposed plans for reconstruction, he went on to say:

> We build not for today but for all the generations to come . . . in the burned districts new buildings will be erected, fire and earthquake proof, of modern architecture and construction, presenting to the view of those who visit San Francisco a city of magnificent edifices. But all of this cannot be done without a great deal of sacrifice; our streets in any case must be widened, some must have the grades reduced and the plan of Mr. D.H. Burnham should be the ideal for which we strive.[7]

After detailing at some length the opposition that had been already expressed by certain vested interests in the city who wished little innovation to be introduced into its planning for the future, the Schmitz statement ended with these exhortatory words:

> Let us therefore put aside all partisan feeling, all feeling of antagonism from whatever cause, and let us determine to lend what aid we can toward the rebuilding of the greater San Francisco, a city second to none and equal to any in the world. We can do this because, in the trying times of the past few months, the courage, perseverance and determination of the people have been proven beyond a doubt; with that courage, perseverance and determination properly directed, we cannot fail, but we must and will see the rebuilding of San Francisco greater, grander and more beautiful than ever—a city that will stand for generations to come as a standard for others to follow.[8]

Obviously, although it was one thing (and a good and necessary thing too) to exhort, there were bound to be a multitude of problems that had to be faced in a resurgent city. Chief among these was that connected with the insurance angle of the disaster and reconstruction period and, even now, there are still some matters in controversy here. Writing in September 1906,

Schmitz expressed his dissatisfaction with the efforts of certain insurance companies to satisfy their obligations to their clients in San Francisco: he wrote that ". . . the property loss was worth fully a half billion dollars, of which amount $250,000,000 was covered by insurance. The attempts of the insurance companies to avoid paying their losses have become a national scandal." He continued:

> Of the hundreds of companies doing business here, those that acknowledged their liabilities and paid in full could be counted on one's fingers. Merchants, householders and all classes of people have suffered greatly and are suffering today because they cannot get their insurance money. In thousands of cases, the amount represented by insurance policy is the sole capital left, and that is impaired—but the people have taken up this question with the same spirit and determination they displayed throughout the catastrophe. Those companies that repudiated their just liabilities will be pursued through the courts and exposed to the world.[9]

Despite his strictures on the insurance companies, Mayor Schmitz was quite enthusiastic, and it would seem with reason, over the picture presented to the world by San Francisco five months after the disaster. In an article that he wrote for a San Francisco periodical the *Independent*, he told of the positive factors as he saw them:

> Notwithstanding the temporary financial distress, the resumption of business as soon as the smoke cleared away was remarkable; buildings arose as if by magic upon foundations yet hot and new houses were raised. During July, over 25,000 men were doing construction in the burned district; some 5,000 temporary buildings and 70 permanent structures were under way; permits for the erection of over 400 additional buildings at an expense of over $3,500,000 were issued. Bank clearings amounted to $160,631,793, an increase of 83.4% over those of July, 1905. By July, more than 200,000 people who had lost their homes and had gone temporarily to suburban towns had returned to the city. Those receiving relief in the bread lines had been reduced from about 250,000 to 17,000; hotels had reopened with first class accommodations and labor was in demand in all quarters; building material was bought up before it reached port and dealers noticed a demand for high class goods; seven theatres were coining money and banks had so much cash on hand that they could now ship several millions to the eastern states. With such conditions only eighty days after the fire, the city is ready, eager, and willing to take

Kearny and Market streets in 1907, showing the Palace Hotel practically rebuilt after the earthquake.

up the matter of rebuilding upon the scale proposed for the greater San Francisco. After what we have gone through, nothing is too great for us to undertake, nothing too difficult for us to accomplish.[10]

Although the amount of insurance could never completely cover all property and personal losses in a disaster of such first magnitude as that of 1906 in San Francisco, it did provide instant means, when, as happened in some cases, it was promptly collected and put to use. It was this money, in great part, which gave impetus to the rebuilding of the city from 1906 to 1909. These years were filled with unprecedented activity; the number of 20,000 engaged in the building trades in prefire San Francisco was doubled by the end of 1906 and continued to grow constantly. A survey made in April 1909, only "three years after," put the value of new construction alone in San Francisco as $150 million. Before the fire, the city had only 27 Class A buildings, i.e. those of steel frames and concrete or stone walls and floors. These had come through the earthquake splendidly and none needed to be demolished. By 1909, all 27 had been restored and complete repairs made when this had been necessary. By 1909, 114 Class B buildings had risen also, these being of reinforced concrete or brick with steel beams; also 1,500 Class C structures, i.e. those concrete, stone, or brick structures that had wooden frames and floors. Finally, to complete the picture of the reconstructed skyline of a substantially reborn city, a city which, indeed, "had been tried and not found wanting," approximately 19,000 frame buildings had been erected during these years of maximum building activity in San Francisco. So, while some 28,000 structures had been destroyed and levelled by fire in 1906, 20,500 buildings, most of them much better constructed than those they replaced, now formed part of the new city. It should also be remembered that many of the buildings that had been destroyed were overdue for such a fate. Many of those in Chinatown, for example, answered this description. The total value of the new structures exceeded that of those burned by almost $50 million and hence it was evident that the apparent and real tragedy of "an earthquake followed by many fires" actually had its good elements. Certainly an improved and first-class system of fire protection came from this experience; other distinguished buildings which now comprise the Civic Center may likewise be considered to be part of the legacy that emerged from tragedy and ruin. It would not be long before San Francisco could consider itself substantially, if not completely, recovered from its days of crisis.

CHAPTER 16

THE PANAMA-PACIFIC INTERNATIONAL EXPOSITION, 1915

. . . Smiling at Fortune's Golden Kiss,
A great, new-born metropolis
That stands, beneath its sun-lit skies,
A monument to Enterprise. . . .

Exposition slogan from poem by David W. Taylor.

F OR ALMOST AN entire year, from February 20 to December 4, 1915, a proudly rebuilt San Francisco was host to the world. The city, over which some had sung a premature requiem in 1906, had decided to celebrate, and this on the grandest of scales, the completion of the Panama Canal to its south as well as its own return from devastation and partial ruin. Even though it had been preceded by the impressive Midwinter Fair of 1894, and was to be followed by the Golden Gate International Exposition of 1939, there is solid room for the opinion that the "PPIE" of 1915 was, all things considered, just about the best of them all. (This, at least, is the verdict expressed by some who, at this writing, remember it well.) The days centering in "Harbor Cove," i.e. the modern Marina district, will always be memorable in the history of San Francisco.

When, on May 1, 1904, construction of the Panama Canal was begun, it found some prominent San Franciscans already planning something special to celebrate its completion, whenever that would be. Earlier, in January 1904, R.B. Hale of Hale Brothers had written to his fellow directors of the Merchants Association of San Francisco proposing an international exposition to celebrate the completion of the proposed canal. The year 1915 had already been set by engineers for the completion of the project and Hale, shrewdly anticipating the rivalry that was sure to ensue between various American cities anxious to host such a commemoration, indicated that 1904 was not at all too early to set machinery in operation with the idea of capturing such an exposition for San Francisco. The merchants promptly and enthusiastically endorsed Hale's proposal, and followed this approval with the appointment of a committee to begin preliminary planning for such an event: $15 million was indicated as a tentative fiscal goal. It was proposed that one-third of this sum be raised by popular subscription, another third be in the form of a federal subsidy, and the final third a city indebtedness to be authorized by the state of California. When, later on in 1904, Congressman Julius Kahn of San Francisco introduced a bill authorizing the federal appropriation, it died in committee for, obviously, other cities would have to be heard from before any such allocation could be made to San Francisco.

With the disaster of 1906 came the thought, at least on the part of some, that the proposed exposition would never come into being because of the urgencies now devolving on a stricken city; however, by December 1906, it had become abundantly clear that San Francisco would indeed rise again and that there was no reason to postpone long-range plans for the 1915 Exposition. First, a Pacific Coast Exposition Company was established and it was decided to have a "trial run" in 1909 in the form of a Portola Festival commemorating the 140th anniversary of the discovery of San Francisco Bay by Don Gaspar de Portola; actually, this exposition was planned to see if a city which it was hoped would be successfully reborn by that time, was ready for an international celebration only six years later. Since the Portola Festival was an unqualified success, a new and more powerful corporation was formed in 1910, complete with thirty directors. This was given the title of the "Panama Pacific International Exposition Company": it was, despite setbacks and obstacles that were to be expected in planning an event of such magnitude, to bring outstanding success to carefully laid plans. When, on April 29, 1910, a mass meeting was held for the purpose of subscribing to the stock of this company, $4 million was subscribed within two hours. On January 31, 1911, the House of Representatives voted, 188–159, to make San Francisco the official site of the exposition, leaving New Orleans, Baltimore, Washington, D.C., and Boston to lick their civic wounds because of the rejection of their respective claims. The victory had not come lightly or wihtout much strategy and planning on the part of determined San Franciscans. This involved a change in fiscal plans: instead of asking the federal government for any direct subsidy, it was proposed that approval of San Francisco as the site was all that would be asked of the federal government at this time. In August 1910, Governor

James N. Gillett called a special session of the California legislature to which he submitted legislation that would permit San Francisco to issue exposition bonds amounting to $5 million while the state of California would help by levying a tax that would yield an equal sum.

Meanwhile, a controversy about the site developed in San Francisco itself. Now that it had been decided to have the exposition located within city limits, there were various proponents of different sections of San Francisco. Six or seven sites were proposed, and it took six months before this question was finally resolved with the selection of the Harbor Cove area (the modern Marina district) adjacent to San Francisco Bay. Since the issue had not yet been resolved when President Taft visited San Francisco on October 14, 1911, he settled (before a throng numbering 100, 000) for a ceremonial breaking of ground in the old stadium of Golden Gate Park; this was understood to be symbolic only and not to serve as a decision as to where, exactly, the project would go.

If the exposition was, in fact, to be international in character, it was necessary to sell the idea to the world. This next step was marked by the careful planning that had characterized earlier thinking; John D. Trask, art critic and collector from Philadelphia, was commissioned to tour Europe in the artistic interests of the PPIE. He was joined by others similarly motivated, and considerable success attended their collective efforts; when the opening day came, about twenty-five countries were represented by pavilions, or some other form of exhibit. All the major countries, as well as others less known, commissioned buildings which, while temporary by design, did much to impart a sense of purpose and beauty to the grounds recovered from swampland on which they were built. Managerial authority was largely concentrated in local hands. A key decision was reached when it was agreed that the major buildings be done in imitation travertine marble. Jules Guerin was selected as the artist in charge of color schemes and his work was successful beyond expectations. Lighting problems were entrusted to Walter d'Arcy Ryan who devised a system of veiled lighting, routine to later generations and known as "indirect lighting," but a considerable novelty at this time. John McLaren, of Golden Gate Park fame, was entrusted with the necessary landscaping and the capable Scot, as usual, rose to the challenge. For several years, he planted and cultivated a supply of trees and bushes; in all, he made use of about 30,000 trees, including the hardy eucalyptus from Australia, to adorn and beautify the exposition grounds. McLaren also went to Europe and was responsible for the eventual arrival of 70,000 rhododendrons from Holland as well as 2,000 azalea plants from Japan and some exotic growths from Africa. Karl Bitter was in charge of sculpture; all the sculpturing took place on the grounds, and one who peruses the books that record this phase of the fair, must be struck at the rich endowment represented there.

When the exposition was in full flower, it was admitted by all that the best vantage point from which to view its splendors was at night at Divisadero and Broadway for, on the brow of that hill, one could see the myriad of buildings as, in all, forty-three states and territories of the United States were represented together with twenty-five foreign countries. It was, truly, an international exposition, more international, really, than its earlier proponents had dared to imagine or dream.

Although, in 1914, the outbreak of World War I caused legitimate apprehension as to the immediate future of the exposition (some thought that the belligerent nations could hardly be expected to send exhibits), steady counsel prevailed with the determination that, come what may, the "show would go on," and it did, right on schedule. Finally, after a mountain of labor had been expended, on Saturday, February 20, 1915, San Francisco, in what was surely one of her proudest hours, opened new portals to the United States and to the world, and the Panama Pacific International Exposition was a reality at last. Not forgotten was the theme announced in the title of the exposition, for visitors were entranced by a five-acre model which was scaled to the landscape of the Isthmus of Panama and which illustrated the Panama Canal itself. Those who so wished could see the exhibits from vehicles that travelled all over the grounds, while many other visitors came repeatedly to walk around at their leisure and view the wonders unfolded before their eyes.

The opening day witnessed a total attendance of 245,143 people. The first ten weeks built up to a total of 4,370,000 and, all through the summer and autumn, the crowds held up and even increased. At the end of the planned ten months, during which little else was talked of in the city than the PPIE, an impressive attendance total of 18,756,148 (many of them repeats) had been reached. No doubt, then, that the exposition had been a success and no doubt either, that San Francisco had demonstrated to its own satisfaction as well as that of the world, that it had definitely recovered from the wounds inflicted upon it less than ten years before. On December 4, 1915, when the PPIE finally closed, with ample evidence that San Francisco had made a success of it all, it was with great civic pride that its citizens bade a fond farewell to the physical aspects of the exposition while fully conscious that its memories would continue to linger on.

It has already been noted that a great many people contributed to the memorable days that marked 1915 in San Francisco; however, several personages were outstanding. First was the civil engineer, Harris de Haven Connick (1873–1965) who bore the title of Director of the Division of Works and therefore was responsible for the "building of the set."[1] From 1911, when Connick received his appointment, he labored successfully in facing the many problems that were his, for he had to create a city within a city with every necessary convenience; among the multitude of his concerns were those centering about sewers, water and gas mains, electrical conduits, wharves, access roads, railroad spurs, fountains, pools, and fire protection. Also, proper housing had to be provided for livestock as well as for human performers, including some aborigines who required special treatment. Connick's drawing boards were already covered with blueprints when the land where all of this was to take place was still under twelve to twenty feet of water. He enclosed seventy acres of the Harbor Cove area by a seawall while the ground was filled from the adjacent bay by means of suction pumps. With the approval of the Secretary of War, Connick made use of additional acreage from Fort Mason and the Presidio, amounting to 588 acres in all. Connick proved to be a great general executive, as the results were to show.

Another man of distinction was the architect, Bernard Ralph Maybeck (1862–1957) who designed the Palace of Fine Arts which, in its completely reconstructed form, still stands as a lone monument to the earlier glories of 1915. Maybeck was serving on the campus of the University of California at Berkeley; there he established the Department of Architecture and was responsible for much of the present campus since he designed some of its earlier buildings. Presumably, both Connick and Maybeck would be quick to acknowledge the invaluable help of many of their confreres; out of their combined efforts came the greatness that was associated with the PPIE.

An idea of the wonderful enthusiasm engendered by the exposition is found in the rhapsodic words penned by the future poet laureate of California, Edwin Markham; he thus described the opening night:

> I have seen tonight the greatest revelation of beauty that was ever seen on the earth. I may say this meaning it literally and with full regard for all that is known of ancient art and architecture and all that the modern world has heretofore seen of glory and grandeur. I have seen beauty that will give the world new standards of art and a joy in loveliness never before reached.

While time and the critical historian might wish to amend some of Markham's rhapsody, it was evident to all who beheld those opening scenes that here was no ordinary spectacle. In commemoration of December 4, 1915, the last night when the lights were finally extinguished, George Sterling, San Francisco poet wrote these appreciative lines which will conclude our treatment of what had, truly, been a "Monument to Enterprise":

> The hour has struck, the mighty work is done—
> Praise God for all the bloodless victories won;
> And from these courts of Beauty's pure universe,
> Go forth in Joy and Brotherhood and Peace.

CHAPTER 17

THE CIVIC CENTER

A MONG THE ARCHITECTURAL distinctions that belong to San Francisco are those that have been awarded it because of its beautiful Civic Center; it has frequently been noted that the city is the proud possessor of one of the most outstanding group of governmental and cultural structures in the nation, surpassed only, if indeed at all, by the national capitol in Washington. It is historically appropriate that these buildings, planned as early as 1904, be considered as true examples of the spirit of San Francisco as well as of the resurgence of the city. We shall treat the various buildings in the order of their dedication.

EXPOSITION AUDITORIUM—dedicated January 5, 1915.

There is an inscription on the cornerstone of this building, occupying the entire block bounded by Grove, Hayes, Larkin, and Polk streets, which requires clarification: "Erected and Presented to the City of San Francisco by the Panama Pacific International Exposition. Anno Domini, MCMXIV." Actually, it would seem that San Francisco's citizens presented a gift to themselves for, while $1 million was allotted for the auditorium's construction from a $5 million bond issue in support of the PPIE, this money ultimately came from the citizens themselves. Additionally, the sum of $322,935 was taken from tax money to face the building with granite so as to bring its exterior in harmony with the other structures planned for the Civic Center. Although it was explicitly provided that the PPIE, which opened six weeks after the auditorium's dedication, should have control of the building during the exposition days, it was stipulated that title to the structure would then revert to the city.

The lot on which the impressively large auditorium stands comprises an area of over 111,437 square feet. Archbishop Joseph Alemany first had title to it in the name of the archdiocese of San Francisco and he sold the property in 1881 to the Mechanics Institute for $175,000. This organization planned to build there a second Mechanics Pavilion to succeed the earlier one which was on leased land on the southeast corner of Eighth and Market streets extending down to Mission Street. In 1882, the new pavilion was opened on the recently purchased site and it played an important part in the history of the city until it was destroyed as a result of the "Ham and Eggs" fire of 1906. Its last use was of a humanitarian nature since it served as a receiving hospital for the injured and sick on the fateful morning of April 18, 1906. By the afternoon of that day, it was necessary to evacuate the structure and to watch its wooden walls being consumed by the fiery holocaust. Since there were already plans to begin a Civic Center, later negotiations between the Mechanics Institute and Mayor James Rolph, Jr. representing the city government, resulted in the acquisition of the site for San Francisco on October 8, 1912. The price was $701,437. Arthur Brown, Jr., already a distinguished architect and destined to go on to greater eminence for other buildings in the Civic Center complex, was chosen to design the building. Construction was under way in 1913 and, by dedication night, January 5, 1915, San Francisco had a beautiful auditorium which has served the city long and well since then.

The Civic Auditorium is a four-story Class "A" building with reinforced concrete floors. The main hall seats about 4,500 with provision for an additional 4,000 portable seats when extra accommodations are required. The Polk and Larkin halls each seat another thousand, and these can be opened in such a way as to implement the seating arrangements in the main auditorium. There are also twenty-six other halls of varying sizes and sixteen rooms designed for committee use. With the memories of 1906 in mind, ample provision was made for wide exits as well as for adequate fire protection. Many notable gatherings have formed part of the history of the Civic Auditorium; outstanding in this regard was the Democratic National Convention of 1920. In 1964, a thorough renovation of the building was accomplished which added much to its value as the city's outstanding meeting place.

To this day, San Francisco's Civic Auditorium remains a notable structure in the impressive area of the Civic Center.

THE CITY HALL—*dedicated December 29, 1915.*

San Francisco has had five city halls, which have culminated in the present noble structure. The first was a rented building located on Montgomery and Merchant streets, which was occupied in 1849, while the second was situated at Kearny and Pacific Avenue on a site which was purchased in 1850. The third city hall was located at Kearny and Washington streets and served until 1895 when it yielded to a new Hall of Justice. Although plans for a newer and larger city hall dated from 1870, it was many years before it came into being. When work on the project, located near the present Civic Center, was begun in 1871 (it was advertised in the City Directory for 1878 to 1879 as "not only the largest and most durable structure in the city but . . . the largest edifice of this description in the United States") it was thought that the building would be completed in several years at a cost of about $1.5 million. It was built on historic ground for it occupied the site of the pioneer Yerba Buena cemetery, a triangular plot of land bounded by Market, Larkin, and McAllister streets. A local historian records that

> Both estimates, as to date of completion and cost, fell far wide of the mark. Seven years later, only one wing of the 800-foot long main building (there was to be a separate Hall of Records) had been completed and its slow progress and mounting costs had become a public scandal. Charges of corruption, including collusion between the builders and city officials, were freely made; meanwhile, the public, impatient at the slow progress, took to referring to it as the "new City Hall ruin."[1]

Even though its cornerstone dated from 1872, this city hall was not yet a completed structure when earthquake damage in 1906 made it necessary to replace the poorly built edifice. This may well be considered to have been a real blessing for the city, since it resulted in the building of our present City Hall.

On March 28, 1912, the voters of San Francisco authorized a bond issue of $800,000 for the acquisition of land for a civic center as well as for the erection of a city hall. Mayor Rolph, newly inaugurated, made the project his particular concern with an announcement that a public competition would be held to select an architect. Over seventy submitted plans, and the firm of Bakewell and Brown was finally awarded the contract by a jury of seven headed by the mayor himself. (This contract also included a prize award of $25,000.) Ground was broken on April 5, 1913, with Mayor Rolph in the finest of fettle on the occasion. The following two years saw the structure rise in grace, strength, and dignity. Unlike its unfortunate predecessor, this city hall was well planned and was marked by superior workmanship matched only by the solid building materials that went into it. On December 29, 1915, one of San Francisco's most memorable days came with the dedication of the newest city hall; the event came only several weeks after the closing of the PPIE. With pardonable pride, Mayor Rolph pointed out that the task of building the city hall had been accomplished in three years and that the cost had been kept within the appropriation of $3.5 million, adding that, actually, some of this money had been returned to the city treasury as unspent.

San Francisco's City Hall rises 308 feet above ground level and, for many years, Mayor Rolph used proudly to indicate to the many guests he entertained on formal occasions on the steps of the rotunda that this same rotunda was "16 feet, 2⅝ inches higher than that of the national capitol."[2] The building is designed in the French Renaissance style and is built of gray California granite; its striking exterior is matched only by its spacious and impressive interior. From 1912 to 1931, during Rolph's long service as mayor, the rotunda and the City Hall itself saw all the world welcomed to its grandeur. Outstanding events included the memorial services for President Warren G. Harding, who died in the Palace Hotel, San Francisco in 1923; appropriately, James Rolph himself lay in state there when, in 1934, he died in office as governor of California. (Surely his spirit was at peace in the familiar surroundings which had formed such a large part of his life.) A stubborn fire in the dome occurred on February 16, 1951, which resulted in damage estimated at $10,000, but it was not long before all was restored and the building back in full operation. The San

Francisco City Hall is, actually, the kind of structure that grows on one as he strolls about slowly and captures some of the undeniable glories which it contains.

THE MAIN PUBLIC LIBRARY—dedicated February 15, 1917.

An appropriate inscription over the main entrance to this building was composed by former Mayor Edward R. Taylor and reads as follows:

> The Public Library of the City and County of San Francisco. Founded 1878. Erected, 1916. May this structure, throned upon imperishable books, be maintained and cherished from generation to generation for the improvement and delight of mankind.

More history is recorded on an inscription on the inside wall of the vestibule:

> This building stands upon a portion of the site of the old City Hall. In its erection, the citizens of San Francisco were aided by a gift of $375,000 from Andrew Carnegie who also gave a like amount for the construction of branch library buildings.

Ground was broken for the Main Library in March 1915; its cornerstone was laid on April 15, 1916, with the dedication ceremonies following on February 15, 1917. The completed structure cost $1,152,167 of which $772,220 came from city funds, with the rest being supplied by the Carnegie gift. Although much criticized now as being a beautiful but hopelessly inadequate building (which is almost certainly true) from the artistic and architectural standpoint, an observant stroll through the building will reveal some interesting features; for example, much of California and local history is recreated in the murals done by Frank DuMond. Originally, these had been executed for exhibition at the PPIE; after this use, they were given to the library by the PPIE directors. One panel, forty-seven feet long and twelve feet wide, is on the wall of the Reference Room and the other is on the wall of the General Reading Room; both are graphic demonstrations of the pioneer spirit which marked the winning of the West. What the future use and disposition of this building will be is impossible to predict; however, for long, it has added to the impressive features that mark the Civic Center.

THE WAR MEMORIAL OPERA HOUSE AND VETERANS BUILDING —dedicated September 9, 1932.

Before mentioning the outstanding structures that comprise the War Memorial Opera House and its adjoining Veterans Building, mention should be made of the State Building, completed in 1923, which rises on McAllister Street and which is quite consonant in design with the rest of the Civic Center. It occupies the half block bounded by Larkin, McAllister, Polk, and Redwood streets. It accommodates the offices of various state boards and commissions together with an office for the governor as well as quarters for the California State Supreme Court. The building cost more than was at first anticipated, $1,560,000. Since its dedication, it has expanded with the addition of two wings. The cornerstone was laid on December 22, 1922, and, since dedication, the California State Building has served its purposes well.

A commemorative plaque in the foyer of the War Memorial Opera House states that the singularly graceful and beautiful structure is "dedicated to the Citizens of San Francisco who have given their lives in the service of their country." It would have been difficult to have erected a more distinguished structure. From early days, San Franciscans have loved good music, including opera, and the plans for the present building were long in mind before its eventual realization. After much preliminary investigation and debate, the present site was chosen, facing Van Ness Avenue, in 1931; Arthur Brown, Jr. was again selected as the architect for the two buildings which were to be built at the same time. Their cornerstones were laid on the same day, Armistice Day, November 11, 1931, and both were dedicated in joint ceremonies on Admission Day, September 9, 1932. (Present at the ceremonies was Governor Rolph who, as mayor, had participated in earlier planning for the two buildings.) The Opera House cost $3.5 million and was formally opened on Saturday evening, October 15, 1932, when the opera *Tosca* was performed with some 4,000 in attendance. Seating 3,285, it well serves a culturally

War Memorial Opera House, Civic Center. Redwood Empire Association

conscious San Francisco. Among the outstanding events, in addition to musical presentations, which have marked the history of the Opera House have been those that occurred April 17 through June 1945, when it and the Veterans' Building served as the birthplace of the United Nations.[3] Commemorative meetings of the United Nations have since been held there, in 1955, and 1965, with a special twenty-fifth anniversary ceremony in 1970. The War Memorial complex is further distinguished by the fact that the Japanese Peace Treaty was drawn up in 1951 in the Veterans' Building and signed in the Opera House. The Veterans' Building features a main auditorium which seats over 1,100, while the remainder of the structure contains numerous meeting rooms which are in constant use by various groups of war veterans. The third and fourth floors are occupied by the San Francisco Museum of Modern Art. The museum's elegant bookshop is now on the ground floor of the building.

All of this contributes to the distinctiveness and cultural attraction of the Civic Center.

CHAPTER 18

UNDER THE HILLS OF HOME:

HOME:

Five Tunnels

S

AN FRANCISCANS HAVE always been aware of the majesty that attends their city from the fact that it is, in good part, built upon hills, forty-two of them, in fact. On the other hand, hills can be annoying when they must be travelled over or around to get anywhere, and this was pretty much the situation in San Francisco before enterprising engineers decided to penetrate some of those hills by tunnelling through them. This has resulted in five such bores; we shall treat them chronologically. But first, for completeness, we should mention some other smaller tunnels.

Since city limits obviously include the Park Presidio approach to the Golden Gate Bridge, brief notice may be taken here of the rather short tunnel which forms part of this approach and which was bored in 1940; the same may be said of the small tunnel through Yerba Buena Island which forms part of the Bay Bridge. Although short, 540 feet, this tunnel has the distinction (since it operates on two levels) of being the tallest bore in the world—it is 58 feet in diameter. Earlier, between 1907 and 1908, the Southern Pacific Railroad Company bored four tunnels, totalling 8,815 feet, between its Third and Townsend Depot and the San Mateo County line. (They have since been relocated.) There is also the 1,500-foot Belt Line Tunnel under Fort Mason, which was dug by order of the State Harbor Commission in 1914. The Southern Pacific tunnels are obviously under private jurisdiction and while the city of San Francisco has assumed responsibility for the formerly state-owned Belt Railroad, this tunnel, limited to commercial use, does not impinge itself upon civic consciousness as do the others.

STOCKTON STREET TUNNEL—1914:
OPENING A DOOR TO NORTH BEACH

Until late in 1952, when the Broadway Tunnel was completed, San Francisco, because of its Stockton Street Tunnel, could claim the unique distinction of being the only city in the world with a double street. The Stockton Street Tunnel extends between Bush and Sacramento streets; for four blocks, there are two streets, one above and one directly through the tunnel with sidewalks for pedestrians on either side, as well as original provision for streetcars, which have since yielded to buses and a steady flow of automobile traffic. The tunnel cut under a portion of Nob Hill, serves as a connecting link between two very distinct parts of the city—the downtown shopping area and Chinatown and the North Beach district. If one enters the tunnel in a northerly direction, the beehive activity of the shopping district centering in Union Square is left behind; in a matter of minutes, one emerges into a very different world. This is among the more notable contrasts of the San Francisco scene. Obviously the completion of the tunnel had an immediate and planned effect on the flow of vehicular and streetcar traffic, now all who wished could go under and through Nob Hill rather than around it.

The steadily growing city of that day had called for just such an improvement and the City Planning Commission met that need by awarding a contract for the tunnelling of a portion of Stockton Street on April 11, 1913. At a total cost of $656,000, the tunnel was completed on December 11, 1914. The tunnel is a short one extending only 911 feet, with approaches totalling 413 feet in all, which brings the final figure to 1,324 feet. The roadway is 34 feet wide with 7-foot sidewalks on either side. Double streetcar tracks long served the Municipal Railroad's "F" line until a later conversion to bus service led to the removal of the tracks. Since the city was still conscious of the possibility of earthquakes, several escape doors (not maintained now) were included which, in the event of the tunnel being caved in at its entrances, would, hopefully, allow egress into the basements of dwellings built above the tunnel. They were never put to use and only serve now to remind us of the thinking of earlier days. The tunnel is 19 feet high and has a moderate grade of 4.29 percent.

Its costs were met by direct assessment of the property owners who were to benefit most from the tunnel. When opened, the Stockton Street bore represented the widest span of streetcar traffic ever undertaken up to that time. On December 29, 1914, with a jubilant Mayor Rolph at the controls, the first streetcar made its way through the newly completed tunnel; this was to be the first of the three tunnels which he would dedicate during his years as mayor.

TWIN PEAKS TUNNEL—1917: OPENING UP THE AREA WEST OF THE PEAKS

When the chief scenic features of San Francisco are mentioned, it is obvious that Twin Peaks quickly come to mind. They are a prime example of what is meant by a consideration of the scenic advantages coupled with traffic disadvantages which form part of the story of the hills of home. The peaks (South Peak, elevation 910.5 feet; North Peak, 903.8 feet) have long served as twin symbols of an oustanding city but, by the early 1900s, were recognized as the principal geographical barrier between older San Francisco and the slowly expanding regions to the west. The streetcar trip of 12,000 feet through the Twin Peaks Tunnel which San Franciscans have taken so much for granted since 1917 was not at all possible before that date. Topography and common-sense engineering forbade running a streetcar line over the formidable barrier provided by the peaks; it became obvious, then, that only a deep and long bore would accomplish the "geographical liberation" of the large section of the city that lay to the west of Twin Peaks. By 1908, determined citizens pressed the case for such a tunnel, since they knew that their property values would skyrocket with its completion. City Engineer M.M. O'Shaughnessy gave much of his time and talents to a consideration of as many as fifteen different sets of plans for the projected tunnel. A Chicago traffic consultant, Bion J. Arnold, was hired and he proposed a composite from features derived from several plans; in substance, the Arnold suggestions were eventually accepted. The financing of such a large project as expected, furnished matter for dispute. It was finally decided that a direct use

Twin Peaks Tunnel, West Portal, before the facade was demolished.

of tax money was not the solution, for many who felt that they would neither use nor benefit by the tunnel would brand it as a colossal real estate deal. Hence, the assessment of those who, like those involved in the earliest Stockton Street Tunnel, stood to gain the most from a penetration of Twin Peaks, was finally settled upon.

A newly organized Twin Peaks Property Owners Association started its efforts to convice those concerned that they should join forces. Estimated cost of the tunnel was placed at about $4 million; of this, the district west of the peaks, which would be the primary beneficiary, was assessed $3,398,972. This district comprised 4,153 acres. The other district, that east of the peaks, with an area of 660 acres, was assessed at $595,316. Both assessment figures were based on a rate of 2¢ per square foot and it was provided that the money could be paid on an installment plan. On October 29, 1913, the city government approved of this key point in the whole project and the construction firm of R.C. Stornie received the tunnel contract with a bid of $3,372,000; the agreement was signed on November 2, 1914, with a stipulation that 1,000 days would be allowed for completion of the tunnel.

Many engineering problems had to be faced in the boring of a tunnel of such length, but they were all faced up to and conquered so that the finished tunnel was the pride of all those who had designed and built it. When finally completed, the Twin Peaks Tunnel was 25 feet wide, and the same high, and 12,000 feet or 2.27 miles long. Of this, the tunnel portion itself is 8,800 feet while the cut and cover section comprises 3,200 feet. The maximum grade is 3 percent while the sharpest curve has a radius of 342 feet. There were two passenger stations, the main one called the Laguna Honda (now Forest Hills) station, and another at the other end of the tunnel called the Eureka station. This last has been discontinued.

The Twin Peaks Tunnel was dedicated on Saturday, July 14, 1917. Mayor Rolph quoted Bishop Berkeley's famous lines: "Westward, the course of empire takes its way," for which saying, a newspaper account recorded:

> The Mayor was rewarded with a kiss by his better half and the crowd dispersed. But not before he had made some predictions with regard to the future of his beloved San Francisco: "With the coming of the rails and the operation of streetcars through the Twin Peaks Tunnel, it will no longer be necessary to move down on the peninsula or across the Bay to Marin or Alameda Counties to find suitable home sites. Enough will be provided west of Twin Peaks."

He then drove the first spike at East Portal to inaugurate the street railway phase of the bore; next he walked the entire length of the tunnel at the head of a jubilant throng. At 2:30 P.M. on Saturday, February 4, 1918, Mayor Rolph, joined by members of the Board of Supervisors and their wives and families, left City Hall in the first Municipal Railroad streetcar to go through the tunnel. Naturally, the colorful mayor, dressed appropriately, acted as motorman, with Timothy Reardon, president of the Board of Public Works, doing honors as conductor. The car was met by huge crowds along the right of way, since this was known to be a great day for the owners and inhabitants, actual and potential, who were to start a new life with their streetcar transportation now an accomplished fact. The Twin Peaks Property Owners Association met the crowded streetcars at West Portal with their automobiles and seized on the gala occasion to take prospective buyers on conducted tours through the emerging residential districts of St. Francis Wood, Forest Hill, Parkside, Ingleside Terrace, and West-wood Park.[1]

Occasionally, voices have been raised about the obsolescence of the Twin Peaks Tunnel, with critics maintaining that it is now an inefficient operation. At the time of writing, this tunnel is in the process of reconstruction. The original facade belongs totally to history and modern design is taking over. Whether for better or worse, the citizens can soon judge.

DUBOCE OR SUNSET TUNNEL—1928: OPENING UP THE SUNSET DISTRICT

Occasionally, some San Franciscans have referred to the outer Sunset district as that area of their city where fog and water meet. However this may be, there was certainly sunshine in the hearts of all who lived there in 1928 with the completion of the Sunset Tunnel which, like the Twin Peaks bore a decade before, was to open up the Sunset district now that fast streetcar transportation to downtown San Francisco was assured.

It may be supposed that in 1898, when Colonel Victor Duboce headed the First California Regiment in the Spanish-American War, he could hardly have known that San Francisco would name a major tunnel after him. This successful project was, in fact, to render accessible one of the finest residential districts in the city. After much preliminary discussion, it was decided that the projected and needed tunnel should bore under Buena Vista Park to the western side of the hill and terminate at Carl and Cole streets. Once again, City Engineer O'Shaughnessy and a capable staff must be credited with bringing an engineering project (not without its special difficulties) to a successful conclusion. When finished, the Sunset Tunnel measured 4,232 feet in length; it is the same height and width as its sister Twin Peaks Tunnel—25 feet. Once again, the assessment plan was used to finance this tunnel; work began on its construction in 1926 and it was finished two years later. Since then, the "N" line has used the facilities of this tunnel. The official opening of the Sunset Tunnel took

Sunset Tunnel, Duboce Park. Going east.

place on Sunday, October 21, 1928. The ceremonies took place at the East Portal located alongside Duboce Park, and were witnessed by 50,000 persons; the ceremonies began at 12:30 P.M. at the climax of a gala parade of streetcars which were the first in service along the new route. Again, it was Mayor Rolph at the controls, complete with a new motorman's cap, and it was noted, with approval, that he handled the controls with a finesse acquired, presumably, from previous experience. In a dedicatory speech, the mayor remarked:

> This is another of those important improvements which benefit the entire city. A new home district is created. It attracts to San Francisco more residents and builders. More people mean more prosperity for the business man. Prosperity for the business man means more employment, a greater and happier prosperity for all.

Since San Francisco was in a particularly happy mood that day, it was appropriate that the day finish with an evening carnival centering at Ninth Avenue and Irving Street in the Sunset district. Once again, a successful bore under the hills of home had been accomplished.[2]

BROADWAY TUNNEL(S)—1952:
TWIN BORES UNDER RUSSIAN HILL

When, on December 21, 1952, a red light at the south of the just completed Broadway Tunnel changed to green, the long-dreamed-of penetration of Russian Hill had been accomplished and one of the most modern tunnels in the world became part of San Francisco. Records show that such a tunnel had been discussed for almost ninety years, for in 1865 and again in 1876, proposals for such a tunnel through Russian Hill had been made to the City Council.[3] Through the years, periodic attempts were made to revive the idea of such a bore, which could render access to the Western Addition so much easier, but it was not until 1946 that the voters of San Francisco approved the plan for its building and authorized a bond issue for the tunnel. When completed, it was really two tunnels for it consisted of twin bores each measuring 1,616 feet from portal to portal; the twin tunnels run between Mason and Taylor streets (East Portal) and Leavenworth and Hyde streets (West Portal). Each of the twin bores is 28½ feet wide, and each provides two lanes for vehicular traffic in a one-way-only pattern with an elevated and protected sidewalk for pedestrians. The whole project took the name of the Broadway Tunnel, since that thoroughfare provides access and egress to the

Broadway Tunnel, Powell Street, East Portal.

bores. The total cost of construction came to $7.3 million; ground-breaking took place on July 28, 1950, with the dedication and opening ceremonies following on December 21, 1952. As in the case of its predecessors, the years of constant use and the flow of traffic have amply justified the planning that brought the Broadway Tunnel into being.

On November 18, 1974, a fifth tunnel was opened for use in San Francisco. This was the Geary Tunnel, 530 feet long, which was built to separate traffic at the busy Geary Street–Masonic Avenue intersection. Together with approach areas, the tunnel runs under Geary Street from Lyon Street to Parker Avenue; it cost $2.4 million.

All five of these tunnels have played significant parts in fulfilling the various objectives that brought them into being.

CHAPTER 19

THE AGE OF THE
FERRY BUILDING

. . . If the Embarcadero has a soul, it's shaped something like the Ferry Building. The world over, it stands for San Francisco the way the Campanile stands for Venice, the Eiffel Tower for Paris, the Empire State Building for New York City. . . .

> Robert O'Brien, *This is San Francisco* (New York, 1948) p. 19.

. . . Oakland Ferry-Railroad Line being now completed from Oakland . . . cars will begin running in connection with the Steamer Contra Costa *on Wednesday, September 2. . . . Every facility is afforded for the safety and speedy transportation of passengers and freight. . . .*

> San Francisco *Alta California*, September 1, 1863.

B EFORE TURNING TO the important details concerned with the construction of the Bay and Golden Gate bridges, it will help to indicate the important part played in the city's past by its world-famous Ferry Building and by the busy fleet of ferryboats that served the Bay Area for many years. Those who remember the Ferry Building at the height of its former activities as well as the imposing fleet of ferryboats that docked in its slips will never forget the integral part played in San Francisco lore, legend, and reality by both the building and the boats. (Although most of the ferryboats are gone, there has been a partial resumption of service and a return, therefore, of some ferryboats; the Ferry Building is far from gone, although much of it is now devoted to various uses.)

With the inauguration of regular ferry service in 1863, it was imperative that a depot be built to accommodate the ferries. In 1873, the State Board of Harbor Commissioners felt justified in appropriating for such purposes that portion of the waterfront lying between the north side of Market Street to the north side of Clay Street and entered into contracts for the construction of four ferry slips and sheds, at an estimated cost of $93,000. It was thought that this would afford superior facilities to the travelling public as the ferries would connect with several of the first railroad lines. By September 1875, a ramshackle sort of structure was sufficiently completed to allow the docking of ferryboats; the next few years saw the addition of several new slips and gradually this first ferry terminal became an accepted part of the Embarcadero scene. By 1888, the Harbor Commissioners discussed the matter of replacing the insufficient facilities with a larger ferry depot, for the "necessities of the travelling public demand better facilities for passing in and out of San Francisco at the foot of

Ferry Landing of the Central Pacific and South Pacific Coast Railroads, about 1886. Site of present Ferry Building. Southern Pacific

Market St. There should be erected a commodious building arranged for the rapid handling of passengers, baggage, mail, express and freight. It should be so constructed as to allow passengers to pass from the upper decks of the ferries through the second story and by a bridge over the crowded and dangerous portion of East St. (Embarcadero)."[1] By 1893, voters had approved an act of the state legislature providing for the sale of bonds sufficient to finance the new terminal. A. Paige Brown, a reliable architect, was employed to draw plans and he decided that the predominant feature, the tower, should be modelled after the Giralda, or Bell Tower, which forms part of the cathedral in Seville, Spain. Although construction of the building was not completed until 1903, enough had been accomplished by 1898 for the building to be opened, with dedicatory ceremonies held on July 13, 1898. The new building received the title of the "Union Ferry Depot." At a cost of about $1 million, San Francisco now had a handsomely designed structure which would in time attain world fame. What was to be familiarly known as the "Ferry Building" was of impressive dimensions, with a frontage of 659 feet and a width of 156 feet.

The large hall of the building has been put to many uses; a famous day saw American President McKinley welcomed there; another witnessed a large banquet after the Spanish-American War, honoring the soldiers returning home from the Philippine Islands. Since it had been carefully and well built on concrete piers, the Ferry Building successfully withstood the earthquake of 1906; it was also spared the fires that followed. Its famous siren was installed in the tower on Christmas Day, 1918, and was first put to use on New Year's Eve a week later.[2] With the completion of the Bay Bridge in 1936, the Ferry Building became at least partially obsolete but it was wisely decided that it should not be razed but rather that it should, after extensive remodelling, be devoted to commercial and other uses. Plans for a World Trade Center were discussed by 1939. However, it was not until May 1956, after the north half of the Ferry Building was rebuilt, with a third floor added to accommodate various import-export firms as well as some foreign consulates, that the World Trade Center was inaugurated. So it is that, even though the original purpose of the building has been considerably changed, San Francisco and San Franciscans are still conscious of the continuing presence of their Ferry Building, an integral part of the San Francisco scene.

It is sometimes related how an Indian chief was the first to create a "ferry boat route" in San Francisco Bay. Dubbed *el marinero,* "the sailor," by the Spanish who observed his activities, he seems to have settled on a small island off San Rafael where he began, on some unknown date and with a small canoe, to ferry persons across the Golden Gate. However, the first regular scheduling of any ferryboat service came in 1850 when Captain Thomas Gray and his small propeller steamer, the *Kangaroo,* sailed twice each week, weather permitting, from San Francisco to San Antonio Creek, later known as the Oakland Estuary. This was the first regular scheduled ferryboat service on the bay. The onrush of people after the discovery of gold made the expansion of any such activity imperative and soon several other pioneer captains and crafts plied the waters of the bay. In 1863, as indicated, in connection with interurban train service, ferryboats began their

Ferry Building, circa 1904.

long years of service in a more regular manner. By the 1870s, the main ferry operations were owned by the major railroad companies whose lines they served. For decades, the ferries flourished but, with the advent of the automobile in the early 1900s, and the overall growth of the Bay Area, they changed with the times and most of them gradually provided service as auto ferries; in 1930, regarded as a peak year for ferryboats, 6 million vehicles and over 40 million people were transported across the waters of San Francisco Bay.

It was not long, however, before the supremacy of the ferries was to be challenged: this came with the construction of the colossal Bay Bridge, completed in late 1936. This, plus the finishing of the Golden Gate Bridge the next year, sounded the death knell of the ferries in loud and clear tones. These bridges served the needs of commerce and of a rapidly growing population in a manner which, at least until recent years, the ferries could not hope to match. By 1939, the ferries to the East Bay had been abandoned and, in 1941, those to Marin County ceased operation. With the completion in 1956, of yet another bridge, the Richmond–San Rafael, the last of the Bay ferry lines succumbed.

Growth and other patterns have brought about a partial return to ferryboat service with the realization that the bridges have reached unanticipated saturation points with regard to the handling of the millions of vehicles that use them. By 1969, the Golden Gate Bridge was carrying nearly 31 million vehicles annually, an increase of 900 percent over its 1938 figures. After much planning, several solutions were proposed, including BART, the increased use of buses to keep more private cars at home, and a new Golden Gate Ferry Line (the latter service, which was started in August 1970, is a commute operation which docks at the Ferry Building and runs to Sausalito on a regular schedule). Just what future patterns will emerge for any further return of the ferryboats to the waters of the Bay is not clear or certain; there are solid reasons to think, though, that this return is more than just a temporary phenomenon. Certainly, a glance backwards makes it evident that both the Ferry Building and the ferryboats have played a memorable part in the history of San Francisco.

CHAPTER 20

THE PORT OF SAN FRANCISCO

. . . The working port of San Francisco is a compact gap-toothed smile of piers whose upper lip is the broad, airy road we call the Embarcadero. . . .

Margot Patterson Doss,
San Francisco at Your Feet:
The Great Walks in a
Walker's Town (New York,
1974), p. 46.

E

VER SINCE THE days of the great sailing ships, San Francisco Bay has been one of the most famous harbors in the world. The romance of the old sea captains, and their frequent agonies, together with the story of the beautiful white-sailed ships they commanded are a part of the past of this natural harbor which was the goal of most of the perilous voyages from the east coast, around Cape Horn, and up the frequently stormy coast of California. In those days, cargoes generally consisted of tools and other things badly needed in California. When the fever of the days of "old, of gold, of '49" began to cool off, the golden era of such ships had passed its zenith; however, the golden era of the port of San Francisco and of the city it served was yet to come.

Soon the more practical steamships replaced the clippers and other sailing ships and, from then until now the procession of vessels of all kinds, sizes, and nations continues to pass through the Golden Gate. The continuing importance of the bay and port of San Francisco can best be understood against the backdrop of the conditions and circumstances under which this port developed.

If one were to seek a date for the beginnings of the port of San Francisco, it could well be that of July 9, 1846, when Captain John Montgomery raised the American flag over the Mexican Plaza which then became Portsmouth Plaza. The arrival of the U.S.S. *Portsmouth* and sister ships in Yerba Buena Cove can be considered as the beginning of the foremost harbor on the Pacific Coast—the port of San Francisco.

California's early days of Spanish (and later Mexican) rule saw little use of the port except by occasional ships of foreign registry, which (illegally) anchored in Yerba Buena Cove to refit and take on supplies, and whaling ships, that stopped only for water, supplies, and repairs. Thus the bay served as little more than a haven for ships engaged in the Pacific trade. The Gold Rush put an end to all this: the harbor's unhurried tempo began to change, although it was immediatley apparent that minimal facilities were available for docking. To help the necessary development, in the early 1850s, the state of California transferred its domain over its beach and waterlot property to the city of San Francisco. Since the city was at the time beset with many problems, it was in no position to undertake extensive waterfront developments; in order to keep facilities as operative as possible, it leased wharf areas to private groups for ten-year periods. These groups were responsible for what, in many cases, amounted to hastily made and impermanent docking facilities or wharves. In 1860, a number of the ten-year leases expired and the private interests involved offered to build a protective seawall and thus to develop better facilities. For this offer, they demanded control of the waterfront as well as authority to collect certain revenues. The bill that they sponsored passed the state legislature but was vetoed by Governor John Downey who sensed unfavorable public reaction to the proposal that San Francisco's port be controlled by private interests. Those holding this view sponsored another bill, one designed to turn the port back to the state. This bill was passed in 1863 and signed into law by Governor Leland Stanford. A board of state harbor commissioners charged with effective administrative control of San Francisco's harbor and port was inaugurated; this important agency was charged with the construction of new wharves, piers, and seawalls and it was also to look to the necessary dredging of the harbor as well as to the collection of all rents, tolls, wharfage and dockage fees. This commission continued as the operating authority until February 7, 1969, when the city of San Francisco once more took charge of its harbor and port.

The first substantial effort on the part of the state to improve the port had come in 1878 with the construction of a 12,000-foot seawall which, by 1908, had stabilized the perimeter of the city's waterfront (it conformed to the sweeping bay currents) and which added 800 acres of land to the city. Much of this is now the heart of San Francisco's downtown financial district.

Most of what has been mentioned here was of a preliminary

Waterfront and Skyline, 1929–30. Southern Pacific

nature, for the story of the port as we have it today really begins around the first decade of the present century. During the period from 1850 to 1910, the stage had been set for what was to become an impressive era of port construction and development. Starting with a $6 million bond issue, in the years between 1911 and 1915, other appropriations were approved which brought the total in Harbor Improvement Bonds to over $19 million. Clearly, by this time, the port of San Francisco was big business. Further improvements were made and, with the coming of World Wars I and II, other necessary and pressing answers were provided to the problems that these conflicts imposed upon the facilities of the port. The trend that developed in World War II years carried over to peacetime when, in 1946, the port entered upon a two-phase, $20 million development program. Major fruits at this time included the $6 million Mission Rock Terminal, which opened in 1950 and provided a 29-acre docking facility that still ranks as one of the largest overwater piers on the Pacific Coast. (Known as Pier 50 on the south central waterfront, the terminal berths cargo liners of many lines.)

However, new facilities were not limited to cargo-receiving

construction but also included the $2.5 million World Trade Center which opened in the reconstructed Ferry Building in 1955. In 1958, the voters approved of a $50 million bond issue and these funds resulted in further modernization of the port; a major feature was the nine-berth Army Street Terminal at the Islais Creek area, itself a 68-acre cargo center. (These as well as many other projects either undertaken or planned serve to gainsay those who maintain that the port of San Francisco has, in modern times, had little of the dynamic or active associated with it.)

The port inherited from nature almost ideal physical conditions; it is, for example, the largest deep-draft port on the West Coast, with the added advantage of an enviable central location. The continuing influx of goods and other materials through the port of San Francisco has contributed tremendously to the growth of the Bay Area and especially to the economy and life of San Francisco. At present, about 12 percent of the total work force of San Francisco is supported by the varied activities directly or indirectly associated with the port. Some 23,000 jobs (4.7 percent of the total city employment) are directly attributable to port activity; these operations involve $195 million in annual payrolls, or 6.2 percent of the total city wages.

Cargo operations are not the only impact of the port of San Francisco. Its effects extend to the manufacturing, commercial, and financial centers. Each year, between sixty and sixty-five thousand persons come by ship to San Francisco and these passengers spend an estimated $1.25 million annually during their sojourns in the city: Fisherman's Wharf and other attractions form part of this picture.

With regard to the too commonly held view that the port of San Francisco is a dying operation (a theme so regularly heard that even staunch San Franciscans sometimes voice it) the sometimes too general assertions made can be directly contradicted by the facts. Reliable figures show that San Francisco is not a "dead" port—which is not to deny that it has many problems yet unsolved and challenges yet unmet.[1] In 1965, shipping revenues amounting to over $5 million revenue tons accrued to the Port Authority. This compares for that same year to $835,000 for Oakland and $630,000 for Sacramento. This cargo tonnage has grown steadily and is expected to grow by 1.5 percent through

1990. It is obvious what a continuing effect this should have upon the economy of the city. An encouraging part of the overall picture, also, is that San Francisco possesses one of the four charters of the federal government's Foreign Trade Zones. It is known as "Zone 3" and means that it is the only port on the West Coast that is exempt from customs duties, taxes, and other such restrictions. Nor has the port of San Francisco lost its title as the maritime gateway to the western United States as well as to the Pacific. While it is true that overall tonnage has followed a somewhat erratic course since the 1930s, with a large amount of bulk general cargo flowing into other West Coast ports, foreign and offshore trade—the highest value trade—has continued to increase. Yet another factor to be considered is that there are more sailings from the port of San Francisco than from any other port on the West Coast.[2]

Despite criticisms of alleged and, in some cases, real deficiencies in planning and execution, the San Francisco Port Authority has a far-reaching program for further and future development of the city's waterfront; this was established and is controlled by a master plan for the physical and economic growth of the port.[3] This plan includes both the construction of new facilities for ships and merchant-related activities, as well as the better use of present resources. It is well to remember, also, that the port is more than just a part of the economic picture, past and present, of San Francisco; a case may be made for the assertion that this same port has been among the most influential factors in the city's growth. It was the port that largely made Gold Rush San Francisco possible; it was the same infant port that contributed to making San Francisco the commercial and financial capital of the West as far back as the 1860s and 1870s. It was the port that kept bringing more and more people to what had become known as the "City"; the color and charm which are justly attributed to the city are in part provided, or, at least, made possible by the port. The bay, which in essence is the port, helps to give San Francisco its moderate weather, its cool winds and, of course, its world-famous fog. It is difficult to conjecture or imagine what San Francisco would be without her bay and her port. The city is inseparable from their joint history.

CHAPTER 21

SYMPHONIES IN STEEL:

Bay Bridge and the Golden Gate

SAN FRANCISCO CAN rightly claim to be one of the skyline cities of the nation. Situated at the tip of a peninsula and built in considerable part upon hills, the city is surrounded on three sides by the waters of the Golden Gate, the bay, and the Pacific Ocean. From the air, one notices a thread leading eastward across the Bay, and another leading northward across the Golden Gate. These two threads are, of course, two of the truly great bridges of the world: the San Francisco–Oakland Bay Bridge, opened in late 1936, and the Golden Gate Bridge, opened the following summer.

A plaque is located at the southeastern corner of Montgomery and Jackson streets in San Francisco; the text of the inscription reads as follows:

> On this site the first San Francisco Bridge was constructed in 1844 by order of William Sturgis Hinkley, Alcalde of Yerba Buena. It crossed a creek which connected Laguna Salada with the Bay and was regarded as a remarkable structure and great public improvement as it shortened the distance to the town's Embarcadero at Clarke's Point.

San Francisco and adjacent areas have come a long way in the matter of bridges since the Hinkley span. Within the 450 square miles of landlocked harbor, San Francisco Bay has eight major highway bridges, including four of the world's greatest steel bridges, as well as two railroad bridges. Four of these bridges, San Francisco–Oakland, Golden Gate, Richmond–San Rafael, and Carquinez Straits, are rated among the ten most notable structures of their kind in the world. Other bridges include the San Mateo–Hayward, Dumbarton, Southern Pacific's Suisun Bay and Redwood City–Newark railroad crossings, as well as the Antioch Bridge. Easily the most important of all these are the two bridges that were completed in 1936 and 1937.

Mention was previously made (Chapter 10) of Emperor Norton; during his quixotic reign as "Norton I, Emperor of North America and Protector of Mexico," he issued a "decree" that San Francisco Bay be bridged immediately. This was to remain unfinished business until long after the emperor, as well as his two dogs, Bummer and Lazarus, had retired from the civic scene. However, when at length the emperor's mandate was fulfilled, presumably even his imperious self would have been satisfied.

The Bay Bridge is the longest steel high-level bridge in the world. As mentioned earlier, the Yerba Buena Tunnel with its diameter of 58 feet, which forms part of the highway between San Francisco and Oakland, is the tallest bore in the world. Additionally, the Bay Bridge can boast of the fact that its construction required the greatest expenditure of funds ever used for a single structure in the history of man. Its foundations extend to the greatest depth below water of any bridge built by man; one pier was sunk at 242 feet below water, and another at 200 feet. The deeper pier is bigger than the largest of the Pyramids and required more concrete than the Empire State Building in New York.

On Thursday, November 12, 1936, at 12:30 P.M. the Bay Bridge was opened to vehicular traffic; its construction had continued for exactly three years, four months, and three days. It was the result of years of discussion and planning on the part of those concerned with providing means of transportation other than by ferry between San Francisco and the East Bay. The Hoover–Young Bay Bridge Commission (named after President Hoover and California's Governor C.C. Young) began sessions in Sacramento in October 1929. With the cooperation of various state agencies, an engineering and traffic study was made. Finally, the present route was agreed upon and the considerable financing of the project was explored. As finally constructed, the Bay Bridge is 43,500 feet or 8¼ miles long, from end to end of the approaches. The bridge proper, including the Yerba Buena crossing, is 23,000 feet or 4½ miles long. On the San Francisco side of Yerba Buena Island, the structure consists of two complete suspension bridges with a central anchorage in the middle. The towers of the suspension rise 474 and 519 feet above water. Over the east channel, the span continues with one main cantilever span of 1,400 feet and, east of this, five truss spans each measur-

Opening of the Bay Bridge, November 12, 1936, as viewed from Four Fifty Sutter.

ing 509 feet. The two cables supporting the suspensions are each 28¾ inches in diameter, and each contains 17,664 wires; the total length of these wires is 70,815 miles, which is enough to encircle the earth three times. The concrete and steel used in building the Bay Bridge would build thirty-five San Francisco Russ Buildings plus another thirty-five Los Angeles City Halls or L.C. Smith buildings in Seattle. Each of the two principal towers represents a construction job equivalent to building a sixty-story sky-scraper.

The chief engineer for the entire project was Charles H. Purcell (1883–1951) whose competency was matched only by his modesty. Assisting him was Charles E. Andrew as bridge project engineer and Glen Woodruff as designer. Total cost of the bridge, including interurban electric rail facilities (since unfortunately abandoned), amounted to $79.5 million. This was financed by sale of 4 and 3 percent revenue bonds, which were purchased by the Federal Reconstruction Finance Corporation. In addition to these bonds, the California State Gas Tax Fund loaned $6 million for the building of the approaches; both sums were eventually repaid from toll revenues. (In 1958, a four-year reconstruction program was undertaken at a cost of $35 million.) Decreasing patronage of the interurban trains had caused the Key System Lines to abandon this service, leaving buses to handle the load exclusively. This reconstruction involved track removals, conversion of each deck (lower and upper) to one-way motor vehicle traffic, and the lowering of the lower deck of the bridge by 16 inches through the Yerba Buena Tunnel. The maintenance of such a colossal structure keeps a legion of persons constantly at work. No matter from what angle the San Francisco–Oakland Bay Bridge is viewed, it will always remain a symphony in steel.

For years, the Golden Gate Bridge held the title of longest suspension bridge in the world. Despite the claims that the Mackinac span, which connects the greater part of Michigan with its upper peninsula across the Straits of Mackinac is longer, the question is best resolved by settling what is meant, indeed, by "longer": actually, the Mackinac suspension is supported by a single span of cables 8,344 feet in length as compared with 4,200 for the Golden Gate Bridge. However, the center span of the Mackinac Bridge is exceeded in length by both the Verrazano–Narrows Bridge in New York City and the Golden Gate Bridge. The claim of "longest" for the Mackinac is based upon the distance between cable anchorages, while the Golden Gate figure is based upon the actual distance between its towers. Rival claims, though, do not seem to be of great importance, since all will admit that, just as is true of its sister span across San Francisco Bay, the Golden Gate is "quite a bridge," the fulfillment of a dream and a vision had by one man: it is the "bridge that couldn't be built."

Triumphantly, then, on Thursday, May 27, 1937, San Franciscans joined other thousands in walking across the newly opened Golden Gate Bridge, all together a huge throng of approximately 200,000. This "preview" was followed the next day by dedicatory ceremonies which culminated in the cutting of a ceremonial barrier, after which an official cavalcade of automobiles traversed the span; the rest of that day was devoted, again, to pedestrian traffic, and the regular flow of vehicular traffic started the next day. It has been written that

. . . Residents of the San Francisco Bay area feel this bridge as an entity and have affection for it. They admire its living grace, and its magnificent setting. They respond to its many moods—its warm and vibrant glow in the early sun, its seeming play with, or disdain of, incoming fog, its retiring shadowy form before the sunset, its lovely appearance in its lights at night. To its familiars it appears as the "Keeper of the Golden Gate."[1]

The Golden Gate Bridge is the result of the long-term determination of the people of six California counties who, eventually, formed themselves into a Golden Gate Bridge District comprising the city and county of San Francisco, Marin, Sonoma, and Del Norte counties, as well as a portion of Napa and Mendocino counties. Since it had long been apparent that the bridging of the Golden Gate, despite the many problems its construction would entail, would mean an effective opening up of the counties north of San Francisco, much planning went into the implementation of the visions and dreams of the members of the Bridge District. In 1928, earlier efforts culminated in the incorporation of the Golden Gate Bridge and Highway District; in November 1930, the voters of the concerned counties passed a $35 million bond issue to finance the building of the bridge, while pledging the property of these counties as security for the payment of the bonds. For many years, Joseph Baerman Strauss (1870–1938), a distinguished engineer with many bridges to his credit, had dreamed of raising a span across the Golden Gate. One who contemplates his many activities realizes that Strauss was much more than merely a competent structural engineer, although he certainly was that: he was also a poet, a seer, and a man of vision and it seems that all these qualities sustained him in the fulfillment of his dream; it is equally certain that he had to live with the skepticism of his peers who kept repeating that "Strauss will never build his bridge, no one can bridge the Golden Gate because of insurmountable difficulties which are apparent to all who give thought to the idea." But Strauss held fast to his vision, and, even though he survived only a year after the opening of his bridge, he did live to bring it to completion.[2]

Construction of the bridge took four and one-half years and the work began on January 5, 1933. The resulting span has been much admired for its magnitude and its graceful beauty. At mid-

Before the Golden Gate Bridge: Fort Point and Marin Headlands.

Golden Gate Bridge on Opening Day, May 27, 1937.

span the bridge is 220 feet above the waters of the Golden Gate;
it is about a mile across and there is only one pier in the water
which, incidentally, was built under most discouraging circumstances, as Engineer Strauss could testify. This pier is only 1,125
feet from shore; the distance between the two towers that support the cables which, in turn, support the floor of the bridge, is
4,200 feet. These two cables are 36½ inches in diameter, the
largest bridge cables ever made. Each cable is 7,659 feet long and
contains 27,572 parallel wires, enough to encircle the world more
than three times at the equator. Fortunately, solid rock was found
at each end of the Gate and huge pockets were excavated in this
rock to form a setting for the concrete anchorage blocks, each of
which contains 30,000 cubic yards of concrete. Among the engineering problems that had to be faced in the building of the
bridge were those that arose from the exposed nature of any such
structure, for it has to withstand winds and gales coming from the
often far from peaceful Pacific Ocean. It was so designed that, in
the most unlikely event of a broadside wind coming at it with a
speed of one hundred miles an hour, the bridge floor at midspan
might swing as much as 27 feet.[3]

Practically all of the Golden Gate Bridge is located within the
city and county of San Francisco (as is the Golden Gate itself).
The two towers rise an impressive 746 feet which means that they
are 191 feet taller than the Washington Monument. In 1884, a
poet thus saluted the Golden Gate:

> Wide Thy Golden Gate stands open to all
> Nations of the world,
> Free beneath its stately portals
> All flags are in peace unfurled.
> Beauteous Gate, when loitering Sunset
> Covers Thee with burnished gold.
> Mighty Gate, when surging ocean Thy
> Strong cliffs alone withhold.
> Treach'rous Gate, deceiving many with a
> Name most fair-Blessed Gate, where millions
> Find the golden boon of liberty.[4]

At the completion of his mighty bridge, Joseph Strauss penned
an impressive ode which he entitled "The Mighty Task Is Done";
it epitomizes his personal travail in building the bridge and makes

Joseph B. Strauss. Brother A. A. Grosskopf, S.J.

of the structure almost a living thing. From his poem, these lines give evidence of the dedication of the man who brought the bridge from his brain and heart as well as from his drawing board:

> At last the mighty task is done;
> Resplendent in the western sun;
> The Bridge looms mountain high.
>   On its broad decks in rightful pride,
> The world in swift parade shall ride
> Throughout all time to be.
>   Launched midst a thousand hopes and fears,
> Damned by a thousand hostile sneers.
> Yet ne'er its course was stayed,

But ask of those who met the foe,
Who stood alone when faith was low,
Ask them the price they paid.
High overhead its lights shall gleam,
Far, far below life's restless stream,
Unceasingly shall flow. . . .

With the completion of the two giant bridges, it was but natural that a proud San Francisco would again wish to call the people of the world to itself; so it was that another world fair, this one called the Golden Gate International Exposition, was planned and brought into being. Several years previously, a movement to develop an airport site by constructing a fill over the shoal area adjacent to Goat Island (Yerba Buena) was started. Although the airport was finally placed elsewhere, the planning resulted in a man made island (called "Treasure Island") on which was staged the exposition.

When the voters of San Francisco decided to have such an exposition, the question of financing the necessary engineering work was happily resolved. In late 1935, the city of San Francisco succeeded in having the project approved as a Works Progress Administration (WPA) project. This authorization, including 20 percent to be furnished by San Francisco, amounted to $3,803,-900. After further study, the WPA concluded that the nature of the work required was such that it could not handle the project. The Secretary of War approved the request that its execution be undertaken by the Army Corps of Engineers. While a group of such specialists applied their talents to the reclamation of the "Yerba Buena Shoals," the day-by-day details were efficiently cared for by Colonel Fred Butler, U.S.A., who had years of army engineering experience behind him at this time. The fill to form Treasure Island was obtained by dredging operations; the island covered an area of 400 acres, 5,520 feet long by 3,410 feet wide.

Meanwhile, the San Francisco Bay Exposition Company was formed with Leland W. Cutler as president. He was greatly aided from the beginning by George Creel, who was appointed United States Commissioner of the Exposition. By 1938, 1,200 men were employed in horticultural work on the newly born Treasure Island; they planted 400,000 bulbs, 800,000 seeds, and 4,000 trees. It then remained for the architects and artisans to accomplish their respective tasks. The international dimension came only gradually as Leland Cutler persuaded those concerned that an invitation should be extended to other countries to join in the celebrations. A subtitle, "A Pageant of the Pacific," was added to the title of the exposition, and gradually its international status was assured.

On Monday, February 18, 1939, the "Magic Isle" as many called it, was opened to an expectant public; special ceremonies were presided over by Governor Culbert C. Olson who appeared before a decorative Golden Gate Bridge portal to the exposition armed with a large key. With the opening of this portal, the exposition commenced. Although not all the exhibition halls had yet been completed, there were enough attractions, plus the novelty of the site itself, to satisfy those who thronged the island on opening day. Notable were the Tower of the Sun with its Elephant Towers, while many came to regard the Federal Building as the most striking of all the buildings. The landscaping and horticultural results attracted much favorable comment. The extensive art work also merited approval; among the best murals were those of Millard Sheets depicting California history. These were supplemented by some borrowed European masterpieces. When one added to the above features the scientific exhibits and recreational areas, it was apparent that there was "something for everyone" in the Golden Gate International Exposition. During its run, the exposition attracted 17 million visitors. However, it was not a financial success; in October 1939, the Pageant of the Pacific closed its gates, six weeks early and $4,166,000 in debt. It was decided to reopen the exposition in 1940 in the hope of recouping these financial losses. This was done in the spring of 1940 when Europe was in the convulsions of war. However, the "Fair went on" as planned; when it finally closed its doors in September 1940, an admirer wrote:

Before we expected it, the day came to close the gates. It was a sad occasion . . . sad especially for the rest of us who had found refreshment on Treasure Island. When the final bills had been paid, it would be recorded that the Golden Gate International Exposition, like so many others before and since, had lost money. The staff compiled a final report, cleaned out the files and drifted away.[5]

Today Treasure Island is owned by the Navy. After Pearl Harbor, the site was turned over to the federal government by San Francisco and it is now one of the West Coast's main naval installations. Three of the exposition's permanent buildings are used by the Navy.

CHAPTER 22

THE "MUNI" RAILWAY TO BART

SATURDAY, DECEMBER 28, 1912, was a significant day in the history of San Francisco. Exactly at noon, a cavalcade of ten streetcars pulled out of the carbarn at Geary Street and Presidio Avenue and proceeded east down Geary Street. When they arrived at the intersection of Kearny, Geary, and Market streets, a small ceremony, deliberately planned as such by Mayor Rolph, took place. (He had said previously: "Let's get the cars going first and toot our horn afterwards!") However, the enthusiasm of the onlookers took over, as about 50,000 San Franciscans filled the surrounding area to hail the advent to the streets of their city of what was to become known as the "Muni."

Mayor Rolph boarded the lead car, deposited one of the first nickels produced by the San Francisco Mint, and took over the controls. Bedlam broke loose; a siren on the roof of the St. Francis Hotel shrieked, and the Municipal Band endeavored to be heard. It was a history-making event, for San Francisco had now undertaken the first public-owned transit system in the United States. In his remarks on the occasion, Rolph said: "It must prove a success," adding in prophetic vein: "I want everyone to feel that this is but the nucleus of a mighty system of streetcar lines which will one day encompass this great city." A local newspaper was moved to this enthusiastic outburst: "San Francisco's Municipal Railway sprang into action yesterday, cutting with its pioneer wheels an indelible track across the page of history." (Financially, the day proved a success as well; on opening day, 15,000 rode the railroad, paying $750 in fares.) Late or "Owl" service was inaugurated the very first night with the initial run, called the Geary "B" line, operating from Kearny, Geary, and Market to 33rd Avenue in the Richmond district. Soon another line, the "A" line, ran along Geary Street with a turn on 10th Avenue in the Richmond

First Car of Municipal Railway to run on Market Street, from Geary to the Ferry, June 25, 1913.

and terminated at Golden Gate Park. Thus a quarter-century dream became a fact.

San Francisco's City Charter, adopted in 1900, had declared for ultimate municipal ownership of public utilities, but no immediate attempt had been made to acquire control of the privately owned transit lines which served the city. However, on December 2, 1902, the first effort was made to purchase the Geary Street Cable Line and to convert it to municipal electric operation when a $700,000 bond issue was put on the ballot. However, this measure failed to receive the necessary two-thirds vote for approval. Finally, victory for the proponents of municipal operation of the Geary Street line came in 1909 when a June bond issue proposal finally won voter approval. This was not accomplished without the open opposition of the management of the Geary Street company; at a banquet of the Merchants Association held at the Palace Hotel on November 12, 1902, President Horace G. Platt gave an address in which he opposed any attempts for public ownership of transportation facilities, maintaining that all such enterprises belonged in the domain of private ownership. He further asserted that government was never able to do any business as economically or as efficiently as private enterprise. "Mu-

Mayor Rolph at controls of first Geary Street car, 1913.

nicipal ownership of public utilities increases taxes without any corresponding benefit to the taxpayer." Platt concluded:

> San Francisco in one respect is financially unique. No other city of the same size in the world is free from debt. And yet, knowing that every bond a city issues is a mortgage on the property of its inhabitants, the people are asked to mortgage their property with the lien of a tax to pay upwards of a million dollars in bonds and thousands upon thousands in interest in order to attempt the experiment of operating a street railroad. Those who advise the step hold out no hope of profit, but simply state that, as the road is a small road, the loss that the city may incur will not be tremendous.
>
> Would not an individual be considered incompetent who mortgaged his property to thus invest in an enterprise that was not compulsory, upon the assurance of a promoter that, whereas there was no probability of a profit, there was at least the hope that the loss would not be tremendous?[1]

However, despite the Platt opposition, the Municipal Railway came into being on December 28, 1912. On June 25, 1913, the Geary line was extended along Market Street to the Ferry Building. A natural priority in the development of new routes came in 1913 with planning for the forthcoming Panama Pacific Interna-

Mayor Rolph driving last horse car on Market Street, 1914.

tional Exposition which was scheduled to open in two years. Accordingly, the privately owned Union Street line was acquired in 1913 while, in 1914, the Stockton Street "F" and the Van Ness Avenue "H" lines were put into operation. By the time the PPIE opened, six lines were providing service to it as well as to the residential areas of the future Marina district and to North Beach. In 1917, service was extended, with the inauguration of the "C" and "J" lines. This most significant transit breakthrough brought fast service as far west as St. Francis Circle. Later this service was extended to form the "K" and "L" lines to meet increasing needs of the growing districts. With the same general idea in mind, the "M" line was started in 1925.

The Sunset district, where the sand dunes were gradually surrendering to rows of homes, was next to reap the benefits of public transportation. This came on Sunday, October 21, 1928, when service on the "N" line started.

While the "N" line marked the end at that time of construction of any major streetcar lines by the Municipal Railway, the same period witnessed the introduction of gasoline powered buses to the streets of San Francisco. They were designed to interlace the city with crosstown lines to supplement the main streetcar lines which were successfully bringing thousands of San Franciscans from the newly created districts west of Twin Peaks to the downtown areas of the city. The first bus line to be established was the Number 1 line, which crossed Golden Gate Park thus connecting the Sunset and the Richmond districts. Later, as the value of the motor coach in providing a system of flexible transportation was realized, this line was extended along 10th Avenue and Fulton Street. By 1928, the Muni had grown to a system of 1,300 employees and 215 vehicles which carried about 240,000 passengers daily. In 1941, it introduced its first trolley buses but World War II interrupted plans for further conversion to trolley coach operations.

For the first thirty-two years of its existence, San Francisco's Municipal Railway operated in competition with other privately owned transit systems. In 1893, a number of these companies had merged in the newly organized Market Street Cable Company. A second consolidation took place in 1902 when the "United Railroads of San Francisco" was created by merging the Market Street Railway, the Sutter Street cable system, and some independent electric lines. Only three cable roads, the California Street, the Union Street, and the Geary Street, remained independent. Of these, the Geary Street line ceased to exist with the advent on that street of the Muni. In 1918, the United Railroad Company was unable to meet its financial obligations. This led, in 1921, to further reorganization when the Market Street Railway Corporation was revived to take over the United Railroads. Now the transit field in San Francisco was virtually narrowed to two systems, with consequent intense competition between the privately owned Market Street Railway system and the Municipal Railway. Over the years, half a dozen attempts to purchase the Market Street Railway were defeated at the polls. Finally, in 1944, the battle between the two systems was resolved when the voters authorized the acquisition of the Market Street system—the purchase price was set at $2 million in cash together with $5.5 million in future earnings of the combined properties.

A milestone date for municipal ownership of the transit system in San Francisco came on Friday, September 29, 1944, for, on that day at 5 A.M. the official merging of the two systems took place. Now all lines in the city were under municipal ownership with the exception of the California Cable Car line which was not taken over by the Muni until 1952. Due to the demands of a wartime economy, it was not possible to proceed immediately with the Muni's plans for modernization. At the war's end, though, a notable change came to Market Street with the removal of the outer tracks (formerly used by the Muni lines) on that thoroughfare. Those who remember the four tracks with their dangerous conditions for the safety of passengers who wished to board cars on the inside track felt both a sense of relief as well as nostalgia with their going. Although this action removed forever the sight of streetcars moving majestically two abreast up and down the city's chief thoroughfare, it speeded up passenger service by providing more space for motor coach movements.

San Francisco felt the full impact of the new Muni on Sunday, July 3, 1949, when streetcars on the No. 5, 6, 7, and 21 lines were replaced by trolley coach operations. On the same day, service was either begun or extended on nine other coach lines. A study of the affected lines showed a 64 percent increase in the frequency of peak-hour service, while the number of seats available during these peak hours was increased by 52 percent. Subsequently, the open-ended pioneer Muni streetcars on the "J," "K," "L," "M," and "N" lines, labelled the "Iron Monsters" by some, were replaced by streamlined, one-man-operated streetcars. The last of the "monsters" operated on a scheduled run on May 9, 1958, and then rolled into honorable retirement; it and its peers had served San Francisco long and well.

It was inevitable that the main problem to be faced by public transportation was the decline of passengers with the increase in private automobile travel. In general, there has been less effect on the patronage of the Muni in San Francisco (at least in comparison with the national picture) because there was an attempt to provide improvements in equipment and service and to retain, at first, a 15¢ (later raised to 25¢) fare. (Even at the present time, the fare is considered to be among the country's outstanding public bargains, largely because of generous transfer privileges.) The reason for attempting to maintain a reasonably low fare is San

Francisco's policy, officially supported, to help solve the ever-increasing problems of traffic in the city with the least cost. The policy, with necessary changes, is based upon the recognition of the Muni as a virtual lifeline between the heavily populated outer districts and the downtown shopping and financial sections, an area small in size but giant in economic proportions since it comprises the major part of the city's tax base. However, even with this sort of planning, the Muni Railway has lost 25 percent of its passengers since the fiscal year, 1967–1968. Statistics reveal that, whereas the Muni had 187,900,000 riders in 1949, the number had diminished, in 1972 to 1973, to 112,600,000. This, obviously, brought a huge deficit in Muni finances. Some have thought that fare increases between 1968 and 1970 (to 25¢) were responsible for most of this loss in revenue but, since then, with the fare remaining the same, patronage has continued to fall. Other explanations given include a decrease in San Francisco's population, the inconvenience long caused by BART construction on Market Street, and the large increase of the number of senior citizens and students who ride the Muni at a reduced rate. In 1973 to 1974, there were 8 million senior citizens and 20 million students on discount fares, out of a total of 112.6 million riders.

By late 1973, the operational deficit of the Muni for the fiscal year, 1974–1975, was projected to increase by $7 million. (This figure was included in the Public Utilities Commission budget for that period.) Most of the increase was attributed by John M. Woods, the Muni's general manager at this time, to greater salaries, wages and fringe benefits, and expanded services arising out of Muni-BART coordination activities.

There will always be instant as well as long-range problems in operating the San Francisco Municipal Railway; however, on balance, in facing them, it would seem appropriate to consider that the Muni has come a long way since its beginnings as a one-line system in 1912 with a cavalcade of cars on Geary Street.

This chapter on public transit in San Francisco would be incomplete without some mention of the part planned and played by the Bay Area Rapid Transit System, commonly called BART. Although most of the 71 miles of track are located outside San Francisco, the fact alone that, at this writing, there are nine stations operational within city limits makes the system of interest here. First, a brief background of how BART came to be.

Myriad problems were due to come with the increase in the number of automobiles in the Bay Area. Urban planners were forced to give the highest priority to efforts to anticipate or solve these problems. After years of discussion, general agreement was reached that a rapid transit system would best help to solve these problems by providing a means whereby people could move quickly around the area without benefit of private car. Since it was generally conceived that San Francisco must be the hub of the system, at least in the sense that fast access be afforded to it from the East Bay, a joint Army and Navy Board recommended, in January 1947, an underwater transit tube beneath San Francisco Bay. By mid-July 1951, the California State Legislature had created a special commission to study Bay Area transportation needs. After many meetings and much discussion of all the factors involved, on June 4, 1957, the Legislature approved the creation of a five-county Bay Area Rapid Transit District—BART. It is not necessary here to go into the many details of the early months and years of planning for the system, since this is all part of a general history of BART which can easily be consulted. Of more interest is the engineering feat which, after several years of very difficult work, resulted in an underbay transit tube 19,133 feet long (3.6 miles) which reaches at its deepest point 135 feet and which is the longest underwater transit tube in the world. Its construction was begun in April 1966, despite the openly voiced prognostications of many that it should not be attempted because of the danger of an earthquake which might disrupt the tube with fatal consequences to any who might be in BART cars at the time.[2] Trial runs were made in early September 1974, when one thousand dignitaries were invited to ride under the Bay into San Francisco. They did so, successfully, in Bart's comfortable cars and thus were witnesses to the first linking of the East Bay and San Francisco as part of the system, much of which had been operating on the other side of the Bay for some time. On Monday, September 16, 1974, commuter service through the $180 million tube began without extraordinary incident; despite the predictions of some, the trains, while full, were not so to overflowing. Most important of all was the final fulfillment of a promise which was years behind schedule and which had been made, in fact, over a decade before.

At the same time, service was opened to Daly City via eight nicely appointed stations in San Francisco; this is mostly, but not entirely an underground operation. The Embarcadero Station was considerably behind schedule because of special difficulties encountered in its construction but the traveller from the East Bay to San Francisco would, after leaving the Oakland West Station, stop first at the Montgomery Street Station. Next came the Powell Street Station which provided several exits to Market Street and adjacent stores with the next stop scheduled at Civic Center. Bart then made a left turn in its continuing right-of-way under Mission Street, with scheduled stops at 16th and 24th streets. Two more stops at Glen Park and Balboa Park saw the route completed at Knowles Avenue, between Niantic and San Diego avenues in Daly City. Also planned but not operational at this writing (the tunnel level is completed, however) are a rerouting of the Muni Railway Streetcars which will no longer run on the surface of Market Street but which will have their separate right-of-way underground, with connections planned for other lines in the future.

Despite the many difficulties which have plagued BART since it first opened in the East Bay on September 11, 1972, it is reasonable to conclude that these and other problems will eventually be solved; in that case, it is safe also to hail BART as a system that will bring considerable benefits toward the solving of San Francisco's transit problems.

CHAPTER 23

WATER:
From Lobos Creek to
Hetch Hetchy

I will make the wilderness a pool of water and the dry land springs of water, the streams whereof shall make glad the city.

Inscription on Water
Temple, Sunol, Alameda
County.[1]

SURROUNDED BY WATER as San Franciscans are, they must necessarily be conscious of what the Greek poet, Pindar, called "the noblest of all elements." Water, as a fundamental need, has a special place in the history of San Francisco. In earlier days, there was no difficulty in obtaining pure fresh water for the city's small population, since the tip of the peninsula on which the future San Francisco was to be located abounded in springs and, later on, in wells.[2] With the influx of additional thousands in the Gold Rush, the providing of fresh drinking water soon became a matter of serious concern. Some earlier sources quickly dried up, as private landowners fenced off springs on their land. Waterboats brought in casks of water from Sausalito springs and the precious cargo was peddled from door to door on the backs of mules; selling for one dollar a bucket or more. It was evident, though, that more adequate and convenient supplies would have to be found. A solution was sought when, in 1855, a petition was presented to the local Board of Aldermen "from Messrs. Perkins, Bensley and Co. asking the right to supply the city with good, pure and fresh water from a stream among the Point Lobos hills and proposing to furnish 1,000,000 gallons a day." A second petition of Lloyd Tevis, J.B. Haggin, and J.B. Overton (styling themselves the Water Works Company of San Francisco) asked for the right to supply the city with water from a lake some twenty miles from the city; their request was laid on the table. The ordinance allowing the Mountain Lake–Point Lobos Company one year from January 1, 1855, to complete their work was referred to a committee of the whole.[3]

On September 16, 1858, the San Francisco Water Works Company began its operations. Tapping Lobos Creek, which ran (it still does) to the north and adjacent to the present Richmond district, the company was able to supply 2 million gallons of water daily through five miles of flume and tunnel along the Golden Gate shoreline to a pumping plant at Black Point near the present Aquatic Park. From this point, the water was pumped to storage places on Russian Hill, the Lombard and Francisco reservoirs, from which it was dispensed for private use by an extensive network of pipes. Small amounts of water were developed elsewhere locally, but the limitations of these sources were realized and a new company, the Spring Valley Water Works, organized in 1860, turned southward toward San Mateo County to begin the development of its Peninsula System. The San Francisco Water Works Company was absorbed by Spring Valley in 1865.[4]

Although a small company at first, the Spring Valley Water Works grew and, by 1864, it brought water by flume thirty-two miles from Pilarcitos Creek in San Mateo County to Laguna Honda (now a reservoir) in San Francisco. Continuing to develop additional water resources in San Mateo County, the Spring Valley Company completed the Pilarcitos Dam in 1867; this was followed by the San Andreas Dam in 1870 and the Upper Crystal Springs Dam in 1878. The same year, Lake Merced, with a pumping station located near the present Fleishacker playfield, came into service. Completion of the Lower Crystal Springs Dam in 1890 finished the well-planned development of the best and most feasible reservoir sites on the Peninsula; subsequent developments of the Spring Valley's system were to be centered in Alameda and Santa Clara counties.

Since early agitation had not been lacking on the part of some San Franciscans aimed at the acquiring of a municipally owned water system, the ensuing decades saw many manifestations of hostility of private interests to such ownership. An attempt to bring about municipal ownership in 1875 was defeated at the polls. However, interested engineers continued to present their ideas about supplying San Francisco's ever-growing water necessities from the Sierra Nevada mountains. As early as 1899 to 1900, the annual report of the United States Geological Survey suggested the Hetch Hetchy region in the Sierra Nevada mountains as a source of supply, estimating that this watershed could supply the city with 250,000 gallons daily, enough for a city of a million inhabitants. In 1901, a survey was made by the city of fourteen possible water sources for San Francisco, extending all the way from Lake Tahoe to the Sacramento, American, and Feather rivers. Soon, though, the investigation established the superiority of the Tuolumne River area, later called the Hetch Hetchy system; among the main reasons proposed were the purity of the water available, as well as the extent of the resources in the area and the possibilities for the profitable generation of electric power within the system.

In 1901, a momentous decision was reached to develop the Tuolumne River watershed, and steps were taken to acquire all necessary rights. Publicity was avoided as much as possible because of conflicting interests; the first applications for water and reservoir rights were made in the name of Mayor Phelan, acting as a private citizen. In 1903, he assigned his interests to the city and county of San Francisco; the next decade was to be marked by conflicts between proponents of municipal ownership as against those favoring private ownership.[5] After incessant and bitter battles, San Francisco, with the passage by Congress of the Raker Act granting permission for the use of the area and its signing by President Woodrow Wilson on December 19, 1913, was assured of success in its plans.[6] In approving the long-desired bill, President Wilson made the following written comment:

> ... It seems to serve the pressing public needs of the region concerned better than they could be served in any other way, and yet does not impair the usefulness or materially detract from the beauty of the public domain. . . .

The Raker Act, which was properly regarded as the Magna Carta for San Francisco's municipally owned water system with its origins in the Sierra Nevada mountains, granted many necessary privileges to the city to enable it to proceed with its plans; included were the use of public lands for the purposes of building "dams, reservoirs, conduits and other structures necessary or incidental to the development and use of water and power." However, there were some explicitly stated conditions to be fulfilled by the city, including the construction of scenic roads and trails in the area of Yosemite National Park, the completion of dam-building at Hetch Hetchy as quickly as possible, and the promise never to sell or give Hetch Hetchy water or power to a private person or corporation for resale.

In 1914, work on the Hetch Hetchy project began in earnest. Luckily, there was an abundance of genuine engineering talent at hand, headed by "the Chief": City Engineer Michael Maurice O'Shaughnessy after whom the major dam was to be named. Numerous obstacles were met and successfully removed; when the project was finally completed, the resultant Hetch Hetchy Aqueduct was 149 miles long, and in a gravity flow carried pure water from the Sierra Nevada mountains to San Francisco and neighboring cities, generating electricity in the process. The heart of the Hetch Hetchy system is O'Shaughnessy Dam, which rises 430 feet across the granite-walled course of the Tuolumne River; it is located high in the Sierra Nevada within the limits of Yosemite National Park. The dam was completed in 1923, and the aqueduct in 1934. Both represented magnificent achievements on the part of those who had dreamed and worked successfully for them. At completion time, the voters of San Francisco had approved water bonds amounting to almost $90 million. However, with continued growth, it was quickly recognized that this sum would have to be supplemented; in 1928, San Francisco voters finally approved the purchase of the Spring Valley Water Company, and the city took over its operations in 1930, paying $41 million for the water rights, reservoirs, and watershed lands, aqueducts and rights of way, and the distribution system in San Francisco. The needs of various communities were served, for San Francisco was not the only beneficiary of the Hetch Hetchy."[7]

A quotation from an informative brochure published in September 1967 would seem to be an apt way to complete this account of how water was brought to a thirsty city; in a letter of commendation written in 1933, to San Francisco and her engineers, J. Waldo Smith, Chief Engineer of the Board of Water Supply of New York City, wrote:

. . . When the project is completed, it will stand as one of San Francisco's greatest assets, and as a lasting monument to the energy on the city and its citizens and to their faith in the future.[8]

Engineer Smith's commendatory words are verified in the present state of the system that supplies water to San Francisco.

CHAPTER 24

THE SAN FRANCISCO AIRPORT:

1919 to Now

. . . San Francisco International Airport clings to the western shore of the land-locked Bay that Nature fashioned as the Pacific's majestic harbor for ships sailing the seven seas. It is a great man-made haven for winged vessels plying the limitless, invisible ocean that is the air. . . .

Mayor Elmer Robinson:
Dedicatory Address, San
Francisco International
Airport, August 27, 1954.

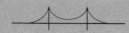

ALTHOUGH SAN FRANCISCO now owns and operates one of the most important airports in the nation, the city was rather slow in realizing the importance of any such facility. Actually, it was not until 1926 that a serious program of construction was undertaken. This was almost a quarter century after the Wright brothers had, on December 17, 1903, successfully flown the first mechanically powered, heavier-than-air machine for a distance of 105 feet in three and a half seconds above the sands of Kitty Hawk, North Carolina. However, the fact that man could fly had earlier been demonstrated in Northern California. Twenty years before the Wright flight, in 1883, John Joseph Montgomery, once a student at St. Ignatius College and later associated with Santa Clara College, made the first successful glider flight in the United States. Other significant "firsts" for the Bay Area came on January 15 and 18, 1911. On the former date, Lieutenant Myron C. Crissy of the United States Army Signal Corps dropped a six-pound bomb in the Tanforan area from a biplane piloted by Philip Parmelee. This was the first explosive missile dropped from an airplane and it detonated a hole in the marshland by the bay three feet wide and two feet deep. Three days later, Eugene Ely successfully landed and took off from a crude wooden platform constructed on the deck of the cruiser *Pennsylvania* which was moored several hundred feet from the San Francisco waterfront. This proved to be the birth of carrier-based naval aviation. (Another "first" was the twin engine for aircraft which was designed and built by Samuel Purcell, a San Jose youth.) But even though each year was to bring further advances in the field, the available and safe landing fields for aircraft in the Bay Area remained few and unsatisfactory. The wooded hills of the Presidio as well as the bordering residential areas made such operations hazardous, and a temporary landing strip was abandoned after the protests of adjacent landowners. Only later, on November 3, 1919 was Crissy field opened as a landing field for the Presidio of San Francisco. Essentially it was closed down on June 30, 1936, with remaining operations transferred elsewhere. It is still used occasionally by U.S. Army helicopters.

Continued agitation on the part of many who foresaw the immediate need of an airport for San Francisco finally brought the matter to a vote in the municipal election of November 2, 1926. Voters were asked to approve of the idea of their city having an adequate airport and they did so by a majority of five to one. City Engineer M.M. O'Shaughnessy proposed the building of such a facility, recommending that it have a 9,000-foot runway, two twelve-plane hangars, adequate lighting facilities, a weather station, service shops, and fire-fighting and first aid equipment. He estimated the overall cost at about $350,000. It was to take many years before such an airport came into being.

Of primary importance was the finding of a suitable site for the needed airport. Some of the suggestions were novel: one proposed the construction of platforms over the piers on the waterfront; still another wanted a huge platform at Third and Townsend streets over the Southern Pacific trainsheds; a prophetic suggestion (one destined to be accomplished later for another reason) suggested the filling in of the shoals off Yerba Buena Island. Eventually, a site was chosen on the Mills Estate in San Mateo County. This location was about fifteen miles south of San Francisco, with the drive there from the core of the city estimated at about twenty minutes. After careful investigation, the city decided to put its airport there. In 1927, funds were voted to buy 1,376 acres of bay-front land in northern San Mateo County. At the same time, with an eye to the future, the city took an option on an adjoining 1,000-acre tract, much of which lay in the shallows of San Francisco Bay. It was agreed that the name of Mills Field be given to the developing facility and two additional bond issues were submitted for voter approval. One called for an indebtedness of $1.7 million for the construction of runways, hangars, and other facilities; the other provided for another indebtedness amounting to $4 million for the immediate increase of the area by the purchase of the acres under option. Both were rejected by economy-minded voters. A recent national stock market crash had made the electorate wary of such financial demands; besides, many were led to believe that the island which would eventually emerge from the shoals adjacent to Yerba Buena Island could supply the location for the needed airport. Despite these setbacks it was decided to proceed with the previously approved plans for Mills Field. On May 7, 1927, a partially completed airfield was dedicated, and regular operations began on June 1 of that year. Frank A. Flynn, a native San Franciscan and World War I military aviator, was appointed first superintendent. He thus records his early memories of the operation:

> The pilot of the first commercial airliner using the field had his choice of three runways. They were described officially as "200 feet wide and 5770 feet long . . . capable of bearing a 20,000 pound weight travelling at 80 miles an hour." Unofficial but none the less authoritative estimates of the field give a somewhat different picture. Paul Isaacs, civilian flyer, recalls Mills Field of 1927 as "a mud hole, just a mud hole." . . .[1]

Despite primitive conditions, Boeing Transport, a predecessor of United Air Lines, began operations at Mills Field on October 15, 1927. After several weeks of intense fog had made regular schedules impossible, the irritated Boeing officials packed up and moved away after only one month's stay. Two other airlines, the Western Air Express and the Maddux Air Lines, made brief appearances on the scene but soon transferred to Oakland. Little or no success, then, attended the first few years of San Francisco's airport. Two bond issues in its support were defeated by the voters in the elections of November 7, 1928, and November 3, 1930. Public apathy and general lack of interest so plagued the whole operation that the San Francisco Board of Supervisors felt themselves powerless to make further expansions and needed improvements. The available airlines remained adamant in their refusal to use the airport in its present condition. In late 1928, the San Francisco Chronicle remarked editorially: "Seeking for a reason for this failure we can find it only in the political management not accustomed to looking at municipal enterprise as a customer-pleasing business."[2] With the worsening of the national economic depression, Mills Field felt further squeezes imposed by the unfavorable economic climate. In 1931, the total traffic at Mills Field consisted of the advent and operation of Century Pacific Lines, Ltd., which, on July 6, 1931, bravely inaugurated passenger flights and continued them for ten months until it became the victim of the still failing economy. A few charter and pleasure flights plus some student instruction operations made up the bulk of the Mills Field business.

When San Francisco went under a new charter, effective on January 8, 1932, provision was made for transferring the airport (and its problems) from the jurisdiction of the Board of Supervisors. It became a special department of the Public Utilities Commission. The final act of the Board of Supervisors was to change the name officially from Mills Field to San Francisco Airport. The new name was accompanied by the selection of a new superintendent; this was Bernard Doolin, who was to take over on June 1, 1932.[3] Events soon proved that this date heralded the turning point in the short history of the airport. Doolin, a native of the Bay Area, had served as a fighter pilot in France during World War I; he quickly imposed strict economies by reducing the small airport personnel from seventeen to eight. He next made an intensive investigation of the entire operation bequeathed to his care and came up with the fact that, whereas San Francisco provided 70 percent of the Bay Area's air passengers, none of the major airlines would schedule flights out of San Francisco Airport. He determined to start a "Sell San Francisco" campaign involving these same major airlines and, after persuading some small operations to move in, Doolin was gratified when Pacific Air Transport, a division of United Air Lines, which was the giant of the industry, signed a contract to make use of San Francisco's Airport facilities. The tide began steadily to change, with other carriers joining the list of those who would make use of these same facilities. A minor embarrassment came when it was evident that the airport had more clients than such facilities, but perhaps Doolin planned this also since he knew that, inevitably, it would bring about the needed expansion.

Evidently the many-sided Doolin was the man of the hour; in 1933, 1937, 1940, and 1945, his bond issues for the needs of the expanding airport met with the overwhelming approval of the voters.

From the physical standpoint, San Francisco's airport was obsolete by 1933. Under Doolin's efficient direction, needed improvements and modernizations were made in 1934 and 1935. With justifiable pride, the 1936 Annual Report of the Public Utilities Commission announced the status of the airport as passing from national to international importance; it was only a question of time, the report said, before international carriers would be using its facilities. Each year saw increased activity under Doolin's direction: in 1940, over 126,000 passengers passed through the portals of the airport and a million and a quarter pounds of mail were handled. When, at this time, United Air Lines announced that it was signing a twenty-year contract with the city establishing the San Francisco airport as its western division headquarters for operations, a new multi-million dollar industry was envisioned and yet another sign was given of the ongoing prosperity of the operation.

With the coming of war in 1941, there was an abrupt and expected change in the operations of the San Francisco Airport. Its facilities were turned over to military control, although some commercial operation was continued on a curtailed basis and private flights were prohibited. The Air Transport Command took over the major part of the operations. However, the war years saw two new very important tenants: they were the Transcontinental and Western Air Lines as well as Pan American Airlines. Both named the San Francisco Airport as the base of their overhaul facilities.

With the approach of the end of the war, San Francisco prepared for an easily foreseen boom in aviation. Engineers thumbed slide rules and began their computations and came up with the figure of $20 million as necessary for further expansion of airport facilities. Edward G. Cahill, Manager of the Public Utilities operations, balked, saying "The runways are long enough!" How he was dissuaded from this view is described by Flynn:

> They talked the unrelenting but unsuspecting Utilities Manager into taking an airplane ride. The plane commander strapped him in the co-pilot's seat, began his takeoff, deliberately held the multi-ton aircraft, moving at two miles a minute, on the ground and refused to let it become airborne until the last possible moment. The onrushing boundary fence loomed so close that Cahill ducked. He was silent as

the plane circled the field and landed. He did not speak until he was back in a swivel chair. Then he said: "I don't want any more arguments about those runways. Build 'em longer! . . .[4]

It would seem that the San Francisco voters needed no such ride for, on November 7, 1945, with a five to one majority, they approved a $20 million bond issue for airport improvements. What the 1936 Public Utilities Report had foreseen now came to pass: this satisfying appropriation meant that the San Francisco Municipal Airport would soon merit the title of International Airport; today, obviously, it is now a Sky Port of Entry in one of the most important trade centers of America.

George M. Dixon replaced Doolin as manager and was responsible for contracts for the six-story administration building with passenger concourses and cargo and mail facilities. The Korean War brought further dislocations but, in the main, added more importance to the airport. For the first time, such foreign carriers as Qantas of Australia, Japan Air Lines, and the Philippine Airlines made use of its facilities. On January 25, 1954, Superintendent Dixon was replaced by General Frederick B. Butler, U.S. Army (retired);[5] a few months later, on August 27, 1954, the new terminal was dedicated by Governor Goodwin Knight. General Butler was able to continue the progressive policies of his predecessors;[6] his efforts were encouraged when, on November 6, 1956, the voters approved an additional $25 million bond issue; $14 million of this generous allotment was used to build a second terminal, with most of the balance given to a lengthening of the runways in anticipation of the needs of the new jet liners. By 1965, the total investment in the airport, including that of the airlines it served, had reached $170 million; always though, were the overriding considerations of future planning—such a project could never really be considered finished. Oscar Lewis thus reports some significant figures concerning the use of the airport:

> . . . By 1965 . . . more than 2,000 acres, much of it land reclaimed from the Bay, were then in use, and an additional 3,000 acres of tidelands were being held in reserve for future expansion. During the fiscal year, from July 1, 1964 to June 30, 1965, 8,349,365 passengers passed through the airport; the amount of air express totalled 13,525,155 pounds, and of air freight 281,854,465 pounds. Operating revenue for the same 12 month period was $9,700,000, an increase of 15% over

the previous year. These figures made clear that San Francisco's airport, like the city's street-transportation and water systems, had become a major operation, one that gave every indication of increasing in size and complexity with each passing year.[7]

By 1971, San Francisco International Airport, together with the airlines and related business and industrial enterprises serving it, had become the Bay Area's biggest business. In 1970, the expanding commercial aviation complex poured about $1 billion into the Bay Area's economy. (This figure does not include the estimated $1 million a day that arriving air travellers spend, mostly in San Francisco and in the northern peninsula.) In 1970, the twenty-six airlines serving San Francisco International generated 14.4 million passengers and about 613 million pounds of freight. This required the services of almost 30,000 employees of the airport itself, concessionaires, and others associated with commercial aviation.

By 1973, a battle royal was developing between those who wanted to see San Francisco Airport prepared to double the number of passengers with a consequent twofold expansion of facilities. Immediately, a growing number of environmentalists opposed such progress, predicting that the battle of the seventies would revolve around this issue just as had the battle of the freeways in the sixties. With a projected figure of $390 million for airport expansion came the opposition in the courts and in the public forum of these same environmentalists. Calling the expansion a "ridiculous boondoggle" and asserting that its approval by the San Francisco Airports Commission and the Board of Supervisors was "unlawful, arbitrary, capricious, unreasonable and an abuse of their or its discretion," the foes of expansion prepared to dig in at all levels and fight their cause. An editorial comment of the *San Francisco Chronicle* noted:

> . . . The extravagance of such assertions makes them less worthy of consideration than the quite plausible complaint that doubling the size of the airport to accommodate 31 million passengers a year and more than a million pounds of cargo per day, might well increase the noise, air pollution and traffic problems already bothersome.
> Many of these problems are now under attack. It is not unreasonable to assume that all will be largely if not entirely solved in the near future. And it is certain that the airplane is here to stay, and that its

contribution to the welfare of San Francisco and the entire Bay Area is essential to their continuing prosperity.[8]

Although hesitant and unsure in its beginnings, the San Francisco Airport has long since come into its own; its continuing expansion is another proof of the constructive spirit that San Francisco has brought to bear on this and similar challenges.

Adolph Sutro.

James Rolph.

Roger Lapham.

George Christopher.

PART 3

PEOPLE, LABOR AND POLITICS

John Francis Shelley.

Joseph Alioto.

CHAPTER 25

ADOLPH SUTRO AND THE SAN FRANCISCO STORY

MANY OF SAN FRANCISCO'S civic "greats" have run their respective courses, lived their lives, and died their deaths—and been buried not only physically but historically as well. Not so with regard to Adolph Heinrich Joseph Sutro (1830–1898) who, among other aspects of a distinguished career, was the city's 24th mayor from 1895 to 1897. One does not live long in San Francisco before hearing the name of Sutro, for it is still prominent and presumably it always will be. A stroll on Sutro Heights overlooking the Pacific Ocean, a look at the site formerly occupied by Sutro Baths, a browsing in the riches of the Sutro branch of the California State Library, or a gaze at the tower now crowning Mount Sutro, all serve to bring the memory of the man into focus. Honored in life and after his death, Adolph Sutro deserves more than passing mention in these pages.

Sutro was born on April 29, 1830, at Aix-la-Chapelle in what was then Prussia. Of Jewish parentage, he received a good education in mining engineering, a training that was to serve him well in future years. At the early age of sixteen, he was considered sufficiently versatile to help in administering a large clothes factory owned by his father. After the latter's death, and partially because of the revolutionary upheavals that marked the year 1848 in European and German history, Sutro migrated to the United States with his mother and other members of the family. This was in 1850. By this time, the news of the discovery of gold in California was a household word but the excitement concerning this find in El Dorado had far from subsided; spurred on by it, Sutro set out for San Francisco by way of the Panama isthmus, arriving in the city on November 21, 1851. For about a decade, he was occupied in the mercantile business. In 1856, he married Leah Harris and six children resulted from this union, although it was not a completely happy one since the two were separated for several years before his death. Sutro's previous mining engineering training caused him to be attracted to the Nevada mines, especially when, in 1859, the Comstock Lode was discovered there. His career in East Dayton, near Virginia City, where he founded the Sutro Metallurgical Works, eventually was crowned with success with the digging of the famous Sutro Tunnel, a more than five-mile-long venture which cost $6.5 million and which Sutro conceived and constructed as a successful means of ventilating the perpendicular shafts of the deep mines that penetrated Mount Davidson and other parts of the Virginia City area. Although he built his tunnel despite the opposition of some of the mine owners who did not want his advice or even his presence on the Comstock, in 1879, when he sold his tunnel interest for a profit of $5 million, he was able to return to San Francisco as a prosperous capitalist.

One who examines the shrewdness that marked Sutro's enterprises in San Francisco must be impressed by this and other qualities which surely included a vision that enabled him to see, in his mind, some of the future of the city he so much admired. How else can one explain or understand the foresight that caused him to buy extensive land holdings in what were then known as the "outside lands" of San Francisco? In the 1880s, the eastern end of the yet young Golden Gate Park was beyond the limits of the designated streets of San Francisco. There Sutro bought a substantial part of what was called the Rancho San Miguel and adjacent lands, amounting to about 1,000 acres in all. Some of the sand dunes and sage-covered hills he planted with eucalyptus trees imported from Australia from which developed Sutro Forest. The crest of this area he called Mount Parnassus but it is commonly called after him rather than by the more classical title. He also bought the land overlooking the Pacific Ocean on which now stands the Cliff House and the adjacent Sutro Heights. When one includes the site on which he was to build the world famous Sutro Baths (unfortunately destroyed by fire on June 26, 1966), it is apparent how important Sutro had become. At the height of his career, he was reported to have had title to about one-twelfth of the whole land area of San Francisco. Some who jeered at "Sutro's Folly" lived to see him go on to yet further

First Cliff House, opened 1863. Southern Pacific

prosperity as a result of these land purchases. He built a fine home on Sutro Heights with an unparalleled view of the Pacific Ocean and planted a splendid garden in the adjacent grounds adorned with much statuary imported from Europe. (Even though his home was torn down in 1931 after the death of his daughter, the grounds remain as a well-kept park area that many San Franciscans visit frequently.)

During this phase of his life, Sutro was a frequent traveller to various European countries where, among other treasures, he collected the nucleus of an outstanding library; he seems always to have had the general idea of bequeathing his possessions to the people of San Francisco. Earlier he acquired the second Cliff House which, in 1864, had replaced the first which had been built in 1858. Sutro rebuilt the entire structure, but saw it go up in flames, and again he was responsible for another rebuilding—this time in 1896—two years before his death. (This was also to be burned in 1907, and a fourth structure was built at the same site.

Cliff House and Seal Rocks, 1887. Southern Pacific

Third Cliff House from Sutro Heights.

Fourth Cliff House from Ocean Beach.

A considerably renovated building, which can be called the fifth
Cliff House, now marks the same site.) The structure that Sutro
built in 1896 was pretty much the measure of the man who,
seemingly, never thought small, for it was in the form of an
elaborate French chateau.

Obviously, one of the outstanding achievements for which
Sutro deserves to be remembered were the Sutro Baths, recalling
the similar accomplishments of the Roman Emperors Nero and
Diocletian, and beloved to many San Franciscans who remember
them well. Completed in 1896 and presented to San Francisco by
Sutro, they were a most acceptable and welcome gift which
brought untold hours of enjoyment to several generations of San
Franciscans. Even though, at the time of their destruction by fire
on June 26, 1966, their character had changed considerably and
an ice rink had, for a time, replaced the six swimming tanks, Sutro
Baths will always be a cherished memory in the history of the city
they enriched.

In 1894, Sutro was persuaded to enter politics and, even though
running on the Populist ticket, he was elected mayor of San
Francisco in 1895. His one term of service (San Francisco mayors
served only two-year terms at this time) found him less successful in the political field than he had been in various commercial
and other endeavors. Indicating his profound opposition to the

Cliff House Train, Sutro's Railroad, 1905.

Southern Pacific interests (he considered them predatory by nature and history) he determined to fight the company in its then undisputed control of the street railways of the city. In opposing the Southern Pacific, Sutro also took on the opposition of the "Big Four," the Railroad Kings Huntington, Stanford, Crocker, and Hopkins, who were then in the last phases of their careers. Establishing his own railroad which came as far as his properties overlooking Ocean Beach on Sutro Heights and, charging a lower fare, Sutro was quickly an object of considerable popularity among those who travelled on his railroad. He is also credited with having projected the idea of what was later to become the Twin Peaks Tunnel and, when one recalls his earlier and successful experience with the Sutro Tunnel on the Comstock, it is easy to believe that this was so.

Mention has already been made that Sutro was a collector of fine books and other such treasures of the mind, and those of his more extensive collection which survived the fire of 1906 now comprise the Sutro Branch of the California State Library which has, since September 1960, found separate lodging in the Gleeson

Library building on the campus of the University of San Francisco. This outstanding collection which, by terms of the Sutro will, must remain in San Francisco, comprises about 100,000 books as well as other notable literary treasures.

Adolph Sutro died in San Francisco on August 8, 1898, aged sixty-eight. For some time he had exhibited weakness both of body and, partially, of mind, though he was able to spend most of his last days in his well-loved home on Sutro Heights overlooking the Pacific. His favorite daughter and then his legal guardian, Dr. Emma Sutro, cared for him in the last phase of a most active life. Final farewell from that life found him dying among the fog-shrouded gardens of Sutro Heights where, as his biographers express it "the plaintive barking of the seals was his funeral dirge." There can be no doubt that Adolph Sutro rates high on the list of those who were distinguished benefactors of San Francisco.

CHAPTER 26

DENIS KEARNEY, AGITATOR EXTRAORDINARY

*The object of this association is to unite all poor and working men
into one political party for the purpose of defending themselves
against the dangerous encroachments of capital on the happiness of
our people and the liberties of our country.*

> Workingmen's Party of
> California: Statement of
> Principles.

*Corruption stalked in city halls and legislative chambers. Railroads
and land monopolies ruled the commonwealth. Under such circumstances a popular uprising was inevitable and, in Kearney, the
people found the kind of leader that suited the occasion.*

> Ira Cross: *History of the
> Labor Movement in California*
> (Berkeley, 1935) p. 72.

ON FRIDAY, SEPTEMBER 21, 1877, at a labor meeting held in San Francisco's Union Hall on Howard Street, an assemblage of about two thousand was addressed by a compactly built man of choleric temperament who was possessed of no little oratorical ability. Speaking in strident terms, his harangue that evening consisted mainly of violent abuse aimed at the "Nabobs," i.e. the rich who resided on Nob Hill, as well as at the Chinese who lived in San Francisco. For the former, he strongly recommended hanging and, for the latter, complete exclusion from California after the deportation of those already in the state had been accomplished. He ended his speech with the words: "Hemp! Hemp!" which were duly repeated and chanted by his henchmen. Then, as usual, came the words of the slogan that will always ring down the halls of San Francisco's history: "The Chinese Must Go! Denis Kearney Says So!" Who was this Agitator Extraordinary and why must his activities find a place in any history of San Francisco?

Denis Kearney was born in Oakmount, County Cork, Ireland, on February 1, 1847, and died, aged sixty, in Alameda on April 24, 1907. In between there were many tempestuous years as well as some other periods hard to reconcile with the violent views he had so completely embraced. He went to sea at the age of eleven as a cabin boy, and by 1868, when he was twenty-one, Kearney held the papers of a first mate. In this capacity, he arrived in San Francisco that same year aboard the S.S. *Shooting Star,* a name that seems completely appropriate, for Kearney's future years were to find him something like a shooting star himself. During the next four years he engaged in coastal sailings until, in 1872, he entered the more lucrative draying business in which he quickly began to prosper. In 1870, he married Mary Ann Leary, and eventually,

Kearney became the father of four children. At this time he was described as a man of considerable temperance in his personal habits since he was opposed to the use of tobacco and of alcohol; he tried by self-efforts to overcome the lack of formal education which had been his and, in the 1870s, was able to enter the ranks of the city's moderately successful businessmen.

The early middle and late years of that decade were marked all through the United States by financial difficulties which first took the form of what was called the panic of 1873. These were accentuated in San Francisco by the serious collapse of the stock market, largely because of the Comstock Lode problems mentioned in the last chapter. As expected, the number of the unemployed rose, with much suffering resulting from a serious and even desperate situation. Whether entirely true or not, some felt that the only two comfortable elements in the restive city were the rich "Nabobs" safely ensconced in their mansions on Nob Hill, and the Chinese who, while not exactly wealthy, seemed able to absorb any economic shocks without any obvious damage to themselves. Since they would and did work for much less money than a white man, and since, at least according to the probably inflated figure used by Kearney in one of his later speeches on his favorite topic, there were 150,000 Chinese in the city, it seemed but natural that they become the target of vituperative abuse at this troubled time.

This had not always been true: Peter Burnett, first American governor of California, accepted the presence of the Chinese (most of whom had come as miners) as a good thing. Indeed, his short-lived successor, Governor John McDougal, referred to the Chinese "as one of the most worthy classes of our newly adopted citizens" and recommended that further immigration be encouraged among them. When, in 1856, the Second Vigilance Committee was organized in San Francisco, while not eligible for membership, the Chinese merchants of the city contributed a considerable sum of money. However, when their patient industry as miners made them unpopular with their Caucasian counterparts and when, gradually, they took up menial positions in the cities of northern California, the opposition began to mount and increase. Finally, in 1869 after the Chinese "coolies" had done yeoman service in the building of the Central Pacific Rail-

Clay Street, Chinatown in early days. Southern Pacific

road, they again found their way back to the cities of northern California where they gradually became engaged as laundrymen and as domestic servants. They would work for such low rates, and could live with such great frugality since their staples were rice and tea, that the white worker could not hope to compete with them.

When the Panic of 1873 and what followed upon it sowed serious discontent and suffering, the stage was set for an explosion of some sort, and that is what Denis Kearney decided to aid and abet. He called and addressed various mass meetings of San Francisco's discontented; this was not at all difficult for him, since he had oratorical gifts as a rabble rouser. At a local meeting held on July 23, 1877, such inflammatory sentiments were voiced that the aging William T. Coleman, the "Lion of the Vigilantes," sent out a call for yet another volunteer organization to aid the police in the event of any rioting in the streets. Coleman ordered the purchase of six thousand hickory pick handles to equip his volunteers, although they determined to keep from using them unless it became necessary. Also, the committee applied to the federal government for arms; their request was immediately granted, and five warships were sent from Mare Island and anchored in the bay, with arms available if necessary. Although there were some skirmishes between the police and Kearney's followers, it would seem that the chief result of this show of strength, in addition to keeping down violence, was to increase the resentment among the dispossessed of the city while, naturally, the demagogic utterances of Kearney and others served to fan the flames of potential strife.

A serious incident occurred on July 25, 1877, when fire broke out at the dock where the Pacific Mail steamers customarily disembarked Chinese emigrants. Despite the opposition of a mob, the firemen were eventually able to bring the conflagration under control. Four men died in the accompanying fracas and, when the rioters were finally dispersed, the damage was set at about $80,000. By this time, it was evident to the more responsible elements in the disturbed city that the Irishman from Cork was the man to watch and, of course, they were right. A large sandlot (now the site of the main branch of the San Francisco Public Library in Civic Center) was used for the Kearney meetings; this proved ideal since it was then possible to view Nob Hill from there. Addressing the "Sandlotters," as they came to be called, from a raised platform, Kearney would turn dramatically in the direction of Nob Hill and shout: "A little judicious hanging would be the best course to pursue with these capitalists. If the ballot fails us, we always have the bullet!" When he turned to the Chinese, among other expressions of hate, he would say: "If John Chinaman don't leave here, we will drive him and his supporters into the sea!" and "We are bent on driving from the state of California these miserable, moon-eyed lepers!" These cocky and boisterous rantings made Kearney sufficiently important for Archbishop Alemany to consider it his duty to forbid attendance at these meetings to all Catholics under his jurisdiction. This he did in a pastoral letter issued in April 1878, which was read from the pulpits of all the Catholic churches of the city. Alemany used strong words: "We, therefore, admonish and even require everyone to stay away from such seditious, anti-social and anti-Christian meetings." By this authoritative action, Kearney's influence was diminished, for many of his adherents were both Irish and Catholic.[1]

Perhaps it was inevitable that Denis Kearney should throw his hat into the political ring. In August 1877, he did so when, his previous application for membership in the National Workingmen's Party having been denied because of some of his views, he formed his own organization calling it the Workingmen's Trade and Labor Union of San Francisco. From this, soon developed his Workingmen's Party of California; though short-lived as a political party, it proved to be an effective force for some years. Kearney had a good cause for it was undeniable that the workingman was exploited by capital as well as by unsympathetic employers. Just as communism did not come out of a void, so, too, the complaints and the political organization of the workingmen in San Francisco by Kearney did not come out of a vacuum. He delighted in his not infrequent arrests as a disturber of the peace. (A Thanksgiving Day parade which he arranged in 1877 caused the Board of Supervisors to pass a "Gag Law" against Kearney; although passed, it proved difficult if not impossible to enforce.)

January 1878, was not only a winter month in San Francisco but a very hard time for the unemployed and other poor of the city. A number of such unfortunate people followed Kearney through the streets chanting such slogans as: "Bread, or a place in the County Jail!" In 1879, Kearney and his cohorts exercised considerable influence in the drafting of California's second constitution in a convention in Sacramento, and he claimed, with reason, that some of the "soak the rich" provisions in it were the result of the political muscle he had exercised with the help of a number of the legislature who had been elected on the Workingmen's ticket. In 1879, when Kearney went to the eastern seaboard to extend there the blessings of his particular brand of Workingmen's Party philosophy, he soon faced repudiation and, even worse, when he returned to San Francisco, he found that he had lost effective control of the party he had brought into being. His announced support of the candidates of the National Greenback Party proved a disastrous mistake and, in July 1880, dissidents even caused his expulsion from his own Workingmen's Party. In 1881, he returned to the drayage business and, while making some efforts to regain his popularity by occasionally declaiming in sandlot style, it became evident that his political clout had gone, together with most of his personal appeal. By this time, the Agitator Extraordinary had, indeed, become San Francisco's "shooting star!" Even his draying business was sufficiently boycotted to make it unprofitable for him to operate. He next turned to the stock market where he had good fortune and, with the gains from it, Kearney purchased a fine home in the Pacific Heights section of the city.

What would appear to be the truest measure of the man, and one that makes it appropriate to designate him as a non-hero in our civic story was his change of attitude toward the working class which came with his affluence. Actually, he seems to have become more than occasionally hostile in his utterances with regard to his former cohorts; certainly the later union labor elements in San Francisco have never found it appropriate or necessary to honor him as a former defender of the rights of the working man. To any who would listen he would now strenuously maintain that the laboring class really lacked the intelligence to overcome problems and that, in fact, it just was not worthy of political representation. Obviously, the divorce was now complete between him and those who had been loudest in his support. By the turn of the century, his style of life had changed completely: gone were the rough clothes of the working-man, gone also was the canvas and leather apron of the drayman. His clothes were now of an expensive cut; he frequented the best restaurants of the city and became a patron of the opera. However, he still maintained that his attitude to the Chinese in San Francisco had been correct, while adding that the exclusion which had been decreed for them was due, largely, to his efforts. (When he found himself listed in the Century Dictionary and even mentioned in Lord Bryce's distinguished history called *The American Commonwealth* as well as in Theodore Hittell's *History of California*, he showed more than usual pleasure.)

From 1901 to 1903, Kearney continued to live the "good life"; strangely, toward the end of 1903, his behavior became erratic, with some evidences of a persecution complex; by 1905, his family worried about him for there appeared to be signs of an imminent mental breakdown. Becoming careless of dress, he showed an alarming lack of self-control, while his conduct even approached the violent at times.

Although never in any real financial difficulties from 1901 until his death in 1907, he fancied that he was, in reality, a poor man; gradually, his robust health began to deteriorate, with complications resulting from a kidney ailment. The San Francisco earthquake and fire in April 1906 dealt him the cruellest of blows when what he called his "beautiful house" and "fine carriage" as well as his "magnificent horses" were destroyed. Purchasing a house on Park Street in Alameda after the debacle, Kearney became somewhat of a recluse. Some months before his death his eyesight failed and his interest in public affairs was now a thing of the past. Not long before his death, however, he made two last statements: one to the effect that the Japanese were worse than the Chinese and the other asserting that the American worker was beneath contempt. He died in his home in Alameda on Wednesday evening, April 24, 1907. At his bedside were his wife, a daughter, and two sons. There were no religious services and his wish that his remains be cremated was respected. A journalist of the day mentioned that, had Kearney died thirty years previously, the event would have been chronicled throughout the world; as it was, his death created little or no stir anywhere, even in San Francisco. Perhaps, though, fairness requires the reflection that the cause he earlier espoused was more important than the man himself; in this connection, one may quote an acknowledged authority on California's history:

Kearney had staunchly pioneered a movement that was most important in the history of American labor. Although the Workingmen were unsuccessful in achieving their whole reform program, they did make labor's wishes publicly known. . . . Into the state's political balance of power had been thrown a potentially strong force—one which . . . would rise again to demand a more specific program for the betterment of labor.[2]

CHAPTER 27

THE TEAMSTERS'
STRIKE OF 1901

I T HAS LONG been true that San Francisco has been and is a citadel of strength for the forces of union labor. The story of how this came about lies deeply rooted in the city's past. In this chapter, an attempt will be made to examine some of the vital details to see how this development affected the future of San Francisco.

The years from 1890 to 1906 cover a somewhat crowded period in the history of the city. Much of the local labor unrest was, at least in part, a legacy of Denis Kearney and his earlier efforts in this regard. However, it should be remembered that what happened at this time in California as well as in San Francisco formed but part of the troubled national scene. Gradually, but not without severe strains and stresses and occasional outbreaks of violence, the labor union movement was coming into its own, although bitterly opposed by many employers who professed to see nothing but radicalism plus communism in the demands, often legitimate, made on them by their employees. Those acquainted with the American past at this time will find, then, only local applications here of what was also occurring on the broader national scene. From 1875 to 1893, various strikes had formed part of the civic picture in San Francisco. Because labor was not at all well organized at this time, it was not too difficult, generally speaking, for management to break the back of any such "infringement on their rights" as they chose to call such disputes. Obviously, they said, if "the laborer doesn't like his working conditions, he can quit and get himself another job—there is no obligation for him to work for us or for us, indeed, to hire the likes of him!" They were to find out differently in 1901. To this year, which was to see a sort of Magna Carta emerge for the cause of unionism in San Francisco, we shall now turn.

In August 1900, a local group of teamsters met in San Francisco to establish an organization with the express purpose of improving their working conditions. That these needed improvement was evident to all, perhaps, except the employers. In the years when horse-drawn drays still formed an essential part of the delivery system in the city, the teamsters occupied a central place in the whole picture. What were their chief complaints? These revolved around the inhumane conditions under which they were forced to fulfill their employment. The average teamster worked from twelve to fourteen hours a day and this not infrequently extended to all seven days of the week or, if he had a day off it was entirely without pay. His wages reached a maximum of $16 a week, with a minimum offered of from $3 to $4. (Even allowing for the more solid dollar of the day, this wage really represented hardly more than a pittance.) Small wonder, that, by the turn of the century, the teamsters of San Francisco felt that the time had come for them to make an effective protest against these intolerable conditions. Every cause, it seems, must have a hero and San Francisco had one at this time.

Teamster Michael Casey was born in Ireland in 1860 and died in San Francisco in 1937. He had come to the city as a lad of twelve and had been a teamster since 1889; obviously, then, he knew whereof he spoke when he addressed his fellow workers on Sunday, August 5, 1900, and put their sentiments into his own eloquent words. The seeds that were sown that day eventually blossomed as the Brotherhood of Teamsters, later known as the San Francisco Teamsters Union, which is still one of the strongest such groups in San Francisco. It was but natural that Casey himself be elected the first "business agent" or negotiator for the newly formed group. Although, as already indicated, these moves represented but the local phase of a movement that was sweeping the nation, they were looked upon with immense disapproval by most of the local employers. The teamsters and their plans immediately excited the ire of the employers' group who determined to give their all to fight this insidious wave of "radicalism" among those who had the good fortune to work for them. Secretly, they banded together under the unpublicized (at least at the beginning) name of the "Employers' Association of San Francisco." Actually, the only reason for this organization was to crush the incipient unionism which threatened their vested interests. By 1901, employing the various economic and political pressures that had been successfully used elsewhere, the employers had succeeded in so pushing the wages and hours dispute into the background as to challenge, indeed, the very notion that their employees had any right at all to organize. A climax was reached when they even refused to meet with representatives of the newly formed Brotherhood of Teamsters, reiterating their stand that no one was forced to work for them. If an employee chose to quit, who would put food into the mouths of his dependents was of no concern to the employers. What, really could any teamster who quit his job do to provide for his family? Certainly, he would be barred effectively from obtaining another job. It was because of this virtual stymie that was not of their choice but that had been forced upon them by the Employers' Association that the Teamsters decided to resort to the weapon of the strike: there appeared little or no possibility of their improving their living and working conditions without putting their beliefs and complaints to the test. So it was that, regretfully but impelled by necessity, the teamsters determined upon a strike call. Their strike, which eventually was to prove successful, must be counted as among the most significant in San Francisco's past.

As was to be expected, the employers had sound financial backing and, cleverly, they determined to pick off, one by one, any group that seemed to militate against their vested interests. While filling the air with their piosities about "free enterprise" the "right of private property" etc., they determined to keep on clipping the coupons of profit while breaking the back of the incipient unionism which they saw as their greatest threat in San Francisco. To this end, they turned with their demands to the "Draymen's Executive Committee" for necessary aid. It was the draymen who owned the large cargo containers called "drays" while it was the teamsters, of course, who operated these drays.

The employers made peremptory demands upon the draymen to "lock out," i.e. not deal with, each and every teamster who refused to accede to their demands that they cease their radical activities in the city. Caught in a considerable dilemma, since they were dependent upon the employers for their contracts, the draymen reluctantly called upon the teamsters to forsake the

union headed by Michael Casey or not to expect any further
work from the draymen's group. The outraged teamsters felt the
knife of unemployment being plunged into their backs, as the
employers, with far from gentle prodding, sought a vital spot to
ensure the death of unionism. But the teamsters were comforted,
at least in part, by the courageous action of the Waterfront Union
which joined them in a strike call—actually, this group was in
pretty much the same condition, since the working conditions of
the longshoremen were also sadly in need of improvement. The
workers demanded what has now long been acknowledged their
right—that of collective bargaining from a position of legitimate
strength in what affected their lives. Obviously, this right was
then questioned by the entrenched employers. (Seldom had battle lines been as sharply defined as at this time in the City by the
Golden Gate.) On Sunday, July 29, 1901, the strike call went out
when the City Front Federation called out all its manpower at the
docks of San Francisco, Oakland, Port Costa, and Mission Rock.
Because the employers were unable, despite some fair and some
foul tactics, to cope with and conquer this strike, the union labor
movement became firmly established in the city, where it has
prospered and developed ever since. However, such gains were
not accomplished without months of intervening strife; charges
of anti-American radicalism were met with counterblasts about
unmitigated and intolerable selfishness on the part of predatory
employers.

During this ominous and crisis-laden period, as has been mentioned, the employers at first refused to meet with the representatives of labor. Strikebreakers, quickly called "scabs" by local
teamsters, were imported from the East Coast and offered inflated
wages to take the place of the striking Teamsters; police protection was afforded to these strikebreakers. Nevertheless, some of
them quickly left the local scene when, with rocks and other
things thrown at them as they drove their drays on the streets of
San Francisco, they decided to return home rather than face the
very real possibility of serious injury and/or death. Local newspapers, such as the *Call*, the *Bulletin*, and the *Chronicle* served up
sympathy for the employers' cause, with William Randolph
Hearst's *Examiner* showing itself as the only local newspaper to
embrace the cause of union labor. Sporadic and almost unavoid-

able outbreaks of violence were, of course, always attributed to the "Communists and other Radicals" among the Teamsters and Longshoremen who were "bent on destroying the traditional American way of life!" In the earliest phase of the strike, about 1,400 teamsters were effectively "locked out" by the draymen. Tempers became even more ugly with the passage of the days and weeks of the strike; the imported teamsters not only objected to the threats and actual examples of physical violence thrust upon them but they also found the San Francisco hills, many of them excessively steep, little to their liking; their woes were at times complicated by property damages accruing to the employers because of accidents resulting from their inexpert handling of the drays under unfamiliar conditions.

Even though Mayor James D. Phelan and his Industrial Conciliation Council, always fearful of even graver consequences, endeavored to mediate the strike, these efforts were rendered ineffective by the continued refusal of the employers to meet with the Teamsters. A stalemate seemed inevitable but the day was saved for labor at this most critical period of the unresolved strike through the efforts of a Catholic priest, Father Peter Christopher Yorke, whose name will always be important in the history of labor in San Francisco. While it would be an over simplification to make Yorke the unique warrior who won this pivotal strike for the Teamsters, for there were others so engaged, it remains true that his intervention and support was given at the right time and by one who could and did successfully withstand the efforts of the now embattled employers to break the power of the Teamsters.

Father Yorke (1864–1925) was, at the time, the editor of the Catholic weekly newspaper, the *Monitor*, and, already, his name was high on the list of courageous and successful controversialists on the scene in San Francisco. (The next chapter will be devoted to a fuller presentation of Yorke's life and career; here we shall confine our treatment to his role in the strike of 1901.) It so happened that a large number of the Teamsters on strike were Father Yorke's co-religionists; when the labor leaders sought his support, it was given after he had carefully studied the situation and tried it against the key encyclical of Pope Leo XIII entitled "Rerum Novarum" in which the pontiff had explicitly stated labor's right to that collective bargaining which was being denied by the Employers' Association in San Francisco. As a consequence, Yorke found it his duty as well as his privilege to fight for the Teamsters' cause in San Francisco. Shrewdly, he decided that the best weapon to wield was that of enlightened public opinion and, after Mayor Phelan had tried unsuccessfully on four occasions to bring the conflicting interests together, Father Yorke openly entered the fray. The priest, so well known because of earlier controversies with which he had engaged in San Francisco, always had an audience waiting for him whether it was in public halls or in the columns of the local press, which, in this case, meant mostly the *Examiner.* Both vocally and in writing, he discoursed eloquently on the rights of labor as well as on the duties of employers, while reminding labor, also, that it too, had its obligations and duties. Never one to pull punches and never at a loss for words or for the apt phrase in his written articles or rejoinders, Yorke openly accused Governor Henry T. Gage of prejudice on the side of capital and big business interests while pointing to the protection of strikebreakers sanctioned by state and local authorities as proof of such unfair attitudes. When an almost disastrous rumour was spread among the workers that all was lost and that, for survival, they had better quickly return to their jobs without the benefits of union organization, it was Father Yorke, with Michael Casey at his side, who exhorted the workers to stand fast. "You are God's people and you are engaged in a struggle for the dearest property of man, your self-respect."

By September 1901, almost 20,000 were unemployed in San Francisco, while nearly two hundred ships were tied up in the harbor. It may be imagined what hardships all of this was bringing to the workingmen involved as well as to their families, since this was long before the day of anything resembling unemployment insurance. A spokesman for California's agricultural interests said that the grain would rot if not harvested soon; the answer of the Employers' Association was a defiant "Let it rot!" To such unbridled defiance, Yorke eloquently replied: "Shall men for whom Christ died to teach them they are free men, with free men's rights, be crushed beneath the foot of the least bright of all the angels that fell from Heaven, Mammon, the spirit of greed?" The Board of Supervisors also endeavored to lend its good offices to resolve the dispute and, for their efforts, they were praised by Yorke who, in a public letter to the Board, again blasted the employers as a "secret society which, by threat of boycott and ruinous competition, forces other employers to lock out their men." A further sag in morale came, though, in September as the effects of the strike became even more apparent. Again Yorke's oratorical efforts were applied as he told the embattled Teamsters and their other supporters: "Don't give up now! You are standing on a gold mine and you don't know it!" On Saturday, September 21, a crowd of about 15,000 tried to find places in the large Metropolitan Temple on Fifth Street between Market and Mission to hear another defense of the strikers by their champion. Yorke's words, though, were not inflammatory, as had been those of Kearney a quarter of a century before him; he urged no violence but rather continued solidarity as they, together, continued their fight for their rights. He also wrote a well-reasoned series of five articles for the *Examiner* defending his position and implementing it with apt words from Pope Leo XIII. He was also one of those who helped organize a strike fund club with headquarters at Powell and Market streets.

On Wednesday, October 2, Governor Gage came from Sacramento to see if he could arrange a solution and informed Yorke that the employers had asked that he call out the State Militia to restore normalcy and safety to the streets of the embattled city. Yorke protested and stated his case again with the results that, within hours, Gage was able to get all the disputants together. In a surprisingly short time, indicating the weariness of all concerned with what had transpired, an agreement was signed on that same day, Wednesday, October 2, 1901. The cause of labor was triumphant; full union recognition was granted with a satisfactory scale of wages and hours completely recognized. Yorke's words were: "The strike is ended to the satisfaction of us all, thank God. Let us have peace!" Union labor in San Francisco has never forgotten the crucial part played in this victory by Peter Christopher Yorke.

CHAPTER 28

SAN FRANCISCO'S "CONSECRATED THUNDERBOLT": Father Peter C. Yorke

. . . That gallant stripling, the victorious chieftain, the matchless warrior, the miraculous boy, that consecrated thunderbolt was Peter C. Yorke. . . .

Attorney John J. Barrett
introduces Father Yorke at
an anti-APA lecture in
San Francisco, 1896.

Father Yorke!—born in Ireland, died in San Francisco, fighting valiantly all the sixty-one years inbetween. You can't write the history of these last thirty-seven years in San Francisco without bringing in the name of Father Peter C. Yorke again and again and again. He was part of this town. He helped to make its years eventful and dynamic. A most remarkable human being was Father Peter Yorke. . . . Turbulent and tender, strong and loyal, vigorous and affectionate, Father Yorke will not be forgotten in San Francisco.

Editorial, *San Francisco Call
and Post*, April 7, 1925.

P

ETER CHRISTOPHER YORKE was born in Galway City, Ireland, on August 13, 1864.[1] His family answered originally to the name of "Jorke" and was of Dutch origin. It appears that, quite early, Peter showed considerable intellectual talent and when he entered the famous Maynooth Seminary outside Dublin in 1882, it was predicted that, with the passage of years, this young seminarian would be heard from. He was to be, indeed— but in an entirely different set of circumstances than was then thought of. After his father's death, his mother decided to emigrate to the United States and, since there was a strong bond between mother and son, Peter decided to continue his priestly studies in America. This he did in 1886 when Archbishop Patrick W. Riordan of San Francisco accepted him for future service in his archdiocese and directed him to report to St. Mary's Seminary, Baltimore, to continue his studies. On December 17, 1887, aged twenty-three, he was ordained to the priesthood in Baltimore by Cardinal Gibbons. In the early months of 1888, he reported to Archbishop Riordan in San Francisco where he was assigned as a curate to St. Mary's Cathedral; in six years, he was appointed by Riordan as chancellor of the archdiocese while, in the next year, 1895, he assumed the editorship of the archdiocesan organ, the *Monitor*.

The next forty years of his life were to result in his solid identification with many separate facets of the ecclesiastical and civil life of San Francisco. It was not long before he brought his outstanding talents as a writer to bear when he directed his editorial artillery against the unfair and bigoted attacks of the American Protective Association in its vilification of the Catholic Church.[2] This group was highly vocal, and their target was especially the "Pope's Irish" since they were, in essence, a nationalis-

Father Peter C. Yorke, 1864–1925.

tic group with the determined objective of "keeping the United States of America safe for white, native Protestant Americans." All this was more than enough to draw the fire of Peter C. Yorke. (Even now, one reading the so-called "literature" of the day is impressed at the bitterness that was characteristic both of the charges and the no-holds-barred refutations which characterized both sides in the controversies between Yorke and some local ministers who were the protagonists of the APA.) The Jesuits, of course, were exposed by some of the latter because of their obviously nefarious (and successful) efforts to corrupt the youth entrusted to their tender care in St. Ignatius College and High School. Yorke, correctly convinced of the undeniable right that was his as well as that of his co-religionists to exist peacefully within the civic and religious fabric of true Americanism, unceasingly challenged the irresponsible statements of his opponents as regards the loyalty of American Catholics. Determined to fight fire with fire (this was hardly an ecumenical age) he seemed to rejoice in his attempts to kill the dragon of bigotry, and a glance at the literary arsenal of ridicule, sarcasm, and other such weapons reveals that the "gallant stripling" did, in fact, become the "matchless warrior" referred to by John J. Barrett. While some today might question Yorke's methods, since, obviously, they were marked by neither courtesy nor charity, they were characteristic of the day and, perhaps, his opponents would not have understood or particularly appreciated any other treatment.

Those who knew Father Yorke have testified that there were really two (at least) "persons" who lived in the one man: one was an essentially calm, though quick-witted, priest whose personal life was marked by an admirable dedication to his calling; in this connection, one who knew him well has testified that he thinks that Yorke should better be remembered as a Christian educator who did more than anyone else to kill the ghosts of bigotry in San Francisco.[3] Father Yorke served many years as a beloved pastor of St. Anthony's Church in Oakland as well as a most efficient and forward-looking pastor of St. Peter's Church in San Francisco; the record in either case is unanimous that he was always the dedicated parish priest and father of his spiritual family. Add to this that he was ever an outspoken and fervent Irish nationalist, and one comes to the conclusion that here was a person who could, and did at times, wear several hats during his busy years in Oakland and San Francisco. His public lectures and sermons betray little of the controversialist for they are calm and well-reasoned analyses of the topics of which he chose to treat. (His piety is evident in such books as *Altar and Priest* and the like.) However, one must be impressed by his vital and lasting contributions to the civic and clerical scene of his day.

On April 18, 1925, Father Yorke died peacefully at St. Peter's Rectory in San Francisco; thousands mourned him and a perusal of the press accounts concerning his funeral indicate that seldom, if ever, had there been a greater outpouring of grief than that which attended the funeral of San Francisco's "Consecrated Thunderbolt." In this connection, it seems appropriate from the standpoint of correct historical perspective, that the words of his biographer, Joseph Brusher, S.J., be quoted here:

The character of Yorke was at once simple and complex. It is easy enough to distinguish his fundamental principles but the man does remain an interesting example of complexity. Ambivalence permeated his life. He was extremely loyal to authority yet had no hesitation in getting around it. He could be a bully in the public forum, even downright mean, but privately he was charming and generous.

If one virtue was to be singled out . . . a virtue that he manifested both in public and in private life, it was moral courage. When he believed in a principle, whether it was tolerance, social justice or nationality, he did not hesitate to go from belief to action . . . no matter whose feet he might tread on in the process, Yorke cared not a whit. And this does call for courage. . . . Without his great moral courage, Yorke would not have thwarted the forces of bigotry, would not have upheld the rights of labor—he might have accomplished a great deal, but he would not have been San Francisco's "Consecrated Thunderbolt."[4]

CHAPTER 29

CORRUPTION:
Abe Ruef
and Eugene Schmitz

A

BE RUEF, ONCE called the "Boodling Boss," was born in San Francisco on September 2, 1864.[1] He was the son of Myer and Adele Ruef, Jewish immigrants from France. His early education was received in San Francisco's public schools from which he went to the University of California at Berkeley where he proved to be a precocious student, graduating, with honors, in 1882 at age eighteen.

Since he had already developed an interest in government, Ruef joined in forming a small club devoted to political reform; two of his associates were Franklin K. Lane, later secretary of the interior in President Wilson's cabinet, and John Wigmore, later the author of the perennial classic known to all law students as "Wigmore on Evidence." (These two became life-long crusaders for better government; Ruef was to become an object lesson in corruption.) He entered Hastings Law School and, as usual, excelled in his studies there. After graduation he started a modest practice of law and gradually emerged as the Republican political "boss" of the district centering around Sansome Street. It seems that his alert eyes soon discovered what many a man before and since has found out—the game of politics, at least as played in many quarters, frequently debasing the noble Aristotelian concept of politics and service of the commonwealth as one of the most worthy functions of man, can be, and frequently is, just plain dirty and sordid.

By 1901, it was apparent to Ruef that he should associate himself with the obvious potentialities of the rising Union Labor party in the city, which became even more important with the settling of the Teamsters strike in that year. His shrewd analysis saw an emergent group not at all sure of itself; indeed he correctly judged it as an uneasy and awkward political entity very much in need of a leader. Ruef determined to be that leader, not in the obvious sense of running for political office but rather as one behind the scenes who would call the plays and thus effectively control the activities of those who would occupy influential office in the city. Even though the Teamsters had won their strike, there was still much unfinished business and there were still wounds to be licked, for labor leaders now felt that they had been betrayed by the Democratic party which had formerly claimed their complete allegiance. The "third party" which emerged, called the Union Labor party, did not have many "free" days; quickly, it was captured by young Abe Ruef, then in his thirties and "rarin' to go!"[2] By this time, Ruef was known as a soft-spoken, well-met, and cultured man of the world who loved and practiced the good life, indulging in gourmet dining and other such comforts.

Although Abe Ruef was determined to get to the top as quickly as possible, he soon became convinced that the method of indirection was the only one for him: although he possibly would not have at all objected to occupying the mayor's seat, sensitive of his Jewish background he thought that, since "politics is the science of the possible" he had better forget such ambitions. (Jewish background had not kept Adolph Sutro from being mayor, but the two were entirely different kinds of men.) Once Ruef had decided that his role would be that of an arranger of things behind the scenes, he began to look around for one who could best serve his immediate purpose, which was to capitalize on the position of labor in San Francisco, and whom he could have elected mayor with labor's support. After some persuasive tactics, he convinced Eugene Schmitz to run for the office of mayor of San Francisco. Correctly, Ruef saw Schmitz as a handsome, personable, and talented man (he was a professional musician), and, also correctly, Ruef knew that Schmitz would not consider himself especially apt in the political arena and thus, presumably he would be amenable to persuasion and training at the hands of the already politically astute Ruef. After election as the 26th mayor in November 1901, Schmitz assumed office the following year and he served as mayor until 1907. During all these years, Ruef, who was to prove his protege's nemesis, acted officially as "legal advisor" to the mayor; actually, it quickly became public knowledge that he was, indeed, the acknowledged power behind the throne and that a word from Ruef would do much toward receiving preferential treatment in the many areas in which he became supreme. (If, at an early moment, Schmitz had made it evident that, while duly grateful to Ruef for bringing him to the position of mayor, he would tolerate no area of special privilege, no vestige of shrewd or corrupt practice, he would have been spared much embarassment later on when, tarred with the same brush as Ruef, he had been made equally guilty of bribe-taking and other offenses.)

One profitable area in which Ruef exercised much power was

Eugene Schmitz.

that which concerned the issuing of liquor licenses. A number of the French and other restaurants of the day found that the acquiring or renewal of such licenses could be expedited if they retained Ruef as their legal advisor, a position that was always accompanied by a substantial fee.

Schmitz stood successfully for a second term in 1903 and again in 1905. In an uncharacteristically wrong assessment of the situation, largely because of adverse publicity in the local press which had already begun openly to question some of the policies seemingly entrenched at City Hall, Ruef decided that his candidate would probably not be reelected mayor and hence he was downright careless in selecting eighteen candidates to run for supervisor; to Ruef's surprise, as well as to that of the eighteen, Schmitz and they were elected to serve again in their respective capacities. In due time, as the courts were to establish, most of the supervisors proved themselves to be voraciously greedy in the matter of accepting "fees for services rendered," having decided that if Ruef could do such things, why not they as well; these are the supervisors known as the "Paint Eaters" since, as Ruef said of them, "they were so greedy that they would eat the paint off a house!" Knowing something of the lucrative Ruef practice, the subtle and to them unconvincing distinction that Ruef drew between his capacity as a private legal counsel in contrast to theirs as sworn public officials seems not to have bothered them at all. Finally, Ruef, very much against his will, was forced to agree to share some of the spoils with a few of the supervisors who, like him, were later to be convicted of bribe-taking.

An example (only one of many) of how Ruef operated may be given here. The Home Telephone Company paid Ruef $125,000 for his influence in obtaining a franchise to establish a competitive system with that of the already existing Pacific States Telephone Company. While Ruef was negotiating, the latter company approached eleven supervisors with an offer of $5,000 to each to vote against the proposed franchise. They accepted, thereby breaking their earlier promise to Ruef that they would not accept money from such sources without first clearing the offer with him. Understandably, Ruef was appalled and enraged, both with the supervisors and the Pacific States Company, for "going over his head." His punishment took the form of seeing to it that the Home Telephone Company was awarded the desired franchise; the supervisors who had accepted bribes from the Pacific States Company were to receive less than half of their money from the Home Company and were told that they must give back half of the money they had received from Pacific States. Only some chose to do so and Pacific States found itself in the compromising and irritating position of having paid substantial bribes to a majority of the supervisors for the granting of a franchise to its competitor. Other payoffs accrued to him from the United Railroads which, wishing to obtain certain privileges regarding the changing of their cable car operations to overhead trolleys, paid Ruef a "fee" of $200,000 to obtain this substantial favor.[3]

When it became apparent that Abe Ruef was fattening and battening on his "fees," the forces interested in civic reform, correctly suspecting that all was not well at City Hall, opened up on him and his cohorts, lumping Mayor Schmitz with him in their damning accusations. Fremont Older, crusading editor of the *San Francisco Bulletin,* went to work, as did others similarly interested in breaking the Ruef stranglehold on the city. Rudolph Spreckels showed interest in the reform movement and William J. Burns of the already celebrated detective agency, was hired (at a stipend of $100,000 provided by Spreckels and former Mayor Phelan) to do the necessary sleuthing so that the malefactors might be brought to the bar of justice. On December 7, 1908, Abe Ruef was convicted on a charge of bribery in the United Railroads case; he was sentenced to fourteen years in the San Quentin penitentiary. After an unsuccessful and long-drawn-out series of appeals, he went to prison on March 7, 1911. (A strange aftermath stems from the fact that Fremont Older, who had largely been responsible for putting Ruef behind bars, later espoused the cause of his parole when he became convinced that it was not right that one man should do all of the atoning for what was, after all, a general malaise and a corrupt condition for which many others were responsible.[4])

Ruef served four years and seven months (as a model prisoner) before favorable action was taken on his behalf by the Parole Board. He left San Quentin on August 23, 1915, and, after an interval in Ukiah, returned to San Francisco to go into business, this time in real estate. He occupied an office in the Sentinel Building (later renamed Columbus Tower and located at the corner of Columbus Avenue and Kearny Street), where a sign on his office door read simply: "A. Ruef, Ideas, Investments, and Real Estate." In January 1920, he received an official pardon from Governor William D. Stephens who explained his action as follows: "My action . . . is in no way predicated upon any doubt as to the justice of his conviction. I have been guided by the manifest spirit of our modern penal reformatory laws. . . . His conduct in prison and on parole has been exemplary and therefore I feel convinced that the exercise of the powers of legal clemency with which I am invested is warranted."

Although a man of wealth for some time, Ruef became almost impoverished when the decade 1925–1935 saw him losing considerable money in bad investments. At the time of his death, which occurred on February 29, 1936, his estate was found to be bankrupt. At the last rites performed in Halstead's Funeral Chapel on March 1, 1936, Rabbi Rudolph Coffee said: "He disproved Carlisle's famous line that 'No man is great to his own valet.' Abraham Ruef was greatest to those nearest him." Walton Bean's thoughtful words, in his authoritative treatment called *Boss Ruef's San Francisco: The Story of the Union Labor Party, Big Business and the Graft Prosecution* may be quoted here: "Had his unquestionably remarkable abilities appeared on the political scene earlier . . . it is interesting to speculate upon the power and success that might have been his." As the historical record has it now, though, it is small wonder that there is no street named after Abe Ruef in San Francisco!

When attention is turned to the place of Eugene Schmitz in San Francisco's history, it becomes evident that his is quite a different story from that of Ruef. Born in San Francisco in the same year as Ruef, 1864, he was the son of pioneer parents who saw to it that his musical education began early. His first employment was as a drummer boy at the Standard Theatre but, by 1900, he had advanced to the leadership of the Columbia Theatre orchestra where he also played first violin. His political life, for which, at first, he seems to have had no ambition or special aptitude, began when Ruef persuaded him to become the Union Labor candidate for mayor in the election of 1900.

Schmitz was an impressive and handsome man, always a commanding figure with a black beard and dignified appearance. Admittedly, his preparation for the position of mayor was not along the customary political lines; in retrospect, an initial mistake was his complete trust in Ruef at the beginning; this can be forgiven Schmitz, though, for Ruef had not yet shown his true colors at this early time. One reads so frequently in the many accounts written of Schmitz that he was unintelligent, and possessed of no real ability and, in fact, was a puppet dangling at the end of Ruef's string. That this was simply not so is amply revealed when one looks at the impressive record made by Mayor Schmitz in his handling the many details of the greatest crisis ever to come to San Francisco, that of the fire and earthquake of 1906. Not for nothing did Victor Metcalf, Secretary of Commerce and Labor in President Theodore Roosevelt's cabinet, report to his chief after a visit to San Francisco a week after the earthquake: "This man Schmitz has turned out pure gold in this emergency." Other similar words of commendation can also be adduced here, yet one seldom, if ever, finds them mentioned in the sweeping and condemnatory accounts of the life and labors of Eugene Schmitz.[5] Practically always he has been tarred with the same brush as Abe Ruef, and this is an historical injustice, for, although it was his misfortune to have been too closely associated with a professional corruptionist, this is hardly the same as making him one also.

When Investigator Burns arrived in San Francisco in June 1906, he quickly applied himself to the process of gathering evidence regarding allegedly corrupt practices in the civil government. A new Grand Jury was appointed in October and this group, after hearing confessions of bribe-taking by various supervisors as well as the testimony of prominent businessmen who gave such bribes, returned indictments against both Schmitz and Ruef. Many allegations of bribery were adduced against both men, and were just as strenuously denied by both; beginning on March 13, 1907, and spreading out over a period of almost three years, the famous Graft Trials brought much unwelcome publicity to San Francisco when the genuinely dishonest practices stemming from City Hall were exposed to public view. As expected, legal maneuvers were liberally resorted to and these were accompanied by the customary delaying tactics; at first, Ruef was granted immunity from prosecution after he confessed his guilt in charges of extorting money from various French restaurants in return for expediting their liquor licenses; however, he was then indicted on sixty-five counts for passing on bribes to some of the supervisors. After two long and stormy trials (which took place in Temple Sherith Israel at California and Webster streets since City Hall had been severely damaged in the earthquake and fire) Ruef, as mentioned, was convicted and sentenced to fourteen years in San Quentin Penitentiary.

On June 13, 1907, Mayor Schmitz was convicted of extortion in the same French restaurant cases. However, on January 9, 1908, his conviction was reversed by the state court of appeals (three judges unanimously concurring) and their findings were sustained unanimously by the seven members of the state supreme court; in this connection, one usually reads that "Schmitz was freed on a technicality," i.e. a faulty indictment that had failed to mention his position as mayor of San Francisco when he allegedly connived in the matter of bribes; however, the record is clear that all ten justices who reviewed his conviction agreed on three things: Schmitz had not received a fair trial; no evidence of a trustworthy character had established the fact, that indeed, he had been guilty of any wrongdoing (something that Schmitz was to maintain publicly and privately until his death); finally, the faulty indictment mentioned above. While denying under oath, and this many times, that he had received any bribes as alleged, the only direct evidence that he had done so was that furnished by Abe Ruef whose perjury became evident as the trials continued. The devious twistings and turnings that marked Ruef's tactics at this time, i.e. his repudiation of previous confessions, caused Prosecutor Francis J. Heney to declare in court that he found it impossible to trust any word uttered by Ruef. One should add to all of the above the additional fact that Frank Dunne, the superior court judge in the Schmitz trial, was hostile to the defendant from the beginning and made little or no pretense of impartiality. It should be noted, too, that in the midst of his long continuing travails, Mayor Schmitz was never without the support of such persons as Father Peter Yorke who, on June

14, 1907, the day after Schmitz's conviction, wrote as follows to the mayor's wife:

> Convey my best regards to the Mayor and tell him to continue to hold himself in the manly way he has during this whole miserable business. He has lost no friends that were worth losing. His enemies have done their worst and the darkest hour is just before the dawn.[6]

Similar sympathy was offered by a prominent Paulist priest of San Francisco, Father Henry Wyman, CSP, who had written to the mayor: "I sympathize with you most deeply because I believe that you are innocent of the crimes with which you have been charged by the Grand Jury."[7] (At a later date, San Francisco's perennial mayor, James Rolph, Jr., said of Schmitz: "I hope that I shall live long enough so that I can put that man [Schmitz] right before the world. He has been treated with the greatest injustice.")

Lest what has been written here, in an overdue effort to set the record straight about Mayor Schmitz, be considered a complete whitewash, it might be well to assert that, while no direct malfeasance was ever established in the Schmitz case i.e. no evidence of bribe-taking, it seems that, whether subjectively culpable or not, Schmitz was objectively guilty of a kind of misfeasance, in the sense that he was not sufficiently prompt in detecting convincing evidence of wrongdoing connected with his administration; after all, presumably he *did* read the newspapers and therefore knew what editor Older was saying about the situation in City Hall. (In this connection, it is tempting to make a general comparison with President Ulysses S. Grant who, in the midst of corruption galore, was not guilty of any direct malfeasance as the nation's chief executive; indeed, his distinguished secretary of state, Hamilton Fish, could write of Grant: "I have never met a man of more sensitive ethical perceptions!") Perhaps some of the political naiveté commonly attributed to Grant might be applied to Eugene Schmitz at this time. That he should have spoken out and completely divorced himself from the nefarious Ruef is abundantly clear now. Perhaps, however, it was not at all evident to Schmitz who seems rather to have gathered strength from his steadfast conviction that he was guilty of no wrong doing either personally or in his exercise of the office of mayor.

That Eugene Schmitz thought himself as innocent, especially after his successful appeal mentioned above, became apparent when he ran again for mayor, evidently in a move of self-vindication, in 1915 and again in 1919; he lost both times because few, if any, could have defeated the popular James Rolph, Jr. However, when Schmitz ran for supervisor in 1917, he was elected (which inspires the reflection that, had the voters of San Francisco been convinced of his prior guilt, they would hardly have returned him to City Hall). He served as supervisor until 1925 when an "economy ticket," such as appears periodically, sent Schmitz and most of the incumbents out of office. Poor health was to mark the rest of his life; although engaged in various business activities, he was by no means a man of wealth; finally, on November 20, 1928, a heart condition brought about his death, at sixty-four, in San Francisco.

Admittedly, the period of the Graft Prosecutions was an unhappy and distressing one in the history of San Francisco. Although over three thousand indictments were returned against some very prominent citizens, the combined wealth of many of these persons together with the tactics of the lawyers they employed, ultimately proved too much for the forces interested in civic reform. At times, bribed witnesses either conveniently lost their memories or disappeared. Finally, when District Attorney William H. Langdon chose not to seek reelection in 1909 (he had been the most prominent in the prosecutions) it became evident that many of those most concerned had become weary of the entire matter. Effectively therefore, the remaining indictments were dismissed. However, the forces of reform had made a lasting mark upon the civil government of San Francisco.

CHAPTER 30

THE STREETCAR STRIKE OF 1907:

Labor's Defeat

THESE PAGES HAVE treated of the successful strike (that of the Teamsters in San Francisco in 1901) which resulted in a Magna Carta for the cause of the workingman in the city. We must now record yet another significant strike, but this one resulted in major losses for that same cause of union labor.

Between 1881 and 1905, 37,000 strikes had been called in the United States. Since the turn of the century had seen considerable gains registered by labor in California, notably, in San Francisco, it was but natural that further attempts be made by labor to redress yet unresolved areas of dispute. In 1900, there were 217 unions in California; by 1902, the number had increased to 495, a 75 percent jump; the total membership of these groups grew by 125 percent. While there were 67,000 union members throughout California, it is revealing to note that 45,000 of this number lived in San Francisco. By 1902, then, the city was approximately 85 percent unionized and the San Francisco Labor Council had assumed a very important place in the local scene. A consequent fear of the rising tide of union labor quickly brought about the resurrection of that Employers' Association which again devoted itself to well-planned, well-financed, and steadfast opposition to any further gains on the part of labor. Against what they chose to call the "twin growing evils of the strike and the boycott," they swore a mighty oath and, against these same evils, they vowed a crusade. It would be only a matter of time before the two irreconcilable forces would be locked in mortal combat.

Among the enterprises hardest hit by the earthquake and fire of 1906 was the United Railroads which owned and operated most of the local streetcar lines. This company was a subsidiary of the United Railroads Investment Company of New Jersey, and this fact enabled the United Railroads to quickly absorb the losses consequent upon the disaster and to return, at least in part, to operation rather soon after the destruction of the mid-April days. Those who operated the cars and who had the best possible case for a legitimate improvement in their working conditions determined that it was now or never for them to settle for better working conditions and for a substantial increase in their low wages. Their chief objectives were an eight-hour day (ten hours still being the normal working day) and a wage increase from the daily $3.10, $3.20, or $3.30 they received according to the length of their service. The demand was not at all unreasonable; the union served notice that it would settle for a wage scale of 30¢ an hour. Although this represented a retreat from its first position which stipulated a wage scale of 37½¢ per hour, it was declared completely unacceptable by the Employers' union, fearful, if it yielded, that it would be at the mercy of its employees who would go on to further demands. It became apparent that a battle royal was shortly to develop between Richard Cornelius, who, in July 1901, had founded Local 205 of the Carmen's Union in San Francisco, and Patrick J. Calhoun, grandson of the famous Senator John C. Calhoun, then serving as president of the United Railroads in San Francisco. A third man of prominence in the dispute was Father Peter C. Yorke, already established as the firm friend of union labor; as founder and editor of the *Leader,* as well as a member of an earlier arbitration board which had heard the complaints of the carmen, Yorke had become convinced of the justice of the carmen's case, which he now supported by speeches as well as by powerfully written editorials in the *Leader.*

President Calhoun was convinced that he could break any strike proposed by the carmen and, indeed, events were to prove him correct. He let it be known that he would bring carmen in from other parts of the country in the event of a strike and it was evident that he meant business when, with just such a strike imminent, he began plans to convert several carbarns into first-aid stations and hospitals and, if necessary, into company arsenals. These would also serve as lodgings for the strikebreakers he would introduce to the city. As an example of his determination to follow through in his plan, it was not long before the McAllister Street carbarn, located between Masonic and Central Avenue, was converted into the appearance of a stockade, complete with a sentry walk for the use of armed guards. Thus complete defiance was the gauntlet laid down by Calhoun as he offered a reduced schedule of wages which the carmen, encouraged by Father Yorke, refused to accept. On May 1, 1907, a mass meeting was held in the Central Theatre where the union grievances were ventilated; the next day saw an uneasy conference between the two parties but no satisfactory accomplishments resulted from this meeting. The shrewd Calhoun correctly estimated that he would have the support of most of the local business interests in his fight to break the power of the Carmen's Union since they joined him in their resentment of the union's growing power. He knew that he was well prepared to do battle since he had arranged, as mentioned, to bring in well-trained carmen who, receiving premium wages (which many of them supplemented with passenger fares), carried weapons and were quite prepared to use them.[1]

After more fruitless negotiations marked by bitterness on both sides, the Carmen's Union called a strike beginning on May 5, 1907: it was to gain the dubious distinction of being the most violent streetcar strike ever seen in San Francisco or, possibly, in any American city. Since both sides were determined to settle for nothing less than complete victory, it was evident that a bitter struggle lay ahead. The calling of the strike meant, of course, that San Francisco's transportation was paralyzed. Coupled with the walkout of the carmen were several other strikes which seriously cut into union funds and which were to prove a contributory cause, eventually, to the loss of the strike on the part of labor. With 2,000 carmen on strike and dependent now on meagre union funds for strike benefits with which to support themselves and families, a time of unrest and violence visited the city. On May 5, President Calhoun gave the strikers two days to return to work; on their refusal to do so, he announced that he had 400 men in readiness to operate the cars while, on May 7, he ordered the strikebreakers to take out six of his cars. In this first attempt, as anticipated, a clash resulted between the armed "scabs," as they were called by the carmen, and the strikers and their sympathizers. The infuriated mob began to hurl rocks and bricks at the cars while the guards began a running gunfight; men fired revolvers from nearby lots, as detectives, guards, and private policemen fired from the sanctuary of the carbarn into the ranks of the enraged strikers. As a result, one young striker was killed and nineteen other men were wounded. This beginning of violence caused the daily papers to call upon the governor of California to send in the state militia to prevent other such incidents. Calling the day "Bloody Thursday," unionists joined with the city's chief of police in denouncing the shootings as a massacre brought about by imported gunmen. When the city administration, acting under pressure from a majority of concerned citizens, decided that calling in the state militia might be a disastrous move, Calhoun's hired hands were disarmed to some extent although there was more violence to come.

When, on May 16, the San Francisco Labor Council endorsed the strike and voted to boycott the cars of the three companies against which the strike had been declared, a period followed in which the daily passenger load dropped by 75 percent; many San Franciscans walked to work or sought other means of transportation to avoid riding on streetcars. It thus appeared that most of the citizens endorsed and, at first, supported the carmen in their legitimate struggle for a living wage. Father Yorke declared that this boycott was "the best guarantee we can have of industrial peace and economic prosperity in San Francisco." The slogan was "Keep Off of Calhoun's Cars!" At first the people did so but, as frequently happens, enthusiasm for the cause diminished as they became tired of walking; it was evident that Calhoun held the key cards for he had both money and time on his side. Sporadic outbreaks of physical violence occurred from time to time but not on the scale of the May 7 incident.

> United Railroads tried to restore normal operations—strikers and their sympathizers responded with boycotts and guerilla warfare. Unions imposed heavy fines on members seen on streetcars and the very real danger of physical harm frightened many cautious citizens away from the cars. Manned by strikebreakers openly wearing revolvers, the moving cars were frequently targets for bricks and, occasionally for bullets also.... Trees were cut down and laid across street car tracks in outlying districts while strikers were accused of greasing the rails on steep hillside sections of track. The United Railroads accident rate had always been high in hilly San Francisco but now it rose to an appalling level.[2]

For a tense three months, the strike continued, with Calhoun boasting that he would never recognize a carmen's union. An already critical condition was considerably complicated by the development of rifts in the ranks of labor, with some leaders supporting the mayoralty ambition of P.H. McCarthy while others favored Dr. Edward Taylor. When the labor leaders focused most of their attention on the coming election, many of the carmen felt that they had been betrayed and, in effect, forced to return to work on Calhoun's conditions. With characteristic honesty, Father Yorke attacked the labor leaders, who he felt were responsible for this turn of events; he felt that these leaders

> had imperilled "the greatest and most gallant fight ever made in San Francisco for the rights of labor. . . ." Calhoun declared that he could provide adequate street car service for the foot weary San Franciscans if the union boycott against his cars was removed. Public interest in the strike was on the wane. The general belief prevailed that the carmen had already lost the strike and public opinion was in favor of the removal of the union boycott.[3]

On September 9, 1907, the General Strike Committee decided on the tactic of lifting the boycott against the United Railroads, even urging their members to patronize the "Calhoun Cars," in an attempt to embarrass Calhoun by showing the public that the United Railroads could not maintain proper and safe service with its strikebreaking employees. However, by this action, in effect, the union and the strikers admitted defeat at the hands of the relentless Calhoun. Although the strike was not officially called off until March 1908, after the Union Labor party had suffered a defeat at the polls in November 1907, many carmen had long since abandoned any hope of success in their struggle. Indeed, on the day after the elections:

> . . . a number of the union carmen reported to the offices of the United Railroads and asked to be reinstated in their jobs. They were reemployed on condition that they would renounce their union. Three weeks later, Calhoun was confident that he had destroyed the Carmen's Union and declared that he would never again recognize Cornelius or his union. . . . Father Yorke was very bitter. The loss of the strike, he asserted, could be attributed to the division of labor over purely political issues. "What all the wealth of San Francisco could not do, what the threats of the Governor and the calling out of the

militia could not accomplish, what the unscrupulous cunning and brute force of Calhoun could not bring to pass, that the labor leaders did with their wretched politics. . . ."[4]

In summary, union labor's loss of this strike had many causes: the local press, especially the *Chronicle,* was procapital in its orientation and showed this bias openly; also the graft trials in progress at the time revealed that some Union Labor party members were involved in corrupt practices while the Carmen's Union ran out of money for strike benefits to its members. However, the immediate cause of the loss of the fight was, as already indicated, the simple fact that the local citizenry grew increasingly tired of walking. In the opinion of Knight:

> The carmen's defeat, however, was chiefly attributed to Patrick Calhoun's determined resistance and to the United Railroads financial ability to sustain the costs involved. "He has wiped us off the face of the earth." The demoralized Carmens Union turned in its charter in 1908 and Calhoun had destroyed one of the largest, best financed and most militant unions in San Francisco. He had convincingly demonstrated the power of a resolute employer and had so completely stifled the Carmens Union that the United Railroads enjoyed twenty-five years of freedom from strong labor opposition.[5]

Before it ended, the Carmen's strike had taken more lives than any other single strike in San Francisco's history. At least six had been shot to death (the number divided between both sides of the controversy) while more than two hundred and fifty had been injured.

CHAPTER 31

CONTRASTING ADMINISTRATIONS:
Edward R. Taylor
and P. H. McCarthy,
1908–1912

I

T WAS EVIDENT that those who occupied the mayor's chair in San Francisco's City Hall after it was vacated by Eugene Schmitz would be of special importance in the history of the city. The two who did so were most different persons in practically every respect yet each left distinctive marks upon the city they governed; one remains somewhat controversial even now.

Certainly one of San Francisco's most cultured and distinguished chief executives was Edward Robeson Taylor (1838–1923) who was mayor "ad interim" for half of 1907 and who served in his own right as 28th mayor from 1908 to 1910. His literary monuments are still enshrined all through the Main Library building in Civic Center and his bronze bust is exhibited directly inside its main entrance: it was placed there through the efforts of one of his predecessors as mayor, Senator James D. Phelan.

Edward R. Taylor was born in Springfield, Illinois, in 1838; in 1862, after serving for a time as printer and editor, he came to California via Panama. After clerking on a Sacramento riverboat, and using his spare time to study medicine, he entered Toland Medical College in San Francisco which, later, became the College of Medicine of the University of California. He graduated in 1865 and interned at St. Mary's Hospital, then located near Rincon Hill. Later, in 1869, he turned to politics when Governor Henry H. Haight appointed him as his private secretary. The governor urged him to study law which he did and, when Haight went out of office in 1871, Taylor was admitted to the bar and became the former governor's law partner. Later, he joined the faculty of Hastings College of the Law, serving as its dean from 1899 to 1910. It was from this latter position that he was persuaded to go to City Hall at a time of great crisis in civil government in San Francisco.

His arrival there in 1907 was the result of an interesting and unique procedure: Mayor Schmitz was convicted of extortion in June 1907 (this verdict was later reversed by higher courts) and, subsequently, the Board of Supervisors declared his office vacant; this was technically correct since under San Francisco's charter a felony conviction automatically deprives a mayor of office. Since it was highly desirable that one be obtained to fill the position who was above reproach in every respect, Dean Taylor, already enjoying a deserved reputation for integrity and known as a successful administrator, was soon considered to be the man of the hour. The supervisors elected him "ad interim," i.e. to fill out Mayor Schmitz's term, and he served in this capacity until January 8, 1908, when he started his own two-year term to which he had been elected in November 1907. Since the entire board which had appointed him resigned, as they were holdovers of the Ruef machine, Taylor had the pleasure of appointing a whole new board of supervisors and, as expected, they were all able and honest men.

He was sworn in as mayor on July 18, 1907. In a statement issued for the occasion, he asserted that "As mayor of this city, every man looks just as tall to me as every other man." Local papers were divided on his appointment: the *Examiner* opposed him and even ridiculed him for his obvious literary attainments for, already, he had shown some talent in the field of the literary essay as well as that of poetry. Unfortunately, he was not spared the sharp pen of Father Peter Yorke who seems also to have been suspicious of a man with such an education as Taylor "descending" into the arena of politics, an example of where Father Yorke could, at times, be very wrong in his judgments.

By the summer of 1907, the regular political organizations of both the Democratic and Republican parties in San Francisco were regarding the graft trials as exceedingly uncomfortable halters around their necks and neither party was overfond of running a reform candidate like Taylor for mayor. Out of this situation came the formation of a nonpartisan group with the appropriate motto of "Citizenship Above Partisanship" which supported the candidacy of the interim mayor. Sensing that he would be a winner, the Democratic party decided to hop on the Taylor bandwagon. A labor leader, P.H. McCarthy, destined to succeed Taylor as mayor in 1910, ran against him on the Union Labor ticket: the November elections saw Taylor winning handily with over 28,000 votes to 17,000 for McCarthy. Since Taylor was not a professional politician and had not the slightest intention of becoming one, he was not at all interested in perpetuating himself in office. Rather he devoted his two years of service, 1908–1910, to his announced objective of giving San Francisco an honest and efficient government. His integrity was known to all and it seems that he appeared, even if briefly, on San Francisco's political stage at just the right time. He did not run for reelection in 1909 but served out his term until January 8, 1910. Always a great lover of the literary arts, and an author in his own right, as a trustee of the Public Library for thirty-three years, Taylor had a major part in selecting the classical inscriptions that are to be found in various areas of the main library building in Civic Center. (While some are of classical origin, others were composed by him but none have his name accompanying them.) He was first married, in 1870, to Agnes Stanford, niece of Leland Stanford; after her death, his second spouse was Eunice Jeffers, whom he married in 1908. He lived many years after his short time of public service and died, aged eighty-five in 1923. Surely the distinguished memory of Edward Robeson Taylor should remain green in the civic and cultural history of San Francisco.

The political picture in general and that of the mayor's position in particular underwent considerable change when Taylor yielded the position to P.H. McCarthy (1863–1933) who served as 29th mayor of San Francisco from 1910 to 1912, and who, unlike his predecessor, retired in the latter year, after one term, with considerable reluctance. Union labor returned briefly to City Hall, then, when Patrick Henry ("PH" he was always called) McCarthy became mayor. When Taylor refused to run for another term, to which, almost certainly, he would have been reelected, politics took over as usual, with McCarthy meeting stiff opposition from his Democratic and Republican opponents. McCarthy received 29,000 of the almost 65,000 votes cast; Thomas Leland, his Democratic opponent, got over 19,000 votes, while the Republican candidate, William Crocker, tallied almost

14,000. As usual, a split ticket of a three-way candidacy brought defeat to the two traditional parties and awarded the mayor's position to P.H. McCarthy. (Surely the mayor-elect was conscious of the fact that more of the citizenry had voted against him than for him.) A word, now, about his background and earlier career and the forces that brought him to political eminence in San Francisco.[1]

"PH" was born in County Limerick, Ireland, on March 17, 1863, and died in San Francisco, aged seventy, in 1933. McCarthy prefaced his years in the city with service as an apprentice carpenter in Chicago, where, in 1881, he arrived from Ireland aged eighteen and where, eventually, he became quite knowledgeable in labor circles. Although his was the trade of carpenter, he seems to have been considerably more interested in labor organizations and the politics connected with them; it was not long before he became involved in endeavors to better labor conditions in Chicago and these experiences included a first hand acquaintanceship with the effectiveness of the strike weapon when it was correctly wielded. Before coming to San Francisco, McCarthy also gained more valuable experience in St. Louis; with other artisans there, he organized the United Brotherhood of Carpenters and Joiners of America which was destined to develop into a body of skilled mechanics with national influence. All this experience was to render him the more acceptable in San Francisco's labor circles when he arrived in the city in 1886. For most of a half century, he was to be intimately (and powerfully) associated with labor unionism in the city. Eventually he worked successfully for the creation of a coordinating agency which emerged as the San Francisco Building Trades Council; he was to serve as the acknowledged leader of this council for almost thirty years. Earlier, he had learned the lesson that, in unity, and in unity only, lies effective strength in the built-in antagonisms that frequently exist between labor and management and he was skillful in using his knowledge in this respect. When, in August 1900, a dramatic lockout of planing mill employees was staged in the area, the San Francisco Council responded by setting up its own mill which was the largest west of Chicago. This novel and successful idea, together with its profitable operation for six months, made the owners of the struck mills decide to come to terms with

McCarthy and his cohorts. It was a notable victory for union labor in San Francisco.

An arbitration board, still much of a novelty at the time, was set up; equal representation of labor and management was provided for and a settlement was reached on February 19, 1901, when labor won the eight-hour day which had been the principal object of its strike. In 1906, still heading the council, McCarthy threw the full weight of the group as well as his own influence into the task of rebuilding San Francisco; the next few years were those of high wages for carpenters and others engaged in associated activities, and McCarthy did not suffer because of this fortunate turn of events. Earlier, in 1896, he had been active in securing a provision in the City Charter, then being revised, granting an eight-hour day to city employees. During this time, Mayor Phelan had also engaged his services as a Civil Service Commissioner.

An area of still unsettled controversy involves the assertion that he was for an "Open Town," the implication being that he was quite willing to tolerate, if not encourage, a loose moral atmosphere for San Francisco. Oscar Lewis thus reflects on the matter:

> One of McCarthy's campaign promises had been to make San Francisco the "Paris of America." This proved to be shrewd politics, for the public, weary of the austerities of the reconstruction period, welcomed the prospect of a return to the light-hearted gaiety that had long been a characteristic of the city. But many came to realize that what the mayor had in mind was a return to the practices of the era before the fire when gambling, prostitution and other rackets had flourished virtually without hindrance. Although the public was in favor of preserving those qualities which had given the earlier town its charm, it was in no mood to incorporate into the new San Francisco the worst features of the old.[2]

Mayor McCarthy openly resented this interpretation of his desires with regard to San Francisco, insisting only that he wished that some of the outstanding cultural and scenic features of the incomparable Paris be brought to San Francisco. He said that his phrase referred to his wish that "a resurgent San Francisco should quickly take its legitimate place once more among the truly great cities of the world." The situation was clouded by the built-in opposition to McCarthy of the more wealthy classes of the city who would have wished for a mayor from the ranks of business rather than labor. Thus, his years in office found "PH" subjected to the strain and misunderstandings that commonly attend the service of the commonwealth. A local history thus comments:

> McCarthy was committed to the policy of liberality towards those phases of the city's life indicated by his euphemistic campaign promise to make San Francisco the "Paris of America." But the citizens proved unwilling to accept this return to an earlier era. . . . It was presently obvious that the phrase was intended in another sense, one that was more fittingly described by another slogan that came into use, making San Francisco an "open town." Here was a phase of the old city that a majority of the inhabitants were quite content to let pass with April 18, 1906. The election of 1911 produced decisive evidence on this point. The ticket headed by James Rolph, Jr. was swept into office.[3]

While it remains entirely possible to interpret the McCarthy slogan in either sense it is doubtful anyone on the political scene at the time in San Francisco could have successfully withstood the rising popularity of one who was to be perennial mayor, from 1912 to 1931, and whose years in City Hall deserve to be known as the "Age of Rolph" in San Francisco's history. To this fascinating person, the beloved "Sunny Jim" Rolph, we now turn our attention. (McCarthy remained important in the labor scene of the city until his death in 1933. He headed the Building Trades Council until 1922, serving as its advisor for some years after. Later, until his death, P.H. McCarthy was in the contracting business.)

CHAPTER 32

PERENNIAL MAYOR:
"Sunny Jim" Rolph

ONE OF THE largest and most affectionate parts played in San Francisco's past was by one who will always be remembered as "Sunny Jim" Rolph, as authentic a lover of the city as can possibly be found. James Rolph, Jr. was born on August 23, 1869, south of Market on Minna Street. Among the many distinctions attending his name and memory is the fact that he was elected 30th mayor of San Francisco to serve five terms of four years each; in 1911, the revised city charter had changed the term of office of the mayor from two to four years. While serving his fifth term, Rolph was elected governor of California, and died in office on June 2, 1934.

Rolph was the oldest of seven children; his father, an employee of the Bank of California, was a man of modest means and Rolph's first source of income was realized form selling newspapers and running errands for his neighbors. After attending public school, he went to Trinity School, which was church-related (Rolph was a lifetime Episcopalian) under the control of Trinity Episcopal Church at Bush and Gough streets. Graduating in 1888, at nineteen, Rolph filled the position of messenger in the firm of Kittle and Company, devoted to the shipping business. His interest here came naturally since his uncle, Augustus Rolph, was a prominent member of the English firm of John Black and Company, a circumstance that brought about the appointment of James Rolph, Sr. as San Francisco's agent for the firm. Young Rolph was never to lose his interest in this type of commercial activity, and he stayed with Kittle and Co. until he was able to start his own firm; this he did when, in 1898, he formed a partnership with George Hind, and Hind, Rolph, and Co. was born: each contributed $2,500 and the pair obtained the temporary use of two ships from Hind's father. The company prospered and soon their blue and white house flag was known from Valparaiso to the Antipodes; by 1908, they possessed a fleet of ten vessels. Previously, in 1903, Rolph had been the founder of Mission Bank which he served as its first president. These busy years saw him recognized, then, as one of the more promising of San Francisco's native sons as his name became better known in commercial and social circles. In 1910, he married Anna M. Reid and he was soon busy with a young family which eventually consisted of a son and two daughters. As yet, Rolph showed no special interest in politics. By 1906, however, the first of the several "Ages of Rolph" came to an end.

Among those whose qualities of leadership were shown when most needed, during and after the days of earthquake and fire, was James Rolph, Jr. He was among the founders of the Mission Relief Association with offices in the Rolph family barn which was located on San Jose Avenue. Hundreds of citizens quickly obtained needed relief through the good offices of this organization. In a sense, his public career began at this time for the press frequently carried his name in reporting relief and other activities. He was prominent in promoting the Portola Festival in 1909 which was staged to show the country and the world that a new San Francisco had indeed risen from the ashes of the old. When he was elected president of the Shipowner's Association of the Pacific, Rolph's prominence caused some friends to insist that the time was at hand for him to enter public service. However, as late as June 1909, he withstood the request of a committee of his friends that he run for mayor, and it was not until 1911 that he was finally persuaded to throw his hat into the political arena. Once in that ring, his hat was to remain there until his death as governor of California in 1934.

Why was Rolph persuaded to run for the office of mayor of his city in 1911? Many who shared the view that Mayor McCarthy was not successful in meeting the problems that confronted the city turned instinctively to the forty-two-year-old, well-liked businessman who, a true lover of San Francisco, was already showing some of that distinctive color and style which was to become his hallmark. Rolph was obviously the man of the hour. Although, a moderately successful businessman and, therefore, a capitalist, he lived among and loved the people of his Mission district. A key to Rolph's perennial popularity was that he never seems to have lost the common touch which flowed out from him with complete sincerity. When Rolph issued an acceptance statement upon filing for candidacy as mayor in 1911, it received the immediate approval of an impressive number of citizens of all classes. On August 31, 1911, Rolph launched his campaign, with a major address at the Globe Theatre in which he told the overflow audience that he had not accepted the nomination for the office of mayor "with a light mind." He then proceeded to show that he had a head as well as a heart and his later distinguished career demonstrated that he put both to good use. That night, a slogan was born: "Sunny Jim Rolph is our man" and he was to be "Sunny Jim" to the end of his life, though his last years as governor of California were marked by illness. His colorful campaign reminded some of the flamboyant tactics used by Theodore Roosevelt for, like the irrepressible "TR," Rolph quickly became the darling of the pressrooms since he always furnished more than abundant copy.

It was evident that P.H. McCarthy could not match this man; election day, September 26, 1911, saw Rolph winning the election by more than 20,000 votes. McCarthy had wounds to lick when he was defeated by Rolph in his own district. The workingmen were embracing the shipowner and this was attributed correctly to the fact that the mayor-elect genuinely liked them as well. This love for the people was a real one, as many an incident was to reveal; even his manner of dressing was distinctive and he was already known as a wearer of natty suits matched by impeccably polished boots, while his lapel was invariably decked with a carnation or some other type of flower. Gradually, it was understood that Mayor Rolph should be greeted publicly at meetings and other events with what came to be regarded as his theme song—"Smiles"—with the words: "There are smiles that make you happy." Rolph would frequently lead the rest of the song himself with or without benefit of baton, thus carrying the tune through to a thunderously applauded conclusion. These were the days, then, of incomparable color in the history of the office of mayor in San Francisco and they matched the past of what has never been considered a dull city.

It is time now to examine another of the Ages of Rolph: his

almost twenty years (a record never since matched) as mayor of San Francisco. During these years, all races and creeds found a good friend in Rolph and most San Franciscans rejoiced that such a large-hearted man was for so long at the helm of the civic ship of state. It would not seem an exaggeration to say that, from 1912 to 1931, San Francisco was, in a measure, "Sunny Jim" Rolph while, in equal measure, "Sunny Jim" represented the best in San Francisco.[1] He was no intellectual genius nor did he pretend to be one; as indicated, however, the record is abundantly clear that Rolph used both head and heart plus a genuine love for San Francisco to the best of his considerable ability. During his earliest years in City Hall, Rolph was a wealthy man, although severe financial reverses were his later on; his monthly salary of five hundred dollars was frequently devoted to charitable uses, as the number of those who sought financial aid increased.

Although Rolph's many years as mayor were marked by memorable events, among the most noteworthy were those associated with the building of a new City Hall during the early years of his rule. From ground-breaking (April 5, 1913) to dedication day (December 29, 1915) Rolph lived the story of the City Hall: on the day of dedication, he proudly told the vast multitude gathered there that "I take pride in this building because it typifies the Spirit of San Francisco. Three times she has been destroyed by fire and, each time, she has risen more magnificently." At the end of his address, a procession was formed while the mayor and his wife opened the doors of City Hall and went to his office. Other distinguished buildings in Civic Center were to adorn the Rolph years: earlier in 1915, on January 5, the Exposition Auditorium was dedicated, with the main branch of the Public Library following on February 15, 1917. Naturally, too, the opening of the Panama Pacific International Exposition in February 1915, was an event tailored to that cloth which was already distinctively Rolph's; he saw to it that he played a major part in all its principal activities until its closing in late November 1915.

No law prevents a mayor of San Francisco from having a private business in addition to fulfilling the functions of mayor; consequently Rolph kept an active interest in his shipping business in his early mayoral years. Although he was to endure a

financial debacle with a loss of about $3 million, he never lost his
debonair smile and never forgot, in the words of the poet:
"Laugh, and the world laughs with you; weep, and you weep
alone." He endeavored to repay all his creditors, and seems to
have pretty well done so by the end of the 1920s only, in 1929,
to witness the beginning of the Great Depression.

This was but the beginning of a most unsettled time in the
history of California and the nation; some political leaders, in
what, in retrospect, may be thought of as an understandable
mistake, seem to have sensed that the pulse of California
would be helped and quickened by the presence, in Sacramento, of an experienced and well-loved man such as
Mayor Rolph. Finally, Rolph was persuaded to run for governor, and after another colorful campaign which found him a
veteran who had not lost his charm, he was elected California's governor on November 4, 1930. Although he was to
serve as twenty-seventh governor of California, he was only
the third native son to occupy the post since 1850, when
American rule came to California. Characteristically, when
inaugurated, he invited the entire state to attend the ceremonies and to participate in the inaugural ball. Also characteristically, Governor Rolph plunged into the many duties of his
new office with enthusiasm; however, it is probable that the
massive problems that were now his, some of them beyond
any solution known to him or to his advisors, made the perennial mayor of San Francisco long for the former days of
happiness that had been his in City Hall. Rolph gradually
broke under the relentless strains of his office and, suffering
several heart attacks, he was ordered by his doctors to un-
dergo a period of complete rest. This he took at Riverside
Ranch near Agnew, Santa Clara County, where an old friend,
Walter Linforth, invited him to recuperate. This was not to
be, for there, on June 2, 1934, Sunny Jim Rolph answered the
call of death.

With Rolph's demise, it was undeniable that someone and
something had passed not easily replaced in either his beloved
city or state. Among the tributes paid him were those of several
associates who knew him well; a lawyer confidante, Thomas
Hickey, said of him: "What finer tribute could be paid to any man

than to be able to say with truth that the number of those who loved him increased with the years?" Another close friend, Judge Matt Sullivan, added these words of affection: "He was the humanest human being I ever knew. He was a man of heart more than head, and whatever his faults were, the reason was that his heart was too big!"

CHAPTER 33

THE
MOONEY-BILLINGS
CASE

. . . There was never any scientific attempt made by either the police or the prosecution to discover the perpetrators of the crime. The investigation was in reality turned over to a private detective who used his position to cause the arrest of the defendants. The police investigation was reduced to a hunt for evidence to convict the arrested defendants. . . .

Statement of the
Wickersham Commission
in 1929 (U.S. Government
Fact Finding Committee
on the Preparedness Day
Bombing).

T

HE LABOR MOVEMENT in San Francisco has had its ebbs and flows. Some of the earlier gains which made the city a citadel of union labor have already been mentioned; here our story centers around a bloody incident which eventually had worldwide repercussions resulting in a cause célèbre that made household words of the names of Thomas J. Mooney and Warren K. Billings.

By 1916, the United States, close to active participation in World War I, was the scene of several Preparedness Day parades; one took place in New York City and was staged with the acknowledged purpose of finding the country prepared in the event that it entered the European war. A second parade was scheduled for San Francisco for Saturday, July 22, 1916. It was denounced as soon as plans for it were made known; anti-preparedness feeling ran strong in San Francisco, as responsible labor leaders as well as radicals and others opposed the idea of fighting a war in far-off Europe for what they considered to be the benefit of the merchant and capitalistic classes. A radical protest put it bluntly: "Our protests have been in regard to the preparedness day propaganda, so we are going to use a little direct action on the 22nd to show that militarism can't be forced on us and our children without a violent protest."[1]

Other tensions involving labor were at a boiling point in California in 1916. Open opposition between the San Francisco Chamber of Commerce and labor unions sprang from mutual distrust; actually, a Law and Order Committee, reminiscent of the earlier Vigilance Committees, had been formed by merchants and others who considered the increasing demands of labor their largest threat. On balance, it looked as though labor was diminishing in political and other clout and this threat to their hard-earned gains served to further complicate the situation. Against this background, the tragic events of July 22, 1916, may be better understood.

Most of San Francisco's civic organizations, with the exception of the labor unions, agreed to participate in what they regarded as a patriotic parade. By mid day of Saturday, July 22, 1916, a large gathering of people, headed by Governor Hiram Johnson and Mayor James Rolph, was preparing to move up Market Street. Suddenly, at 2:06 P.M., near the intersection of Steuart and Market streets, not far from the Embarcadero, there was a bomb explosion, which caused the death of ten people and injuries to forty more. Prompt investigation traced the explosion to a bomb wired to a clock; both had been concealed inside a suitcase that was deposited against the wall of a building at Steuart and Market streets. The shock and sadness felt by San Franciscans and others was of such a nature that it was imperative that the police produce the guilty person or persons. They professed to do so in the persons of two who were already known as extreme radicals —Thomas J. Mooney and Warren K. Billings.

Tom Mooney (1882?–1942) had long been known in San Francisco as a left-wing radical completely dedicated to the revolutionary cause. This put him high on the list of suspects with the commission of any terroristic act. Mooney had employed the services of Warren K. Billings (1893–1972), another radical who also had, by 1916, served a term in Folsom Prison as a conspirator with Mooney in a case involving the unlawful transportation of explosives. Police, conscious of Billings's past, charged him almost immediately, like Mooney, with guilt in the Preparedness Day bombing. Sacrificial victims were quickly called for in the hysteria that marked San Francisco after the bombing. Within several days, Mooney, his wife Rena, Billings, and two others were arrested and jointly indicted for the murder of Hetta Knapp, one of the victims. Billings was tried first; he was convicted and sentenced to life imprisonment—the death penalty was not asked for by the prosecution since their view was that Billings had been but a tool of a smarter man, Mooney. He was the next to be tried and, at the end of thirteen days of trial, during which 154 witnesses testified, the jury returned a verdict of guilty of murder in the first degree without recommendation of clemency. Mooney was sentenced to be hanged; this was the beginning of a long campaign on his behalf. It was to continue during the twenty-two years that Mooney was a prisoner in San Quentin. In 1939, both Mooney and Billings were released from prison (Billings had been at Folsom). The latter was released by way of parole, while Mooney received a full pardon, something for which he and his friends had been working for many years. Mooney did not live long to enjoy it; he was in poor health and, after spending much time in a local hospital, he died in San Francisco in 1942. Billings, who had been a watchmaker by trade, returned to this work; for many years he had his own business in the Grant Building on Market Street, and later he worked part-time in a jewelry store on Maiden Lane. He died in Redwood City on September 4, 1972.[2] Both men, seemingly with reason, protested their innocence of the crimes which had kept them so long behind bars.

It is now virtually certain, from exhaustive and scholarly work done on the case, that the two, while hardly model Americans and while probably never without revolutionary designs, were, in simple fact, not guilty of the San Francisco Preparedness Day bombings attributed to them. Essentially, the evidence against them rested on the testimony of two men; they were an Oregon cattleman, Frank C. Oxman, and an itinerant waiter, John McDonald. While Oxman testified that he had seen the two at the scene of the crime, it was later proven that he was in Woodland, California, at that precise hour. McDonald later admitted to perjuring himself in what he had said about the two men. Even though Oxman had been thoroughly discredited by 1921, when efforts were continuing to "Free Tom Mooney" as the slogan had it, the State Supreme Court, in a singularly bad decision, allowed the use of his testimony. In 1928, Judge Franklin A. Griffin, a distinguished jurist who had presided at the Mooney trial, wrote a letter to Governor C. C. Young in which he said: "Every witness who testified against Mooney has been shown to have testified falsely. There is now no evidence against him. There is not a serious suggestion that any exists." When, in 1929, the United States Government Wickersham Commission, which had been appointed to review

Tom Mooney with his sister, Anna Mooney, left, and his wife, Rena, right, leaving San Quentin. San Francisco Archives, Public Library

the entire case, reported its findings, it used strong language concerning the type of witness in the case.

> . . . a weird procession consisting of a prostitute, two syphilitics, a psycopathic liar and a woman suffering from spiritualistic hallucinations.

Earlier, in 1917, President Wilson had sent a Mediation Commission to San Francisco to investigate. In due time, the group reported that there was no evidence of Mooney's guilt. Since Mooney was still under sentence of hanging, President Wilson wrote to Governor Stephens for a stay of execution. In November 1918, Mooney's sentence was changed to life imprisonment. But it was to be a long uphill fight before final vindication came in 1939.

Naturally, San Francisco newspapers carried full coverage of the "Mooney-Billings Case" as it was known. A pro-labor paper, the *News,* had this to say at the time of the pardon:

> Thus the Mooney case came to be a blot upon the fair name of the fairest state in the Union. Court after court, Governor after Governor, perpetuated the strain by failure to recognize the essential truth that the evidence upon which Mooney was convicted was, from beginning to end, a flimsy tissue of lies, perjury and doubt. . . . Tom Mooney in prison was a symbol of injustice, a martyr to the cause of human liberty. He can no longer be a martyr. But he can be a powerful voice in advancing the cause of workers everywhere.[3]

The pardon issued to Mooney in 1939 by Governor Culbert L. Olson, who kept a campaign pledge that he would issue it were he elected, expressed the governor's emphatic view that there had been a massive miscarriage of justice which he was determined to rectify. This he did by granting "a full and unconditional pardon of the crime of murder in the first degree to Thomas J. Mooney."

In retrospect, the Mooney-Billings case appears to represent one of the most tragic miscarriages of justice in American legal history.[4]

CHAPTER 34

MARITIME AND GENERAL STRIKE OF 1934

O
N MAY 27, 1851, the *San Francisco Daily Alta California* carried the following item:

CITY INTELLIGENCE—A STRIKE—A lot of stevedores and longshore sailors struck for wages yesterday, raising the banner of $6.00 a day and paraded the streets during the morning.

This appears to be the first example of a strike affecting the waterfront of San Francisco. Out of it and similar agitation came, on July 25, 1853, the formal organization of the Riggers and Stevedores Union Association; however, this was a trade union that refused to organize unskilled labor. From this beginning came years of struggle and a widening gap between maritime and allied workers and management. However, with the 1880s came some years of accomplishment for the cause of the "stevedores and longshore sailors." Several more unions came into being to counter this. In 1886, the Shipowners Protective Association was organized in San Francisco and this became the first group of employers in America to specifically ally themselves against labor. At the turn of the century, the Longshore Unions affiliated with the AFL International Longshoremen's Association and, in 1901, organized the City Front Federation to represent the sizable number of about 15,000 longshoremen, seamen, and teamsters in San Francisco.[1]

The next decade was marked by continued maneuvers on the part of both the unions and the employers to obtain their different objectives. As an example, in 1914, the employers, in another attempt to eliminate the closed shop, formed the Waterfront Employers Association. The basic strategy was one of the oldest known in such matters: separate the longshoremen and seamen's unions and crush each separately. The moment came in June 1916, when the ILA called a coastwide strike in an attempt to gain higher wages and a coastwide closed shop. The union failed to get needed support and went down to defeat. The greatest significance with regard to San Francisco was that the local Chamber of Commerce for the first time launched an active campaign on behalf of the employers. A California labor historian wrote as follows:

> The strike, as is usual in water-front labor conflicts, was marked by violence, forty-five cases of assault being recorded. The San Francisco Chamber of Commerce then reversed its policy of non-interference in labor disputes and organized a Law and Order Committee, hoping by this means it might free the employer interests of the city from union domination.[2]

Another disturbance came in 1919 when the longshoremen again struck and were again defeated. Cross records what happened: "A split then occurred in the ranks of the Union and a company union, the Longshoremen's Association, was formed with the aid of the shipowners. During the next fourteen years this was the only longshoremen's union recognized and dealt with by the shipping interests."[3] The closed shop had perished on San Francisco's waterfront. This union became known as the Blue Book Union, after the color of their dues book, and, in December 1919, signed a five-year contract under open shop conditions. By 1921, the maritime unions of San Francisco had been virtually crushed. Another commentator puts it this way:

> The years between 1921–1933 saw less activity of labor unions than at any other period of San Francisco's history. For once it was a long period of industrial peace. The labor unions had been destroyed. San Francisco was an open shop town. No longer was it possible for labor to control the commerce in and out of the harbor. . . . Ironically enough these were the years when the Port of San Francisco suffered most. . . .[4]

These same years were those of discontent on the waterfront. The overall picture saw the era as one of too little work coupled with special privileges which discouraged many who were not their recipients. "Star Gangs" composed of about one thousand available stevedores got most of the work and the highest wages while the "casuals" (the remaining three-quarters) got what was left. Gang bosses demanded and received kickbacks and other such favors. Speedups and lack of overtime pay were other complaints. When the depression of the early 1930s came, discontent reached its peak. Among others, radicals, communists and IWW members harangued the discontented longshoremen and goaded them to demand needed reforms. Since the time appeared ripe, a combination of these factors led to the determination to reestablish the old International Longshoremen's Association. The new ILA quickly gained strength and, in October 1933, struck against the Matson Navigation Company. The strikers were both delighted and surprised at the ease with which they won this latest of strikes. Camp remarks:

> Water front workers claimed that conditions in the Port of San Francisco were the worst in the world and when Dr. Paul Eliel, speaking for the Employers, made this admission, it added great weight to the claims of longshoremen, in the troublous years which followed. . . . The "Blue Book" Union did nothing to improve conditions along the water front and its death in 1933 was admittedly the best thing that had happened there in many a year. . . .[5]

The next year, 1934, was to prove critical, resulting, eventually, in a general strike. The industrial peace of the city was threatened by several factors. Depression spawned an army of unemployed with bitter competition for any sort of work. (Some of these unemployed were to provide a future reserve of strikebreakers.) Profits were down and the shipping companies depended for existence upon government subsidies. These companies correctly foresaw that a strong maritime union would make demands which they professed themselves unable to meet. In 1933, they determined once more to move in on the new ILA after its initial victory. With 4,000 longshoremen and only about 1,300 available jobs, the stage was set for a bitter struggle, which was not long in coming. Injustices provided abundant fodder for radical demagogues. Even though the actual extent of their infiltration into the maritime unions is probably overestimated, their influence and prodding was very real.

By early 1934, the feeling was growing that the day was near at hand when conflict was inevitable; determined opposition to union demands was met by as much determination to press these same claims. What had been long a dormant volcano on San

Francisco's waterfront was due to erupt. All that was needed was an occasion for active confrontation. It soon came. In February 1934, the resurrected ILA decided to challenge the Waterfront Employers Association. Calling a convention of maritime workers to meet in San Francisco on February 24, delegates representing all the Pacific Coast ports responded; a set of union demands, which included an hourly wage of $1, a thirty-hour week, a six-hour day, and the regulation of all hiring through the union hall, was submitted to the employers who were told that they had until March 7 to accept the demands or a strike vote would be taken. The employers, realizing the implications behind the demands, rejected the proposals. In advertisements in San Francisco newspapers, they defended their right to hire whomever they pleased, adding that they had no authority to authorize such a coastwide agreement. On March 7, the ILA voted to strike the ports of the West Coast on March 23. On March 22, answering an appeal from President Roosevelt to delay the strike until an impartial, fact-finding investigation could be made, the strike was postponed. A fact-finding board was appointed and met, but its efforts came to naught. More conferences were held and deadlocked until the union set May 7 as a new deadline. On May 8, the district president of the ILA issued a statement that "no one, not even President Roosevelt, can stop this strike now except an agreement on the part of our employers to conform to our demands." The strike was set for the next day. It came off on schedule when

> ... as dawn came that morning, longshoremen in Seattle, Bellingham, Tacoma, Aberdeen, Astoria, Gray's Harbor, San Francisco, San Pedro, Stockton, Oakland and San Diego arose as usual and went toward the waterfronts. They gathered as usual at piers and waterfront sheds but they did not report for work. The strike was solid, all up and down the coast. It was estimated that more than 12,000 men quit work that day.[6]

Employers were quick to use strikebreakers in an effort to keep the ports open; they probably would have succeeded in this move were it not that the Teamsters Union, San Francisco Local 85, ordered its members not to haul to or from the docks. (In this sympathy gesture, they were returning a similar favor which had

been paid to them by Bay Area maritime workers in the Teamsters strike of 1901.) Other unions now joined in support of the
strikers; when, on May 13, the national president of the ILA,
Joseph Ryan, asked the strikers to modify their demands and
came from New York to further this request, he made the fatal
mistake of by-passing the rank-and-file membership of the local
ILA, persuading their officers to join him in dealing directly with
the employers. An agreement was drawn up with the employers
which was promptly rejected when put to the rank-and-file vote.
This repudiation of Ryan was followed by a yielding of the more
conservative members of the ILA as they gave way to the more
persuasive influence of the liberals led by Harry Bridges.

On June 18, Bridges was responsible for the organization of a
Joint Marine Strike Board consisting of five members from each
of the striking unions. Bridges was chairman, of course, and from
then on he directed the strike. The longshoremen announced
their intention of never concluding a separate agreement; while
public opinion did not, at the outset, favor the strikers, this began
to change and President Roosevelt was called on to appoint a
mediation board. He did so, with the respected Archbishop Edward J. Hanna of San Francisco as chairman and Assistant Secretary of Labor E.F. McGrady and O.K. Cushing, a San Francisco
lawyer, named to serve with him. While some questions were
settled, an agreement could not be reached on the union demand
that they, and they alone, control the hiring halls on the water-
fronts. This time, though, the unions announced that they would
arbitrate this question provided the employers would deal with
all the unions involved, and not merely the ILA. Since this condition was unacceptable to the employers, the latter decided that
the time had come to use any and all efforts to crush the strike.
From May 9 to the end of June, tensions mounted as clash after
clash occurred between strikers and strikebreakers. Here is how
these days were described:

> Everywhere assaults were increasing in number and viciousness.
> Steamship executives, employees and strikers were under constant
> threat: bricks and milk bottles full of creosote flew through windows,
> beaten and mutilated bodies floated in the Bay. Docks became so
> congested that strikebreakers could no longer work. The one month
> strike cost San Francisco $300,000,000.[7]

General Strike, 1934. San Francisco Archives, Public Library

The commerce of San Francisco was virtually paralyzed, with thousands of tons of perishable goods left rotting on the docks; it was estimated that the losses accruing to all concerned amounted to about $700,000 each day the waterfront was closed.[8] A rumor, not without foundation, that city authorities had decided to open the port by using all necessary means further inflamed the longshoremen who were convinced of the justice of their cause; it was evident that if any attempt was made by local authorities, it would be resisted by the thoroughly aroused strikers. This was to bring San Francisco to a crucial and sad day in its history—the so-called "Bloody Thursday" of July 5, 1934.

The movement to open the port had begun as early as June 2, when the San Francisco Chamber of Commerce had written a letter to the Industrial Association, the same organization that had broken the earlier strike of 1919. The letter requested that, because of the enormous losses being sustained by the continuing strike, a movement be spearheaded by the association joined with civil authorities to open the beleaguered port. By July 1, this request had become a demand for action and the Industrial Association decided to open the Port of San Francisco. Mayor Angelo J. Rossi promised ample police protection since he considered the move a necessary one. The association organized the Atlas Trucking Company, manned its trucks with strikebreakers and, in a proclamation in the press, informed San Franciscans that:

THE PORT IS OPEN

Beginning July 3, the Industrial Association is moving goods to and from the waterfront. We will do this only until citizens are at full liberty to move their own goods. The San Francisco waterfront is public property. All citizens are entitled to use it without interference. The port of San Francisco is now open to the business of San Francisco.[9]

The first test came on the morning of July 3, 1934, as police cleared pickets from the front of Pier 38 and the operation began as planned. As the trucks attempted to leave the pier, they were met with an onrush of strikers who were repulsed by tear gas and the night sticks of the police. Thirteen police and a dozen strikers were the casualties of this first day, but this was but a prelude to what was to happen two days later in a tension-filled city.

Wednesday proved to be a lull before the storm. By daylight of July 5, on what was to become known as "Bloody Thursday," thousands of longshoremen, sailors, and other maritime workers roamed the Embarcadero in an ugly mood. This was to result in the most important day of the strike. Ira Cross indicates the sequence of events:

> With trucks manned by strikebreakers, goods were moved from the docks to the warehouses but no farther. Strikers and their sympathizers were too active. Trucks were overturned; some were burned; goods were dumped into the street; police and pickets clashed; a riot occurred. Tear gas and pistols were met with cobblestones and brickbats. More than a hundred were seriously wounded and other hundreds were injured.[10]

Accounts of the exact circumstances that resulted in the shooting and death of two union men on "Bloody Thursday" are still controversial; it is enough to indicate here that the death by gunfire of two longshoremen, Howard Sperry and Nicolas Bordoise, further inflamed the passions of their co-workers. Governor Merriam was presented with a petition from the San Francisco Junior Chamber of Commerce to proclaim martial law in the city; while refusing (Mayor Rossi was opposed to such a declaration mindful, perhaps, that San Francisco had come through her days of crisis in 1906 without resorting to martial law) the governor sent 500 National Guard troops to protect state property along the Embarcadero. The presence of the National Guard, the use of the police force and their protection of strikebreakers caused the San Francisco Labor Council to appoint a Strike Strategy Committee which recommended that a General Strike vote be put before the various unions.

The death of the two workers, angrily attributed to deliberate police action by the strikers, served to prove a turning point in the strike. Up to that time, public opinion had been divided; however, after a solemn funeral procession in which 10,000 men marched up Market Street in silence led by a uniformed honor guard of World War veterans, opinion shifted in favor of the strikers. The employers once again offered to arbitrate all issues but remained adamant in refusing to deal with any others but the longshoremen. Refusing to abandon the other unions who had supported them, the stage was set for a general strike. It came between July 16 and 19, 1934. Although the date set for the beginning of a general strike was Monday, July 16, it was anticipated by four days when, on July 12, the Teamsters struck prematurely. Five hundred strikers blocked the access highways into San Francisco, allowing only emergency vehicles to pass into the city. Governor Merriam ordered the State Highway Patrol to convoy all food trucks into the city. On July 16, 1934, the main general strike began:

> Panic seized the citizens of the Bay Region. Grocery stores were jammed by persons eager to obtain supplies to carry them over the crisis. No one knew how long it might last. Long lines of automobiles blocked service stations . . . hysteria gripped the populace.[11]

All public transportation ceased at the beginning of the strike; all theatres, and practically all restaurants (only nineteen out of 200 remained open) as well as all liquor stores closed. Practically all the activities of a busy city came to a halt.[12] Rapidly organized "vigilante" groups began raiding suspected radical meeting places as violence again threatened to erupt.

On balance, it would appear that the chief purpose of labor in calling the general strike was to protest the stubborn stand of the Industrial Association. On the first day, July 16, carmen were authorized to return to work by the General Strike Committee in order to protect their civil service status. The next day similar authorization was given to fifty-nine restaurants, while the following day saw most other restrictions lifted. With the return of the Teamsters to work, labor had made its point. Even though the immediate occasion of the strike of July 16 to 19, 1934, was the presence of the state militia on the waterfront, a more fundamental and root cause was the legitimate fear that what was left of trade unionism in San Francisco would be destroyed by the tactics of the Industrial Association. It is no exaggeration to say that labor unionism was fighting for its very life in San Francisco at this time.

On July 21, two days after the general strike, the employers submitted a proposal to arbitrate all the issues with *all* the waterfront unions. Since these unions now felt that they had obtained their objective, they quickly agreed, by a four to one vote, to accept the proposed conditions. All outstanding issues were submitted to arbitration, with the National Longshoremens Board selected as the agency of arbitration. On July 29, the ILA returned to work in San Francisco and the other ports of the West Coast; two days later, the other unions returned to work. This now meant that 12,000 longshoremen as well as 13,000 workers had returned to their jobs. On October 12, the Longshoremens Board announced its decisions—in essence, they were favorable to the union demands. Some compromises were necessary but the key issue of the hiring hall was solved in a manner satisfactory to the unions. Also, satisfactory compromise in wages and hours was achieved; longshoremen were to receive 95¢ an hour straight time, $1.40 an hour for overtime, and a six-hour day. Waterfront peace was to exist for two years on the basis of these awards; it was but logical that the longshoremen should claim substantial victory in the strike. After many years of struggling for recognition, the Longshoremens Union had now come to a position of prominence. (Union strength was growing and more trades were being organized into unions.) Gone forever, it was hoped, were the disrupting tactics employed by strikebreakers: the great defeats of 1919 had been reversed.

Other significant results of the 1934 strike can now be seen in the light of history: not until 1948 (fourteen years later) did the strike return to the San Francisco waterfront; it was not to have such conditions again until 1972; hence the waterfront, which had been plagued by many disturbances before 1934, had some substantial years of peace which must be ascribed, in great part, to what had been accomplished in 1934. Also there has been significant cooperation between employers and longshoremen; these have resulted in such improvements as the introduction of more modern equipment in the handling of cargo and the like. From all of which it may be said that the stirring (and disturbing) days of 1934 loom large in the history of labor in San Francisco.

CHAPTER 35

SAN FRANCISCO'S CITY CHARTERS—AND MORE MAYORS

T

HE THIRD CHAPTER of this book treated of the origins of civil government in San Francisco in the period that preceded American control. Mention was also made of the Consolidation Act passed by the California State Legislature which declared the city and county of San Francisco a coterminous area as of April 19, 1856. Here we shall take up the story of the city charters which have been the city's organic law from 1856 until the present; we shall also look at some of its mayors.

The unique Hawes Act of 1856, providing for consolidation, was, in effect, a new charter for San Francisco.[1] On balance, it seems that the good points of the new charter of 1856 were outweighed by its weaknesses which gradually became evident. Three of its features have been retained until now. *Consolidation,* which was to provide for greater economy and efficiency of both local governments; *Reduced Boundaries* which, as Hawes saw it, permitted a "closer watch of rascality" and reduced the costs of government; *A Unicameral Board of Supervisors,* which replaced the former two boards of aldermen and the one county board of supervisors. However, later generations of politicians successfully circumvented some of the Hawes built-in safeguards by appealing occasionally to the State Legislature. Some students of the subject think, though, that the 1856 charter was, in essence, too rigid in form. However, with regard to ways to get around it, Mayor Andrew J. Bryant declared in his inaugural message early in 1876:

> . . . It has been the custom for heads of departments in the city government, and sometimes even their subordinates, to ignore the Board of Supervisors and make direct application to the legislature in furtherance of schemes not designed for the public good so much as to increase their own profit, power and patronage.

In 1880, a group of charter reformers in San Francisco could point out that, between 1857 and 1878, the State Legislature had passed a total of 456 laws affecting the government and local administration of the city. A later study in 1898 revealed that over 400 amendments to the charter had been made, thus effectively reducing about one-half of the charter of 1856 to dead wood. Many newly created offices were made appointive at the state level so that, by 1898, the governor of California had 590 appointments in San Francisco at his pleasure, exclusive of some 2,000 notaries public. It was evident that San Francisco needed a new charter but attempts to get it were defeated by small votes in 1880, 1883, 1887, and 1896. Finally, in 1898, by a small majority vote, a strengthened mayor-council type of charter patterned after that of New York City was adopted; it was put into effect in 1900. James D. Phelan, last mayor under the old charter and first under its successor, was the leader in the successful attempt to adopt a new municipal constitution.

The new charter proved quite an improvement over the obsolete, amendment-ridden "rags and tatters" Consolidation Act. It gave the mayor more power, and, while increasing the number of boards and commissions, made them appointive by the mayor instead of the governor. Most important of all, it meant the end of special charter and state legislation for San Francisco. Now the politically emancipated people of the city were able, through their home rule charter and power of amendment, to order their own changes and thus to control their own municipal destiny. However, in its operation, the new charter failed to live up to all expectations. The crucial days of 1906, with the many problems resulting from earthquake and fire, emphasized old problems while producing many new ones. In later years, the 1900 charter was referred to as the "horse and buggy charter" which could not, it seemed, adapt itself to a more modern age. During the 1920s it became increasingly evident that the charter was indeed inadequate; the effects of the economic crash of 1929 served only to confirm the inadequacies of San Francisco's instrument of government. There was a gradually emerging civic consensus that other municipalities had met their problems with radical changes in their form of government throughout the 1920s. The city manager, rather than the commission type of municipal government, appealed to many political thinkers. Several organized attempts were made by concerned groups to bring the fundamental law of the city up to date by amendment or complete revision. Finally, in 1930, continued and vigorous action by a citizens' committee forced the Board of Supervisors, acting largely out of political self-defense, to call for the election of a board of freeholders. The charter framed by them was completed in a short time (since much thought had been given to it by its proponents) and was adopted by the voters on March 26, 1931; it went into effect on January 8, 1932.

The charter of 1932, like the act of 1856, represented a distinct departure from conventional types of municipal government. It has been frequently designated as "The San Francisco Plan." It is a compromise between the strong-mayor and the city-manager types of council government with a touch of commission rule. This is brought out by the relative positions of the mayor and the chief administrative officer. Actually, despite the title, the latter is hardly the "chief" administrative official in the sense of the traditional city manager or strong mayor. The mayor is still the chief executive of San Francisco both in name as well as in power. Realistically, those who drew up the charter of 1932, acknowledged that many of the day-by-day functions of municipal government were quite routine. They sought to draw up a formula which resulted in the present division of duties and responsibilities between the mayor and the chief administrative officer. In summary, the charter, under which San Francisco still operates, has continued the consolidation within the framework of a new and modern form of local government which is the essence of the "San Francisco Plan."

It is not surprising that this charter, as its predecessors, has developed substantial weaknesses. In his first term as mayor (1948–1952), Elmer Robinson appointed a "little Hoover Committee" to study the daily workings of civil government in relation to provisions of the city charter. (Actually, at the behest of successive boards of supervisors, the 1932 charter was studied for revision in 1936, 1946, 1950, 1959, and from 1968 to 1972.)

In the late 1960s a hard-working Committee for Charter Revision, composed of twenty-one members, held many meetings on charter study and revision; it was a considerable disappointment, then, when in the election of 1969, the voters rejected the suggestions of the committee with regard to charter revision. Rightly interpreting this as a vote of no confidence, many of the members of the committee, including its chairman, resigned. A further attempt to return to the matter of charter revision was made when Mayor Joseph Alioto asked Timothy McDonnell, S.J., professor of government at the University of San Francisco, to act as chairman of a new committee on charter revision. This new group did not ignore or divorce itself from all the hard work of those who had served on it previously; finally, though, in 1972, in a self-denying decision which attracted much attention, the committee presented a final report and went quietly out of business —even returning an unexpended surplus of $60,000 to the city treasury! A major reason for this unusual move was the decision reached by Father McDonnell and his associates that, after nearly five years of study on its part and that of its predecessors, the city should not again attempt to revise its charter through an appointed citizens' committee. The report said: "Experience has proven it to be unsuccessful. In the future, charter revision should start with mandatory Charter Education in San Francisco's secondary schools while including the election of a Charter Commission."[2] Although a modest proposal by the latest committee to renumber charter sections and eliminate archaic language was approved by the voters in 1971, the group did not feel that its further efforts would win approval at the polls. Indeed, so many varied interests were represented on the committee that it admitted difficulties in obtaining needed and desirable consensus within its own ranks. The committee also recommended in its final report that the mayor and the board of supervisors use powers already available to them in the existing charter to move toward changes in the budgetary process and departmental structure. Since past grand juries had several times proposed many charter changes, the committee declined to make any recommendations, adding that "it is difficult to evaluate these proposals because they are observations and recommendations of sub-committees which are not supported by adequate evidence and arguments included in either the reports or the files of the Grand Jury."[3] At the present time, then, San Francisco still operates under the charter law which has been in effect since 1932.

We turn now to a consideration of the mayors of San Francisco who have served since the colorful years of "Sunny Jim" Rolph (1912–1931, which have been discussed in Chapter 32). His successor as 31st mayor of San Francisco was Angelo J. Rossi (1878–1948) who served from January 8, 1931, to January 8, 1944; this was to be the second longest incumbency in this position, since Rossi's thirteen years were exceeded only by the nineteen years of Mayor Rolph.

Angelo Rossi was born in the Mother Lode mining town of Volcano, Amador County, and came to San Francisco with his parents as a boy of twelve. He was educated in the public schools in the city, and, in 1887 started work as an errand boy in the family florist business; he worked himself up as an employee there and finally became partner and owner of the A.J. Rossi Floral Company. He had no college education, although, in 1935, while mayor, he expressed his gratitude at being the recipient of an honorary Doctor of Laws Degree awarded him by the University of San Francisco. Rossi's long years of public service began in 1914 with his appointment as a member of the San Francisco Playground Commission. He was elected to the Board of Supervisors in 1921 for a four-year term; although not reelected in 1925, he was back on the board in 1929 for another four-year term; He was not to finish this term, for in 1930 when Mayor Rolph was elected Governor of California, the Board of Supervisors chose Supervisor Rossi to fill the position of mayor. He was inaugurated on January 8, 1931, and was chosen for a second term in 1935, and reelected in 1939. In 1943, he was defeated in another try for the office by Roger Lapham; probably, Mayor Rossi had hoped to rival James Rolph's years of service. But this was not to be; in a three-way race in which he was pitted against George Reilly and Roger Lapham, he was defeated for reelection.

Mayor Rossi's years at City Hall were characterized by industry and devotion for he openly said: "I love being your mayor!" He had his days of crisis when, in 1934, San Francisco was visited by a general strike; when shipowners and others demanded that he call upon the governor to send state militia into the city, he refused to do so, preferring to address a plea to both sides of the dispute calling for moderation in their moves. By 1940, Rossi was regarded as "San Francisco's Number One Salesman," with substantial popularity among his assets. He was mayor in another crisis, starting with Pearl Harbor and the many problems resulting from World War II in the port city of San Francisco. At the time of his death he was eulogized as one who "reared in the hard school of adversity, had the outstanding characteristics of kindliness and honesty, holding aloft the torch of integrity in public places" (W. McGovern, Memorial Services, City Hall, April 7, 1948). Another paean of praise was accorded him in the same memorial service held in the rotunda of his beloved City Hall when Dion Holm, a prominent lawyer, said of Rossi: "He loved San Francisco and all of California inordinately and unselfishly gave long and arduous hours of labor for the betterment of all. Long before the expression 'minority group' became current in our language, Angelo J. Rossi was the exemplification of tolerance to all groups."[4] Mayor Elmer Robinson, serving at the time of Rossi's demise, added that "he served during those terrible years of depression and war—to the very end he remained a generous and able public servant." An editorial in the *San Francisco Chronicle* summed up his person and career:

> Like his predecessor, Sunny Jim Rolph, he discharged his duties as a good human with a strong sense of loyalty and affection for the city and its people. During his many years as Mayor, he made definite contributions to the city's progress. He surrounded himself with competent subordinates and commissions and kept a wary eye on the tax rate and lost no opportunity to spread the fame of San Francisco far and wide. In his passing, the city he loved so well bids him an affectionate "vale."[5]

Rossi's successor was quite a different type of person and mayor. Roger Dearborn Lapham (1883–1966) was born in New York City and served as 32nd mayor of San Francisco from 1944 to 1948. (He had promised not to run for reelection; "Four years will be enough," he said.) His was a wealthy background and he was a graduate of Harvard University after which he joined the family-organized and owned American Hawaiian Steamship Company. Rising through the ranks, he served as president of the line for thirteen years. He was described as a "big, broad-shouldered man, square-jawed, deep-voiced and possessed from early years of a great shock of white hair." In 1920, he decided to settle permanently in San Francisco and, in 1925, was responsible for moving the main office of his steamship company to the city. As conditions became more critical along San Francisco's waterfront (and, in general, along the West Coast), the vigorous Lapham emerged as spokesman for the shipping interests. While acknowledging that there was much room for improvement in the lot of those who worked either longshore or aboard ship, he was adamant in refusing to submit to what he considered the inordinate demands of the maritime unions which were then headed by Harry Bridges. With the advent of the paralyzing strike of 1934, his personal courage led him to a public debate before a not overly friendly audience in Civic Auditorium; his opponent that evening was the same redoubtable Harry Bridges. His attitude then all throughout what later came to be called "One Hundred Days of Crisis" won for him the grudging but real respect of his opponents. He was regarded as a frank and honest man and this reputation suggested to his business associates and other admirers that he bring these same qualities to the service of his city. When first approached to run for mayor, he professed no interest, saying that he simply was not the political type. Finally, though, he was persuaded to throw his hat into the political ring; he did so, as already indicated, with the statement that, while he thought it was time for a change at City Hall, if elected, he would serve only one term.

In November 1943, the shipping magnate was elected mayor and took his oath of office on January 8, 1944. When he became mayor, his statement was characteristically forthright: "I am under no illusions. I am now at the height of my popularity!" He had been elevated to the post of mayor by a plurality of 93,000 votes and, among other things, his election was regarded as the overturning of a long-established political machine to which he did not belong. As an efficient businessman, he was convinced that it was economically absurd to have two competing streetcar systems in San Francisco, the "Muni" and the privately owned Market Street Railway Company, and vowed to put an end to this situation. This move made him many enemies among those who opposed this change. There were many San Franciscans who, convinced of the efficient management behind the privately owned Market Street Railway System, opposed unification of the competing systems; they sought to remind Lapham that, as a successful businessman, he would be expected to remember that competition frequently makes all rivals better public or private servants; they added their belief that, if the proposed unification went through as Lapham wished, the resultant conditions in the local transportation system would deteriorate under public ownership. In 1946, Henry Budde, a local newspaper owner and editor, started a recall petition against Lapham since the mayor had brought about the consolidation of the two systems and had announced a fare increase of 3¢. Lapham was among the earliest signers of the petition for his own recall, not because he believed in it but because, as he explained, he wanted the matter brought out into the open and submitted to the voters. The recall petition was easily defeated and Lapham had the consolation of knowing how he stood with San Francisco's voters. He also aroused opposition by his call for the abolition of the city's cable cars. His terse epigram: "Discard them" won no general acceptance, as he might well have known, and perhaps did. However, it was completely in character that he express his views.

Mayor Lapham was at the civic helm during the important days when the United Nations Organization met in San Francisco. He was an enthusiastic host and, after the signing of the charter of the world-wide organization, went to great lengths in an endeavor to capture the permanent headquarters for the United Nations for San Francisco. In this he was unsuccessful.

When, in 1948 Roger Lapham left City Hall in fulfillment of his promise, he returned to his many business interests but joined these with service as economic advisor to various American foreign missions. He died quite suddenly in San Francisco on April 16, 1966, at the age of eighty-two; his had been the fullest of lives and he had frequently expressed his satisfaction with the domestic and other happiness that had marked his long life. Harry Bridges had this to say about his former foe:

> I never had anything but admiration for him. We had our bitter fights but there was never a doubt in my mind that he honestly represented his class and, whenever we reached agreement, his word was good.[6]

The editorials that commemorated his passing verified what has been said here concerning Lapham's personal and civic character. The *San Francisco Chronicle* remarked:

Roger Lapham was one of that rare breed of men who achieve distinction easily and wear it naturally. He distinguished himself in whatever he undertook. As Mayor he eminently liked and acted the part and is to be rated along with the revered Phelan and Rolph as burgermeisters who shed lustre on the office. His death at 82 has called up eulogies from all who knew him in which he is described as "great, forthright, fearless, honorable and unselfish." He was a San Franciscan of the old tradition.[7]

When Mayor Lapham came to the end of his term, among those who determined to run to succeed him at City Hall was Superior Court Judge Elmer E. Robinson (1894–) who was to serve as San Francisco's 33rd mayor from 1948 to 1956. Robinson was a native San Franciscan and received his early education in the public schools; after law school in 1915, he was admitted to the California State Bar. For fifteen years, he had a thriving private practice in the city; in 1930 he manifested considerable interest in politics with his support of Mayor Rolph's candidacy for governor of California. Although some influential Republicans began to suggest him as Rolph's successor as mayor should the latter win his gubernatorial post, the Board of Supervisors chose their confrere, Angelo J. Rossi, to succeed Rolph. Later in 1935, Robinson was appointed a municipal court judge; after six months he was elevated to the Superior Court bench in San Francisco. While serving in this capacity, Judge Robinson became known as one of the more influential Republicans in the city. When Mayor Rossi lost his bid for reelection to Roger Lapham in 1943, Robinson was generally recognized as the leader of the local Republican party. In 1947, he decided to run for mayor; his opponents were another Republican, Supervisor Chester MacPhee, and Democratic congressman Frank Havenner. Judge Robinson emerged as the winner after a vigorous race. During a successful first term, Mayor Robinson was responsible for organizing San Francisco's first attempt at slum clearance, under a redevelopment agency. Also, San Francisco's southern boundaries were extended by the acquisition from the state of some coastal and fringe lands in the area adjacent to Lake Merced; these were put to use by the Department of Public Works and the Police Department which established a pistol firing range near Lake Merced. Seemingly the voters liked what they saw for, in

1951, they reelected Mayor Robinson when he ran against two supervisors, George Christopher and J. Joseph Sullivan. During his eight years as mayor, (1948–1956) Robinson was official host to the returning General Douglas MacArthur as well as to the signatories of the Japanese Peace Treaty; in 1955, at the tenth anniversary commemoration of the signing of the United Nations Charter, he played the same role. He was also involved in planning an expanded airport for the city. While grand juries are more frequently critical of incumbents than otherwise, when his term of office ended, Mayor Robinson was praised by the San Francisco Grand Jury:

> The incumbent Mayor, the Honorable Elmer E. Robinson, now concluding two terms as Mayor of San Francisco, deserves particular mention for what is felt have been outstanding accomplishments of the various city departments in direct service to the people of San Francisco during his administration.[8]

Among the other projects that marked the Robinson administrations were those which concerned the Fire Department and the Public Library system. At the close of his eight years of competent service in City Hall, the *San Francisco Examiner* said of him: "Because of Elmer Robinson's leadership, this city is a finer place in which to live, to work, to play. We salute him and wish him a well earned rest."

San Francisco was still rebuilding from the destruction of 1906 when George Christopher (1907–) arrived in the city. He was born in Arcadia, Greece, and in 1911 moved with his parents to San Francisco, where his father opened a "seven-stool" restaurant at Third and Minna streets in the south of Market area. George attended Lincoln Grammar School and, while a sophomore at Galileo High School, was forced to leave school because of his father's serious illness. For eight years he worked full time at the *San Francisco Examiner* and took evening courses to complete his high school education; finally, he earned a degree of Bachelor in Commercial Science in accounting at Golden Gate College. In 1929, he opened his own accounting office. An investment in a dairy resulted in his establishment of the Christopher Dairy Farms of which he became president. Christopher first entered politics in 1945 when he was elected supervisor. He was reelected in 1949, leading all other candidates with 183,000 votes, a record endorsement. In 1951 in a very close race, he made an unsuccessful try for the position of mayor against the incumbent Elmer Robinson. His years as supervisor saw him constantly in the public eye for he was outspoken and forthright in his stand on various problems and issues. In 1955, he announced that he would again run for mayor in the November election.[9] His opponent was George Reilly; Christopher received 162,280 votes to Reilly's 77,085. The *Chronicle* reported it as "the biggest margin ever given a candidate for Mayor here." Slightly more than a year after this electoral triumph, Mayor Christopher made an unsuccessful bid for the Republican nomination for the United States Senate seat vacated by William F. Knowland. In the June primary election, he was defeated by Governor Goodwin Knight.

Christopher's first years as mayor found him interested in bringing more efficiency to the Police Department as well as to all other departments of city government.[10] He was enthusiastic in his endorsement of a rapid transit system for the San Francisco Bay Area.[11] Mayor Christopher also sponsored a $6.5 million bond issue to finance the San Francisco Parking Authority which resulted in various public garages: he was especially proud of an ordinance that he sponsored in 1958 called the Fair Employment Practices Ordinance which outlawed racial and religious discrimination by employers and unions in San Francisco.[12]

In 1959, Mayor Christopher ran successfully for reelection against City Assessor Russell L. Wolden. Again, he tasted electoral triumph with 145,009 votes against Wolden's 92,252. He announced: "Just because this is to be my last four years, I'm not going to coast." He acknowledged mistakes in his first administration adding that "the man who makes no mistakes does nothing." In 1960, he made a much-publicized trip to Russia; he had been invited by Premier Khrushchev to return a visit which the Soviet leader had made to San Francisco in the previous year. This visit resulted in a considerable increase in the popularity of San Francisco's mayor. However, on May 13, 1960, the returning mayor had to face a major crisis, with a confrontation by a mass of students and others who noisily protested the hearings in City Hall of the United States House Subcommittee on Un-American Activities. After other efforts failed and after severe provocations, Christopher supported the vigorous police action which removed the group from City Hall. In this action, extreme as some called it, he won the support of many San Franciscans who deplored its necessity but were grateful that action had been taken in a critical moment. It should be mentioned, too, that Mayor Christopher considered as an outstanding accomplishment his sponsoring of the $200 million Golden Gateway, revolving around the decaying commission district close to the Embarcadero.[13] In 1962, near the end of his imaginative and generally productive two terms as mayor, Christopher ran for lieutenant governor of California on the same ticket as Richard Nixon, who aspired to be governor. Both were defeated. When succeeded by John F. Shelley as mayor in 1964, George Christopher resumed control of his dairy interests. As a retired mayor he continued his interest in politics as what he considered to be "an interested observer not without experience."

It had been a long time since one associated with the cause of union labor had occupied the mayor's chair in San Francisco. This now happened with the election of John Shelley (1905–1974) who served as the 35th mayor from 1964 to 1968. He was born in the South Park district of the city, the first of nine children; after grammar grades, he was tall and lanky enough to obtain a berth as a seaman and, until 1929, he went to sea off and on, rising to the rank of first mate; between trips, in 1923, he was graduated from Mission High School. He next took a job as driver of a bakery wagon; his interest in their union made him seek more education and he attended evening classes at St. Ignatius College, now the University of San Francisco. He graduated in 1932 with a degree in law, although he chose not to practice. In 1937, Shelley, at thirty-two, became the youngest president of the San Francisco Labor Council. He held this key post until 1948 when he became President of the State Federation of Labor, a position that he held for two years. Later he served as state senator from San Francisco, and his constructive work in Sacramento was appreciated by those who proposed that he run for Congress. In 1949, following the death of Representative Richard J. Welch, a Republican, Shelley ran successfully for this position in a special election. His record in Congress was so good that, at two-year intervals, he was returned to Washington until he decided to run for mayor of his native city in 1963. By that time he was a member of several important congressional committees, including the powerful Appropriations Committee on which he served for nine years. He was responsible for legislative action favoring some key projects in San Francisco, including the retention of Hunters Point Shipyard and the obtaining of federal funds for such projects as BART, and medical care for the aged.

A significant moment in the Shelley City Hall years came with his inauguration as mayor on January 8, 1964, in the rotunda of the City Hall. A reporter caught the spirit of the day by writing: "Shelley, his spare six-foot-four figure towering above the rostrum, intoned his inaugural speech in his finest labor hall tenor, concluding: 'I intend to plan San Francisco's future with a heart as well as a bulldozer!' " It was not long, though, before he complained that San Francisco's main problem was "too much action and not enough planning." After one year of what was to emerge as a turbulent four-year term, he also remarked, with characteristic bluntness: "I feel like a mountain goat leaping from one crisis to another." Crises aplenty he had, and he is supposed to have wryly reflected more than once that he missed the more peaceful (and, in some ways, more influential) scene of which he had formed a part in Washington. His first year saw him facing massive sit-in demonstrations over minority employment; however, he was successful in playing a key role in negotiating settlements and keeping violence at a minimum. Here his reputation as a dedicated and fair-minded servant of union labor stood him in good stead. In this regard, he remarked: "I'm not afraid to take my lumps and I have some scars to prove I've taken them." Shelley showed considerable personal courage by going to a Hunters Point riot in 1966 which broke out because of the unfortunate slaying of a young car-theft suspect by a policeman; as a result of his prompt visit to the troubled area, he was given credit in bringing about a quick settlement of the violent outbreak. His action here was matched by a forthright statement which he made about the matter:

> I fully realize that I am placing in jeopardy my entire public career but the medieval practice of discrimination by labor unions is just as sorrowful and just as unfair as the archaic attitudes of members of employer groups. It is time to start curing this sickness.

When other crises came and went during Mayor Shelley's turbulent term, one observer said: "Jack Shelley may not be the best Mayor San Francisco ever had or the worst—but he has certainly been the unluckiest!" A source of much criticism was the fact that city spending rose by 33 percent during his term; his critics pointed out that the Shelley budgets were constructed so loosely that a Board of Supervisors largely unfavorable to him cut them by a total of $19 million; this was compared unfavorably with a budget trimming of $8.3 million during Mayor Christopher's last term in office. As he approached the end of his first term and had to face the problem of whether he should run again, his sense of practical realism, coupled with bad health, made him decide not to seek the office once more. Preliminary polls taken in September showed Republican State Senator Harold Dobbs running ahead of Mayor Shelley. Then Shelley, with a history of heart disease and other internal disorders, went to the University of California Hospital. He issued a statement saying that his doctors "are not afraid I might lose the election. They are afraid I might win. The clear terms are that it is a simple choice for me of life or death." A City Hall political reporter had this comment:

> It is not that Shelley was bad for the Mayor's office. Officials agree he was honest, intelligent, humane. But those closest to him grew to recognize that the Mayor's office was bad for Shelley. The daily demand for action ran counter to his life experience.

About two months after he had finished his term as mayor, Jack Shelley was honored by 1,600 "luminaries of the business, political and labor worlds" with a civic banquet at the Fairmont Hotel. Harry Bridges then described him as an "unflinching comrade in the bitter labor battles of the 1930s" and there were messages from President Johnson and Vice-President Humphrey. The newly inaugurated mayor, Joseph L. Alioto, praised his predecessor for his "passionate concern for solving current social problems." Shelley punctured the solemnity by remarking that "I come here tonight not to bury Shelley—it will be a long time before they do!" He later became the city's official lobbyist at Sacramento; his political experience served him in good stead there although he had personal problems arising from deteriorating health. He died on September 1, 1974, at St. Mary's Hospital where he had undergone several operations. Mayor Alioto had this to say of him:

> Jack Shelley served the city faithfully and he served it well. He was a champion of working people all his life, and, through his devoted advocacy, he brought them a better life and a more hopeful future. We will miss him: San Francisco will be ever in his debt.

His successor was again to bring different qualifications to the office of mayor.

Joseph L. Alioto was born in the North Beach section of San Francisco on Febuary 12, 1916. He was the second child and the only son of four children. His father, Giuseppe, was a Sicilian who had come to San Francisco as a fisherman. His mother was a native-born San Franciscan of Sicilian parentage. His first schooling was at Sts. Peter and Paul School in North Beach, after which he attended Sacred Heart High School from which he graduated in 1933. He next enrolled at St. Mary's College, Moraga where he majored in philosophy and English, and was elected student body president and valedictorian of his class. In 1937, he graduated with highest honors and won a scholarship to study law at the Catholic University of America in Washington, D.C. After completing law school there, he worked for the federal government in the antitrust division of the Department of Justice. At the end of World War II, Alioto returned to his native city and opened the law office which bore his name, announcing he would specialize in antimonopolistic cases. He was quickly a success in this phase of the practice of law; in the course of some years, he won more that $60 million in damages for his many clients. (Branch offices of the firm were established in Chicago, Salt Lake City, and Honolulu.) Gradually, he became involved in other business endeavors which he grouped under a parent corporation called Alioto Enterprises. His entrance into public life came with his appointment to the Board of Education in 1948; in 1953, he became its president. He won favor with local teachers by working tirelessly for their salary increases as well as becoming involved, in the role of an attorney, in a significant civil liberties case, which enabled teachers to take part in the election of school board members.

Alioto entered the electoral arena almost by accident. Long an active Democrat, he decided at first to support the candidacy for mayor of another Democrat, Eugene McAteer, until the latter's untimely death in 1967. Alioto then decided to try for the position himself. With Mayor Shelley's support, Alioto was pitted against a conservative Republican, Harold Dobbs, with the race becoming complicated by the candidacy of a liberal Democrat, Jack Morrison, who threatened to split the Democratic vote and thus ensure Dobbs's victory. Alioto, although relatively unknown in the political arena, quickly and astutely, after only fifty-five days of campaigning, assembled what he called "a kind of New Deal coalition of labor and minorities, plus flag-waving Italians." On November 7, 1967, Alioto was elected mayor with a margin of 15,000 votes over his nearest opponent. (In some areas of the city, notably North Beach, Alioto lead by an over three to one majority.) On January 8, 1968, in a very special kind of inaugural ceremony at the Opera House, Joseph Alioto was sworn in as the 36th mayor of San Francisco.

Although extremely energetic from the beginning (within a month, he had successfully negotiated an end to a local newspaper strike) he seems quickly to have been attracted to a higher position than was his at City Hall; by July 1968, there was talk of his being the vice-presidential candidate of the Democratic party. This did not materialize and he turned his gaze to the state capital where Governor Ronald Reagan would soon be running for reelection. Soon, a sensational article in *Look* magazine accused him of connections with the notorious Sicilian Mafia gang and, even though he cleared himself of these charges, they appeared to have hurt his general image in the minds of many. (Later Alioto brought a $12.5 million libel suit against the publishers of *Look* magazine.) In 1973, it was evident that San Francisco's mayor was again interested in being California's governor. However, he remarked that "the life of a Mayor has not been uncomfortable for me. San Francisco is an exciting city." By that time, Alioto had managed to accumulate some political foes who charged that he had not done well as mayor. By that time also, San Francisco voters had disagreed, as earlier, in 1971, they had returned him to City Hall for a second term.

In 1975, Mayor Alioto approached the end of his second term in office. Ineligible by city charter for a consecutive third term, he was to be succeeded by State Senator George Moscone after what proved to be a hotly contested battle.

George Moscone, born in San Francisco in 1929, was educated in local schools and, after some time at the then College of the Pacific in Stockton, won an academic scholarship to Hastings College of the Law, where he finished among the top five in his class. After service in the Navy, in 1956, he began his practice of law in San Francisco. He was elected to the Board of Supervisors in 1963 and went on from there as state senator to Sacramento in 1966. He proved quite vocal and prominent in this capacity and was reelected in 1970 and again in 1974 by large majorities. In 1967, his colleagues in Sacramento elected him state senate Democratic majority leader. In his race to be Alioto's successor, his main opponent was Supervisor John Barbagelata, a conservative real estate broker. On November 4, 1975, Moscone finished first in a field of eleven candidates but, since he had not obtained a majority, a run-off election was held on December 11, in which he defeated Barbagelata (his only opponent now) by 4,443 votes, which amounted to only two percentage points over his opponent. Barbagelata was admittedly not gracious in his narrow defeat and it was evident that he would spearhead continued opposition to Moscone. In the course of the now concluded "no holds barred" campaign, many accusations of both a political and personal nature had been made concerning Moscone; to these he replied by calling them all untrue, adding that "I believe that I am fitted for this office on the basis of my ability and character." Among others, outgoing Mayor Alioto endorsed Moscone, saying of him that "he is a man of his own mind. . . . He is an experienced politician who is bright and will make a first-class mayor."

On January 6, 1976, George Moscone became the 37th mayor of San Francisco; his short inaugural address made it clear that he had many plans for his native city, that he considered himself a hard-working public servant and that he would demand equal dedication from his associates. Lacking some of the charisma which had marked the frequently dramatic rule of his predecessor, the new mayor seemed determined to preserve a much lower profile than had Alioto. Some of his appointments to key positions met with much opposition but, accustomed to the ways of politics, this did not seem to worry Moscone. On February 21,

1977, after more than a year in office, he proposed to answer some of his critics in the public press. To those who had expressed disappointment in what they called his "track record" he replied that, while freely admitting that much was yet to be done, he felt that he could stand on his record in such matters as the lowering of the city's unemployment record by 1.4 percent. He also listed what he considered significant steps forward in port planning as well as an increase of 1,630 in the number of new business enterprises during his year in office. His statement concluded:

> I sought the office of Mayor because I felt that I owed San Francisco something. I want to repay this city of my birth by doing what I can to make it a better city. When elected, I asked your help in achieving a better city. I am greatly encouraged by many of the important achievements of 1976, which included the commission appointments as well as saving the Giants baseball franchise for San Francisco. I am not discouraged by some of the disappointments nor by the efforts of those—in and out of politics—who do not know the facts and who would destroy the morale of our people. We have problems, to be sure. We've solved some and failed to solve others. But we are moving forward and I must continue to count on your help.

On August 2, 1977, Mayor Moscone figured largely in a special election, along with the issues to be decided that cost the taxpayers over $400,000. It was hardly surprising that this election came about as a result of the initiative process which was backed principally (although there were other supporters) by Supervisor Barbagelata. The special election ballot had just two measures. Proposition A called for a straight repeal of the district election of supervisors which had been approved only in the November 1976 election and had not yet been put to the test. Proposition B was more complicated and proposed that the four-year term of Moscone, as well as that of Sheriff Richard Hongisto and District Attorney Joseph Freitas be cut in half and that new elections for those offices be held in November. "B" also had its own proposals for electing supervisors. The newly created eleven districts should be kept, it said, and the supervisors should live in separate districts but each of them should be elected by all of the voters. Moscone's comment on "B" reminded him, he said, of Christmas tree legislation he had seen in Sacramento . . . "providing a little present for everyone."

It would seem that the glittering package proposed by Bar-bagelata and his supporters merited the comment of a veteran campaigner that its proponents put too much into the package, when it might have been able to "pull off a straight recall of Moscone." Seldom had San Francisco seen such a melange pro-posed to its electorate. After a confused campaign which was marked by vicious personal attacks and by great personal activity on Moscone's part, it became evident that his supporters from all over California were outcontributing Barbagelata's friends by a ratio of about five to one. Nearly $150,000 was spent for televi-sion commercials by opponents to Proposition B, while the oppo-sition barely scraped together funds to issue some posters.

When the results of this unique election were tallied, 57 per-cent had voted against Proposition A—five percent more than the plan had received in 1976. Proposition B did even worse, with 64 percent of the public voting against it. A careful analysis revealed that Proposition A was defeated in every part of the city except for three wealthy areas; Proposition B carried only one of these. Jerry Burns, a veteran political reporter for the *San Francisco Chroni-cle,* had some thoughtful comments which he incorporated into an article in the *California Journal,* a monthly that specializes in analyses of state government and politics. Asking the question: "Who won in the election," Burns noted that Moscone and the others whose positions were at stake had certainly received what amounted to a vote of confidence and that this should make him a more effective mayor. The district election principle having been upheld, only the future would tell how this would work out in practice. Burns asked another question: "Did the election mark a victory for radicalism on the local scene?"; he answered that it was considerably unlikely that Moscone would participate in such a transformation or, indeed, that the voters would send an entirely radical ticket to City Hall via the supervisorial route. (Barbagelata had proven himself, as might be expected, a "prophet of doom" in lamenting that San Francisco would never be the same again and that it might well veer in the direction of "radical Berkeley!") Burns considered such predictions quite premature: evidently, they were not verifiable at the time. For the Board of Supervisors, the election results meant that all eleven supervisors, because of the defeat of the two propositions, would have to appear before the voters at the next November election. Quickly, at least six announced their decision to run for reelection from districts; all would obviously have the advantage customarily accruing to incumbents. A sound guess, wrote Burns, was that moderate to liberal candidates would win in the new districts. He predicted that the old expensive television and media campaigning would be replaced in a notable way, by door-to-door district campaigning. Burns's final remark is worth quoting: "It's all going to be confusing for a while but that's San Francisco politics!" At the very least, Mayor George Moscone had sufficient reason for elation in what had happened to him.

PART 4

MORE MODERN
TIMES

HOST TO THE WORLD:
San Francisco and the Birth of the United Nations Organization in 1945

Oh what a great day this can be in history!

President Harry S.
Truman at the signing of
the Charter of the United
Nations, San Francisco,
June 26, 1945.

I
N 1944, WHEN World War II was coming to an end, representatives of China, Great Britain, the Soviet Union, and the
United States, met at Dumbarton Oaks, an estate in Washington,
D.C., and engaged in preliminary discussions regarding the formation of a world organization of nations determined to preserve
world peace. These deliberations took place between August 21
and October 7, 1944. From this meeting, with further input after
the Yalta conference in February 1945, came an agreement that
representatives of various nations would be invited to a conference in San Francisco, with the initial meeting on April 25, 1945.
It was agreed that two kinds of nations would be invited to the
conference: those who had signed the United Nations Declaration by February 5, 1945, and those so-called "Associated Nations" who had declared war on the Axis powers and who would
adhere to the United Nations Declaration by March 1, 1945.

Naturally, it was a cause of considerable satisfaction to San
Franciscans when their city was singled out as the locale for such
an unprecedented and important meeting. Its selection seems to
have been based largely on its accessibility to many of the participating countries; likewise, San Francisco's location across the
continent from the nation's capital would symbolize nationwide
concern with the progress of the conference. Also, the undeniable
scenic charms of the city and its compactness appealed to the
planners of the conference. It was not long before emissaries of
the State Department came west to plan the many details that
would have to be considered in inviting the nations of the world
to the City by the Golden Gate. When the State Department
announced that it would welcome letters from any and all Americans with suggestions concerning the format and purposes of the
conference, the result was both surprising and encouraging: just

before the opening of the San Francisco meeting, the State Department was receiving almost 20,000 letters a week, which were read, and the contents sorted and funnelled to those most immediately concerned. From April 15 to 24, 1945, delegates from all over the world poured into San Francisco; the Army Air Transport Command provided over sixty airplanes, nine special trains made up of one hundred Pullman cars brought more participants, and others arrived by ship. Registration revealed that there was a total of 282 delegates from 46 nations accompanied by 1,444 assistants serving in various capacities. In addition, representatives of the following organizations attended: the League of Nations, the Permanent Court of International Justice, the International Labor Organization, the United Nations Interim Commission on Food and Agriculture, the United Nations Relief and Rehabilitation Administration, and the Pan American Union. Truly, San Francisco was destined to be the temporary capital of the world during the next few weeks.

On Wednesday afternoon, April 25, 1945, the "United Nations Conference On International Organization" held its first session in the San Francisco War Memorial Opera House. Since President Truman found it impossible to leave his many concerns in Washington for this opening session, he addressed those present by radio from the White House; after assuring all of a warm welcome, he said: "If we do not want to die together in war, we must learn to live together in peace." The opening addresses stressed that this was not a peace conference as such; the united nations were still at war with the Axis powers, although Germany's surrender was to come shortly. The primary task was envisioned as the drawing up and completion of an outline of a world charter which had been tentatively agreed upon at the Dumbarton Oaks meeting. Out of this charter, it was hoped, would come an organization of "peace loving nations"; it is interesting to note that the sponsoring powers agreed on approximately fifty points in the first week at San Francisco, although it was inevitable that some areas of dispute and disagreement would surface as the days went on. However, it was solid cause for satisfaction that any measure of agreement at all resulted.

Although the United Nations could claim the presence of no Woodrow Wilson, George Clemenceau, or David Lloyd George, three persons quickly became prominent. They were Vyacheslav Molotov of Russia (who had requested special police protection for himself and entourage), Harold E. Stassen of the United States, and Australia's Herbert Evatt. As the days went on, Stassen was outstanding in his frank and perceptive comments. (Secretary of State Edward Stettinius, while present and participating, does not seem to have attained equal status with Stassen.) Newspaper reporters filed about 150,000 words from San Francisco each day; 170,000 feet of motion picture film and many thousands of still pictures were taken. (This was before the advent of television.) A thousand typists worked day and night to keep things flowing; 800 Boy Scouts served as messengers and couriers, and high school students served as ushers. The total cost to the United States as the host nation was $1.5 million. It was reckoned that, on an average day, the secretary of the conference, Alger Hiss, authorized the release of thousands of pages of mimeographed material. When finished, it was discovered that the documentary material amounted to about twenty tons.

The signing of a United Nations Charter took place on Tuesday, June 26, 1945. The charter was printed in five languages, English, French, Spanish, Russian, and Chinese. At last, after two full months of discussion, debate, and full expression of disagreements, the time had come for San Francisco to give birth to the United Nations Organization. It was indeed a proud day in the history of the city.

It was arranged to have the big powers sign first with the exception of the United States which, as hosting nation, reserved the privilege of signing last. China, as the nation that had suffered the longest from Axis aggression, would be the first to sign; followed by signatories representing Russia, Great Britain, France, and then down the line alphabetically starting with Argentina. The signings continued for four and one-half hours when, as planned, President Truman marched down the aisle, accompanied by thunderous applause, to place his name on the charter for the United States. By this formal action, the signatories, in the words of the charter itself "have agreed to the present charter of the United Nations and do hereby establish an international organization to be known as the United Nations."

San Francisco has hosted several significant anniversary commemorations of the birth of the United Nations. In 1955, due observance was made of the tenth anniversary of the charter's signing and again, in 1965, the twentieth anniversary was observed. For the latter event, Mayor John F. Shelley invited representatives from the 114 nations comprising the United Nations Organization to gather in San Francisco; most did so and various programs were held at the Palace of the Legion of Honor as well as at the War Memorial Opera House. The final address was given by Adlai Stevenson, who bore the title for the occasion of "Ambassador Extraordinary and Plenipotentiary, Permanent Representative of the United States of America to the United Nations."

Yet another commemoration, this time of the 25th anniversary of the signing of the charter, took place on June 25 to 26, 1970. After an official reception in the rotunda of the City Hall, the delegates, headed by Secretary General U. Thant, were guests at a ceremonial commemorative session in the Opera House, and the day's events concluded with a civic banquet at the Fairmont Hotel. Greetings were extended by Mayor Joseph L. Alioto, who said:

> At first there were fifty member nations; now there are 126, all proud and independent and yet bound by a common commitment to find orderly ways to settle international disputes without the ultimate tragedy of bloodshed. War, sadly, has not been eradicated; nor, significantly, has the will for peace. This yearning for peace prevails throughout the world and finds its lasting and most persuasive expression in the United Nations.

Despite many vicissitudes and a continuing turbulent history, the United Nations at its founding provided San Francisco with one of the proudest pages in its own colorful past.

CHAPTER 37

SOCIAL CHANGES IN THE CITY:
Beatniks, Hippies, and the Haight-Ashbury Generation

I N THE MID-1950s the term "Beat Generation" became widely known in San Francisco as well as throughout the United States. The term referred to men and women in their teens and early twenties who alienated themselves from the mainstream of American society. Their activities were marked by a quest for new life styles and patterns joined with a rejection of conventional values and standards. These attitudes were reflected at the outset in poetry and later in prose form, theatre, and motion pictures, as well as in painting, sculpture, and other arts.

The principal leader of this movement and the one who gave it its name was Jack Kerouac, born in Lowell, Massachusetts, in 1922. He was of French-Canadian and Catholic background; after service in the merchant marine, he spent time in the Navy but was discharged because of what was judged to be a "schizoid personality." After hitchhiking across the United States and Mexico several times, he settled in the North Beach section of San Francisco and used the city as a kind of base of operations. After attracting some disciples to him and to the City Lights Bookstore on Columbus Avenue, Kerouac suffered a repudiation of his ideas when, in 1959, the *Saturday Review* reported that "True Bohemians in San Francisco have deserted Beatnikland by the score and want no part of the bearded nihilists who are its inhabitants."[1]

After evidence of disorientation and more wanderings, Jack Kerouac settled in St. Petersburg, Florida, where he died in October 1969, aged forty-seven. His death received little publicity; a national magazine commented as follows:

As a shaman of the Beat Generation, Kerouac was a forebear of today's hippie and radical counter-culture. But he would not or could not translate himself into the 1960's. A little before he died last week at 47, Kerouac was muttering at both straight society and the rebellious young, the military-industrial complex and the Viet Cong. "You can't fight City Hall," he wrote. "It keeps changing all the time."[2]

Even though Kerouac did not associate himself permanently with San Francisco, his influence was felt in the local Beatnik movement; "Beats" involved themselves in civil rights controversies, peace movements, and campus "anti-multiversity" and free speech demonstrations. While some onlookers applauded their efforts as a sign that American society was being regenerated, others deplored them and their activities. However, San Francisco became closely identified with the Beat Movement, as many somewhat prominent artists chose the relatively permissive atmosphere of the city for their home. Gradually, San Francisco became the mecca of this vanguard of American society.

Probably the most far-reaching effect of the Beat Movement was its influence on the Hippie phenomenon which was to surface shortly in San Francisco. The Hippies were to take their place in the history of the city because, among other things, of their geographical location in the Haight-Ashbury district not far from Golden Gate Park which quickly became their "People's Park." The part of the city in which the Hippies located lacked the colorful history of the older parts of San Francisco but part of the area, known as Ashbury Heights, possessed some natural beauty spots; it has been thus described:

> To the North are the steep slopes leading up to Lone Mountain ... to the South are the even steeper slopes of the majestic Twin Peaks which dominate the city, banked by Sutro Heights to the West and Buena Vista Park and Mt. Olympus to the East.[3]

This area first formed part of the earlier Rancho San Miguel which was owned by the Noe family. Gradually, as the city developed, some of these lands became residential, with a distinctive type of dwelling gradually marking the district; some of these sturdy and interesting homes still remain and were, for a time, invaded by the Hippies. Dramatic changes began with World War II when housing was at a premium in San Francisco. Commodious old dwellings and roomy flats, formerly occupied by one family, began to house several families, with occupants coming and going in quick succession. Some of the older home owners, observing the resultant neighborhood blight, sold their property and moved away, particularly after the war, when they joined the flight to the suburbs. The stage was then set for the entrance of minority groups and movements into the Haight-Ashbury district.

At first, this entrance was spearheaded by those remaining Beatniks who were not wanted in the North Beach area: it seemed that a perfect spot lay waiting for them—the Haight-Ashbury district. The area comprised about eighty-five square blocks named after the intersection of its main street (Haight) with a key side street (Ashbury). Plush greenery in nearby Golden Gate Park awaited the newly arriving dwellers while the connecting strip of grass and trees of the Panhandle stretched eight blocks from the park to the east where some wealthy families (like the Magnin department store family) lived. Another park that was used by the Hippies was Buena Vista, rising on a steep hill and marked by adjacent Victorian homes with beautiful views of the city and the bay.

An increasing number of young men and women, including many blacks, began "dropping out of society" and moving into what they quickly came to call the "Hashbury District." By the fall of 1965, there were enough long-haired newcomers for the local press to take notice; in September, a series of articles appeared in the *Examiner* which used the word "Hippies" to describe these people.[4] The *Examiner* articles described how many of the new arrivals moved from North Beach to the Haight-Ashbury in search of cheaper places in which to live as well as larger dwellings where they hoped to share communal living. Some were already under the influence of habit-forming drugs and other hallucinatory agents while still others opted for the study of Buddhist and Hindu philosophy. As early as spring 1967, the word about Hippies had spread among property owners and real estate agents and it was not a favorable one: "They're both dirty and destructive, and don't sell or rent to them." When the Hippies quickly verified the fears entertained about them by the unsanitary, even filthy, ways in which they seemed content to live, San Francisco's director of Public Health, Dr. Ellis D. Sox (promptly named "LSD Sox" by Hippies) ordered a general clean-up which was immediately called "unwarranted harassment." This was quickly refuted by Dr. Sox with a listing of particular conditions which he believed threatened not only the health of the Hippies but that of other dwellers in the area, and, in general, of all San Franciscans who might come in contact with them. (A newspaper account remarked: "Like a bejeweled matron with a social reputation to maintain, San Francisco had never brought itself to embrace its hairy, soiled offspring, the Hippie.") At least, however, the phenomenon brought San Francisco, willy-nilly, to the attention of the rest of the country as well as to other parts of the world. An article in a local newspaper described the scene as of April 2, 1967:

> Week by week, the press of cars slowly cruising down Haight Street increased, their occupants ogling the Hippies, readily identified by their colorful ponchos, beards, bare feet, long and usually unkempt hair. The police and merchants had not responded with loving understanding to the "love" that the Hippies said they had for everything and everyone. Because Hippies loved LSD, marijuana, sex, not paying rent, drawing on walls and sidewalks, making noise whenever they felt like it (including 4 a.m.) not all their neighbors in the Haight-Ashbury district "dug" the hippies. The Municipal Railway complained that heavy auto and pedestrian traffic along Haight Street on weekends delayed motor coaches for as long as 30 minutes. It was consequently announced that buses would be re-routed on weekends. Cheerful predictions were made by Hippies that maybe 100,000 of their kind from elsewhere would tune in and drop out of the blue into Psychedelic Avenue with no glue but plenty of pot.[5]

By 1967, it was estimated that between 6,000 and 8,000 Hippies, either real or fake, had moved into the area; they were from all parts of the United States, and later investigations revealed that some of them were far from indigent but came rather from well-to-do families with which for various reasons, they had become disenchanted. *Newsweek* hazarded a guess as to the numbers by quoting a source "who is familiar with the distribution pattern of LSD, the psychedelic drug that activates the Hip world; he estimated that between 25,000 and 30,000 weekend Hippies, who can loosely be defined as teenagers, sporadically switched on. About 5,000 of this estimated figure include full-time San Francisco Hippies."[6]

Despite the hazards of drug use, a good number of the Hippies were characterized by completely peaceful intentions and conduct; only later did the problem of hard-core and other crime emerge. Among them were some college graduates, on leave from American society, which had, as they said, left them "unfulfilled." Some worked regularly and some little or not at all. The common bond was their mutual revulsion against established authority and against the whole "system." The Hippies also experimented with new forms of family styles—in some cases, communes consisting of as many as two dozen persons lived together; problems were automatically created by such arrangements, of course. In 1967, when word got about that a large influx of Hippies was planned for the summer, Mayor John Shelley stated his strong opposition to such a seasonal migration. He reminded those who planned to come that "existing ordinances will be strictly enforced and such migratory persons cannot be permitted to sleep in public parks or otherwise violate laws involving public health and the general peace and well-being of this community."[7]

By 1968, there had been a radical change of scene in the "Hashbury." The former Flower People or Love Children who had called their area the "Spiritual Capital of the Love Generation," had now been replaced by other more sinister elements and, according to one report, the area had become a "tension filled ghetto, simmering with hostility that bursts out in violence against authority—fights, holdups, muggings, rapes are common in the Haight."[8] The police reported that robberies in the area were up "300% in the first nine months of 1968. Aggravated assaults increased to 150% and rapes by 25%. Three people had been reported murdered in the year."[9] Obviously the original relatively inoffensive (save for personal hygiene and sanitation) flower people were no longer resident in great numbers in the district. A school crossing guard at the corner of Haight and Ashbury streets summed up what had happened:

> This used to be one of the nicest streets in the city. Look how run down its gotten. There used to be nice stores, but it's a ghost street now as far as business is concerned. When the first Hippie kids came here a couple of years ago, they were not too bad. Now there's every element . . . mug men . . . dope peddlers . . . and the filth! It looks nice now, but just come this afternoon and there'll be litter, beer cans and wine bottles all over. And the Hippies—all they do is walk back and forth, up one side and down the other.[10]

By the middle of January, 1969, the Haight-Ashbury district was described as a "totally distressed area, the poor man's underworld, Tenderloin West and a psychedelic ghetto."[11] Some of the discouraged original residents who had remained through it all spoke of their district in sorrowful terms as "moribund except for garbage strewn streets, defunct business and assault, rapine and pillage after dark." A 1969 survey revealed that the six-block sector which was the heart of the area "was characterized by thirty-seven vacated stores, eighteen boarded or steel-grated business enterprises, and more than a score of shops and bars whose plate-glass windows were cracked or shattered, five more establishments that are filthy wrecks, deserted without cleanup or an apparent backward glance by their former owners." The survey also referred bitterly to the presence "of the largest assemblance of sprawling, lunging, leaning, dormant and semicomatose characters in the city!" Some veteran Haight-Ashbury property owners were interviewed; one said: "We are desperate. We know that this is bottom. Five years ago, I owned the business I've got now and the liquor store next door. I sold the liquor store for $35,000; the guy who bought it went broke in eighteen months. . . . The only people who keep me going are the old settlers like myself; people who believe that some day the district will rejoin the union and civilization. The flower children were a set of Brownies compared to the people who roam the streets now."[12]

In a remarkable and, for San Francisco, unprecedented series of events, the Haight-Ashbury district has, since 1971, undergone a substantial change amounting to a return, in part, to former days. A number of "Veterans of the Haight," as they were dubbed, among property owners and businessmen, decided that their persistence in remaining while others fled the area merited a reward and they petitioned the Board of Supervisors for a rezoning or "downzoning" of part of the district which would enable owners to be sure that their investments would be protected from the coming of high-rise and other types of building which they did not favor; in 1971, they managed to transform a highly argumentative and divided group of young and old, white and black, Hippie and straight, owners and tenants, into a block of unity revolving around the rezoning question. What happened was a tribute to their determination to deliver their area from the myth that it was irretrievably lost to recovery; they pointed out that both the flower children and the speed, or drug, freaks had mostly left, and the dwellings that they had left should not be the victims of wreckers' balls and replaced with revenue buildings; this would destroy some of the former and undeniable architectural charm that had marked many of the old Victorian dwellings. One who spearheaded the movement said that: "While rezoning is only the first step, it is a necessary one to serve notice on real estate speculators, developers and the hospitals that dominate the Haight, that there is no longer going to be any large scale high rise development. The people who live in the Haight are going to determine what happens in the Haight."[13]

This was by far the largest attempt ever made by a group of San Francisco residents to downzone an area comprising seventy-two acres and nine hundred parcels, and it met unexpectedly quick acceptance at the hands of the Planning Commission as well as, ultimately, by a vote of the Board of Supervisors. One of the supervisors who voted for the protective downzoning plan, said that "the Haight is setting an example for many other neighborhoods in San Francisco." By December 1, 1972, a cautiously optimistic report presented to the Planning Commission indicated that an economic upswing was already in progress. It credited improvement of the Haight's financial picture to a reduction of major crime in the area as well as to the appearance of many new business enterprises and a shopping environment decidedly superior to that which had prevailed. The report noted that, since 1968, there had been a steady reduction in the crime rate which had put the district below the city average; however, it was pointed out that the recovery was far from complete. Significantly, though, it was very much on the way. Perhaps it was and is not an "impossible dream" to hope that the much afflicted area would or will gradually return to the normal and civilized conditions it previously enjoyed.

CHAPTER 38

CHANGING SKYLINE

. . . You architects who have visited San Francisco before may wonder where the city has gone. It's here somewhere, cowering behind hills and down alleys that form the new skyline that is almost indistinguishable from Pittsburgh's, Houston's or Atlanta's.

Herb Caen, *San Francisco Chronicle*, May 6, 1973.

W

HEN, ON JANUARY 30, 1847, the sleepy pueblo of Yerba Buena changed its name to San Francisco, it consisted of relatively few structures, mostly of primitive frame variety. Other clusters were at Mission Dolores as well as at the Presidio. Growth followed quickly with the Gold Rush; between 1849 and 1869, San Francisco developed into a sizable city of 150,000 inhabitants, already meriting the title of the principal city of the Pacific Coast. Many buildings of this period were designed in the Greek Revival or Classical mold, with an occasional intermingling of other architectural styles. During these two decades, the landscape was also enriched by some well-designed business structures, often built in granite or sandstone. This earlier period of styling is frequently forgotten in the light of the Champagne Days of the 1870s and 1880s. However, the earlier age deserves to be acknowledged as the city's first major period of architectural design.[1]

In 1869, with the completion of the transcontinental railroad, joined with the wealth from the Comstock Lode silver mines in Nevada, a new and quite flamboyant style of architecture gradually became part of the San Francisco scene. Some remnants of this period still exist in the Mission district as well as in the Western Addition, Nob Hill, and Pacific Heights districts. From 1870 to 1895, a sort of "San Francisco Style" evolved, an elaborate exhibition in wood of exterior facades that was of the essence of what is now referred to as "Victorian San Francisco."[2] Styles changed by the middle 1890s when the levelling and stabilizing effects of a manufacturing economy made themselves felt; by this time, San Francisco's population was around 340,000. Now, dwellings called "flats" made their appearances in quantity with the influence of the massive neoclassic styling of the 1893

World's Fair in Chicago becoming apparent. (This was joined with an occasional interest in the earlier California Mission style.) Obviously a highly significant change came once more, from 1906 to 1909, with the rebuilding of San Francisco. By 1915, with the advent of the Panama Pacific International Exposition, new forces were let loose in the city. These years saw the beginning of steel structures for commercial uses and the flowering of the "California style" in the work of such architects as Bernard Maybeck and other distinguished men. Many commercial buildings which joined fine design with expensive materials came into being during this period. The use of granite and bronze was prominent.[3]

The two decades of the 1960s and 1970s were to bring spectacular and not always appreciated departures from traditional San Franciscan ways in the matter of new construction. The observations of the authors of the authoritative *Here Today: San Francisco's Architectural Heritage,* ring a bit hollow in the light of what has since transpired:

> The survival of the (San Francisco) spirit down to this day would also seem to be the result of its historical flavor; it has not been a spirit contingent upon the latest building boom. It is no accident that San Francisco was the first great city in the country to resist violently the encroachment of the freeway builders. In their conscious appreciation of the character of their city, many San Franciscans are highly aware of the importance of both the past and the physical qualities their city draws from the past. . . . The double decker freeway in front of the Ferry building symbolizes the bankruptcy of this traditional approach as does the wholesale destruction of a large part of the Western Addition in the name of "Redevelopment."[4]

Not since the years of reconstruction after the fire and earthquake of 1906 had San Francisco witnessed such an era of building as it did in the 1960s; this activity also characterized the next decade, as early in 1971 Harold Gilliam, a long-term observer of the local scene, wrote: "San Francisco is a disappearing city. Some kind of city will remain here, of course, but many of the qualities that have made this a unique and incomparable metropolis are vanishing." Warming to his theme, Gilliam continued:

> Take the architecture, for example. One of the greatest pleasures this city has to offer is to walk the streets of its neighborhoods observing themes and variations in the designs of its houses. . . . Inevitably most

of these buildings must disappear. A house does not last forever. . . . But most of the newer houses throughout the city are totally without the verve and vigor of the buildings they are replacing. Take a walk through the eastern end of Pacific Heights where turreted and gabled old Queen Anne houses, Brownstone mansions, Tudor, Spanish, Renaissance and colonial houses are being replaced by stark, bland apartments lacking in eye catching texture, ornamentation or detail. Of course there are some brilliantly outstanding exceptions, but, on the whole, the new dwellings appear utterly lacking in character and interest; monotonous, box-like, mass-produced products of an age of conformity.[5]

Gilliam also had occasion to bemoan the city's disappearing hills. He correctly observed that picturesque old view houses on Telegraph and Russian hills were being replaced by skyscraping apartments on the hilltops. He sadly observed that a sort of Chinese Wall of tall apartment buildings on the bottoms of these hills was further complicating the scene. "The ultimate result will be to turn San Francisco into a counterpart of Manhattan Island, its hills disappearing behind walls of skyscrapers." Many will now agree that these words were quite prophetic and that what Gilliam predicted has now come to pass in San Francisco.

When the prestigious American Institute of Architects met for

Nob Hill today.

Mark Hopkins Hotel, Nob Hill.

their convention in San Francisco in early May 1973, they were set right by local columnist Herb Caen as to what they would find in the city. Blaming them in a corporate sense, at least, for what some of them had done to his city as well as to other American urban complexes, Caen told those whom he called the "Titans of the T Square who have given us such wonders as pyramids with cars, filing cabinets in the sky, vertical ice trays, 60-story decks of cards" that they have made us what we are today, "very, very nervous!" Sadly this long-time observer and commentator on matters San Franciscan lamented that "it's the San Francisco of yesterday that has been lost in the crush. Something charming, perishable and, it turns out, unique is being trampled to death by those to whom less is more and ugly is beautiful." Recalling the oft-quoted words uttered by Frank Lloyd Wright twenty-five years previously: "Only a city as beautiful as San Francisco could survive what you people are doing to it." Caen evoked historical memories of some of the truly distinguished architects whose earlier work had so tastefully adorned San Francisco:

> Willis Polk formalized the elegant San Francisco town house, gracious and spacious. Arthur Brown put his Beaux Arts stamp on City Hall and Opera House and, in the downtown areas, buildings arose that had a decent respect for their neighbors. Unlike the present day Bank of America and Transamerica, there was not a single "look at me ego trip on the skyline" which rose naturally and with dignity from the hills.

The *Chronicle* columnist went on to point out that the Russ Building, which had been the largest in the city for decades, made an harmonious connection with such other structures as the Shell Building, Mills Tower, and the old Standard Oil Building. In a final admonition to the visiting architects, Caen concluded: "If there is still a heart in San Francisco, you will probably find it throbbing in a cable car slot, not in an elevator shooting at 1,000 feet a second to the 52nd floor. So please be kind."[6]

Similar and equally trenchant criticisms of the changing San Francisco skyline were expressed in an article syndicated by the *New York Times* which concerned itself with what was happening in the city. Reference was made to the many huge buildings on their way to the sky "shaping a skyline that Herb Caen recently said was 'almost indistinguishable from Pittsburgh's, Houston's or Atlanta's.'" It was but natural that obvious comment would come from a consideration of the Transamerica Pyramid, since it was a giant building and the tallest in the city.[7]

The move toward high-rise buildings began in San Francisco near the end of the 1950s, and continued through the next dec-

Market Street with tallest building in 1890: Claus Spreckels (Call) Building.

ade; during this time some forty new skyscrapers were built. This finally led to a "ballot box rebellion" in 1970 when aroused voters attempted to force a seven-story height limit on buildings in San Francisco. Although the initiative measure failed to pass, it did result in height limits being established in most neighborhoods. However, downtown, skyscrapers still continued to rise. Critics had praised the earlier and successful attempt of J.D. Zellerbach which resulted in a distinguished building in 1959. It has been recognized as among the best examples of post-war office building design anywhere in the world and it provided hope, not completely realized, that other structures would learn from its success. It still exhibits a combination of elegance and warmth

Bank of America Building.

unprecedented in San Francisco's office building past. Partially
due to Zellerbach's success as well as to the economic forces of
the expanding 1960s, other buildings began to rise in the financial
district. Along with this came a new step in urban growth, the
Golden Gateway Center, which was the first major large-scale
redevelopment project for downtown San Francisco. This center

replaced the run-down wholesale produce district with many imaginative new structures of various designs; forty-five acres were involved in the change. Gradually an impressive 2,300 dwelling units, in high-rise blocks, towers, and rows of town-houses placed on a raised pediment, came into being; eventually garage space for 1,300 cars as well as assorted shops were to form part of the Golden Gateway Center. Here seemed to be proof that, with proper planning and restraint, an area of any city can be satisfactorily changed for the better.

This brief overview of the changing architectural scene in modern San Francisco is concluded with the hope that sensitive planners, developers, and architects may combine their professional skills to make San Francisco a more beautiful place than it is even now.

CHAPTER 39

REFLECTIONS ON THE CONTEMPORARY SCENE

WHEN ONE APPROACHES the consideration of the contemporary scene in San Francisco, the conviction comes quickly that, inevitably, much of the historical dimension must be lacking. Evidence with which to correctly assess the passing scene is incomplete or, in some cases, mostly absent. However, an attempt will be made here to consider some of the present problems of San Francisco. In 1976, the city observed its bicentennial year, and a few observations extending into 1977 will conclude this treatment of the San Francisco story.

Modern American cities have this much in common: the larger among them must deal continually with a never-ending cycle of problems which stem from the very nature of their urban existence. Inadequate housing, urban renewal, redevelopment, crime, quality education, ethnic problems—all form part of the city scene in America, and elsewhere too, it may be supposed. Obviously, San Francisco has and will continue to have its share of such problems. First, some consideration on the number of those who currently live in San Francisco.

More than a century ago, according to the federal census of 1870, San Francisco had a population of 149,473. The subsequent decades saw a steady rise with the highest population recorded in the census of 1950, when 775,357 was given as the number dwelling within the city and county of San Francisco. Since then there has been a consistent drop as more and more inhabitants have either left the area or, in the familiar phrase, "fled to the suburbs." In 1960, there were 742,855 inhabitants; by 1970, this number had decreased to 715,674; by 1973, it was estimated the city's population had decreased by 4.8 percent, with the largest decline coming in the white population, down 43,686 or 8.5 percent while the city's nonwhite population increased by 4.5 percent. Estimates made by the Population Research Unit which is associated with the Department of Finance (under the jurisdiction of the California Department of State) gave clear indication that the city's population declined, from 705,700 in 1971 to 662,-700 as of January 1977. The last figures available from the Federal Bureau of the Census in San Francisco placed the city's population on July 1, 1975, at 664,520. Despite the not over large discrepancy here, the fact remains that, as already indicated, San Francisco has lost steadily in population during the last decade.

The 1970 figures caused some editorial comment in the *San Francisco Chronicle* which did not see the decrease in an entirely unfavorable light. Pointing out that the population density of San Francisco was second only to that of New York, the editorial remarked that "it is not bad news, per se, that San Francisco lost 5 percent of its population in the 1960's":

> It will prove to be bad news only if the complete census breakdown, yet to come, could show that the decline was accompanied by a relative increase in the socially dependent families on welfare, aged persons without means, immigrants lacking skills or without knowledge of the English language, etc. . . . The losses will be more than offset by the gain in the quality of the life a less crowded San Francisco can provide its citizenry, if there is also an easing of the very costly burdens of crime, welfare and education of the underprivileged.[1]

Not all agreed with the above editorial opinion. In 1973, Harold Gilliam, a veteran and competent observer in such matters, wrote that "The city is in deep trouble. Like most urban centers, San Francisco faces steeply rising costs of operation and diminishing residents to pay the bills."[2] He then proposed at considerable length some suggested plans to remodel San Francisco so as to attract another half million people. The plan was that proposed by a local architect, William Blackwell, and, as expected, it drew much criticism and comment from all kinds of experts and amateurs as well as from those who simply considered themselves true lovers of the city. At least these comments indicated that there were still very many who cared about the future of San Francisco.

Several years earlier, in 1967, the San Francisco Chamber of Commerce had set up a committee of four to "find out just what was going on in San Francisco." In a matter of months, the committee told San Franciscans that:

> It is essential that every effort be made to raise the standards of education and motivation and to take steps to encourage merit employment of people in minority groups so that they may fully participate in the economic life of the city.[3]

The city's future, said the committee, depended largely on how the minority residents were treated and what they did to help themselves. Pointing out that 56 percent of the city's 91,359 children belonged to minority groups—24,051 Blacks, 16,057 Asians, 11,089 Spanish-speaking—the committee observed: "The consequent effect, real or imagined, on the quality of public education is driving some parents who can afford it to move to the suburban school systems." Noting further that the white middle class was moving to the suburbs, "because manufacturers moved, drawing workers with them," the report concluded as follows:

> Perhaps the city will never get much larger than it is today. If we really conceptualize San Francisco to be the capital of the region, then our concern and planning must be for continuous upgrading of its population and our living and working environment.[4]

Enough has been indicated here to establish the fact that the San Francisco of the recent past and of now faces immense and complex problems. Unemployment rates increase while serious crimes multiply; racial tension is ever present and, frequently, even the best-intentioned plans for urban renewal and redevelopment result merely in displacing ghetto residents, usually black or other minority groups. Slum areas such as were present in the Fillmore district can be torn down much more quickly than they can be rebuilt; buildings go down overnight but there remain, and frequently for extended lengths of time, many vacant lots. These are only some of the more evident details connected with the problem of urban housing in San Francisco. It is evident that they will continue to occupy the attention of both civic planners and other interested San Franciscans. The great and continuing debate in the city today would seem to concern itself with the pros and cons of suitable ways and means to preserve the flavor of old San Francisco—whether in fact, such a flavor can be maintained while city planners attempt to update San Francisco and make it a clean, livable, modern space-age city. Understandable and inevitable tensions have resulted as various groups have endeavored to implement their divergent views.

The educational system is surely among the most important institution in any city, state, or country. The far-reaching influence it has over the minds of future leaders is evident. A study conducted by teachers and school administrators of the Bay Area was reported as follows:

> We (San Franciscans) are far from our goal of equality/quality education . . . increasingly difficult problems are a legacy of racial, cultural and economic isolation which the school district has willed itself . . . every additional day of delay will only further reduce what faith remains in the school district's willingness to move ahead.[5]

As elsewhere throughout the nation, the problem of segregation exists in San Francisco's school districts. Economic and social sanctions formerly guaranteed a uniformly white middle-class student body in some areas and a black minority group student body in other sections of the city. Bond issues for improvement of educational facilities in certain areas such as Hunters Point have gone down to defeat more than once; this has helped to increase unrest among those most affected by this refusal of the voters to improve conditions in a depressed area. Just what solutions to this and kindred problems the future will bring is unknown; since the area's city government, large and small business, research and industry and, indeed, the very fabric of family life is dependent to a notable extent on the San Francisco school system, the most crucial challenges to be faced by the city lie in the field of education.

Mention must be made of the problem of crime as it has concerned the recent history of San Francisco. A 1972 report of the San Francisco Grand Jury asserted that it was no longer possible to walk the streets of the city in safety and this would seem even truer in 1977. While the crime picture in 1961 was unspectacular (forty murders were reported, some few of which turned out to be "justifiable homicides" with police having to handle about 33,500 major crimes in all), the situation had changed very much for the worse ten years later. By 1971, major crimes reported were up to 72,655, more than double the 1961 figure, and the Police Department budget had soared from $13 million to $46 million. Many reasons were given by as many persons as to why this epidemic of crime had come to San Francisco. Some blamed it on the increased use of drugs (probably a major contributing factor) while others said that it was "all because of the blacks: the more blacks in the city, the more crime." A veteran police captain told of his belief that "it is the liberal courts and the parole board. The judge gives a convicted felon six months in the county jail and frees him on probation. Or he goes to state prison and he's paroled back to the streets to commit another crime." Others have claimed that the welfare policies of the state joined with redevelopment projects had succeeded only in creating new ghettos which always seem to provide an environment suitable for crime. Some observers join such comments with remedies which they consider as sure to reduce the incidence of crime—included among such persons are sociologists, criminologists, politicians, the police, and prosecutors. Meanwhile, the crime situation remains a pall upon the city as it does in many cities today.

Urban redevelopment has been a part of the local scene since 1945; problems that had come to light during war years now called for long-term study in the hope that solutions might be found. A Postwar Planning Committee viewed San Francisco with a critical eye and deemed the situation "serious but far from hopeless." Investments by such nationally known firms as Macys, Woolworth's, and Sears pointed to the fact that there was still abundant business faith in San Francisco's ability to meet its problems. A six-year program was formulated which included 277 projects, totalling over $130 million. High priority was given to improvement of transportation, off-street parking facilities, and to plans to improve local parks and playgrounds. A Master Plan was adopted by the committee to guide future development in the city. In the late 1940s, parts of the Western Addition were designated as "blighted areas" and a Redevelopment Agency was appointed by the Board of Supervisors to undertake the project of renewing the areas concerned. Redevelopment was hindered by a law requiring the relocation of the displaced families before the deteriorated buildings could be cleared. Since there was an acute shortage of housing at this time, the only solution seemed to be the building of new housing elsewhere in the city. Various sections, such as Diamond Heights, were surveyed with a view as to their place in the plan. However, it was not until January 1956, that the Federal Housing and Home Finance Agency approved a loan and capital grant to assist the San Francisco Redevelopment Agency in its plans for Diamond Heights. As was expected, controversies hinging upon many factors as well as financial problems served to slow down progress in this important matter. Gradually also, environmental problems impinged themselves on an ever more complicated scene. While some of the major perplexities gradually yielded as some solutions were found, there still remained much disagreement among San Franciscans as to whether the overall policies of redevelopment in the city had been for better or for worse. Possibly the answer lay somewhere between two extremes. Meanwhile it has long been apparent that controlled growth and efficient development do not come easy in San Francisco.

In 1963, Thomas Creighton, an architect with considerable professional training, joined several others as a vice-president of John Carl Warnecke and Associates, a local firm of architects and planning consultants; he soon published a thoughtful article in the *San Francisco Magazine* (August, 1963). Indicating that he shared with many others a keen interest in the city as well as a similar interest in preserving the unique atmosphere and character of San Francisco, Creighton outlined his tentative Five Point Program which, if followed essentially, would, he thought, enable San Francisco to avoid falling into the pitfalls that had marked situations in other American cities.

He conceived a major hazard to be that of sacrificing the city's distinctive character for so-called "practicality"; to him this meant, among other things, the replacing of the beautiful French Renaissance structures with concrete slabs. This he called the "uglification program." His first point of the five suggested that an in-depth study should be conducted of the unique character of San Francisco. This, if done properly, would, he hoped, help to develop a "San Francisco Philosophy joined with a program for planned growth." From this would come a new Master Plan. Creighton saw as an absolute necessity a restudying of the vital role of the San Francisco Planning Commission which, at the time, was powerless without the approval of their decisions by a highly political Board of Supervisors. Concentrated and unselfish effort should be able, Creighton thought, to coordinate the planning efforts of all the boards and agencies that dealt with relevant and constantly changing problems. This should also have the welcome result of putting San Francisco in the fore in regional and area planning.

While critics were not slow to express reservations with regard to what Creighton wrote, some said that, at the very least, the various points represented serious efforts to confront the future and to continue the solving of some of the more urgent problems of San Francisco. The past few years have seen other plans offered by similarly concerned San Franciscans and all, or at least most, of this would seem to be for the good.

As San Francisco approached its bicentennial year of 1976, various civic groups as well as interested private citizens made preliminary plans to commemorate this important year in the city's history. As early as August 13, 1972, Robert Commanday, music critic for the *San Francisco Chronicle,* wrote an extensive article in which he mentioned that proposed plans were already incorporated in an unofficial report which had been presented to Mayor Alioto; it was the work of a committee of twenty-five citizens from various civic organizations and some governmental agencies. Probably because of this and other similar articles that appeared in the local press, it was not long before things started to move, (although not in any spectacular fashion). In 1974 an official organization called "San Francisco Twin Bicentennial, Inc." was formed which announced its purpose as:

> planning and implementing a 200th birthday commemorative program during 1976 which honors San Francisco's proud past, challenging present, and promising future in conjunction with the American Revolution Bicentennial. We seek to enlist the broadest community participation recognizing the unique character of San Francisco's ethnic diversity and dramatic setting. We will not overlook any opportunity to reflect with appreciation on our past progress and, at the same time, to create new ways to improve the quality of life for those who live in and visit San Francisco.

The *San Francisco Progress* on July 2, 1974, furnished more information about this emerging group:

> The formation of San Francisco Twin Bicentennial began in September, 1973, at the initiation of Mayor Alioto. It was subsequently organized as a nonprofit corporation under the laws of California. Its funding for initial planning has came from city hotel tax revenue, with $60,000 appropriated for the fiscal year July 1, 1974–June 30, 1975. Additional governmental and private grants are being sought.

Because of the very nature of the planned observances, it was essential that a History Committee be appointed to correctly honor the city's past; fortunately this committee was headed by Albert Shumate, M.D., member of a prominent San Francisco family and himself an intimate student and lover of San Francisco's past. Approximately 40 persons representing all manner of historical and related organizations were appointed to serve on this pivotal committee which, during the many months of its operation, met regularly and provided an important "control," from the standpoint of historical accuracy.

The first event of note heralding the coming of 1976 with its important commemorations honored Fernando Rivera y Moncada and Father Francisco Palou, L.F.M., who, on December 4, 1774, camped at Lake Merced and proceeded to Point Lobos, making them the first Europeans to view the Golden Gate at close range. Exactly 200 years later, on December 4, 1974, the Twin Bicentennial organization dedicated a plaque near the original site commemorating this pioneer event with Dr. Shumate serving as chairman.

Foremost among the numerous events that marked 1975 in connection with the bicentennial observances was the commemoration of the 200th anniversary of the arrival of the small Spanish packet boat, *San Carlos,* which, on August 5, 1775, entered the Golden Gate under command of Captain Juan Manuel de Ayala. Several Ayala days were observed; a Mass was offered at Mission Dolores Basilica on Sunday, August 3, and this was followed later in the day by the dedication of a historical kiosk at the newly renamed "Lt. Ayala Vista Point" at the north end of the Golden Gate Bridge. On August 5, exactly 200 years to the day since the Ayala entrance, a large luncheon was held at the Fort Mason

Officers Club which was followed by the dedication of a California Historical Landmark Plaque at Aquatic Park commemorating the Ayala entrance into the bay. Principal speakers included Mayor Alioto and the Spanish Ambassador to the United States, His Excellency Jaime Alba, with a large audience viewing the ceremonies.

On March 28, 1976, another commemoration of considerable significance was held. This was an accurate re-creation of Colonel Juan Bautista de Anza's trek to the site of the future San Francisco in late March 1776. In an elaborate ceremony, de Anza and key members of his party again came to the "White Cliff" above where Fort Point now stands and, in an elaborate reenactment, this event was significantly commemorated.

Finally, what the *Examiner* called the "city's biggest week in 200 years" came in late June 1976. On Sunday, June 27, Archbishop McGucken was joined by a full congregation when he offered Pontifical Mass in Mission Dolores Basilica: the present basilica, adjacent to the old mission which dates from 1791 and which is not far from the original mission dating from October 9, 1776, was a fitting place to have this liturgical commemoration. In the afternoon, the Golden Gate Park Music Concourse was the scene of a special concert which, among other events, saw another reenactment of the 1776 first settlers, complete with de Anza's arrival on horseback. On June 29, the annual birthday Mass was offered in old Mission Dolores and an overflow luncheon was had, as is traditional each year, in the newly expanded Officers Club at the Presidio. The principal address was given by the Reverend Floyd Lotito, a Franciscan friar who was well chosen to tell the story of what was being commemorated during these June days. Other celebrations included a large downtown Interfaith Parade on June 27.

It was with a feeling of legitimate pride that the many who had contributed to these varied events looked back on the bicentennial celebrations in San Francisco.

For the ever-present critics of the local scene whooping constantly that "San Francisco is not what it used to be," it would seem that they were and are merely voicing a truism which applies to just about every major American city. It is enlightening to record here as we bring our story to a close that, according to official figures of the San Francisco Convention and Visitors Bureau, more than four times the number of people visited the city in 1976 than those who live here. It was estimated that more than $661 million were left in the city by these same tourists. The report also noted: "Tourism is San Francisco's biggest business and, during 1976, earnings were up to 193 percent over 1975. That was despite a drop-off in the number of conventions due to the lack of a major convention center here. However, local hotels and motels received 2,912,000 visitors, of whom 753,785 attended conventions."

It would appear that without blinking at or ignoring the many serious problems that face San Francisco, it is permissible or, perhaps, even required to conclude with the observation that the City by the Golden Gate with its unique and storied past will continue to occupy a privileged position among the great cities of the world.

A SURVEY OF SAN FRANCISCANA

I T WILL COME as no surprise to the multitudes who love San Francisco that the long-standing object of their affections has attracted much comment in the past, just as it still does. The list of books, articles, poetry, and the like which concern the city is an impressive one; a modest attempt to list some of the more enduring sources will be found in an appendix. Here, since the historical dimensions of the city have now been drawn to 1977, we shall assemble a representative sampling of what has been written about San Francisco.

First, for a quick dip into some sayings about San Francisco, we may list the following for what they are worth. Richard Henry Dana, famous for his *Two Years Before the Mast,* first published in New York in 1840 and generally regarded as a minor American classic, called San Francisco "the sole emporium of a new world, the awakened Pacific." Bret Harte, in an oft-quoted phrase said of San Francisco that she was "serene, indifferent of fate," while Rudyard Kipling asserted that the city "has only one drawback, 'tis hard to leave." George Sterling, poet of the city and possessed of an especial affection for it, wrote that "Her gaze is ever West in the dream of her young unrest" while "her heart is a song and a star," there the "winds of the future wait at the iron walls of her gate." (Most frequently quoted of the Sterling sayings, perhaps, is that where he called San Francisco his "cool grey city of love.") Gene Fowler, a later literary light, enthusiastically wrote that "Every man should be allowed to love two cities, his own and San Francisco." A different brand of praise came from the visiting Nikita Khrushchev who said, "Of all the cities of the United States I have seen, San Francisco is the most beautiful." This potpourri of praise was added to by Robert Louis Stevenson when he wrote: "San Francisco is not herself only. She is not only the most interesting city in the Union and the hugest melting pot of races. . . . She keeps, besides, the doors of the Pacific." Ina Coolbrith, poet laureate of California, wrote in "The Argonauts": "I have dreamed of San Francisco all the way." Will Rogers had a characteristically frank comment about cities: "Cities are like gentlemen, they are born, not made. You are either a city, or you are not. I bet San Francisco was a city from the very first time it had a dozen settlers!" After the fire and earthquake days of 1906, a famous old-time boxer, Willie Britt, opined that he "would rather be a busted lamp post on Battery Street than the Waldorf Astoria." Speaking of hotels, Innkeeper Conrad Hilton is on record as saying that "In all my travels, I have never seen the hospitality of San Francisco equalled anywhere in the world." So much for some of the many quotable sayings about the city.

In 1849, a certain F.P. Wierzbicki, M.D., achieved literary distinction by issuing what is believed to be the first book published in San Francisco. It was called *California As It Is and As It May Be: A Guide to the Gold Fields.* Here is the medico's impression of the still undeveloped town:

> When this uneven slope of the hill on which the town is situated shall be built up with fine and solid houses, what now looks dreary and desolate will then look very picturesque and smiling . . . but, as yet, one needs a little philosophy to bear him through the present that he may lean on the future.

This present book has borrowed more than once from what must certainly be regarded as one of the classics in the literature of San Francisco history, *The Annals of San Francisco,* by the famous trio of Soule, Gihon, and Nisbet, which appeared in New York in 1855. In this still important and extensive literary treatment, the authors enter upon many judgments regarding the city whose annals they have chosen to compile; all throughout their effort, it is quite evident that they feel that what they are doing is worthwhile because of the nature of San Francisco itself. An early chapter refers to the "magnificent bay and harbor which are now called San Francisco."[1] That same bay is again referred to, this time as "incomparable,"[2] with the authors opining that "the Bay of San Francisco is so extensive . . . that many more harbors than the one at the city of that name will hereafter be formed."[3] More extensive, though, and more inclusive are these words which were penned in connection with what had happened in the city in 1853:

> The San Franciscans are proud of their noble city that sits enthroned besides calm waters and, as Queen of the Pacific, receives homage and tribute from all seas and oceans. Her buildings are becoming palaces and her merchants, princes. Wealth, gayety, and luxury characterize her people. She is fast approaching that peculiar and regal character which in days of old was borne by the great cities of the Mediterranean. . . . She is very young yet and has a long age of growing grandeur before her. Her spirit is "Go Ahead!" We have seen her, but a few years since, only a barren waste of sand hills, a paltry village, a thriving little town, a budding city of canvas, then of wood, and next a great metropolis of brick. . . . After the wonders we have already seen, nothing seems impossible in the progress of San Francisco. Her future will be far more glorious than even the present.[4]

One of the most widely quoted sources on early San Francisco is Bayard Taylor's *El Dorado, Or Adventures in The Path of Empire* which appeared in both London and New York in 1850. It has been reprinted many times because of the shrewd comments of the author about a myriad of things he saw in his "El Dorado." (At the time of his visit, Taylor was a twenty-four-year-old correspondent for the *New York Tribune.*) He wrote:

> Every new comer to San Francisco is overtaken by a sense of complete bewilderment. . . . One knows not whether he is awake or in some wonderful dream. Never have I had such difficulty in establishing, satisfactorily, to my own sense, the reality of what I saw and heard.[5]

Another early source on things San Franciscan is the social history written by B.E. Lloyd and published by him in 1876 as *Lights and Shades in San Francisco.* In a brief preface dated September 1, 1876, called "Why," Lloyd remarks:

> Life in San Francisco is intense and has marked peculiarities. It is not passive in a single particular. The manners, customs, business and pleasure of the people are opposed to inactivity, at all seasons and in all things. The growth of San Francisco has been rapid, perhaps unprecedented. The exciting causes that have led to this have formed her characteristics. There is some romance surrounding her development and, mingled in it, there was much vivid reality. But it has been purely San Franciscan.[6]

Continuing the spectrum approach to what people have written about San Francisco, the thoughtful reflection of Charles Caldwell Dobie may be mentioned here:

The past is bound up in any proper appreciation of San Francisco's present. Most present day San Franciscans have a confused sense of its gold-rush history, but of its very beginning, they know next to nothing. The descendants of American pioneers take proper pride in the covered wagon exploits of their ancestors, but they are ignorant or scornful of the heroic exploits of the early Spanish settlers who also marched through a wilderness to achieve the promised land. The Spanish pioneers of San Francisco may not have endowed it with a striking material legacy but they provided an additional strain of romantic fortitude which deserves recognition.[7]

Denis Brogan, a professor of political science at Cambridge University in England who has visited America many times and written about it in several books, contributed his impressions of San Francisco in an article in *Harper's* magazine in 1950: here is how he felt about the City by the Golden Gate:

The special position of the European tourist in America may best be illustrated, I think, by considering what it is in the American city that appeals to him most. I don't think that there is much difficulty in determining what city that is. Yes, it is San Francisco.

I don't think that I know any foreign visitor to America, with adequate grounds of comparison, who hasn't preferred San Francisco to any other great American city and to most small cities or towns. Some of the grounds are obvious enough and are common to American and European visitors alike. There is the magnificent site; there is the celebrated though, in chilly fact, less magnificent climate; there is a romantic past; there is a romantic name; there is an amiable population; there is the remoteness on the Pacific coast away from the gray, tormented, all too familiar Atlantic. The visitors from Scranton, Paisley, Saint-Etienne, Eindhoven, Akron may all feel these things, but they feel them in different ways.[8]

Brogan commented on each of the facts he mentioned in the above quotation. The site thrilled and impressed him. "For a patriotic American, San Francisco Bay is the most magnificent harbor in the world, just what a city needs." After further analysis, Brogan reflects:

But it is not, I think, the romance of the port that wins one to San Francisco. It is the stability, human and material, San Francisco has a gratifying air of being finished. . . . Most American cities sprawl. Indeed one could say of some regions what Whistler said of a bad picture: "It may be finished but it certainly wasn't begun." Almost alone among big American cities (quite alone among those I know and I know most) San Francisco is defined. Defined by the Bay, by the Golden Gate, by the Twin Peaks. "Across the Bay," "Down the Peninsula" these common phrases give the atmosphere of this geographically beleaguered city. You can think of it standing a siege. I think this stability, this possibly irritating self-centeredness, is reflected in the citizens, native and adopted. No city is less a victim of the booster spirit. . . . It is a relief, or at least a change, to come to a city where most citizens don't seem to know or care how big they are or how much the Bureau of the Census has betrayed the truth in its latest returns. . . . It is surely significant of something that the "cri de coeur" of the exiled native son: "California, here I come" makes it plain that it is to San Francisco, not to Bakersfield, Pasadena, Santa Barbara or anywhere else that he is returning. So say all of us who are not merely not native sons, but not even ordinary Americans. . . .[9]

An indication of the continuing interest in San Francisco is shown by an article which appeared in the very first issue of *Holiday* magazine, published in 1946. The author comments on the city as changed and yet, in many respects, unchanged, by World War II. He concludes that San Francisco still remains "cosmopolitan (even more so than before the War) funloving, exotic, gateway to the Pacific, that's San Francisco!" A final reflection is thus phrased: "The greatest change in San Francisco is the way the War has turned the town around, at least in outlook. A few years back, the City by the Golden Gate was the western end of the transcontinental railways and the Lincoln Highway . . . now it's the crossroads of the new American empire. . . ."[10]

In at least three more issues, *Holiday* returned to its comments and coverage on matters San Franciscan. The September 1953 issue of *Holiday*, which proved to be a sort of warm-up for two later issues, had a dozen pages devoted to the *Holiday* way of "discovering" cities. The first article remarked:

Although it will not be argued that San Francisco is heaven itself, there is a general agreement among its approximately 800,000 inhabitants that a happier steppingstone to Heaven could not be found. Countless other Americans, moreover, lean to the same point of view.

Of all the cities in the United States, San Francisco comes closest to being everybody's town.[11]

Again, the entire issue for April 1961, was devoted to this theme. Its appearance was hailed in various manners in the city itself; Herb Caen called it "narcissism run amok" but the issue quickly surpassed 32,500 sales in a city where normally the "slick paper travel magazine" sold about 2,000 copies each month. The magazine's 220 pages were wholly devoted to photographs and articles about San Francisco, many of the latter by Bay Area professionals. The editorial foreword glowed: "All that they have said of San Francisco has turned out to be true. The spell bewitches so many, it cannot be dismissed as a figment. The place deserves a name not lightly bestowed—metropolis."[12] The city's Chamber of Commerce quickly got into the act with the pronouncement that "It is absolutely impossible to gauge the importance of this issue." Despite Caen's comment, he was one of the contributors in his role as "Mr. San Francisco" and he was reported to have led thousands of San Franciscophiles in admiring the production.[13] The Chamber of Commerce had only one cautionary remark: it implored San Franciscans not to hold on to their copies, rather, they should look to it that these be sent, presumably after reverent perusal, to non-Bay Areans, adding: "We don't want this to be a mutual admiration society." However, William Hogan, Book Editor of the *Chronicle,* had his reservations about the issue. Mentioning that *Holiday* was a travel magazine which never stressed the unpleasant or the sordid or tawdry, Hogan remarked: "That is *Holiday*'s viewpoint, and a successful one it is."[14] However, he wrote that he did not intend to send his copy on, "For the San Francisco I read about and looked at in *Holiday*'s exotic tribute seemed as remote as the Emerald City of Oz." He added:

As one who has lived in the Bay Region for lo, these 150 years (!) *Holiday*'s idea of the city seemed glib and superficial. Nothing dishonest, understand, merely superficial. No viscera, no sinew, no reality. The City is both less and more than the one *Holiday* reflected. On the other hand, it simply isn't that good; on the other, it is a richer, more dignified, more human region than this sensationalized mockup suggests. . . . You can send your copy on to friends in Mason City or Tulsa, if you like. I'm afraid if I had friends in Tulsa, they would never find the mirage which *Holiday* found at the Golden Gate, and after such conditioning, they may not like the exhilarating and real community that most of us know and live in.[15]

Seemingly, *Holiday* chose not to learn anything from these criticisms for, in March 1970, less than a decade afterward, it issued *San Francisco: A Special Issue.* The approach was essentially the same, consisting, in this case, of a dozen articles exploring various aspects of the San Francisco of the past and present.

The *Tomorrow* magazine, issue of March 1950, continued an earlier series of articles with the general title of "Hometown Revisited." Number 16 in the series was on San Francisco and was written by the well-known author (and native San Franciscan) Irving Stone. After recalling his earliest years there, Stone wrote:

> San Franciscans, like the amazing hills they have climbed these several generations, are a hard, stony people astonishingly like New Englanders: stubborn, proud, wilful, self-contained, tenacious, fiercely independent, rooted in rocky tradition, not the kind of hardness that is mean or uncharitable, but rather the kind that demands so terribly much of itself. . . . All the things are true about San Franciscans. But a lot more is true, too.[16]

After an extensive analysis of the San Francisco he best recalled, Stone discussed the contradictions that he found in its story. For example, the fact that while friendly, hospitable, and charming, San Francisco was "always a tough labor town, just as willing to settle its arguments with stones, clubs or brass knuckles as with conciliatory words." Stone's final words are memorable: "But some part of San Francisco will never be changed: the core of the city, built, like Rome, on many hills. In fact, and in legend, this core will never be destroyed."[17]

Another literary great whose works are well known is William Saroyan. In 1940, he was moved to write an article for the *San Francisco Chronicle* in which he recorded his views about the city. He called San Francisco the "genius of American cities," which he regarded as "the wild-eyed, all-fired, hard-boiled, tender-hearted, white haired boy of the American family of cities. It is the prodigal son; the city which does everything and is always forgiven, because of its great heart, its gentle smile, its roaring laughter, its mysterious and magnificent personality. . . ."[18] Saroyan went on:

> It is not the easiest city in the world to like at first. It is not an easy city to know. The city is cold. It is hard. It is ugly(!) It is indifferent. But, at the same time, it is also warmer than any other city; it is gentler; it is more beautiful; and it is kindlier. It is a city with its head in the clouds and its feet in the valleys. San Francisco is a world to explore. It is a place where the heart can go on a delightful adventure. It is a city in which the spirit can know refreshment every day.[19]

John Steinbeck, although born in Salinas, professed a fondness for San Francisco in an *Examiner* article which was published in 1958. Describing his first contacts with what he had early learned to call "The City," Steinbeck then recalled he had learned much of his craftmanship in San Francisco, concluding with these words: "We learned in the magic heaped on the hills of San Francisco. And you know what it is? It's a golden handcuff with the key thrown away. Ask anyone about San Francisco and the odds are that he'll tell you about himself and his eyes will be warm and inward, remembering."[20] Again, Steinbeck thus expressed his admiration for San Francisco:

> San Francisco put on a show for me. A city on hills has it all over flat-land places. New York makes its own hills with craning buildings, but this gold and white acropolis rising wave on wave against the blue of the Pacific sky was a stunning thing, a picture of a medieval Italian city that can never have existed.[21]

In November 1961, another "slick" national magazine appealing to the carriage trade, *Town and Country,* saluted San Francisco:

> People who deal in superlatives soon run out of their stock in trade when they come to deal with San Francisco. This is a city that literally has everything. If ever there was an "alabaster city" as the song, "America, the Beautiful," proclaims, this is it. . . . However, it is not the physical attributes of San Francisco that spell its greatest merit. It is the spirit and character of the city. A spirit and a character that are different from any other city in the country. It is a vibrant city and a city of great energy and excitement. It is at once one of the most American of all cities and one of the most cosmopolitan.[22]

It has already been noted that foreign visitors have occasionally made comments about San Francisco. Here is what a British reporter, John Gold, wrote in the *London Evening News* in 1958 after a 6,900 mile rail journey across the United States.

They call San Francisco the Queen of the West Coast. It is a city that sparkles like a jewel besides the shimmering Pacific. We broke our journey there for two days and two nights. . . . There was only one thing wrong during our visit. Despite the Chamber of Commerce, which claims that the city is never too hot in summer, never too cold in winter, San Francisco was locked in the fiery fingers of a heat wave! On that single afternoon, 120 baseball fans fainted at the Stadium!

San Francisco is the most European city in the country. This is surprising since San Francisco is about as far as you can get from Europe while standing on American soil. Yet the buildings and the people have an appearance of solidity which you do not find in many areas of the country.[23]

An interesting comparison as to San Francisco's place among other cities of the world appeared in an article in the *National Review* in June 1968. The author, William A. Rusher, mentioning that travel was his hobby and that he had visited, "if not all, then very nearly all of the principal cities of the world," added:

I know of two (Rio and Hong Kong) whose physical sites are even lovelier than San Francisco's. I will go further: San Francisco is no match for the special qualities of a number of famous cities; the exquisite loveliness of Venice; the brilliant caravan colors of Marrakesh; the sheer power of New York; the grandeur that still is Rome. But when all is said and done, when all the pluses and minuses have been toted up, I take my stand: San Francisco is, for me at least, and as a visitor, the queen city of the world. . . . She will last my time, thank Heaven. And as long as I am physically able and can afford it, I will return to her whenever I can, to admire her, and smile with her, and savor life's joys with her, and re-learn what it can mean to be civilized.[24]

Another literary apostrophe is the following tribute published in 1934 by Glenn C. Quiett in his *They Built The West:*

She (San Francisco) has distinction, beauty, charm, and many lovers. One must envy the good fortune of those who are yet to come under her spell. When such a one comes for the first time to this glamorous city, he will learn to love her cool, gray beauty; he will delight in seeing her rise ghostlike on her high hills—an uneven, sawtoothed Whistler silhouette, dimly outlined against an indefinable sky. And sometime he will watch from a ferry at sunset these startling color changes which turn the sky from flaming apricot to blue and then to that cool, compassionate, all-enduring gray which lays its mask over the city like a visible hush. At the Golden Gate he will see the sun lie low in a bed of cherry coals, flaming between black headlands. And then, suddenly, the city will be swallowed up in darkness, and all will vanish save the flashing jewel of Alcatraz, fantastic island castle of a pastry-cook's dream.[25]

It is not surprising that San Francisco should be the subject of songs. In fact, since 1969, it has had an official song, made so by "City Ordinance No. 307–69," signed by Mayor Joseph Alioto on October 29 of that year. It is, of course, "I Left My Heart in San Francisco." But this song was preceded by several others; for example, in 1922, the *San Francisco Examiner* commissioned composer Victor Herbert to set a contest winning lyric to music. The lyric was by John L. Consadine and it was called "San Francisco of My Heart."[26] But a much earlier, possibly the first, tune was that published in 1856 and known as "The Fireman's March" dedicated to the San Francisco Fire Department. A decade later, the "San Francisco March" appeared while Emperor Norton rated his own song in 1880. The next big rush of such songs came after the fire and earthquake days in 1906, when lyricists grieved for a stricken city with songs such as "Of Earthquake and Fire," "The Stricken City," and "San Francisco, Our Beloved, Arise, Arise!" Tin Pan Alley composers did well enough in 1915 with the Panama Pacific International Exposition to sing about; "Meet Me at the San Francisco Fair," "The Fair of the Golden West," and "The Grand Old Frisco Fair" were among songs which then appeared. Florenz Ziegfeld boosted the city in 1915 with "Hello, Frisco" in his Follies. (Alice Faye and John Payne revived this tribute in their 1943 film, "Hello, Frisco, Hello.") The International Exposition of 1939 brought about the "Golden Gate March."

There were also some predictable love songs such as "The Bells of Treasure Island" and "Two Bridges That Bridged Two Hearts." The cable car has been immortalized several times in the lyrical genre; examples are the 1939 "On a Little Cable Car for Two," and in 1947, which was a critical time for those who would save the cable cars for the city, perhaps the sentimental "Dinky Little Cable Car," designated the official song of the "Savers," helped along a worthy cause. As for plain old "San Francisco" there have been at least four songs with the title, in 1906, 1917, 1932, and

1936. (The last was the rousing title song of the Jeannette Mac-Donald, Clark Gable film classic which still surfaces from time to time.)[27]

This sampling of what has been written about San Francisco would be incomplete were it not to mention that there have been some outspoken and even sincere critics, also. Some of their views were written in answer to the question, "What's Wrong with San Francisco" which was posed by the *San Francisco Examiner;* Barnaby Conrad, artist and author, opined that the "New York box type buildings we are beginning to see all around should not be allowed." (It would appear that Conrad lost out here!) George Killion, the president of the American President Lines, stressed the necessity for a rapid transit system, which BART has now fulfilled, in part at least. He also wrote that the city should exercise a unified control over bridges, airports, and marine terminals with the consequent benefit of mature planning. "Finally, we need a redeveloped, modernized city to meet the demands of our date with destiny." Howard Gossage, an advertising executive, answered that "San Francisco needn't be so narcissistic. Yet, it's an old cult here. She is too self-centered to realize her own faults." Anthony Sotomayor, a local artist, made a plea for more natural beautification, "more trees, more shrubs, more flowers. Take Market Street as an example. It needs more trees." (It now has them.)

Dick Nolan has been a long-term columnist for the *San Francisco Examiner;* his columns have been marked by many a trenchant expression of criticism of the city which he professes, at heart, to love and admire. Here are some examples of the Nolan type of critique: In 1963, he opined that "the trouble with this city is that the hard, dynamic men who made it great" have given way to "timid disciples of the half measure, men who want to buy half a horse":

> San Francisco is no one horse town. It is a half horse town. It is the haven of half horse politicians and the home of the half horse solution. It took a long time for San Francisco to develop from genuine one horse status to coach-and-four elegance, and it has taken it perhaps as long to decline to half horse imbecility.[28]

Most of the examples adduced by Nolan clearly regard the ever-changing political atmosphere; the "City Fathers" he accuses of consistent shortsightedness which is obvious, he thinks, to those who study their devious ways. The situation had far from improved four years later according to Nolan. This time his *Examiner* contribution was entitled "Disgusting City!":

> San Francisco on a smoggy day is so emphatically not the City Beautiful, but the City Disgusting. And, if San Francisco can be so regularly, routinely and perennially disgusting, what hope is there for ordinary cities. Smog is but a symptom. The disease lies deeper. . . . With maniac dedication, we have been building yesterday's city, pausing only occasionally to wonder why it doesn't work today.[29]

Another example of the continuing Nolan pique came in his contribution of December 1, 1974, entitled "A Loser's Lament." He returned to a favorite theme, it seems, with these introductory words: " 'I Left My Heart in San Francisco' is a pretty soup ballad, but it contains truth. A lot of us left our hearts in San Francisco. We got here just in time to make the deposit, before they rolled up the town and took it away. San Francisco is missing, you know." He continued his lament:

> Of Oakland they keep quoting the Gertrude Stein pronouncement about there being no there there. Well, in San Francisco, there is here here, and it has to be the herest kind of here, the nowest kind of now. It has all been a ghastly mistake, really.[30]

About the only legitimate conclusion to be drawn from the evidence here presented is that people have found a bit of about everything to comment on regarding San Francisco. More, many more, persons have been admirers rather than critics; as usual, the complete truth about the city seems to lie somewhere inbetween. Whatever the case, here, at the end of the literary trail (with historical dimensions) which this book has sought to be, most will still agree that "San Francisco has something for everyone, and enough for all!" We are, indeed, citizens and/or residents of "no mean city!"

Bibliography

ALTHOUGH EACH OF the chapters has several key bibliographical references, which are listed with the notes at the end of the book, it may be well to include here a few of the books in the field of San Franciscana.

Basic is the volume called *The Annals of San Francisco,* first published in 1855 but now, since 1966, available in improved dress. This reprint, with additions, is so well done that its title-page entry should be indicated here: *The Annals of San Francisco* by Frank Soule, John Gihon, M.D., and James Nesbet *Together with the Continuation Through 1855* (compiled by Dorothy Huggins). *Being a True Facsimile of the Celebrated Original Work First Published in 1855 and 1939, Respectively, To Which Have Been Added an Introduction* by Richard Dillon, *A Treatise on the Engravings* by James A. Baird, and a *Complete Index* by Charles H. Goehring (Palo Alto, 1966). All of which represents an updated and excellent presentation of the *Annals.* Important background and new material on the authors give the *Annals* renewed life. The original work was not intended as critical history but rather as year by year "annals" of the growing city. It is a source book in that many of the things were noted by contemporary observers as well as by the authors. Although not trustworthy in places because of the obvious prejudices manifested, e.g. hostility to the Franciscan mission system, the *Annals* undoubtedly have their own flavor. (Their statement that the missionaries "do not appear to have done any good to humanity" would not find many sharers today.) Once the reader gets the picture on this and other questionable statements, the *Annals,* perused with that needed grain of salt, provide a unique and indispensable background to knowledge of the growth of the city.

One of my favorites is an early and readable attempt at the social history of San Francisco. This is Benjamin E. Lloyd's *Lights and Shades in San Francisco* (San Francisco, 1876). In these pages will be found sprightly comments on the passing scene from the 1850s to publication date. One can, delightfully, go back to a completely different era when reading these accounts. They have a flavor of their own.

In 1875, Oscar Tully Shuck published a sturdy volume (still available in libraries) called *Sketches of the Leading and Representative Men of San Francisco, Edited by Eminent Editors and Authors of California.* This was a continuation of his earlier *Representative and Leading Men of the Pacific* (San Francisco, 1870). The volume continues to have permanent value as a reference work.

San Francisco or Mission Dolores by Zephyrn Engelhardt, O.F.M. (Chicago, 1924); as usual the pugnacious Franciscan (who was called by someone in a hard moment for Fr. Zephyrn: "The Franciscan Bancroft," i.e. H.H. Bancroft, whom he disliked intensely and professionally) dug well into sources and presented his results in what he considered to be an honest manner. However, he is every bit as opinionated as Bancroft and, indeed, the authors of the *Annals*. (Those who know Engelhardt from his four-volume *Missions and Missionaries of California* will scarcely be surprised!) Until a calmer *Mission Dolores* is essayed, Engelhardt will continue to hold the fort, which, presumably, would please him very much.

Having made mention of some of the worthier but earlier, treatments, we may note some of those that have followed from then to now. A general guide of real help is the new revised (1973) edition of *San Francisco, the Bay and Its Cities,* edited by Gladys Hansen, the knowledgeable Head of Special Collections, San Francisco Public Library. Within its almost 500 pages will be found a veritable treasure trove of information on matters San Franciscan. Helpful also is Lawrence Kinnaird's *History of the Greater San Francisco Bay Region,* 3 vols. (New York, 1966). Interestingly written and a challenge to "history on the hoof" fans is Margot Patterson Doss's *San Francisco At Your Feet: The Great Walks in a Walker's Town* (New York, 1964). Strolls around the city with "Doss in hand" are bound to prove both rewarding and healthy. Oscar Lewis's *San Francisco Mission to Metropolis* (Berkeley, 1966) has some interesting pages accompanied by apt illustrations. Earlier, the then *Chronicle* columnist, Robert O'Brien, caught the spirit of his adopted city with *This is San Francisco* (New York, 1948). Also noteworthy (despite some inaccuracies) is Cora Older's *San Francisco: Magic City* (New York, 1961). (This is by the widow of the celebrated editor, Fremont Older.) Mention must be made of several books by Herb Caen, perennial newspaper columnist: *Baghdad by the Bay* (New York, 1949); *Don't Call It 'Frisco* (New York, 1953); and *Herb Caen's New Guide to San Francisco* (New York, 1958). Of general interest also are Joseph Henry Jackson's *The Western Gate: A San Francisco Reader* (New York, 1952), as well as Oscar Lewis's compilation *This Was San Francisco: Being First Hand Accounts of the Evolution of One of America's Favorite Cities* (New York, 1962). Special mention should be made of *San Francisco: A Sunset Pictorial,* by the Editors of Sunset Books and *Sunset* Magazine (Menlo Park, 1966). Included in this professedly affectionate treatment (criticized by some as "not telling it like it is") are some outstanding pictures in color and black and white. The accompanying text is well done and other features include "Highlights in the Life of San Francisco" as well as "Historical Landmarks of the Bay Area"; there is also an interesting if incomplete glossary of street and other names and an annotated bibliography by Richard Dillon. Those who seek a sociological treatment of present and pressing problems should look elsewhere; it was simply never the intention of the editors to supply this need. (In dispute, perhaps, might be the dust jacket statement that "in a sense, this book is the most complete picture ever presented of San Francisco." "Among such treatments" would, perhaps, have been a better way of stating it.)

What follows here will be a mixtum-gatherum of titles that seem worthy of mention. They treat of a multitude of persons and things and are not presented in chronological order. Eugene Black's *The Immortal San Franciscans For Whom The Streets Were Named* (San Francisco, 1971) helps to fill a need, since many ask about the naming of the city streets. The overall research that went into the making of this book is quite impressive. Richard Dillon has done well in his *Embarcadero* (New York, 1959), *The Hatchet Men* (New York, 1962), on the Tong Wars of Chinatown, and *Shanghaiing Days* (New York, 1961). All make rewarding reading. Certainly praiseworthy are the specialized volumes by Harold Gilliam on the natural history of San Francisco and vicinity; noteworthy are his *San Francisco Bay* (New York, 1957), and *The Natural World of San Francisco* (New York, 1967), Gilliam's collaboration with Phil Palmer, *The Face of San Francisco* (New York, 1960) is outstandingly successful in both text and sensitive choice of illustrations. Notable also is an excellently presented picture book of San Francisco which was published in 1975. Called *San Francisco* and edited by Scott Blakey, the book, which was printed abroad and published under the rubric of "Les Editions du Pacifique," contains much intelligent text combined with an array of full-page illustrations in color which make this an interesting and worthy addition to its genre.

Those wishing a succinct account of the city's government should consult Martin W. Judnich *San Francisco Government. A Summary of the San Francisco City Charter, the Laws and Ordinances and the Works of the Various Departments* (San Francisco, 1967). An ambitious attempt sponsored by the Junior League of San Francisco resulted in the valuable *Here Today: San Francisco's Architectural Heritage* (San Francisco, 1967) which, within a year, went into five printings. This is the most complete survey ever made, with a multitude of pictures, of the important architectural heritage of the city. As an historic sites project, this merits substantial praise, indeed.

Some other titles that have worn well are the earlier *Portsmouth Plaza: The Cradle of San Francisco* by Catherine Coffin Phillipps (San Francisco, 1932). Oscar Lewis and Carroll Hall contributed a thoroughly enjoyable volume in their *Bonanza Inn* (New York, 1939) the story of the Palace Hotel. Herbert Asbury's *The Barbary Coast* (New York, 1969) is still regarded as standard on the subject. Also worthy are William Camp's *San Francisco, Port of Gold* (New York, 1947) and Felix Reisenberg, *Golden Gate* (New York, 1940) which is a survey of the port story, 1769–1939. Still very worthwhile is Herbert E. Bolton's *Outpost of Empire: the Story of the Founding of San Francisco* (New York, 1931). Of a popular nature are three books (first presented as radio scripts) by Samuel Dickson, *San Francisco Is Your Home* (Stanford, 1947), *San Francisco Kaleidoscope* (Stanford,

1949), and *Tales of San Francisco* (Stanford, 1957). Finally, an informative account of the literary history of San Francisco is the standard *San Francisco's Literary Frontier* by Franklin Walker (New York, 1939), as well as the thoughtful treatment by Kevin Starr, *Americans and the California Dream, 1850–1915,* which has several well-written and rewarding chapters on this important aspect of San Francisco's past. An interesting and well-received and reviewed book is that by T.H. Watkins and R.R. Olmstead, *Mirror of the Dream* (San Francisco, 1976). It is a long book with more than 450 illustrations.

It remains true, of course, in the San Francisco story as elsewhere, that, "of making many books, there is no end." This has been no more than an attempt to indicate some titles for those who would read on, and on. May their perusal make for many hours of reading for pleasure as well as for lasting profit.

Sources and Notes

Chapter 1
GEOGRAPHY: THE LAY OF THE LAND

Sources

As indicated, the sources for the geography of San Francisco are neither abundant nor complete. Three of some help are James E. Vance, *Geography and Urban Evolution in the San Francisco Bay Area* (Berkeley, 1964). Quite informative is Harold Gilliam's *The Natural World of San Francisco* (New York, 1967). A practical guide of considerable value is *The Hills of San Francisco*, no authors listed but the book was "compiled from a series of articles which appeared in the *San Francisco Chronicle*" (San Francisco, 1959).

Notes

1. The following islands, with their dimensions, are located, either wholly or in part, within the city and county of San Francisco: Treasure Island (0.63 sq.m); Yerba Buena (Goat) Island (0.24 sq.m); Alcatraz Island (0.34 sq.m); Angel Island (only a small part of which is in the city and county) (0.014 sq.m); Red Rock Island (a portion of which marks the northern boundary of the city and county) (0.004 sq.m); the Farallones (part of the city and county since 1872 (1.091 sq.m).
2. San Francisco was first incorporated as a city on April 15, 1850. On that day the first charter was approved by the state legislature and the boundaries of the city were set as follows: "The southern boundary shall be a line two miles distant in a southern direction from the center of Portsmouth Square, and which line shall be parallel to a street known as Clay St. The western boundary shall be a line one mile and a half distant in a westerly direction from the center of Portsmouth Square which line shall be a parallel to a street known as Kearny St. The northern and eastern boundaries shall be the same as the county of San Francisco."

The present boundaries of the city and county of San Francisco, which were established as such on April 19, 1856, are as follows:

Beginning at the SW corner, being NW corner of San Mateo County, in the Pacific Ocean, on the extension of Northern line of township three south, of Mount Diablo base; thence northerly along the Pacific coast to its point of intersection with Westerly extension of low water line on Northern side of the entrance to San Francisco Bay, being Southwest corner of Marin and NW corner of San Francisco; thence

Easterly, through Pt. Bonita and Pt. Cavallo, to the most SE point of Angel Island, all on the line of the Marin, as established in Section 3,929; thence Northerly, along the Easterly line of Marin, to the NW point of Golden Rock (also known as Red Rock), being a common corner of Marin, Contra Costa and San Francisco Counties; thence due SE four and one-half statute miles to a point hereby established as the corner common to Contra Costa, Alameda and San Francisco Counties; thence SE of the Western line of Alameda County to a point on the North line of township 3 S, range 4 W Mount Diablo base and meridian; thence Westerly on township lines and an extension thereof to the place of beginning.

The 82.38 sq. miles which comprise the watery part of the city and county of San Francisco can be broken down into (1) Bay waters (including the Golden Gate, all of which are within the limits of San Francisco) 53.95 sq. miles; (2) Pacific Ocean—28.43 sq. miles—San Francisco's limits here extend to the customary three miles offshore.

Here is a convenient way to recall the approximate dimensions of the Golden Gate: the strait, which was given its present name by John Charles Fremont in June 1848 (The Spanish had given it the descriptive name of *La Boca del Puerto de San Francisco,*) is about one mile wide from Fort Point to Lime Point, i.e., the extent of the Golden Gate Bridge; it is about two miles long from Point Lobos to Point Bonita and about three miles long, respectively, from Point Bonita to Lime Point and from Point Lobos to Fort Point. The "1-2-3" relationship, then, is a convenient method of measuring the Gate.

3. An interesting and early appreciation of the hills of San Francisco is found in a report, submitted to the Common Council in 1854 by a Board of Engineers which had been appointed to study the matter of street grades:

The hills are certainly not deformities. The stranger, on his first approach to San Francisco, cannot fail to be struck with the singular and peculiar beauties of the site. The varied outlines of its hills, covered with smiling residences to their very summits; the changing aspects which they present as the steamer passes, in succession, the North Beach, Clark's Point, and reaches the harbor—all conspire to form a panorama which no other city in the world can rival. The stranger can scarce refrain from exclaiming: How incomparable among cities will San Francisco be when those lovely hills shall be covered with permanent residences and ornamental grounds.

Chapter 2
ORIGINS: PRESIDIO, MISSION, AND PUEBLO

Sources

Although many informational items have appeared concerning the Presidio of San Francisco (much is available at Army Headquarters there) outstanding from the historical aspect is Theodore Treutlein's *San Francisco Bay: Discovery and Colonization* (San Francisco, 1968) which is a gold mine of precise information and updated scholarship; it also settles several formerly controversial points.

Those who wish equally precise information about Mission Dolores need look no further than Maynard Geiger, O.F.M., "New Data on the Buildings of Mission San Francisco," *California Historical Society Quarterly,* vol. 46, no. 3 (September 1967) pp. 195–205.

For the story of Captain William A. Richardson and the Founding of Yerba Buena, cf. John Bernard McGloin, S.J., "A Study of San Francisco's Neglected Pioneer: William A. Richardson, Founder and First Resident of Yerba Buena," *Journal of the West,* vol. 5, no. 4 (October 1966), pp. 493–503.

Notes

1. Maynard Geiger, O.F.M., *The Life and Times of Junipero Serra, O.F.M.* or *The Man Who Never Turned Back (1713–1784)* (Washington, 1959) II: 141.
2. On the basis of Anza's designation of about 200 varas for the Presidio, it would seem that the original area embraced about 900 sq. feet. The Presidio now comprises about 1,540 acres or about 67,169,520 sq. feet.
3. Font's words are quoted in Herbert E. Bolton, *Outpost of Empire: The Story of the Founding of San Francisco* (New York, 1931), p. 333.
4. Bolton, *Outpost of Empire,* p. 334.
5. The oldest building in San Francisco is the present Mission Dolores, dedicated on August 2, 1791, and still very much in use. As indicated, all that is left of the Presidio "Comandancia" is a small adobe wall which dates from 1791, but this is hardly to be thought of today as a building.
6. cf. Maynard Geiger, O.F.M. "New Data on the Buildings of Mission San Francisco," *California Historical Society Quarterly,* vol. 46, no. 3 (September 1967). This is an immensely valuable article in which Father Geiger convincingly demonstrates many important points which have been either obscured or disputed in the Mission Dolores story. Much of what is here presented is based upon the careful scholarship of Father Geiger.
7. Zoeth S. Eldredge has an interesting comment about the laguna in his *The Beginnings of San Francisco* (San Francisco, 1912), 1:330:

> The Laguna de Los Dolores covered the present city blocks bounded by 15th, 20th, Guerrero and Howard streets, now closely built up by residences. . . . The Arroyo (i.e. rivulet or creek) had its rise on Twin Peaks and flowed about the line of 18th St. into the Laguna. Bayard Taylor, who saw the mission Valley in 1849, remarked in his *El Dorado:* "Three miles from San Francisco is the old mission of Dolores situated in a sheltered valley which is watered by a perpetual stream fed from the tall peaks towards the sea."

Eldredge also indicates that this laguna or lake was discovered by de

Anza on March 28, 1776, and by him named the *Laguna de Manantial* or "running, flowing lake." The lake afterwards became known as *Laguna de los Dolores.* . . . The laguna is shown on the map of La Perouse made in 1786 but had disappeared before the earliest American settlers appeared upon the scene, leaving no memory.

8. On Captain Richardson, cf. John Bernard McGloin, S.J., "A Study of San Francisco's Neglected Pioneer: William A. Richardson, Founder and First Resident of Yerba Buena," *Journal of the West,* vol. 5, no. 4 (October 1966), pp. 493–503.

Chapter 3
FROM YERBA BUENA TO SAN FRANCISCO: 1835–1847

Sources

Old but still serviceable is John S. Hittell's *A History of the City of San Francisco* (San Francisco, 1878), as well as Catherine C. Phillips, *Portsmouth Plaza: The Cradle of San Francisco* (San Francisco, 1932). Lewis F. Byington and Oscar Lewis amassed considerable material on early San Francisco in their *The History of San Francisco* (Chicago, 1931), 3 vols.

Notes

1. The name *Yerba Buena,* "Good Herb," is first mentioned in a letter of Hermengildo Sal, Commandante of the Presidio of San Francisco, to Governor Jose de Arillaga at Monterey; Sal reported that Captain George Vancouver from England had anchored "about a league" (c. three miles) below the Presidio in a place they called *Yerba Buena* on November 14, 1792. This anchorage was in the general vicinity of what is now known as North Beach. (Perhaps Sal's "league" was an approximation.) Specifically, *Yerba Buena* refers to a variety of wild mint that grew profusely and widely in the area. The name, *Yerba Buena,* is still the official name of the island commonly called Goat Island, because of the wild goats once roaming it.

2. Rezanov's name will always be associated with his celebrated romance with Maria de la Concepcion Arguello (1791–1857) daughter of Don Jose Arguello who, at the time of the Russian's visit in 1806, was the comandante of the presidio. The most complete treatment of the affair (which is mentioned, with frequent inaccuracies, in most books on California's past) is in a M.A. thesis, "Concepcion Arguello in the California Story: Fact versus Fiction," by Sister Mary Jane Mast (University of San Francisco, 1962).

3. The so-called "Pueblo Question" has always been of some interest in the San Francisco story. Ordinarily, military garrisons or presidios were intended, in the Spanish method of colonization, to give rise to "presidial pueblos" which, in time developed into established towns or cities. Other pueblos which so developed in California were those at San Diego, Santa Barbara, and Monterey. Because of the deterioration of the

Presidio of San Francisco, though, the pueblo of *Yerba Buena* supplanted
the Presidio and the modern city of San Francisco may correctly be
said to have developed from the *Yerba Buena* settlement of Captain Richardson.
4. The second resident on the shores of the cove of Yerba Buena was
Jacob P. Leese (1809–18?) who, on July 1, 1836, took up residence
adjacent to Richardson. His distinction lies in the fact that he was the
first native born American (Richardson was English although he had
acquired Mexican citizenship before 1835) while Leese was born in
Ohio. However, Leese had also become a Mexican citizen.
5. This brief synopsis is from *Inside City Hall: A Guide to San Francisco City
and County Government* (San Francisco: League of Women Voters, 1974),
pp. 2–3.
6. *Annals of San Francisco* (San Francisco, 1855), pp. 178–179.

Chapter 4
DAYS OF "OLD, OF GOLD, OF '49" . . .
Sources
Many of the over 1,200 books and pamphlets about the Gold Discovery
in California also furnish information about its effects upon San Fran-
cisco. A good overview is William M. Camp, *San Francisco, Port of Gold*
(Garden City, N.Y., 1947). Also good is Joseph H. Jackson, *Gold Rush
Album* (New York, 1949). A vivid picture of San Francisco at this time
is in Bayard Taylor's *El Dorado: Or Adventures in the Path of Empire* (New
York, 1850).

Notes
1. Cf. George Groh, *Gold Fever: Being a True Account, both Horrifying and
Hilarious, of the Art of Healing, So Called During the California Gold Rush* (New
York, 1966). Groh's book is an informative and amusing account of this
particular aspect of the Gold Story.
2. These figures were published in the *San Francisco Daily Alta California*,
January 31, 1850.
3. Theodore T. Johnson, *Sights in the Gold Region and Scenes by the Way* (New
York, 1851), p. 104.
4. Samuel C. Upham, *Notes of a Voyage to California Together with Scenes in El
Dorado, 1849–1850* (Philadelphia, 1878), pp. 221–222.

Chapter 5
RELIGIOUS BEGINNINGS
Sources
Old but still among the best with regard to the Catholic story is Zephyrn
Engelhardt, O.F.M., *Missions and Missionaries of California*, 4 vols. (San

Francisco, 1908–1915), cf. especially volume 4 on the American period. "On the Pioneer Congregations in San Francisco," an interesting and reliable series of eleven articles was published in the (biweekly) San Francisco *Progress* from November 30, 1974 to December 14, 1974. The author, Dan Borsuk, gives many details about eleven congregations (one is Catholic, but the other ten are Protestant) which have survived intact in San Francisco from Gold Rush days. On the Jewish story, cf. Michael Moses Zarchin, *Glimpses of Jewish Life in San Francisco* (2nd ed., rev., Oakland, 1964).

Notes

1. *San Francisco Daily Alta California,* December 1, 1849.
2. Frank Soulé, John Gihon, and James Nisbet, *The Annals of San Francisco* (New York, 1855), p. 701. (New ed. Palo Alto, 1966.)
3. On Alemany, cf. John Bernard McGloin, S.J., *California's First Archbishop: The Life of Joseph Sadoc Alemany, O.P., 1814–1888* (New York, 1966).
4. Several commemorative brochures have been published concerning St. Francis Church. But by far the most complete treatment is that of Peter Commy (unpublished, a copy is in the USF archives) "Queen of the Avenue: The Story of San Francisco's Patronal Parish of St. Francis of Assisi, 1849–1949."
5. On the St. Patrick–Holy Cross story, cf. John Bernard McGloin, S.J., "San Francisco's Oldest Frame Church Building," St. Ignatius Church Bulletin, March 1972, pp. 5–11.
6. McGloin, *California's First Archbishop,* pp. 161–162. On Old St. Mary's, cf. Thomas D. McSweeney, *Cathedral on California Street, The Story of St. Mary's Cathedral, San Francisco, 1854–1891* (Fresno, 1952).
7. Quoted in B.J. Morris, "Protestant Beginnings in San Francisco," *Academy Scrapbook* (Fresno, October, 1953) p. 86.
8. *Ibid.,* p. 87.
9. On the Reverend Williams, *ibid.,* p. 88.
10. *Ibid.* (November, 1953) p. 123.

Chapter 6
EDUCATION AND CULTURE: 1847–1862
Sources

On one of the most important aspects of cultural life in San Francisco, cf. Edmond M. Gagey, *The San Francisco Stage: A History* (New York, 1950). A picture of the early educational scene in American San Francisco is in John Bernard McGloin, S.J., *Jesuits by the Golden Gate: The Society of Jesus in San Francisco, 1849–1969* (San Francisco, 1972). The educational picture is also portrayed in William W. Ferrier's *Ninety Years of Education in California, 1846–1936* (Berkeley, 1937).

Notes

1. Bolton's essay was printed in the *American Historical Review,* Vol. 22, no. 31 (October, 1917) 42–61.
2. Millie Robbins, "Adding Culture to Dad's Dough," *San Francisco Chronicle,* February 9, 1972.
3. The San Francisco City Directory for 1868 also records the fact that, where one public school with two teachers served the city in 1850, by 1860, there were eleven schools with sixty-eight teachers.
4. *San Francisco Daily Alta California,* August 1, 1859.
5. For the Jesuit story in San Francisco, cf. John Bernard McGloin, S.J., *Jesuits by the Golden Gate: The Society of Jesus in San Francisco, 1849–1969* (San Francisco, 1972).
6. For an interesting commentary on San Francisco as viewed by the authors of *The Annals of San Francisco,* cf. pp. 14–18, passim.
7. *San Francisco Daily Alta California,* October 6, 1851.

Chapter 7
THE VIGILANCE MOVEMENTS: 1849, 1851, AND 1856
Sources

Still standard on the Committee of 1851 is Mary T. Williams, *The History of the San Francisco Committee of Vigilance of 1851. A Study of Social Control on the California Frontier in 1851* (Berkeley, 1921). Best on the second or "Great Committee" of 1856 is an excellent study with illuminating comments by Doyce Nunis, Jr., The *San Francisco Vigilance Committee of 1856. Three Views: William T. Coleman, William T. Sherman, James O'Meara* (Glendale, 1971). For a characteristically opinionated account of the movement, cf. Hubert Howe Bancroft's *History of the Pacific States of North America,* vols. 36 and 37, *Popular Tribunals* (San Francisco, 1884–1890).

Notes

1. On the Committee of 1851, cf. Mary T. Williams, *The History of the San Francisco Committee of Vigilance of 1851. A Study of Social Control on the California Frontier in 1851* (Berkeley, 1921). The same author also published a volume of the papers of this committee. Her work supplanted to a notable extent the earlier and occasionally inexact treatment of Hubert Howe Bancroft who entitled volumes 36 and 37 of his *Works,* "Popular Tribunals."
2. John S. Hittell, *A History of the City of San Francisco and Incidentally of the State of California* (San Francisco, 1878), p. 243.
3. Casey's last words were published in the *San Francisco Daily Alta California* on May 23, 1856.
4. Professor Bean's review was published in an advertisement for the "Three Views" volume which appeared at the time of publication (1971)

of this important contribution to the literature of the Vigilance Movement in San Francisco.

Chapter 8
SIX FIRES OF THE FIFTIES
Sources
The best single source is Frank Soulé, John Gihon, and James Nisbet, *The Annals of San Francisco* (originally published in 1855. Cf. new edition, Palo Alto, 1966). Chapters 8–17 contain contemporary descriptions of these fires. Cf. also Part 3—"The Great Fires." Chief Frederick J. Bowlen published a valuable "San Francisco Fire Department History" as a series of articles in the *San Francisco Chronicle*, May 14, 1939 to July 13, 1939. Pauline Jacobsen, *City of the Golden Fifties* (Berkeley, 1941) is of some help here. (Badly needed is a complete and critically written account of the San Francisco Fire Department.)

Notes
1. *The Annals of San Francisco*, p. 599. The fires discussed in this chapter have found no better treatment than that given them by the authors of the *Annals* who witnessed them and their effects.

Chapter 9
THE TERRY-BRODERICK DUEL
Sources
An old account, still of value because of its detailed description of the duel, is Ben Truman's *The Field of Honor* (New York, 1884). Jeremiah Lynch told the Broderick story in his *A Senator of the Fifties: David C. Broderick of California* (San Francisco, 1911). The duel is also discussed and its implications noted in David A. Williams, *David C. Broderick, A Political Portrait* (San Marino, 1969).

Notes
1. *San Francisco Times*, September 14, 1859.
2. *San Francisco Times*, September 14, 1859.

Chapter 10
THE BONANZA AGE: 1860–1900
Sources
On Emperor Norton, another one of San Francisco's "Peculiar Institutions", cf. A.S. Lane: *Emperor Norton: the Mad Monarch of America* (Caldwell,

Idaho, 1939). Some good information on the Bonanza Years is in A.R. Neville, *The Fantastic City* (Boston, 1932). Oscar Lewis's *The Big Four* (New York, 1938) is a splendid portrait of these important moguls of the Bonanza Age.

Notes

1. One observation about the Emperor Norton saga should be mentioned here: it is that an exaggerated "cult" has resulted in a kind of "Emperor Norton approach" to this part of San Francisco's past. This is an unfortunate distortion for many more substantial and significant persons than the "Emperor," sane or demented, have dotted the pages of our civic past. In this connection, I have pointed out many times in class lectures that there was a sort of poetic justice in the locale of the "Emperor's" death. This happened directly across the street, at California and Dupont streets (the latter is now Grant Avenue), from the first St. Mary's Cathedral; this caused my comment that there is more, much more, solid San Francisco history embodied in that building, which dates from 1854, than in the whole of the exotic story of the "Emperor."
2. Later, a local muse was to express his opinion of the Nob Hillers as follows:

> They're San Franciscans of the Nob Hill crowd,
> Of course, they're wealthy and, of course they're proud,
> Their names only show a few slight signs,
> Of inelegant beginnings in the placer mines!

3. Margaret Clark Griffis to "her family" written from San Francisco sometime in 1872, clipping (undated) from the *Oakland Tribune.*
4. A complete life of "Blind Boss Buckley" remains to be written; a good portrait of the man and of his activity will be found in Alexander Callow, Jr.'s article: "San Francisco's Blind Boss," *The Pacific Historical Review* (August, 1956) pp. 261–279.
5. Lewis Byington and Oscar Lewis in *The History of San Francisco,* 3 vols. (Chicago, 1931) I:350, remark: "The event was commemorated by the most elaborate celebration the city had yet seen. Parades, torchlight processions and orations fittingly marked the close of the city's first century." *Our Centennial Memoir* published in San Francisco in 1877, (no author indicated) gives a good account of these important days.
6. The outstanding critic of the Midwinter Fair was the recently appointed Superintendent of Golden Gate Park, John McLaren. He did not welcome anything of a commercial nature to "his park" and, when the fair was over, it was a matter of only a few days before the site was cleared and the area restored to what McLaren considered its proper uses (see chapter 12).

Chapter 11
WILLIAM CHAPMAN RALSTON:
BUILDER OF A CITY

Sources

Two full length biographies of Ralston are Julian Dana's, *The Man Who Built San Francisco: A Study of Ralston's Journey with Banners* (New York, 1937), and the earlier Cecil Tilton, *William Chapman Ralston: Courageous Builder* (New York, 1936). Another study is George D. Lyman's, *Ralston's Ring: California Plunders the Comstock Lode* (New York, 1937.)

Notes

1. Julian Dana, *The Man Who Built San Francisco: A Study of Ralston's Journey with Banners* (New York, 1937); and Cecil Tilton, *William Chapman Ralston: Courageous Builder* (New York, 1936).
2. The Comstock Lode, including how it affected San Francisco's fortunes, is treated of in several studies: cf. George D. Lyman, *The Saga of the Comstock* (New York, 1934). The Silver Kings are treated of by Oscar Lewis in a book with that title (New York, 1947).
3. This would seem to constitute a rather murky side of an otherwise reasonably honest career; perhaps all that need be said is that Ralston formed a part of the "Age of the Robber Barons" about which much has been written.

Chapter 12
GOLDEN GATE:
THE PEOPLE'S PARK OF SAN FRANCISCO

Sources

The most detailed and accurate account of the park is an M.A. thesis by Roy Lee Cox, "San Francisco's Golden Gate Park, 1870–1970: A Centennial Evaluation" (University of San Francisco, 1970). Also of interest are Katherine Wilson, *Golden Gate: The Park of a Thousand Vistas* (Caldwell, Idaho, 1947), and Guy and Helen Giffin, *The Story of Golden Gate Park* (San Francisco, 1949).

Notes

1. *Sonoma Democrat* (Santa Rosa, California) January 25, 1873. "By a San Francisco Correspondent."
2. Another area that forms part of Golden Gate Park is now known as Park Presidio Boulevard and extends in a north-south direction from Fulton Street to Lake Street. It embraces 23 acres and is one of the busiest boulevards, trafficwise, in the entire city because it is used as an approach to and from the Golden Gate Bridge. A 1910

city map, in corroboration of an earlier Park Commission's Report, mentions it as an area of "several blocks of land, each block 600 feet long and 240 feet wide, or nearly one mile extending from the northern boundary line of Golden Gate Park to the south line of the military reservation at a point not far from the old U.S. Marine Hospital."

3. Olmstead's letter is included in the *Annual Report of the Park Commissioners, 1910,* quoted in Roy Lee Cox, "San Francisco's Golden Gate Park, 1870–1970: A Centennial Evaluation," (M.A. thesis, University of San Francisco, 1970) p. 120.

Chapter 13
THE STORY OF THE CABLE CARS
Sources

On Hallidie, their promoter, cf. a penetrating article by David F. Myrick, "Andrew Smith Hallidie: A Remarkable Man," in *La Peninsula, Journal of the San Mateo County Historical Association,* Vol. 17, no. 1 (February, 1973), n.p. An informative and accurate brochure of their favorite attraction was published by the San Francisco Municipal Railway: *The Cable Cars of San Francisco* (no author indicated, no date of publication). A rewarding brochure with good illustrations is that by Phil and Mike Palmer, *The Cable Cars of San Francisco* (Berkeley, 1959).

Notes

1. John P. Young, *San Francisco, a History of the Pacific Coast Metropolis,* 2 vols. (San Francisco, 1912) II:575.
2. David F. Myrick, "Andrew Smith Hallidie: A Remarkable Man," *La Peninsula: Journal of the San Mateo County Historical Association,* vol. 17, no. 1 (February, 1973), n.p.
3. This statement is incorrect: a part street car, part cable car line, the London and Blackwell Passenger Railway, predates Hallidie's venture by thirty-seven years; it first operated in 1836.
4. *The Cable Cars of San Francisco* (no author indicated) a brochure distributed by the San Francisco Municipal Railway, (n.d.), pp. 4–5.
5. It may be of interest that I called the attention of the Cable Car Centennial Committee to this difference in dates; after verification by another checking of local newspapers, the correct date was honored in the official centennial commemoration which took place on August 2, 1973.
6. "The Little Old Car That Could," *San Francisco Chronicle,* October 5, 1974.
7. "Cable Cars 100th," *San Francisco Chronicle,* August 2, 1973.

Chapter 14
1906: EARTHQUAKE AND FIRE

Sources

Unsurpassed is William Bronson, *The Earth Shook, The Sky Burned* (Garden City, 1959). Two contemporary accounts of merit are Charles A. Keeler, *San Francisco Through Earthquake and Fire* (San Francisco, 1906), and David S. Jordan (ed.), *California Earthquake of 1906* (San Francisco, 1907).

Notes

1. B.E. Lloyd, *Lights and Shades in San Francisco,* (San Francisco, 1876), p. 324.
2. Frank Soulé, John Gihon, and James Nisbet, *The Annals of San Francisco,* p. 165.
3. B.E. Lloyd, *Lights and Shades,* p. 319.
4. I am indebted for this information concerning the loss of life in 1906 to Mrs. Gladys Hansen, Archivist of the City and County of San Francisco and director of Special Collections, San Francisco Public Library. Mrs. Hansen, while enrolled in my history of San Francisco course, kindly responded to an invitation to do a research paper on this subject. Called "Loss of Life—April 18, 1906," it is a detailed account of this important aspect of the fire and earthquake story.
5. *San Francisco Municipal Report for 1905* (San Francisco, 1906), p. 702. On April 17, 1956, in an issue commemorating the days of 1906, the *San Francisco News* had the following:

Charles Richter, the famed seismologist at the California Institute of Technology, has estimated that the energy released in a few short seconds by the San Francisco earthquake of 1906 had a force which would take a billion A-bombs of the size that destroyed Hiroshima to equal it.

6. San Franciscans need not fear a repetition of this breakdown in fire alarm communications. For many years now, the "nerve center" of the city has been located in Jefferson Square, a block bounded by Laguna Street on the west, Gough on the east, Eddy to the north, and Turk to the south. The Central Fire Alarm System is located in a special building with no structures near it. It has recently been modernized, thus providing even greater security in any time of crisis in the city.
7. This third fire was started by a person who unfortunately lit a fire in her home in the Hayes Valley area; she, it seems, wanted her breakfast and started a fire in her stove in the early middle morning on the first day of the holocaust, April 18. (This is why it is commonly called the "Ham and Eggs Fire.") The chimney flue was out of line because of earthquake damage and escaping sparks fanned by a wind from the west brought fire and ruin to St. Ignatius Church and College, located at Hayes and Van Ness Avenue, and yet another fire to add to the north and south fires which were already raging.

8. Although St. Mary's Cathedral was spared at this time, it finally succumbed to a destructive blaze on September 7, 1962.
9. The adobe Mission Dolores, dating from 1791, came through the ordeal of these days relatively unscarred. Slight earthquake damage (a few minor cracks in the walls) was eventually repaired; however, the brick parish church adjacent to the mission, which dated from the 1870s, was so severely damaged because of falling bricks, etc. that it had to be demolished; it was first replaced by a temporary church which finally yielded to the present Mission Dolores Basilica.
10. Major General Adolphus Greely, *Report on the Earthquake in California, 1906* (Washington, D.C., 1906) p. 6. Since I have heard so many solemn assertions to this effect that martial law *was* declared in San Francisco at this time, in addition to the Greely Report, which should be conclusive, it may be well to quote other sources on the matter. Aitken and Hilton, in their *History of the Earthquake and Fire in San Francisco, An Account of the Disaster of April 18, 1906 and Its Immediate Results* (San Francisco, 1906), p. 91, are emphatic here: "No more erroneous report of affairs gained credence than this. The army and, later, the navy, the national guard, and the cadets from the state university, throughout the entire time of their service in the city, were affiliating forces only, subject to orders from the Mayor. Never did the city pass out of hands of the municipal authorities."
General Greely's report has these added details (p. 17):
In matters of purely military control, including the guarding of Federal buildings and property, my own actions and orders were supreme. As regarded what might be called non-military duties, it was clearly set forth that the Army was in San Francisco for the purpose of assisting municipal authorities to maintain order, protect property and, especially, to extend relief to the destitute and homeless. All operations in any of these directions were to be strictly confined to such methods and measures as might be either formulated or endorsed by the Mayor as necessary to the public interest. In short, the military force was to be strictly subordinate to the municipal authorities.
I submit that the weight of evidence presented here should settle forever the question of the existence of martial law in San Francisco in 1906.

Chapter 15
RELIEF AND RECONSTRUCTION
Sources
An informative report on a vital part of this story is in Archibald MacPhail's *Of Men and Fire: A Story of Fire Insurance in the Far West* (San Francisco, 1948). A complete and authoritative account, with much

information on the relief picture is in the special report of Major General
Adolphus Greely, *Earthquake in California, April 18, 1906* (Washington,
D.C., 1907). A good account of the relief picture is in Richard Living-
ston, *A Personal History of the San Francisco Earthquake and Fire in 1906* (San
Francisco, 1941).

Notes

1. Archbishop Riordan's remarks were quoted in the San Francisco *Call,*
April 28, 1906. Patrick William Riordan (1841–1914) served as second
archbishop of San Francisco, 1884–1914. Succeeding the pioneer Archbishop Alemany, Riordan, a native of New Brunswick, Canada, came
to San Francisco after successful service in the archdiocese of Chicago.
His years as second archbishop proved him to be a person of distinction
in both the ecclesiastical and civic life of San Francisco. His thirty years
as archbishop were marked by a close attention to the educational
concerns of his church as well as to its general upbuilding. A noted
orator, Archbishop Riordan was described by one who knew him as,
truly, a "prince among men who never lost the common touch and was
loved and respected by those whom he served as archbishop." On
Riordan, cf. James Gaffey, "The Life of Patrick William Riordan, Second
Archbishop of San Francisco 1841–1914," (Ph.D. dissertation, Catholic
University of America). (Monsignor Gaffey's excellent life of Riordan
was published in 1976. It will furnish a substantial addition to the
literature of Catholicism in San Francisco.)
2. A printed copy of the Schmitz proclamation is in the historical archives of the University of San Francisco (Schmitz Papers).
3. Mayor Schmitz to the "Citizens of San Francisco," May 11, 1906.
Copy in Schmitz Papers, USF Archives.
4. Mayor Schmitz to President Theodore Roosevelt, San Francisco, May
22, 1906. Copy in Schmitz papers as above.
5. Lawrence Harris, a San Francisco businessman in 1906, proved to be
among the poet-historians who commemorated the days of crisis and
what followed upon them. His poem: "The Damndest Finest Ruins"
attracted considerable attention, and merits partial quotation here. Harris recalled, at a "Fifty Years After" luncheon of the California Historical Society, which was held at the Sheraton-Palace Hotel in 1956, that
he had walked down California Street on the way to his office in the
commission district and watched the advancing fires and observed the
buildings already damaged by earthquake. His poem was a salute to the
stricken city; he wrote:

> Put me somewhere west of East St. (the Embarcadero)
> Where there's nothing left but dust,
> Where the lads are all a bustlin' and where
> Everythings gone bust-
> Where the buildings that are standin' sort of blink

And blindly stare

At the damndest finest ruins ever gazed on anywhere.

After saluting the city in several stanzas, Harris concludes:

Why, on my soul, I would rather bore a hole

And live right in the ashes that ever move to Oakland's mole;

If they'd all give me my pick of their buildings proud and slick

In the damndest finest ruins, still I'd rather be a brick!

(At the luncheon mentioned above, I heard Mr. Harris recite his poem from memory, even though he was in advanced age. He received a prolonged and standing ovation from the hundreds present for the occasion.)

6. The USF Historical Archives houses various examples of such charred records which were removed from the large safe at the site of St. Ignatius College at Hayes and Van Ness Avenue.

7. Schmitz Papers, USF Archives. Schmitz's reference to the "plan of Mr. D.H. Burnham" should be explained here. Daniel Hudson Burnham (1846–1912) was already a leading light in the American architectural world by 1906; he was successfully associated with redevelopment plans for the improvement of Washington, D.C., Cleveland, Chicago, and Manila. He had earlier received deserved acclaim for his work as chief architect of Chicago's World Fair in 1893. In 1904, former Mayor James D. Phelan and other leading citizens formed an "Association for the Improvement and Adornment of San Francisco." Cognizant of the dangers inherent in nonplanning for the future, they invited Burnham to come from Chicago as chief consultant for plans affecting San Francisco's future. Arriving here in September 1904, he took up residence in a bungalow provided for him by the Association on the slope of Twin Peaks which afforded him a panoramic view of the city. With his aid, Edward H. Bennett, Burnham set to work on what he considered his most important project. After a year, he presented his "Burnham Plan" at a lavish banquet at the St. Francis Hotel where he explained his vision of the future to the members of the association and their guests. (The report is a rather rare item now; it was called: "A Report on a Plan for San Francisco" and was published in San Francisco in 1905.) The projects it described were bold and ambitious in the extreme and most of them were not put to use because of conflicting ideas among the citizens of San Francisco. In a general sense, though, some of his ideas have been realized: although the Civic Center is located several blocks from where he put it, his idea of a grouping of government buildings was respected. Likewise the modern Marina Boulevard as well as the Park Presidio Boulevard were part of his plan. Some smaller aspects of his plan were also implemented but not as part of the general and quite grandiose plan that he had for San Francisco. Burnham's Plan was far ahead of its time, it would seem, but it did present solutions to many pressing problems of the day as the distinguished Burnham saw them.

8. Schmitz Papers, USF Archives.

9. Mayor Schmitz's comments here are in a typed, undated copy (probably written about September, 1906) which is preserved in the USF Archives. While somewhat justified in his strictures regarding the insurance picture in the months following the catastrophe, it is now possible to present a more complete picture. In an illuminating volume by Archibald MacPhail, *Of Men and Fire: A Story of Fire Insurance in the Far West* (San Francisco, 1948), the author admits that there were indeed, some "six bits" companies (i.e. those who paid only 75¢ on the dollar to claimants); however, he is adamant in asserting that there were also many "dollar for dollar companies." He points out, also, that fire insurance companies paid close to $200 million in claims at this time. In another treatment, Oscar Lewis asserts that "in excess of $170,000,000 was owed to San Francisco policy holders and it was estimated that about $120,000,000 would eventually be paid." (Some of the smaller and weaker companies could not meet their obligations.) Lewis adds that, "in fact, about $163,000,000 was paid, with a net loss of only about $7,000,000." His final conclusion is that "the majority of companies, both American and European, met their obligations fairly and squarely, thus rendering more conspicuous some companies which sought to avoid full payment." (Lewis Byington and Oscar Lewis, *History of San Francisco* [Chicago, 1931], I:434).

10. The Schmitz Papers, USF Archives, contain a typed copy of this article which was intended, a notation indicates, for the San Francisco *Independent* and was written by Schmitz himself.

Chapter 16
THE PANAMA-PACIFIC INTERNATIONAL EXPOSITION,
1915

Sources
As is appropriate, the literature of the PPIE is quite abundant. Most complete is the official account by Frank M. Todd, *The Story of the Exposition: Being the Official History of the Celebration Held at San Francisco in 1915 to Commemorate the Discovery of the Pacific Ocean and the Construction of the Panama Canal,* 5 vols. (New York, 1921). The PPIE Company published *The Legacy of the Exposition* (no author indicated) in San Francisco in 1916, shortly after its close. Also contemporary and quite informative is John D. Barry's, *The City of Domes* (San Francisco, 1915).

Notes
1. Harris deHaven Connick was born in Eureka, California, in 1873 and died in Oakland in 1965. A graduate engineer from Stanford University in 1897, he was the chief designer of the sewer system in San Francisco where he served as chief assistant city engineer shortly after the turn of the century. As indicated in the text, he was in charge of the construc-

tion and operation of the PPIE; twenty years later, Connick was appointed chief director of the 1939 Golden Gate International Exposition, a post that he held for more than a year.

Chapter 17
THE CIVIC CENTER

Sources
Details regarding the various buildings of the Civic Center are in the revised edition of the valuable guide edited by Gladys Hansen, *San Francisco: The Bay and Its Cities* (New York, 1973). Elizabeth Gray Potter's *San Francisco Skyline* (New York, 1939) devotes some pages to the topic. On the Opera House in particular, cf. Robert F. Gagey, *History of the San Francisco Stage* (New York, 1951).

Notes
1. Oscar Lewis, *Mission to Metropolis* (Berkeley, 1966) pp. 160–161.
2. Actually, although one of Rolph's best-known and oft-repeated statements (as his auditors craned their necks to see the top of the rotunda) he was somewhat inaccurate in its measurements. The correct figure is 11 feet, 7 inches.
3. While most of the meetings and conferences were held in the Veterans Building, it was on the great stage of the Opera House on June 26, 1945, that President Harry Truman and other dignitaries signed the Charter of the United Nations.

Chapter 18
UNDER THE HILLS OF HOME: FIVE TUNNELS

Sources
A satisfactory treatment of the three earlier tunnels is in Vincent D. Ring, "Tunnels and Residential Growth in San Francisco, 1910–1930" (M.A. thesis, University of San Francisco, 1971). Official records of the planned tunnels are in City Engineer Bion J. Arnold's *Report on Transportation Facilities, City of San Francisco* (San Francisco, 1913). There is abundant newspaper material on the dedication of each of the tunnels.

Notes
1. The ultimate value of the Twin Peaks Tunnel to the western area of San Francisco is confirmed by the fact that, before its opening, ninety-two acres there were assessed at $164,150, while, four years later in 1921, this figure had risen to $340,000.
2. A bizarre incident concerning the Sunset Tunnel happened on the evening of November 15, 1968, when four bandits held up a street car

in the middle of the tunnel and forced its thirty-one passengers to surrender their money and other valuables.

3. A principal objection to the proposed tunnel under Russian Hill was that such a project would prove to be a menace to health since "people entering a dark, damp tunnel from the open air would be subject to colds!"

Chapter 19
THE AGE OF THE FERRY BUILDING

Sources

Robert O'Brien had a good appreciation of the place of the Ferry Building in San Francisco history in *This Is San Francisco* (New York, 1948). Excellent on the ferryboats is George H. Harlan's *San Francisco Bay Ferryboats* (Berkeley, 1967). Colorful also is *Of Walking Beams and Paddle Wheels* by George H. Harlan and Clement Fisher, Jr. (San Francisco, 1951).

Notes

1. Biennial Reports (1886–1888) of California State Board of Harbor Commissioners for San Francisco (Sacramento, 1888). These reports furnish a complete guide to all waterfront activities from the creation of the State Board of Harbor Commissioners in 1863 to 1890.

2. The famous Ferry Building siren, so well known to generations of San Franciscans, was finally replaced by chimes on March 7, 1974. The present author, a veteran of the climb to the top of the Giralda, the bell tower of the cathedral of Seville in Spain, can testify to the fact that it indeed furnished architectural inspiration for our Ferry Building.

Chapter 20
THE PORT OF SAN FRANCISCO

Sources

An earlier account is Edward Morphy, *The Port of San Francisco* (Sacramento, 1923). Cf. also Cyril C. Hermann and D. Gruen, *The Port of San Francisco: An In-Depth Study of Its Impact on the City, Its Economic Future, the Potential of Its Northern Waterfront* (San Francisco, 1966). The continuing series of reports of the State Harbor Commission (Sacramento) furnish much information.

Notes

1. In an interesting and wide-ranging interview in the *San Francisco Chronicle* of December 4, 1972, Cyril Magnin, then serving as president of the San Francisco Port Commission and its predecessor, the State Harbor Authority (he had served in these capacities since 1955), la-

mented the dismal picture presented by many with regard to the port. While quite willing to admit present and serious difficulties which called for immediate action leading to effective solution, his words were, "We have made mistakes. We have been accused of everything under the sun, but there's life in the old horse yet! Running a port, you know, is a highly competitive business; you fight for everything." Among Magnin-backed activities were his efforts to regain some tonnage for San Francisco by establishing a new LASH (Lighter Aboard Ship) terminal at Islais Creek (since opened) which, said Magnin, "would give San Francisco the most modern of all facilities on the Pacific Coast. And soon we're going to have roll-on, roll-off capacity (for ships on which cargo is simply driven on by trucks). Some of our critics are uninformed and hurtful both personally and towards the port."

2. Something taken too much for granted, perhaps, is the fact that the very existence of the port of San Francisco lends an undeniable international and cosmopolitan atmosphere to the city; this dates back certainly to Gold Rush days, if not, at least in part, to before.

3. These plans were treated of in two articles in *San Francisco Business,* one in the March, 1973, issue: "Clearing the Fog at the Port—A New Course is Plotted by the Mayor's Port Committee" by Jim Belden, and in the March, 1975, issue: "The Big Squeeze: Does the Port Have Room to Move?" by Paul Van Slambrouck. Both articles are blunt in stating problems, but they both join Cyril Magnin in asserting that these problems can be solved. What is needed, they imply, is less political interference and more competent leadership. This would seem to be the reason for choosing Thomas Soules in early 1975 as new director of the port. Soules accepted the position after ten years of service in a similar capacity in Boston's port—before this, he had an international maritime career. In an interview soon after his arrival (*San Francisco Chronicle,* February 9, 1975) Soules expressed his optimism that the port's problems could be solved. "I think it's almost impossible to kill a port, although you can beat and bruise and damage it. . . . If everything was going well, the port wouldn't have needed to bring in a man from the outside. I think it's an opportunity for me because the public is aware that something has to be done. People want the port to start being successful. I don't think a head-on competition with Oakland is fruitful. I'm going to look into more of a cooperative Greater San Francisco Bay attitude." The new port director will be paid $44,000 a year. On February 19, 1975, the *San Francisco Examiner* had a challenging article by former Mayor George Christopher in which he proposed a businessman's approach to port problems. (It was just this approach which had made Christopher's two terms as mayor, 1956–1964, so successful.) After analyzing the problems as he saw them, which, he stated, did not admit of easy or instantaneous solutions, Christopher made a plea for cooperation with the new director: "The port has belatedly retained a new director, highly reputed as an expert. He should be given a free hand, devoid of political

considerations, to operate the port on a businesslike basis." His lengthy and quite specific suggestions for such solutions found the former mayor concluding his observations as follows: "No one has the total solution, and I offer my suggestions in concert with others, hoping that some of these suggestions may prove beneficial." Time alone will reveal whether these confident words are justified: "The new day is here. Now. The day San Francisco confidently resumes its rightful role as the Pacific's most important, best equipped port." Advertisement for the Port of San Francisco in *Golden Gate Atlas,* published (no date indicated) by the Maritime Exchange of the San Francisco Bay Region, p. 16.

Chapter 21
SYMPHONIES IN STEEL:
BAY BRIDGE AND THE GOLDEN GATE

Sources

While journalistic sources are abundant for both bridges, neither has yet had as complete accounts as they deserve. On the Bay Bridge, cf. *The San Francisco–Oakland Bay Bridge* (no author indicated, Chicago, 1936). On the Golden Gate Bridge, best so far is Allen Brown, *Golden Gate: Biography of a Bridge* (New York, 1965). On the Golden Gate International Exposition which celebrated the completion of both bridges, cf. Richard Reinhardt, *Treasure Island: San Francisco's Exposition Years* (San Francisco, 1973).

Notes

1. These appreciative words are in a mimeographed release published by the Golden Gate Bridge District (no date, no author indicated) which contains much information about the bridge.

2. Appropriately, Strauss's statue has been erected in an area close to the bridge. The inscription reads as follows:

> 1870 Joseph B. Strauss 1938
> "The Man Who Built the Bridge."
> Here at the Golden Gate is the
> Eternal Rainbow that he conceived
> And set to form, a promise indeed
> That the race of man shall
> Endure unto the Ages.
> Chief Engineer of the Golden Gate Bridge
> 1929–1937

3. A dramatic test, which the Golden Gate Bridge passed successfully, came on Saturday, December 1, 1951. Between 5:55 P.M. and 8:45 P.M. the bridge was closed to traffic because of a violent storm which generated a gale with a velocity of seventy miles an hour. The deck of the bridge swayed twenty-four feet from side to side and five feet in the perpendicular dimension. Since the bridge was designed to sustain a twenty-seven-foot sway, no serious effects came from this dramatic

moment. Close examination of the structure later indicated only minor damage.
4. Poem: "Mission Dolores" in *A California Pilgrim* (no author indicated, San Francisco, 1884) p. 114.
5. Richard Reinhardt "The Great Exposition" in the *San Francisco Chronicle,* October 14, 1973. This article is an adaptation of his book, *Treasure Island* (San Francisco, 1973).

Chapter 22
"MUNI" RAILWAY TO BART
Sources
As expected, there are large official files concerning the railway. In 1921, the Bureau of Engineering of the Board of Public Works (no author indicated) published a valuable study: *The Municipal Railway of San Francisco, 1912–1921* with an accurate account of the beginnings of the system. The Bay Area Rapid Transit System—BART—has not lacked for available literature; Bay Area newspapers and magazines, as expected, have devoted much space to its trials, tribulations, and occasional triumphs.

Notes
1. Horace G. Platt, "Address Against the Municipal Ownership of the Geary Street Railroad," pamphlet (San Francisco, 1912). Copy in USF Archives.
2. A public relations man put it this way: "The toughest thing we had to sell was the underwater tube. A lot of people were afraid they'd get caught in it in an earthquake and drown." His comments are in an article "A Magic Metal Carpet Called Bart to Streak Through Baghdad-by-the-Bay," in the periodical *Government Executive* for October, 1969. After some weeks of service, the *San Francisco Chronicle* printed a cheerful report based upon a statement of Chuck Pelton, structure foreman for the tube, who had been constantly inspecting it since the opening run. He said: "I'm happy to announce that the tube is holding up very well. We've had very few problems with the tube or leaks or anything." *Chronicle,* December 23, 1974.

Chapter 23
WATER: FROM LOBOS CREEK TO HETCH HETCHY
Sources
Excellent is *Hetch Hetchy and Its Dam Railroad,* by Ted Wurm (Berkeley, 1973). Just before his death, the creator of Hetch Hetchy, City Engineer M.M. O'Shaughnessy, published his authoritative *Hetch Hetchy: Its Origin and History* (San Francisco, 1934). Background and details of the earlier

story are in *Reports on the Water Supply of San Francisco 1900–1908* (no author indicated, San Francisco, 1908).

Notes

1. The Sunol Water Temple was designed by Willis Polk, who was inspired by the ancient Temple of Vesta at Tivoli, Italy. Immediately below the classical dome is a deep circular enclosed area through which flows a torrent of water from the Sierra Nevada en route to San Francisco by way of Crystal Springs Lake in San Mateo County.
2. It is of interest to note that the water supply for the earliest hand-drawn fire engines of San Francisco came either from the Bay or from large cisterns (the word is of Latin derivation, *cisterna* meaning a "box") built at a number of street intersections. However, the various fires of the fifties (cf. Chapter 8) proved the insufficiency of such provisions.
3. Dorothy H. Huggins, *Continuation of the Annals of San Francisco, Part I. From June 1, 1854 to December 31, 1855* (San Francisco, 1939) p. 98.
4. The name "Spring Valley" was derived from a spring that was located near Washington and Mason streets in San Francisco.
5. The name "Hetch Hetchy" is probably of Indian origin and is usually applied to the entire water project: actually the name is more properly applied to a small mountain valley north of Yosemite Valley.
6. The important Raker Act took its name from its proponent, Congressman John H. Raker.
7. Oscar Lewis, *Mission to Metropolis,* p. 230, mentions the significant fact that, from 1930 to 1960, the amount of Hetch Hetchy water delivered for use rose from 52 million to 168 million gallons daily.
8. Quoted in *San Francisco Water and Power,* a brochure published by the city and county of San Francisco, 1967, p. 47.

Chapter 24
THE SAN FRANCISCO AIRPORT: 1919 TO NOW

Sources

As indicated, the essential story is well told in William Flynn, *Men, Money and Mud: The Story of San Francisco Airport* (San Francisco, 1954). Various reports of the San Francisco Public Utilities Commission provide more data on the airport story. Journalistic accounts are numerous also.

Notes

1. William Flynn, *Men, Money and Mud: The Story of San Francisco International Airport* (San Francisco, 1954), p. 16.
2. *San Francisco Chronicle,* November 10, 1928.
3. Bernard Doolin, who was appointed as Superintendent of the Airport on June 1, 1932, was a native of Berkeley who had trained as an Army

pilot at the Berkeley Ground School and at Rockwell Field, San Diego. After service in France in World War I, Doolin had flown from the Marina field and became involved and interested in a better airport for San Francisco. He was also a trained engineer in the employment of Standard Oil of California. The two qualifications that stood him well in his new and responsible position were his acquaintanceship with men determined to make United States commercial and military aviation a real power in the world, and his background and experience as an engineer. According to Flynn, *Men, Money and Mud,* p. 22, it was Doolin "who was to become the man who mixed the money and mud that built San Francisco Airport." His career of service was a long and distinguished one, indeed. On November 14, 1932 the *Chronicle,* calling him "Twelve Hat Doolin" because of his many jobs, wrote as follows:

In front of his name he is entitled to write "Superintendent." Doolin doubles in brass. He is a grease monkey, head janitor, peanut butcher, phone operator, dispatcher, chauffeur, log keeper, garderner, ditch digger, pilot inspector as well as Superintendent. He has a different hat for every job and he is not "official" until he gets on the right hat!

After years of service, Doolin was succeeded by George M. Dixon, an oil company executive.

4. Flynn, *Men, Money and Mud,* p. 41.

5. General Butler came to his new responsibilities after a long career in the Corps of Army Engineers. Flynn writes of him: "It fell to the veteran soldier to finish the job that had been started almost twenty years previously. His major responsibility was achieving the greatest benefits possible from operation of the utility." General Butler served as Superintendent until December, 1956, a period of almost three years.

6. In an enlightening conversation, General Butler recalled with the author that, after the August 27 dedicatory ceremonies, first service started at 12:01 A.M. on Monday August 30, 1954, when a Pan American flight departed westbound to the Orient.

7. Oscar Lewis, *Mission to Metropolis,* p. 234.

8. *San Francisco Chronicle,* September 23, 1973.

Chapter 25
ADOLPH SUTRO AND
THE SAN FRANCISCO STORY

Sources

A rewarding study of Sutro is that by Robert E. Stewart, Jr., and Mary Frances Stewart, *Adolph Sutro: A Biography* (Berkeley, 1962). A contemporary account is by Eugenia K. Holmes, *Adolph Sutro: A Brief Story of a Brilliant Life* (San Francisco, 1895). For Sutro's prominent part in the story of the Comstock Lode, cf. Oscar Lewis, *Silver Kings* (New York, 1947).

Chapter 26
DENIS KEARNEY, AGITATOR EXTRAORDINARY

Sources

There is much need of a complete and objective study of Denis Kearney, none has been written to date. However, he is treated at some length in such standard accounts as those by Andrew F. Rolle, *California: A History* 2nd ed. (New York, 1969); Walton Bean, *California: An Interpretive History* (New York, 1968); and John W. Caughey, *California: A Remarkable State's Life History* (Englewood Cliffs, New Jersey, 1970).

Notes

1. An interesting part of the Kearney story is the continued hostility he showed toward religion. From his first years in San Francisco, he declared himself opposed to organized religion in general and to the Catholic faith in particular. While conclusive evidence is lacking as to the ultimate reasons for such a stance, perhaps some of it came when, while trying to educate himself, he became fond of the writings of Darwin, Spencer, and others whose religious views were quite different from the Catholic faith which, originally, had been Kearney's. Religion continued to be anathema to him until his death; all religions, he said, were "systems to delude the common fools who were the members of them."

2. Andrew Rolle, *California, A History*, 2nd ed. (New York, 1969), pp. 426–427.

Chapter 27
THE TEAMSTERS STRIKE OF 1901

Sources

The strike is detailed in Ira B. Cross, *History of the Labor Movement in California* (Berkeley, 1935). It receives treatment also in Bernard C. Cronin's, *Father Yorke and the Labor Movement in California* (Washington, D.C., 1943). An in-depth article by Robert M. Robinson, "The San Francisco Teamsters at the Turn of the Century" is in *The California Historical Society Quarterly*, vol. 35, nos. 1 and 2 (March, June, 1956), pp. 59–70, 145–153.

Chapter 28
SAN FRANCISCO'S "CONSECRATED THUNDERBOLT":
FATHER PETER C. YORKE

Sources

As indicated, the only complete biography of Father Yorke is the authoritative work by Joseph Brusher, S.J., *Consecrated Thunderbolt: Father*

Yorke of San Francisco (Hawthorne, New Jersey, 1973). Bernard Cronin's *Father Yorke and the Labor Movement,* mentioned in the previous chapter, is good here also. For Yorke's dramatic part in the APA controversy, cf. Donald L. Kinzer, *An Episode in Anti-Catholicism: The American Protective Association* (Seattle, 1964).

Notes

1. A much-needed life of Father Yorke was published in 1973. Entitled *Consecrated Thunderbolt: Father Yorke of San Francisco* (Hawthorne, New Jersey, 1973) it was written by Joseph Brusher,S.J., who had devoted many years of careful research to preparing this study of the most famous priest in San Francisco's history. His volume is well written and fills a real need.

2. This avowedly anti-Catholic organization was formed in Clinton, Iowa, in 1887 and, by 1896, it purported to have a membership of over a million. It first appeared on the San Francisco scene in September, 1893; within a year, it claimed a membership in the city and environs of about seventeen thousand. (However, Father Yorke who made it his particular business to study the APA, gave it as his considered opinion that, while there were probably about eighteen thousand affiliated with the group throughout California, their membership in San Francisco never exceeded four or five thousand.)

3. This was the opinion expressed to the author by Monsignor Robert I. Falvey who had served as a young priest with Father Yorke in St. Peter's Church, San Francisco, and who, while there, administered the last rites of the church to him.

4. Brusher, *Consecrated Thunderbolt,* pp. 269–270.

Chapter 29
CORRUPTION: ABE RUEF (1864–1936)
AND EUGENE SCHMITZ (1864–1928)

Sources

Cf. Walton Bean's *Boss Ruef's San Francisco: The Story of the Union Labor Party, Big Business, and the Graft Prosecution* (Berkeley, 1952). A more popular account is Lately Thomas, *A Debonaire Scoundrel: An Episode in the Moral History of San Francisco* (New York, 1962). A detailed and good study of Schmitz is Robert Del Pippo, "Eugene Schmitz, Twenty-Third Mayor of San Francisco, 1901–1907: An Historical Assessment" (M.A. thesis, University of San Francisco, 1965).

Notes

1. An interesting treatment of Ruef and Schmitz is the entertaining article by Bruce Bliven in *American Heritage* for December, 1959. Entitled

"Boodling Boss and Musical Mayor" the account outlines, in a general way, the activities of both.

2. Abe Ruef is almost always referred to as "Boss Ruef." I have so called him many times in presenting lectures about him. However, in the Spring 1972 issue of the *California Historical Quarterly,* an excellent prize-winning article appeared written by James P. Walsh, a former student. It bears the challenging title "Abe Ruef Was No Boss: Machine Politics, Reform, and San Francisco." A careful perusal makes me agree with the Walsh thesis, i.e. that Ruef was certainly not a "boss" in the sense in which this term is applied to most American political chieftains. In appearance, he was about as much different from the stereotyped boss as possible; the important point, though, is that, deliberately and contrary to the methods of other such politicians, Ruef sought to establish no machine nor to control or manipulate large numbers of votes; rather, he preferred to exercise influence in a quiet but effective manner on such as Mayor Schmitz and a few others. So it would seem that the Walsh article provides a compelling corrective to the portait usually furnished of Abe Ruef. Rather than a boss, Ruef was a political opportunist of great influence until his downfall.

3. An interesting and true story was related to me by a good friend, David B. Torres. Employed at this time as a clerk in the Pacific States Telephone Company's office in San Francisco, he told of doing what at first looked like some routine bookkeeping work. Two vouchers for $50,000 each were to be entered by him in the proper books—they were made out to the "Public Relations Representative of the Company." When Torres inquired as to how precisely he should make the entry, his superior officer merely smiled, saying: "General Expenses-Miscellaneous, Dave!" Only later did he realize that this involved the amount charged the company by Ruef to obtain a desired franchise for itself. (A voucher is a receipt in payment of a debt.)

4. Editor Older visited Ruef several times at San Quentin. Eventually, he was responsible for the publication, in the *San Francisco Bulletin,* of Ruef's memoirs which were entitled *The Road I Travelled.* They consist of not much more than a whitewash written by Ruef in which he endeavored to vindicate himself of the main charge brought against him. They are an interesting addition to the literature of self-justification.

5. An example of such commendation is found in the following lines written by a prominent San Francisco rabbi, Jacob Voorsanger:

Whilst doctors and lawyers and clergymen were busy at the Pavilion, Mayor Schmitz and a number of young men had rallied at the old City Hall, the Hall of Justice. Schmitz became the man of the moment and the hour. There were two opinions about Eugene Schmitz before the earthquake; his friends and enemies were many; they attributed to him the maximum and minimum of political sagacity and competency. There is but one opinion of Mayor Schmitz today in our stricken city. His courage and presence of mind in the hour of danger, his splendid capacity for organization, his remarkable cheerfulness in the midst of trying conditions, his quick perception of the needs of the hour—these qualities have justly earned the appreciation of all citizens, regardless of rank or political affiliations. There were a number of clerical calamity-howlers in our city, who, like Titus Oates in London in 1665, had attributed to our chief magistrate the cause for all the real and imaginary troubles, physical, ethical and moral, that had made their appearance in our midst. These self-same calamity-howlers now recite Schmitz' praises in wondrous unison. It is uncertain how long this theological amity will continue; possibly until the next municipal campaign, for the emotions of politics are as unstable as quicksilver; but meanwhile the quill of the historian has traced the name of Eugene Schmitz and his fame has become independent of the shifting passions of selfish men or time-serving clerics and politicians. It is the fame of a man qualified to meet the demands of the hour, therefore a man out of a million, and the distinguished leadership he has exhibited has determined the position of our "earthquake mayor" in the annals of the greater San Francisco.

Rabbi Voorsanger's comments first appeared in the June 1906 issue of *Out West;* they were reprinted in an article entitled "The Relief Work in San Francisco," published in the *Western States Jewish Historical Quarterly* (April 1976), pp. 246–247.

6. Peter C. Yorke to Mrs. E.E. Schmitz, Oakland, California, June 14, 1907. Original in Schmitz papers in the University of San Francisco Archives.

7. Henry Wyman, CSP, to Eugene Schmitz, San Francisco, November 24, 1906. Original in USF Archives.

Chapter 30
THE STREETCAR STRIKE OF 1907: LABOR'S DEFEAT

Sources

Excellent here is Robert E.L. Knight, *Industrial Relations in the San Francisco Bay Area, 1900–1908* (Berkeley, 1960). Cf., also, Bernard Cronin, *Father Yorke and the Labor Movement in San Francisco,* 1900–1910, and Ira Cross, *A History of the Labor Movement in California* (both previously listed).

Notes

1. The June 8, 1907, issue of the weekly San Francisco *Star* thus illustrated the tactics of one of the strikebreakers:

These strikebreakers fully understand the position of the company and do not fail to take advantage of it. A story is told that a conductor on the Sutter Street line recently turned into the company $7.40 at the end of his day's work. The Superintendent, who knew that the average cash collected by each conductor amounted to $60, asked him if

that was all he had. The strikebreaker answered "Yes." The superintendent then said: "I guess we will have to dissolve our partnership."
The strikebreaker replied: "All right, but I want to thank you for the
use of the car!"

2. Robert E. L. Knight, *Industrial Relations In the San Francisco Bay Area,
1900–1908* (Berkeley, 1960), p. 193.

3. Bernard C. Cronin, *Father Yorke and the Labor Movement in San Francisco,
1900–1910* (Washington, D.C., 1943), p. 137.

4. *Organized Labor* (San Francisco weekly organ of the Labor Council)
May 25, 1907.

5. Knight, *Industrial Relations,* pp. 196–197.

Chapter 31
CONTRASTING ADMINISTRATIONS: EDWARD R. TAYLOR AND P.H. McCARTHY, 1908–1912

Sources

The only complete life of Taylor is the well-done *The Life and Times of
Edward Robeson Taylor* by Kenneth M. Johnson (San Francisco, 1968).
While there is no full-length life of P.H. McCarthy, there is an M.A.
thesis treating of his administration: Millard R. Morgen, "The Administration of P.H. McCarthy, Mayor of San Francisco, 1910–1912" (M.A.
thesis, University of California, Berkeley, 1948). A perceptive treatment, quite critical in places, of his rule as mayor is in Robert Knight,
Industrial Relations in the San Francisco Bay Area, 1900–1918 (Berkeley, 1960).

Notes

1. There is need of a carefully done and objective biography of P.H.
McCarthy because of the controversy that surrounds his name. As of
this writing, there is no such published account.

2. Oscar Lewis, *San Francisco: Mission to Metropolis* (Berkeley, 1966), p. 213.

3. Lewis Byington and Oscar Lewis, *The History of San Francisco,* 3 vols.
(Chicago, 1931), I:449.

Chapter 32
PERENNIAL MAYOR: "SUNNY JIM" ROLPH (1869–1934)

Sources

There is no satisfactory and complete biography of Rolph. A study in
admiration for a close friend is by David W. Taylor, *The Life of James Rolph,
Jr.* (San Francisco, 1934). There is an unpublished and quite well-done
M.A. thesis by Sister Clementia Marie Fisher, "James Rolph Jr., 1869–
1934, An Estimate of His Influence on San Francisco History" (University of San Francisco, 1965). A short article with illustrations rescues his

name and fame: Moses Rischin, "Sunny Jim Rolph: The First Mayor of All the People," *California Historical Quarterly*, vol. 52, no. 2 (Summer 1974):165–172.

Notes
1. In this light, it is impossible to agree with the words of an otherwise competent California historian about Rolph. John Caughey, in his *California: A Remarkable State's Life History*, 2nd ed. (Englewood Cliffs, New Jersey, 1970) p. 511, writes: "In his long tenure as mayor of San Francisco, the major qualifications Rolph had evinced were as official greeter, hand shaker and parade reviewer." He was all these things, of course, but he was many other things also, as a study of his years of service to San Francisco reveals.

Chapter 33
THE MOONEY-BILLINGS CASE
Sources
Close to a definitive account of the bombing is Richard Frost's *The Mooney Case* (Stanford, California, 1968). Louis Adamic's *Dynamite: The Story of Class Violence in America*, rev. ed. (New York, 1960) provides colorful details. A thoughtful review of the entire incident is Albert F. Gunn's "The Mooney-Billings Case: An Essay Review," *Pacific Northwest Quarterly*, vol. 60, no. 3. (October 1969).

Notes
1. Richard H. Frost, *The Mooney Case* (Stanford, California, 1968) p. 82.
2. On April 23, 1968, I visited Warren Billings, (he was then 75 years old) at the Maiden Lane Jewellers, 47 Maiden Lane, San Francisco. I told him of my long-standing interest in his case, which had been shared by some of my students, one of whom had visited him and talked quite extensively with him. Recalling her visit, Billings proved quite friendly. Upon my saying how good it was that he had lived to see his "rehabilitation" he smiled and said that there had never been any need for his "rehabilitation," since he was not guilty of any of the accusations made against him in connection with the Preparedness Day affair. We both agreed that Curt Gentry's book, *Frame-Up, the Incredible Case of Tom Mooney and Warren Billings*, which had been published in 1967, the year previous to my visit, was properly named. We parted with a friendly handshake. On checking back again at the Maiden Lane Jewellers on April 20, 1972, I was told that Billings, now 79 years old, no longer was employed there. He died at Kaiser Hospital, Redwood City, on September 4, 1972. I always considered myself fortunate in having met one of the principals in this famous case.

3. The San Francisco *News,* January 7, 1939. In the same issue, the *News* quoted Governor Olson as follows:

I have made an extended study of the voluminous record of this case and am convinced that Mooney is wholly innocent of the crime of murder for which he was convicted and that his conviction was based wholly on perjured testimony presented by the representatives of the State of California. In view of my convictions, I deem it my duty to issue a pardon to Thomas J. Mooney . . . therefore I, Culbert L. Olson, Governor of the state of California, do hereby grant Thomas J. Mooney a full and unconditional pardon of the crime of murder in the first degree.

4. While several theories have been advanced (they are all interestingly discussed by Frost in *The Mooney Case*) as to the culpability of those involved in the Preparedness Day bombing, none appears to have sufficient weight of evidence to solve the case. It now appears, after the extensive studies of Frost and others, that the responsibility for San Francisco's Preparedness Day bombing will never be known.

Chapter 34
MARITIME AND GENERAL STRIKE OF 1934

Sources

The strike is well covered in Paul Eliel's, *The Waterfront and General Strike: San Francisco, 1934* (San Francisco, 1934). Cf. also Mike Quin (pseudonym for Paul W. Ryan) *The Big Strike* (Olema, 1949). Harry Bridges' career has been colorfully treated by Charles P. Larrowe in *Harry Bridges: The Rise and Fall of Radical Labor in the United States* (New York, 1972).

Notes

1. A previous chapter (16) has treated the Teamsters Strike of 1901 when the City Front Federation attempted to close the port of San Francisco in support of the Teamsters; however, strikebreakers, recruited partly from the University of California students as well as unemployed farmhands, broke this part of the strike.
2. Ira Cross, *A History of the Labor Movement in California* (Berkeley, 1935), p. 235.
3. Cross, *A History,* p. 235.
4. William M. Camp, *San Francisco, Port of Gold* (New York, 1947), p. 437.
5. Camp, *San Francisco,* p. 431.
6. Camp, *San Francisco,* pp. 459–460.
7. Felix Reisenberg, *Golden Gate, The Story of San Francisco Harbor* (New York, 1940), p. 316.
8. While some have called this an exaggerated figure, it is certain that the losses were substantial.
9. Paul Eliel, *The Waterfront and General Strike* (San Francisco, 1934), p. 229.

10. Cross, *A History of the Labor Movement in California,* p. 257.
11. Cross, *A History,* p. 258.
12. This was only the third such general strike in American history. The first was in Philadelphia in 1835 and the second in Seattle in 1919.

Chapter 35
CITY CHARTERS—AND MORE MAYORS
Sources

On the general history of the charters, cf. John D. Bollens and Stanley Scott, *Governing a Metropolitan Region: The San Francisco Bay Area* (Berkeley, 1968). Cf. also Martin W. Judnich, *San Francisco Government: A Summary of the San Francisco City and County Charter, the Laws and Ordinances, and the Works of the Various Departments* (San Francisco, 1967). An excellent study of the mayors of San Francisco is William Heinz in collaboration with Gladys Hansen, *The Mayors of San Francisco,* 2 vols. (Gilbert Richards, Limited Editions, Woodside, California, 1975).

Notes

1. This is evident from the title of the Hawes Act: "An Act to Repeal the Several Charters of the City of San Francisco, to establish the Boundaries of the City and County of San Francisco and to consolidate the Government Thereof." The new charter provided for a district-elected, twelve-man Board of Supervisors, presided over by a president who was elected at large and who could vote only to break ties. The president was given the title of "Mayor" in 1861. A major concern of the new charter was control of the graft which had prevailed in the city's administration thus far.
2. This final report was quoted in an article in the *San Francisco Chronicle,* November 15, 1972, "Parting Advice of S.F. Charter."
3. The report, quoted in the above-mentioned *Chronicle* article, also stated that the committee specifically urged changes to a "program and priority budget," rather than the line item approaches now used, adding that it had no specific proposals for changes in city departments.
4. The eulogy was delivered by William McGovern as part of the memorial service held in the rotunda of the City Hall on April 7, 1948. As indicated, Dion Holm's words were spoken at the same time.
5. *San Francisco Chronicle,* April 6, 1948.
6. Bridges' words are to be found in the Lapham File, Special Collections, San Francisco Public Library.
7. *San Francisco Chronicle,* April 19, 1966.
8. Annual Report, Grand Jury of San Francisco, 1955. In an interesting interview which I had with Judge Robinson on March 10, 1975, he recalled his days as mayor, reminiscing that, perhaps, he was destined to be a mayor of San Francisco! When I asked him why, he said that his

mother had told him of meeting the then mayor, Adolph Sutro, with her son, Elmer. She told him that Mayor Sutro patted young Robinson (about three or four years old at the time) and smilingly remarked: "Who knows, Mrs. Robinson, we may have here a future Mayor of this city!"

Judge Robinson mentioned how different and more simple and admitting of easier solutions were the problems which he faced as mayor, 1948–1956, when contrasted with those which must, in a changed and changing city, be faced by present-day mayors.

9. In 1953, an amendment to the City Charter became effective which prohibited more than two successive terms as mayor to any individual. Consequently, Mayor Robinson was ineligible for a third term.

10. When Christopher took office, the press of the city were loud in their criticism of the Police Department which they referred to frequently as the "Blue Gang." The new mayor appointed a new chief, Francis J. Ahern and, on his sudden death, Mayor Christopher appointed Thomas Cahill to succeed him. Both of these chiefs gave constructive and good service under Christopher's leadership.

Mayor Christopher came to his years as mayor well equipped with a business background and a decade of service on the Board of Supervisors. In an interview which he gave me on March 13, 1975, he recalled that, during each of the eight years as mayor, he set aside, annually, $16 million for what he called "rehabilitation"; this was money used to acquire new equipment for the fire department, for the refurbishing of some drab police stations, and the like. By so doing, he was able to avoid putting a bond issue on the ballot to provide for such necessary maintenance. and repairs.

11. Not only was Christopher an active supporter of the idea of rapid transit but he caused legislation to be introduced and passed in Sacramento establishing a Bay Area Rapid Transit District, which has now developed into BART.

12. This was the first legislation of its kind enacted in California. At this time also, Mayor Christopher won the gratitude of the many sport lovers in San Francisco when, after much private negotiation, he persuaded the New York Giants to transfer their baseball franchise to San Francisco.

13. In the interview referred to above, the former mayor told me that, on balance, he considered his determination to replace the rat-infested slum produce market district with a more representative development the outstanding feat of his administration. He was opposed by several "slum landlords" and, only after a private solicitation of his part of $55,000 in donations from eleven public-spirited citizens, was he able to finance a study of the blighted area which resulted, eventually, in the removal of the commission markets elsewhere and the beginning of the outstanding Golden Gateway section of San Francisco which is surely to be counted among the better developments in the modern city. "It

was made possible" said the former mayor, "by my policy of co-operating with and asking the support of major business leaders. This approach led to the formation of the Blythe-Zellerbach Committee (an informal private sector organization headed by the late George Blythe and the late J.D. Zellerbach) which put up the money to study key problem areas in San Francisco," recalled Christopher.

Chapter 36
HOST TO THE WORLD:
THE BIRTH OF THE UNITED NATIONS ORGANIZATION
IN 1945

Sources

The general story is well told in Herbert Evatt, *The United Nations* (Cambridge, 1948); Hamilton Fish Armstrong, *The Calculated Risk* (New York, 1947); and R.B. Russell, *A History of the United Nations Charter: The Role of the United States, 1940–1945* (New York, 1958).

Chapter 37
SOCIAL CHANGES IN THE CITY:
BEATNIKS, HIPPIES, AND THE HAIGHT-ASHBURY

Sources

Jack Kerouac had special credentials to write his *On the Road* (New York, 1957) since he himself was a leader of the Beat Generation. The Hippie story is covered in *Voices from the Love Generation* (Boston, 1968), a series of interviews with the leaders of the Haight-Ashbury Hippie community. Cf. also, Burton H. Wolfe, *The Hippies* (New York, 1968).

Notes

1. Barnaby Conrad, "Barefront Boy with Dreams of Zen," *Saturday Review*, May 2, 1959, p. 23.
2. *Time*, October 31, 1969.
3. Cf. Sister Mary Bernardette Giles, *A Changing Urban Parish. The Study of Mobility in St. Agnes Parish, San Francisco* (San Francisco, 1959).
4. The term "Hippy" is of English origin and is derived from "hip-clothes" which are described as tight-fitting, hip-hugging pants which were worn by some English young men in the 1950s; gradually these became known, in current English slang, as "Hippies."
5. *San Francisco Examiner*, April 2, 1967.
6. *Newsweek*, February 6, 1967.
7. *San Francisco Examiner*, April 2, 1967. As any San Franciscan could have told the potential invaders, the not-at-all secret weapon which would

militate against them was the generally cold and foggy climate that marks the Haight-Ashbury and adjacent areas of the city in the summer months: some indeed, discovered this upon arrival and did not long remain as problems for the police.

8. *San Francisco Examiner,* July 21, 1968.

9. *San Francisco Chronicle,* October 1, 1968.

10. *San Francisco Chronicle,* October 1, 1968.

11. *San Francisco Examiner,* January 14, 1969.

12. This comprehensive report, which benefited from several interviews with long-term dwellers in the district, was published in the *San Francisco Examiner,* January 14, 1969.

13. *San Francisco Examiner,* April 23, 1972.

Chapter 38
CHANGING SKYLINE

Sources

Much information will be found in the Junior League of San Francisco's publication, complete with illustrations, *Here Today: San Francisco's Architectural Heritage* (San Francisco, 1968). A study in indignation is Bruce Brugmann and Greggar Sletteland, *The Ultimate Highrise: San Francisco's Mad Rush to the Sky* (San Francisco, 1971). An article written at the beginning of this period of change is Allan Temko's "San Francisco Rebuilds Again" in *Harper's Magazine,* April, 1960.

Notes

1. A still remaining and prominent example is the United States Mint at 5th and Mission streets; it was constructed from 1869 to 1874 and is built of granite and sandstone; it is the last remaining important Greek Revival structure in California.

2. An outstanding example of this period is the Pacific Union Club on Nob Hill. Originally built as a residence for the James Flood family, it is of brownstone and designed in the Italianate style. It has the distinction of being the last remaining mansion of its kind on Nob Hill. It was gutted in the fire of 1906, but its walls stood and it was rebuilt according to the plans of the distinguished architect, Willis Polk.

3. A prominent example here is the Ferry Building, which was built in the middle 1890s. The Hibernia Bank at McAllister and Jones streets (at Market) dates from 1890 and remains substantially unchanged; this neoclassical building is remarkable in its use of fine materials both in its exterior and interior.

4. Roger Olmstead and T.H. Watkins, *Here Today: The Architectural Heritage of San Francisco* (San Francisco, 1968), pp. 3–5.

5. Gilliam's informed comments appeared in the *San Francisco Examiner,* February 12, 1961.

6. *San Francisco Chronicle,* May 6, 1973.

7. Although the Transamerica Pyramid, sometimes referred to as the "Needle," has but forty-eight floors of rental space, its tower, which is reserved for housing the building's utilities, etc., enables it to surpass in height the fifty-two-floor building which is known as the World Headquarters of the Bank of America. The Pyramid rises to an impressive 853 feet, exceeding the World Headquarters by fifty-three feet. While conceding that even some of its critics admit that, at night, the illuminated Pyramid inspires awe and may even be called a breathtaking sight, Herb Caen goes on to comment that "from a distance, Manhattan looks good at night too!"

Chapter 39
REFLECTIONS ON THE CONTEMPORARY SCENE
Sources

The redevelopment scene in San Francisco is described in Margot Patterson Doss's, *San Francisco Redevelopment at Your Feet* (San Francisco, 1973). The best source for more information on the crime picture in the city is to be found in the *Annual Report, Statistical Summary* (San Francisco Police Department). The educational and school situation is best researched in the *Proceedings and Annual Reports of the San Francisco Board of Education.* As might be expected, the problems concerning each of the above subjects receive abundant contemporary journalistic coverage as well as editorial comment.

Notes
1. *San Francisco Chronicle,* August 2, 1970.
2. *San Francisco Chronicle,* March 18, 1973.
3. *San Francisco Chronicle,* March 12, 1967.
4. *San Francisco Chronicle,* March 12, 1967.
5. Terry Link, "The New Schools," *San Francisco Magazine,* September, 1969, p. 22.

Chapter 40
A SURVEY OF SAN FRANCISCANA

Notes
1. *Annals of San Francisco* (New York, 1855) p. 46.
2. *Annals,* p. 144.
3. *Annals,* p. 144.
4. *Annals,* p. 491.
5. Taylor's words are quoted in Oscar Lewis, *This Was San Francisco, Being*

First Hand Accounts of the Evolution of One of America's Favorite Cities (New York, 1962) p. 85.

6. Benjamin E. Lloyd, *Lights and Shades in San Francisco* (San Francisco, 1876), Preface, "Why?" (no page indicated).

7. Charles C. Dobie, *San Francisco, A Pageant* (New York, 1933).

8. D.W. Brogan "Tourist in America," in *Harper's* Magazine, December 1950, p. 36.

9. Brogan, "Tourist," pp. 37–38.

10. Frank J. Taylor, "San Francisco," *Holiday,* Vol. 1, no. 1 (March 1946), no page indicated.)

11. *Holiday,* September, 1953, pp. 27–28.

12. *Holiday,* "San Francisco Issue," April 1961, p. 67.

13. *San Francisco Chronicle,* April 1, 1961.

14. *San Francisco Chronicle,* March 28, 1961.

15. *San Francisco Chronicle,* March 28, 1961.

16. Irving Stone, "Hometown Revisited. 16. San Francisco" in *Tomorrow,* March, 1950, p. 23.

17. Stone, "Hometown" p. 27.

18. *San Francisco Chronicle,* January 28, 1950. "The Beauty and Ugliness of San Francisco Moves William Saroyan To Say A Few Words."

19. Saroyan, "The Beauty, etc."

20. *San Francisco Examiner,* 1958 (date not indicated on clipping), John Steinbeck, "The Golden Handcuff, John Steinbeck Writes About San Francisco."

21. John Steinbeck in "San Francisco Quotes" (Chamber of Commerce, San Francisco) no date given.

22. "Salute to San Francisco" In *Town and Country,* November, 1961, p. 109.

23. John Gold, "The Best City in the World" *London Evening News,* October 15, 1958.

24. William A. Rusher, "One More Vote For San Francisco," *National Review,* June 4, 1968, p. 567.

25. Quoted in Robert G. Cleland's *California in Our Time, 1900–1940* (New York, 1947) pp. 124–125.

26. Victor Herbert said he hoped the people of the city "would like it, especially since it contained no jazz. I couldn't write jazz, for I am a musician, and no real musician ever wrote jazz."

27. Some of the information here given forms part of an article in the *San Francisco Examiner,* November 10, 1974: "The Songs of San Francisco" by Eleanor Knowles.

28. *San Francisco Examiner,* November 10, 1963. Dick Nolan's "San Francisco's Spineless Generation."

29. *San Francisco Examiner,* November 8, 1967. Dick Nolan's "Disgusting City."

30. *San Francisco Examiner,* December 1, 1974. Dick Nolan's "A Loser's Lament."

Index

Accessory Transit Company, 97
Airport, 420–421
Alameda, 250
Alcatraz, 391
Alemany, Archbishop Joseph Sadoc,
    O.P., 39, 61, 64, 91, 165, 248
Alioto, Joseph L., 325, 335–338, 349,
    376–378
    allegations of Mafia connections,
        337
    and bicentennial commemoration,
        376–378
American Federation of Labor,
    International Longshoremen's
    Association, 310–314, 319
American Institute of Architects,
    1973 Convention, 362–364
American Protective Association
    (APA), 262–263, 423
American Theatre, 52
Annals of San Francisco, 39, 50, 69, 133,
    383–384
Antioch Bridge, 196
Aquatic Park, 378
Architecture, 360–362, 364
    height limits, 365
    since 1960, 367
Area, of city, 4–6, 399–400
Army Street Terminal, 193
Arnold, Bion J., 176
Arson, 71, 72
Asians, 372
Australian immigrants, 54

Baker, Senator Edward B., 82
Bank of America Building, 8, 364,
    366, 433
Bank of California, 97–98, 101
Banking, 87, 98
Baptist Church, 42

Barbagelata, John, 338–340
Barrett, John, 338–340
Bay, San Francisco, 196, 215, 383
Bay Area Rapid Transit (BART)
    System, 188, 334, 392, 419
    construction, 214–216
Bay Bridge, 174, 184, 186, 187,
    195–199, 418
Beat Movement, 352–353
Bella Union, 51
Belt Line Tunnel, 174
Bernal Heights, 30
Bicentennial celebrations, 376–378
Big Four Railroad Kings, 99, 241
Billings, Warren K., 303–308, 427
Black Friday, 101
Blacks, 372, 374
Blackwell, William, 371
Bloody Thursday, 316–317
Blue Book Union, 311–312
Blue Mountain. See Mount Davidson
Board of Supervisors. See
    Supervisors, of San Francisco
Bolton, Herbert E., 46
Bonanza Age, 83–93
Bonanza Kings, 100
Boundaries, of city. See Area, of city
Bourdoise, Nicolas, 317
Brannon, Sam, 46, 47, 55, 58, 71
Brick buildings, 71, 72
    and earthquakes, 136
Bridges, 195–206
Bridges, Harry, 314, 328, 329, 335
Broadway Tunnel, 175, 181
Broderick, David C., 78, 82
Brogan, Denis, 385–386
Brooks, Benjamin H., 123
Brouillet, John B., 40
Brown, A. Paige, 185
Brown, Arthur, Jr., 169

Brutus, Junius, 52
Bryant, Andrew J., 322
Buckley, "Boss" Chris, 90
Budde, Henry, 329
Buena Vista Park, 109, 179, 354
Bulletin. See *San Francisco Bulletin*
Burnett, Peter, 245
Burnham, Daniel Hudson, 413
Burns, William J., 272, 274

Cable Car Barn, 128
Cable cars, 117–130, 329, 409
  centennial, 128
  in other cities, 125–126
Caen, Herb, 359, 363–364, 387, 433
Calhoun, Patrick J., 281–285
California, 190
  American conquest, 26
  architectural style, 361
  banking, 98
  early schools, 46
  earthquakes, 132–133
  as Mexican province, 24
  State Building, 169
  State Legislature, 322, 323
  Supreme Court, 306
California Collegiate Institute for
  Young Ladies, 48
California Journal, 340
California Midwinter Fair, 114, 156
California State Library, Sutro
  Branch, 236, 241–242
California Street Railroad, 126
Camps, relief, 146–147
Cantil Blanco, 13–16
Carmen's Union, 281–285, 318
Carnegie, Andrew, 168
Carpenters, 291, 292
Carquinez Straits Bridge, 196
Casey, James, 59, 61
Casey, Michael, 255, 257, 259
Catholics. *See* Roman Catholics
Centennial, of San Francisco's
  founding, 84, 91
Central Fire Alarm System, 137
Central Pacific Railroad, 245–246
Central Tower, 92

Chamber of Commerce, San
  Francisco, 304, 311, 316, 371,
  387
Chilenos, 55
Chinatown, 175
Chinese, 244–246
Christopher, George, 331–332, 417,
  430–431
Chronicle. See *San Francisco Chronicle*
Chronicle Building, 92
City Charter, 292, 322–325, 429
City Front Federation, 257, 310
City Hall, 140, 144, 166–168, 275,
  299
City Lights Bookstore, 352
Civic Auditorium. *See* Exposition
  Auditorium
Civic Center, 153, 163–172, 415
Civil government, 90, 324–325
  beginnings, 25
  chief administrative officer, 324
  corruption, 270–272, 274–276
  and martial law, 141
  Vigilance Committees, 55–66
Class A buildings, 152, 165
Claus Spreckels Building, 365
Clay Street Hill Railroad Company,
  120, 123, 124
Cliff House, 237–240
Climate, 34
Clippers, 190
Coit, Lillie Hitchcock, 73
Coit Tower, 73
Coleman, William T., 63–65, 247
College of Notre Dame, 97
Columbus Tower, 273
Committee of Fifty, 145
Committee of Public Safety, 141
Committee of Safety, 141
Comstock Lode, 98, 237, 245, 360,
  408
Congregation Sherith Israel, 44
Connick, Harris de Haven, 160,
  414–415
Consolidation Act. *See* Hawes Act of
  1856

Constitution, of California, 248
Convention and Visitors Bureau, San Francisco, 379
Cora, Charles, 59
Cornelius, Richard, 281
Corruption, in city government, 270–277
County of San Francisco, 4–6, 322, 399
Creighton, Thomas, 375–376
Crime, 53–66, 356, 358, 373, 374
Criticisms, of San Francisco, 393
Crocker, William, 99, 241, 290
Crocker Mansion, 87, 139
Cultural Development, 51–52
Customs House, 71, 72

Daly City, 216
Dana, Richard Henry, 382
de Anza, Juan Bautista, 12, 13, 401–402
de Ayala, Captain Juan Manuel, 377
Del Norte County, 200
Dennison's Exchange, 68
Depression, of 1929, 300, 312, 323
de Young Museum, 92
Diamond Heights, 375
Doolin, Bernard, 227–228, 420–421
Doss, Margot Patterson, 189
Downey, John, 191
Draymen, and Teamsters' Strike of 1901, 256–258
Drugs, 354–358, 374
Duboce Tunnel, 179–180
Dueling, 61–62
  Terry-Broderick duel, 77–82
Dumbarton Bridge, 196
Du Mond, Frank, 168
Dunne, Frank, 275
Dupont Street, 69. See also Grant Avenue

Earthquakes, 132–133, 175
  earthquake-proof buildings, 150
  of 1868, 86–87
  of 1906, 131–142, 250, 280, 323

and fire, 136–141, 410–411
  Mission Relief Association, 297
  Tokyo, 1923, 136
East Street, 138, 184, 185. See also Embarcadero
Educational system, 46, 372, 373
El Dorado, or Adventures in the Path of Empire, 384
El Marinero, 186
Electric wires, and 1906 fire, 138
Embarcadero, 183, 189, 196. See also East Street
Emperor Norton I. See Norton, Joshua A.
Empire Number One, 74
Employers' Association of San Francisco, 255–256, 259, 280, 281
Emporium, 48, 92
Episcopal Church, in early San Francisco, 43
Escape doors, from Stockton Street Tunnel, 175
Eucalyptus, 159
Examiner. See San Francisco Examiner
Exposition Auditorium, 164–166, 299
Exposition bonds, 158
Expositions, and fairs, 91, 204, 205, 391
  Midwinter Fair of 1894, 114–115, 156
  Panama-Pacific International Exposition, 1915, 155–161, 164, 168, 299, 361, 391, 414–415

Fair Employment Practices Ordinance, 332
Fairmont Hotel, 144
Ferry Building, 136, 183–188, 193, 416, 432
  dimensions, 186
Ferryboats, 184, 186, 197
Fillmore Street, 149
Fire departments, 70–73
Fire-fighting equipment, 69
Fireproof buildings, 150

Fires, 136, 406
  of 1849–1851, 57, 67–75
  of 1906, 131–142, 250, 274, 280
  Chicago, 1871, 137
First Baptist Church, 43
First Congregational Church, 43
First Presbyterian Church, 72
Fisherman's Wharf, 193
Flood Mansion, 87
Foreign Trade Zones, 193–194
Fort Gunnybags, 64
Fort Mason, 174, 377
Fort Point (Fort Winfield Scott), 16,
  378
Freeway, 361
Freitas, Joseph, 339
Frontier justice, 54–66

Gage, Henry T., 259, 260
Geary, John White, 28, 70
Geary Street Cable Line, 209
Geary Street, Park, and Ocean
  Railroad, 126
Geary Tunnel, 182
Giants, 339
Gilliam, Harold, 361–362, 371
Giralda, of Seville, 185
Goat Island. See Yerba Buena Island
Gold Rush, 32–35, 403
  Alaskan, 93
  Californian, 32, 236
Golden Gate, 202, 377, 291, 400
Golden Gate Bridge, 174, 184,
  186–188, 196, 199, 377, 418–419
  construction, 202
  height, 8
  opening, 199
Golden Gate Bridge District, 200
Golden Gate Ferry Line, 188
Golden Gate International
  Exposition of 1939, 156, 204,
  205
Golden Gate Park, 107–115, 209,
  212, 237, 408
  and Hippies, 353, 354

Park Commission, 109
  windbreak design, 111
Golden Gateway Center, 333,
  366–367
Governors, of California:
  Burnett, Peter, 245
  Downey, John, 191
  Gage, Henry T., 259, 260
  Haight, Henry H., 288
  Johnson, Hiram, 305
  McDougal, John, 245
  Merriam, Frank S., 317
  Olson, Culbert L., 308
  Rolph, James, Jr., 169, 300
  Stanford, Leland, 191
  Stephens, William D., 273, 307
  Young, C.C., 306
Grace Cathedral, 87
Grace Episcopal Church, 43
Graft Trials, 274–275, 277, 285
Grant Avenue, 9, 69
Great Committee, 55, 58
Griffin, Judge Franklin A., 306
Groh, George, 33
Guadalupe Hidalgo, Treaty of, 16,
  26, 55

Haight, Henry H., 288
Haight-Ashbury district, 353–358
Hall, William Hammond, 109–110,
  112
Hallidie, Andrew Smith, 121–125,
  409
Hallidie Ropeway, 122–123
Hangings, 54, 58
Hanna, Archbishop J., 314
Harbor, San Francisco, 190–191, 196
Harbor Cove, 156, 158, 160
Harbor Improvement Bonds, 192
Harding, Warren G., 167
Harper's, 385
Harte, Bret, 382
Hastings College of the Law, 288
Hawes Act of 1856, 322–323, 429
Hayes Valley, 92, 139
Hearst, William Randolph, 257

Heney, Francis J., 275
Hetch Hetchy, 220, 420
Hibernia Bank, 432
Hills, 7, 174, 400
Hills of San Francisco, 7
Hippies, 353–356
Hiss, Alger, 348
History of the San Francisco Disaster, 141
Hittel, John S., 63
Hogan, William, 387
Holiday, 386–388
Holladay, Ben, 87
Holy Cross Church, 40
Home Telephone Company, 271–272
Hongisto, Sheriff, 339
Hoover-Young Bay Bridge Commission, 197
Hopkins, Mark, 99, 126, 241
Horse-car transit lines, 126
Hounds. See Society of Regulators
Housing, shortages, 374–375
Hunt, T. Dwight, 42
Hunters Point, 30, 334, 373
Huntington, 99, 241

Indians, and Mission Dolores, 19
Industrial Association, 316, 318
Insurance, after 1906 disaster, 150–152
International Exposition of 1939, 391
International Workers of the World, 312
Irish, 244, 248, 262, 264
Iron Monsters. See Streetcars
Islands, 399

Japanese, 250
Japanese Peace Treaty, 170, 331
Japanese Tea Garden, 115
Jenny Lind Theatre, 52, 71–72
Jesuits, 263, 405
Jews, 44, 269
Johnson, Governor Hiram, 305

Kearney, Denis, 243–251, 422
Kearny, General Stephen W., 27

Kerouac, Jack, 352–353
Khrushchev, Nikita, 332, 382
King of William, James, 59–61
Kipling, Rudyard, 382
Knickerbocker Number Five, 75
von Kotzebue, Otto, 24

Labor movement, 254, 304–305, 308, 388
  and Denis Kearney, 243–251
  and John Shelley, 333–336
  Maritime and General Strike of 1934, 310–319
  and P.H. McCarthy, 291–292
  Streetcar Strike of 1907, 280–285
  Teamsters' Strike of 1901, 255–260
  Workingmen's Party of California, 248–249, 251
Laguna Puerca, 6
Lake Merced, 6, 79, 219, 330, 377
Land grants, 28–30
Langdon, William H., 277
Langlois, Anthony, 40
Lapham, Mayor Roger Dearborn, 326–330
Law and Order Committee, 304
Leader, 281
Leo XIII, 258, 260
Library, Main, 168–169, 247, 288, 290, 299
Lombard Street, 8
London Evening News, 390
Longshoremen, 258–260. See also Strikes, maritime
Look, 337
Lovett, Angelina, 46

MacArthur, General Douglas, 331
McCarthy, P.H., 284, 290–293, 297–298
McDonald, John, 306
McDonnell, Timothy, S.J., 325
McDougal, John, 245
McGucken, Archbishop, 378
MacGuire, Tom, 52
MacGuire's Opera House, 52

Mackinac Bridge, 199
McLaren, John Hays, 109, 112–115,
    158–159, 407
Macondray, F.W., 56
Mafia, 337
Magic Isle. See Treasure Island
Magnin family, 354
Maraschi, Father Anthony, S.J., 64,
    71
Marin County, 188, 200
Marina district, 211. See also Harbor
    Cove
Maritime and General Strike of
    1934, 313–319
Mark Hopkins Hotel, 87
Market Street Railway Company,
    126, 212, 328
Markham, Edwin, 161
Marshall, James W., 24, 32
Martinez, Maria Antonio, 20
Masset, Stephen C., 51
Matson Navigation Company, 312
Maybeck, Bernard Ralph, 160, 361
Mayor, duties of, 324–325
Mayors, of San Francisco:
    Alioto, Joseph L., 325, 335–337
    Bryant, Andrew J., 322
    Christopher, George, 331–334,
        430–431
    Lapham, Roger Dearborn, 327–330
    McCarthy, P.H., 290–293
    Moscone, George, 338–341
    Phelan, James D., 258, 259, 323
    Robinson, Elmer, 324, 330–332
    Rolph, James, Jr., 276, 277, 293,
        296–299, 326, 327
    Rossi, Angelo J., 316, 326–327
    Schmitz, Eugene, 144–147,
        269–277
    Shelley, John F., 333–336
    Sutro, Adolph, 240–241
    Taylor, Edward Robeson, 288–290
Mechanics Institute, 165
    Eleventh Industrial Exhibition, 91
Mendocino County, 200
Merriam, Governor Frank S., 317,
    318

Methodist Church, 41, 51
Midwinter Fair of 1894, 114–115,
    156
Mill employees, lockout of, 291–292
Mills Tower, 364
Mining, 236, 245
Minorities, 334, 372, 373. See also
    Racism
Mission Bank, 297
Mission district, 148
Mission Dolores, 17–19, 118, 140,
    378, 401, 411
    dedication, 18–19
    and education, 46
Mission Relief Association, 297
Mission Rock Terminal, 192
Mission San Francisco de Asis. See
    Mission Dolores
Molotov, Vyacheslav, 348
Monitor, 258
Montgomery, John B., 26
Montgomery, John Joseph, 224
Monumental Number Six, 75
Mooney, Thomas J., 303–308
Mooney-Billings Case, 303, 305–308,
    427–428
Mormons, 41, 46
Moscone, George, 338–341
Mount Davidson, 5, 7
Mount Sutro (Mount Parnassus),
    236, 237
Mount Sutro Towers, 8
Municipal ownership:
    of railway system, 208–210, 213
    of water system, 219–220
Municipal Railway (Muni), 199,
    207–216, 328, 355, 419
    low fares, 213–214
    maiden run, 208
Museum of Modern Art, 171

Nabobs, 244, 245
Napa County, 200
National Greenback Party, 249
National Review, 390
National Workingmen's Party, 248
Neri, Joseph, S.J., 90

New York Times, 364
New York Tribune, 384
News, 308
Newsweek, 355
Nob Hill, 87, 126, 175, 244, 245,
    247, 362, 363
Noe, Jose de Jesus, 30
Noe family, 353
Nolan, Dick, 392–393
North Beach, 175, 211
    and Beatniks, 352, 354
Norton, Joshua A., 84–86, 197, 407

Oakland, 393
O'Farrell, Jasper, 120
Old St. Mary's, 40–41
Older, Fremont, 272, 276
Olson, Culbert L., 308, 428
O'Meara, James, 65
Omnibus system, 119
Opera House, 169–171
Origin, of city, 12
O'Shaughnessy, M.M., City
    Engineer, 176, 179, 221, 225
Owen, Patrick, 109, 110
Oxman, Frank C., 306

Pacific Coast Exposition Company,
    157
Pacific Mail, 247
Pacific States Telephone Company,
    271–272
Pacific Union Club, 87, 432
Paint Eaters, 271, 272
Palace Hotel, 98
Palace of Fine Arts, 160
Palou, Reverend Francisco, L.F.M., 6,
    12, 18, 377
Panama Canal, 156, 159
Panama-Pacific International
    Exposition, 1915, 155–161, 164,
    167, 168, 299, 361, 391, 414–415
    opening day, 159
    transit system, 210–211
Panhandle, 354
Panic of 1873, 245–246
Park Presidio, 147

Parks, and playgrounds, 107–115,
    209, 374, 408
People's Court, 66
People's Park, 116
*Personal History of the San Francisco
    Earthquake,* 138
Phelan, James, Sr., 87
Phelan, James D., 145, 220, 258, 259,
    272, 288, 292, 323
Phelan Building, 92
Pier 50. *See* Mission Rock Terminal
Platt, Horace G., 209
Point Lobos, 377
Police department, 332, 374
    volunteer, 71
Political parties:
    Democrats, 269, 289–290
    National Greenback Party, 249
    National Workingmen's Party, 248
    Populists, 240
    Republicans, 289–290, 330
    Union Labor Party, 268–269,
        284–285, 290
    Workingmen's Party of California,
        243, 248, 249, 251
Polk, Willis, 420, 432
Population, 27, 89–91, 119, 370
    decline in, 371
    and Gold Rush, 33–34
Populists, 240
Port, of San Francisco, 14, 189–195,
    416–418
    problems, 193–194
Portola Festival, 157, 297
Portsmouth Plaza, 26, 69, 81, 92,
    108, 118, 129, 144, 190
Potrero Nuevo, 30
Preparedness Day Bombing, 303,
    305–308
Presbyterian Church, in early San
    Francisco, 42
Presidio, of San Francisco, 13–17,
    224–225, 378, 402
    aid during 1906 fire, 139, 141
    relief camps, 147
    Spanish-American War, 93
Presidio and Ferries Railroad, 126

Presidio Lake, 6
Press:
    anti-labor bias, 257, 285
    and Mooney-Billings Case, 308
Pueblo de Yerba Buena. See *Yerba Buena*
Purcell, Charles H., 198

Racism, 55, 244, 250, 262, 334, 373,
    374
Railroad companies, 126, 186, 241,
    245–246
Railroad Kings, 99, 241
Ralston, William C., 86, 87, 95, 102,
    408
Rancho San Miguel, 237, 353
Real estate, 353, 358
    during bonanza years, 98–99
    values, 177
Reconstruction and relief, after 1906
    disaster, 143–153
Red Cross, 147
Redwood City-Newark Bridge, 196
Report of the Earthquake in California,
    1906, 411
Religion, in early California, 38–44
Restaurant workers, in Maritime and
    General Strike of 1934, 318
Richardson, Captain William A., 19,
    25, 403
Richardson, William H., 59
Richmond district, 212
Richmond-San Rafael Bridge, 188,
    196
Riggers and Stevedores Union
    Association, 310
Riordan, Archbishop Patrick
    William, 412
Riots, 247, 334
Robinson, Elmer, 324, 327, 330–332
Robinson's and Evrard's Museum,
    51
Rogers, Will, 383
Rolph, James, Jr., 165, 167, 176, 178,
    180, 208, 232, 277, 293,
    296–301, 305

as governor, 169, 300
as mayor, 296–299
Roman Catholics, 39, 248
    attacks on, 262–263
    and *San Francisco Bulletin,* 60
    and Teamsters' Strike of 1901, 258
Roosevelt, Franklin D., 313, 314
Rossi, Angelo J., 316, 317, 326–327,
    330
Ruef, Abe, 223–224, 268–277
    conviction for bribe taking, 275
    and Union Labor Party, 268–269
Russian Hill, 140, 181
Ryan, Joseph, 314

Saint Francis Church, 46, 404
Saint Ignatius Academy, 49
Saint Ignatius Church, 50
Saint Ignatius College, 48–50, 90,
    139, 224, 263, 333. *See also*
    University of San Francisco
Saint Mary's Cathedral, 41, 139
Saint Mary's College, 46
Saint Patrick's Church, 40
San Andreas Fault, 134
San Francisco at Your Feet, 189
San Francisco Bay, 196, 215, 383
    underbay transit tube, 215
San Francisco Bay Exposition
    Company, 204
San Francisco Building Trades
    Council, 291–293
San Francisco Bulletin, 257, 272
San Francisco Business, 417
San Francisco Chronicle, 340, 359, 364,
    376, 387, 388
    anti-labor bias, 257, 285
    Chronicle Building, 92
San Francisco College, 48
San Francisco Examiner, 259, 260, 331,
    378, 389, 391, 392
    and Edward R. Taylor, 289
    and Hippies, 354
    and labor movement, 257
San Francisco Gothic architecture, 92
San Francisco Grand Jury, 331, 373

San Francisco International Airport, 223–231
San Francisco Labor Council, 280, 283–284, 317, 333
San Francisco Magazine, 375
San Francisco Market Street Railway, 119
San Francisco Mint, 208, 432
San Francisco Parking Authority, 332
San Francisco Planning Commission, 375
San Francisco Port Authority, 193–194, 416
San Francisco Progress, 377
San Francisco Redevelopment Agency, 374, 375
San Francisco Twin Bicentennial, 376–377
San Mateo County, 225
San Mateo-Hayward Bridge, 196
Santa Clara College, 48
Saroyan, William, 388–389
Saturday Review, 352
Sausalito, 188
Schmitz, Eugene, 269–277, 289
    and Earthquake and Fire of 1906, 141, 144–147, 150, 151
    and Ruef corruption, 275–277
Segregation, in schools, 373
Seismograph record, of 1906, 135
Sentinel Building, 273
Sharon, William, 98, 101
Shell Building, 364
Shelley, John F., 333–337, 349, 356
Sherman, William T., 65
Shipowners Protective Association, 310
Silver City, 86
Sisters of Mercy, 61
Skyscrapers, 362, 364–365
Slums, 372, 430
Smog, 393
Social Number Three, 75
Society of Regulators, 55
Songs, about San Francisco, 391–392

Sonoma County, 200
Soules, Thomas, 417
South Park, 121
Southern Pacific Railway, 241
Spanish-American War, 93, 186
Spanish-speaking people, 372, 385
Sperry, Howard, 317
Spreckels, Rudolph, 272
Spring Valley Water Works, 219, 221
Squatters, 108, 109, 115
Standard Oil Building, 364
Stanford, Leland, 87, 99, 126, 241
    as governor, 191
Stanford Court Hotel, 88
Stassen, Harold E., 348
State Building, 169
State Harbor Authority, 416
Steamships, 190
Steinbeck, John, 389
Stephens, William D., 273, 307
Sterling, George, 382
Stevenson, Adlai, 349
Stevenson, Robert Louis, 382–383
Stockton Street Tunnel, 175, 176
Stone, Irving, 388
Strauss, Joseph Baerman, 200, 202–204
Streetcars, 176, 178, 208, 213
    strike of 1907, 280–285
    underground, 216
Street railroad. *See* Cable car; Municipal Railway
Strikes, 254, 280, 337
    maritime, 310–319
    Streetcar Strike of 1907, 280–285
    Teamsters' Strike of 1901, 256–260, 268–269, 280
Suburbs, 370, 372
Suisun Bay Bridge, 196
Sunol Water Temple, 420
Sunset district, 212
Sunset Tunnel, 177–180, 415–416
Supervisors, of San Francisco, 289, 322, 324, 330
    election of, 339–341

Paint Eaters, 271–272
and Teamsters' Strike of 1901, 259
and urban redevelopment, 376
Sutro, Adolph Heinrich Joseph, 232,
236–242, 269, 421
career as mayor, 240–242
land holdings in San Francisco,
237–238
library, 238, 241–242
Sutro Baths, 236, 237, 240
Sutro Forest, 237
Sutro Heights, 236, 238, 241, 242
Sutro Metallurgical Works, 237
Sutro Tunnel, 237, 241
Sutter's Mill, 24
Sydney Ducks, 55

Tammany Hall, 78
Taylor, Bayard, 384
Taylor, Edward Robeson, 132, 168,
288–290
Taylor, Zachary, 28
Teamsters:
beginnings of union, 255–256
and City Front Federation, 310
in Maritime and General Strike of
1934, 313–314, 318
Strike of 1901, 256–260, 268, 269,
314
Telegraph Hill, 55, 73, 140
Temple Emanu-El, 44
Terry, David S., 78–79, 82
Terry-Broderick Duel, 406
Thant, U, 349
Theatre, 51–52, 151
Thorne, Louisa, 96–97
Tomorrow, 388
Tourism, 379
Town and Country, 389
Transamerica Pyramid, 8, 364, 433
Transcontinental railroad, 87
Transportation systems, 118, 121,
123, 126, 199, 328–329, 374, 392
Bay Area Rapid Transit (BART),
188, 334

first publicly owned, 208–210
problems, 214, 215
rapid transit system, 332
steam, 126
See also Municipal Railway
Trask, John D., 158
Treasure Island, 204, 206
Treaty of Guadalupe Hidalgo, 16,
26, 55
Trinity Episcopal Church, 43, 47
Trolley buses, 212
Truman, Harry S., 345, 347, 348
Tunnels, 173–182, 237, 241, 415–516
Twin Peaks, 4, 7, 176, 212
Twin Peaks Tunnel, 176–179, 241,
415
Tycoons, 87

Unemployment, 372
Union College, 48
Union Ferry Depot. See Ferry
Building
Union Labor Party, 268–269, 284,
290
Union Mill and Mining Company,
98
Union Square, 47, 175
Unions, 280, 334. See also Labor
movement
United Brotherhood of Carpenters
and Joiners of America, 291
United Nations, 170, 329, 331,
345–349
United Railroads of San Francisco,
212
in fire and earthquake of 1906,
280–281
payoffs to Ruef, 272
and Streetcar Strike of 1907,
281–285
United States House Subcommittee
on Un-American Activities,
332–333
United States Mint, 208, 432
University of San Francisco, 50, 242,
325, 333

Urban redevelopment, 330, 371, 372, 374–376, 430, 433

Van Ness Avenue, 139
Vancouver, Captain George, 24
Vanderbilt, Cornelius, 97
Vaults, after Fire of 1906, 149
Verrazano-Narrows Bridge, 199
Veterans Building, 169–171
Victorian San Francisco architecture, 92, 360
Vigilance Committees, 245, 247, 304, 405
    of 1851, 55, 56–58
    of 1856, 58, 63
Vigilance movements, 53–66
Violence:
    against Chinese, 247
    in strikes, 257–258, 282–283, 285, 314, 316–317
Volunteer Company Number Five, 73
Volunteer police department, 71

War Memorial Opera House, 169–171, 347
Washerwoman's Lagoon, 6
Washington Monument, 202
Washington Square, 73
Water, 217–221, 419–420. See also Fires
Water supply:
    in 1906 earthquake, 136–137
    for Golden Gate Park, 111
Waterfront, of San Francisco, 191, 310–319, 328, 339
Waterfront Employers Association, 310, 313
Waterfront Union, 257
Western Addition, 148, 181, 361, 374
Whitcomb Hotel, 144

Wickersham Commission, 303, 306–307
Wierzbicki, Dr. F.P., 383
Wilson, Woodrow, 220, 307
Windmills, 111
Wire rope, 121–122
Wooden frame dwellings, 153
    and earthquakes, 136
Woodworth, Selim E., 58
Workingmen's Party of California, 243, 248, 249, 251
World Trade Center, 186, 193
World War I, 129, 212–213, 314
World War II, 192, 347
Wright, Frank Lloyd, 364
Wyman, Father Henry, C.S.P., 276

Yerba Buena, 12, 16, 360, 402
    founding, 19
    renaming of, 26
Yerba Buena Island, 174, 197, 204, 225
Yerba Buena Tunnel, 197, 199
Yorke, Father Peter Christopher, 261–265, 422–423
    defense of American Catholics, 262–264
    as editor of Monitor, 258, 262
    as founder and editor of Leader, 281
    opposition to Edward R. Taylor, 289
    and Streetcar Strike of 1907, 281–285
    support of Eugene Schmitz, 275–276
    and Teamsters' Strike of 1901, 258–260
Young, C.C., 306

Zellerbach, J.D., 365–366
Ziegfield, Florenz, 391